村上文子同學共勉

梁伯華

於新州

二〇〇三年五月八日

# Political Leaders of Modern China

## A Biographical Dictionary

EDITED BY
Edwin Pak-wah Leung

An Oryx Book

GREENWOOD PRESS
Westport, Connecticut • London

**Library of Congress Cataloging-in-Publication Data**

Political leaders of modern China : a biographical dictionary / edited by Edwin
Pak-wah Leung.
    p.  cm.
   Includes bibliographical references and index.
   ISBN 0–313–30216–2 (alk. paper)
   1. Politicians—China—Biography—Dictionaries.  2. China—Politics and
government—19th century—Biography—Dictionaries.  3. China—Politics and
government—20th century—Biography—Dictionaries.  I. Leung, Pak-Wah, 1950–
DS755.3.P64  2002
951'.03'0922—dc21     2002016615

British Library Cataloguing in Publication Data is available.

Library of Congress Catalog Card Number: 2002016615
ISBN: 0–313–30216–2

First published in 2002

Greenwood Press, 88 Post Road West, Westport, CT 06881
An imprint of Greenwood Publishing Group, Inc.
www.greenwood.com

Printed in the United States of America

The paper used in this book complies with the
Permanent Paper Standard issued by the National
Information Standards Organization (Z39.48–1984).

10 9 8 7 6 5 4 3 2 1

*To my parents, Leung Liu and Lee Shui*

# Contents

# Preface

This dictionary, unlike my two historical dictionaries (*Historical Dictionary of Revolutionary China, 1839–1976* and *Historical Dictionary of the Chinese Civil War*), focuses only on political leaders in modern China. As such, it is a biographical book in nature. It provides up-to-date and comprehensive coverage of major Chinese political leaders during the modern period from the Opium War (1839–1842) to the beginning of the twenty-first century. It should be pointed out that there are other reference books on China's political leaders, such as Arthur W. Hummel, ed., *Eminent Chinese of the Ch'ing Period, 1644–1912*, 2 vols. (1943–1944); Howard L. Boorman and Richard C. Howard, eds., *Biographical Dictionary of Republican China*, 5 vols. (1967–1979); Donald W. Klein and Anne B. Clark, eds., *Biographic Dictionary of Chinese Communism, 1921–1965*, 2 vols. (1971); and Wolfgang Bartke, *Who's Who in the People's Republic of China* (1987). But these books are outdated and do not provide comprehensive coverage of modern China. In comparison, the present dictionary has a much broader time frame, covering the late imperial, Republican, and Communist periods in modern Chinese history. It also provides a comprehensive chronology and an introductory essay on the nature and characteristics of modern Chinese political leadership. In addition to the general bibliography, each entry in the book also comes with a "References" section to provide the reader with further bibliographical suggestions. The first time an entry refers to a person discussed in another entry, bold type is used to indicate a cross-reference. Romanization of Chinese names and places follows the *Hanyu pinyin* system, with only a few commonly accepted exceptions such as Confucius and Sun Yat-sen.

About 30 scholars from all over the world participated in this book project, making it a truly international academic endeavor. Their names appear in the list of Contributors. In addition, my research assistants/graduate students Jennifer Cucchisi, Thomas Radice, Keping Niu, and Jie Shen helped with some of the work. Seton Hall University Research Council provided a research grant, and the Centre of Asian Studies at University of Hong Kong provided assistance during my stay there as a Research Fellow. To all of them, I must record my heartfelt appreciation.

Finally, I want to thank my Greenwood editor, Cynthia Harris, for her patience and encouragement, and my wife, Vera, and son, Immanuel, for being so supportive of me during the preparation of this book.

# Abbreviations

| | |
|---|---|
| CC | Central Committee |
| CCP | Chinese Communist Party |
| CPGC | Central People's Government Council |
| CPPCC | Chinese People's Political Consultative Conference |
| DL | Democratic League |
| DPP | Democratic Progressive Party |
| GMD | Guomindang or Chinese Nationalist Party |
| MAC | Military Affairs Committee |
| NPC | National People's Congress |
| NRA | National Revolutionary Army |
| PLA | People's Liberation Army |
| PRC | People's Republic of China |
| ROC | Republic of China |
| SAR | Special Administrative Region |
| UN | United Nations |
| YL | Youth League |

# Introduction

Confucius has said: "the rule of virtue can be compared to the Pole Star which commands the homage of the multitude of stars without leaving its place" (*Analects* 12.1). This saying is significant insofar as it refers to one aspect of Chinese political leaders (both ancient and contemporary), namely, the desire for order through the authority of one key figure: the ruler. This introduction discusses the characteristics of the political leaders of the late imperial period, the Republican period, and the Communist period. Though each period is marked by different specific ideological elements, all three periods reveal their common heritage in a tradition that favors a strong central government. While this belief is not necessarily unique to the Chinese per se, its expression, through a deep historical understanding of what it means to be "Chinese," is. And this reverence for Chinese culture reveals how even the most radical elements of contemporary politics did not shake off the residue of some traditional Chinese values and ideas.

## COMMON CHARACTERISTICS

One common characteristic of these leaders that should not be too surprising to anyone familiar with the political history of any culture is the desire for power. None of the major political figures in each of these three periods, no matter how virtuous or ruthless, was free from the overwhelming desire to control China's fate. Of course, not everyone who aspired for power succeeded in attaining it. Hong Xiuquan, the leader of the Taiping Uprising of the 1850s and 1860s, led a religious/social rebellion against what he saw as an unworthy, corrupt government. Though his motives may have been mostly or partly religious, there is no denying his desire to control China. He may have wanted to bring China salvation, but his self-proclamation as the "Heavenly King" of a new dynasty demonstrated an ulterior motive of power.

Another example of power lust is the similarly brief and failed attempt by Yuan Shikai to start a new dynasty in the early Republican period. Yuan saw the opportunity to take advantage of the budding republic for his own personal gain. Unlike most of China's modern leaders, Yuan did not seem to be driven by any sense of nationalism toward China, but only by his own desire for power. He defied constitutional procedures and dissolved parliament in an attempt to consolidate his power. It was indeed a tragedy in China's early Republican history.

By far, the most famous battle for power in recent decades was between Jiang Jieshi (Chiang Kai-shek) and Mao Zedong in the civil war of the 1930s and 1940s. Both sides painted noble pictures of their struggles for the people of China. But behind the scenes lay a fight for control not only between the parties, but also within the parties themselves. After the Communist take-over and subsequent exile of the Nationalists to Taiwan, Jiang ruled the island with an iron fist. It was not until his son, Jiang Jingguo, came to power that Taiwan began to move toward democracy. Likewise, on the mainland, Mao struggled to consolidate his power, becoming "deified" in the eyes of the people. As some in the party and in the general public became disillusioned with Mao's failed "Great Leap Forward," he sought to regain authority by sowing the seeds of the Cultural Revolution of the 1960s and 1970s, which attempted to reenergize support for Mao. During this time, Mao, who had been brought up with Confucian values, ostracized all of those with traditional Confucian ideals. As Mao grew older his main focus seemed to stray from doing what was best for China and turned toward maintaining his own power.

Most recently, in 1989, the struggle for power in China was plastered on television screens around the world during the student demonstrations at Tiananmen Square. But the Tiananmen Square demonstration also points to another more fundamental characteristic of Chinese politics from the late imperial period to the present: a desire for reform. In fact, "reform" embodies the tone and nature of not only the political climate of these periods, but also the social and intellectual climates as well. It is widely accepted that China is now in a period of rapid change and development, which has been sparked by recent desires for improved social and political conditions.

Even in the mid-nineteenth century, the theme of reform was evident. Lin Zexu, for example, pushed for reform by trying to rid China of foreign influence, especially in the opium trade. Lin was given orders to rid China of the addicting substance in whatever way possible. Unfortunately, he was eventually made the scapegoat of the Chinese government when Great Britain retaliated against his heroic efforts to destroy the opium coming into

China. However, subsequent generations hailed him as a hero of social reform.

Reform can also be seen as a driving force for the other political leaders. Hong Xiuquan, through the Taiping Uprising had a mission to change China, and also rid the country of corruption and foreign influence. The fall of the Qing Dynasty in 1912 and the rise of Republican China came out of the spirit of reform. Sun Yat-sen and Jiang Jieshi after him envisioned a new republic rather than a new dynastic system. But with reform inevitably came disagreement as to what kind of reforms should be implemented. Again, the dispute between the Nationalists and the Communists was ideological insofar as both sides envisioned different remedies for China's ills. And even when the Communists prevailed in 1949, Mao still faced internal opposition to his own ideas of reform, since many of them had failed.

After Mao's death in 1976 and until 1989, Deng Xiaoping was hailed by many as a great reformer. Deng's pragmatism led to the opening of China to modernization, despite his aversion to democratization. His main concern was economic reform, which led him to coin the phrase "socialism with Chinese characteristics," an idea that is still promoted by Chinese political leaders today.

## THE UNIQUENESS OF THE CHINESE POLITICAL LEADERS

The special emphasis on "Chinese characteristics" was a common trait among the late modern and contemporary political leaders in China, which made them unique in world politics. It stemmed from a deep sense of cultural heritage and history. These leaders recognized and took pride in China's long and rich political and cultural legacy, and made it a staple of their reform efforts. No matter how China needed to change, China always needed to remain "Chinese."

The "Chineseness" of the reformers came in two broad categories: conservative and liberal. In the conservative category were reformers who wanted to take China back to a "golden age" of moral integrity. Many leaders during the Qing saw a corruption in the original moral order of society caused by some (usually foreign) element that needed to be exterminated. For Lin Zexu and others, it was opium, which profited foreign traders while it plagued the Chinese people. Opium enslaved the common people into addiction and corrupted government officials, who squandered the people's money in search of a constant drug-induced "fix." The key for Lin was to rid China of this social ill, and thereby return to a more idealized, a more "purified," social condition—one that was free from foreign influences.

In the liberal category were leaders like Mao and Deng, who both tried to reform China not by rejecting foreign influences, but rather by embracing them—but with a catch. The Chinese Communists could not pride themselves in rejuvenating an "old world" China. Socialism was a new idea, a foreign idea, an idea that appeared to reject everything the Chinese had tried before. But in order to make it palatable to the common people, the Communists had to show that it could be adapted to the Chinese context. Hence "Marxism" became "Maoism," which led to Deng's "Socialism with Chinese characteristics." Both Mao Zedong thought and Deng Xiaoping thought were far from classical Marxism, according to which China was far from ready for a Socialist revolution. But Mao's faith in the power of the Chinese peasant class and Deng's pragmatic concerns for China's specific economic problems provided grounds for enough adaptation of classical Marxist theory to make it work.

## THE IMPACT OF TRADITION

But what exactly does it mean to be "Chinese"? A truly satisfactory answer is too complex for this chapter, but suffice it to say that there is an element of indigenous tradition, especially Confucian tradition, in what brings out the "Chineseness" of the culture. Of course, the Confucian tradition is a long and complex one involving political, moral, and even religious elements, so to say that China has remained somewhat "Confucian" throughout the ages is vague. It is best to specifically point out the "family resemblances" of diverse individuals which make up a composite "Confucian" tradition.

The most obvious examples came out of the Qing with individuals who explicitly styled themselves Confucian. Lin Zexu's moral crusade against opium was a distinctly Confucian crusade. Lin and others such as Zeng Guofan and Li Hongzhang were schooled in the Confucian classics and were trained to view the world through the lens of Confucian moral and political discourse. This discourse, since its beginnings in the Warring States period (468–221 B.C.), viewed proper government as a moral government, a government structured with ritual codes of conduct. And the government itself was supposed to be a monarchy that operated within the "dynastic system."

Even in Qing rebellions, such as that of Hong Xiuquan and the Taipings, the residue of Confucianism remained. Though Hong considered himself Christian and even destroyed Confucian temples, his creative "misunderstanding" of Christianity revealed his Confucian upbringing. Hong's view of the Trinity, for example, interpreted the three persons of God not as one substance, but as a "holy family," much like what was prevalent in traditional Chinese ancestor worship.

But what of the periods after the Qing? Did they not abandon Confucianism for more progressive worldviews? They did if Confucianism were strictly defined as an inherently hierarchical system of government that entailed monarchy. But first of all, traditions like Confucianism, which have evolved over millennia, tend to be flexible. Second of all, it is almost impossible to abandon any cultural tradition completely.

One Confucian cultural element that was never abandoned completely in both the Republican and Communist periods was the notion that social stability presupposed homogeneous thought patterns throughout society. In other words, "pluralism" was not acceptable. The notion of "choice" was never dominant in Confucian thought, so the idea that one had some fundamental "freedom" of thought or "right" to think never arose. Basically then, since the institutionalization of Confucianism, there were two ways of thinking: the right way and the wrong way, and there was only *one* right way.

This idea did not die with the end of the dynastic system. It remained popular to both the Nationalists and the Communists. As mentioned above, both Jiang Jieshi and Mao Zedong strove to consolidate their own power within their respective parties. But they and their parties also strove to maintain control over the people. Jiang kept Taiwan under martial law and firmly resisted local desires for democracy, which carried with it the danger of potentially numerous dissenting voices within society.

The Communists were just as controlling on the mainland. Dissension from the party line was not tolerated, especially within the general public. Mao did appear to support free expression with his "let a hundred flowers bloom, let a hundred schools contend" policy, but neither he nor the party tolerated any harsh criticism. Many critics were persecuted. Similar persecution occurred under Deng Xiaoping's reform movement, which involved allowing the people to speak out about reform. But as the "Democracy Wall" became more critical than Deng could tolerate, it was quickly shut down.

Even though the Nationalists and especially the Communists rejected Confucianism as an explicit solution to China's problems, both reverted back to strong government-controlled systems. Social harmony meant getting the people to think in the "right" way, and any deviation from this rigid standard was seen as a threat to social order. Though Confucius was absent in name, his spirit lingered on in different forms.

## CONCLUSION

Chinese political leaders from the late imperial period to the Communist period were, on the whole, complex personalities who strove for their own personal gain while also fighting for China itself and trying to work within China's own particular social and intellectual circumstances. Although many Chinese leaders did not consider themselves nationalistic, their main interest seemed to lie in doing what was best for China. This nationalistic sentiment seemed to be a common bond among most of China's leaders, past and present. The tradition of Confucianism also carried through the generations of leadership. While none truly attained the "Pole Star" status that Confucius idealized for the rulers, many of them made remarkable attempts to steer China into its present status as a world power. And as China continues to develop politically and economically, it is clear that present-day and future Chinese political leaders will not only shape Chinese history, but also world history.

# Political Leaders
# of Modern China

# B

BO GU (Qin Bangxian, June 24, 1907–April 8, 1946). Russian-trained Chinese Communist Party (CCP) leader; one of the so-called "Twenty-Eight Bolsheviks"; general secretary of the CCP between 1932 and 1934.

Born in Hangzhou, Zhejiang province, Bo Gu was **Qin Bangxian**'s pen name. It was taken from the Chinese transliteration of two syllables of his adopted Russian name. Qin Bangxian was born into a declining scholar-official family. His father died when he was nine. He was brought up in Wuxi, Jiangsu province.

In 1925, Qin Bangxian went to study in the English Department of Shanghai University and joined the CCP. In 1926, he was sent to the **Sun Yat-sen** University in Moscow with other young Chinese Communists. At the university, he was known as one of the Twenty-Eight Bolsheviks led by **Wang Ming**, and wholeheartedly believed and followed the policies of the Comintern and Wang Ming.

In March 1931, Qin Bangxian replaced Wen Yucheng as the general secretary of the Communist youth. In September 1931, Qin joined the provisional Politburo, which was formed after Xiang Zhongfa was arrested. Qin became the secretary of the CCP in November, after the Politburo decided to abolish the general secretary position. After Wang Ming left for Moscow and **Zhou Enlai** for the Central Soviet Region, Qin became the head of the CCP. He blindly followed the Comintern's policies and, on a few occasions, simply carried out the orders of the Shanghai Comintern office.

Because of the Comintern's hostile attitude toward middle-of-the-road forces (its "closed-doorism"), the provisional Politburo could not survive in Shanghai and was forced to move to the Central Soviet Region in 1933. In Ruijin, Qin combined the provisional Politburo and the Central Bureau of the

Central Soviet Region into the CCP Central Bureau. Qin became the secretary and head of the Central Bureau. Before Qin moved to Ruijin, he requested the Comintern to allow Li De (Otto Braun) to go with him as a military adviser.

In February 1933, Qin launched a campaign against Luo Ming, the secretary of the Min-Yue-Gan Provisional Party Committee, who did not follow Qin's policy of military advance and adopted a more realistic guerrilla-warfare strategy. **Deng Xiaoping** was among four other leaders being criticized and removed from their positions. At the same time, Qin adopted a policy to discriminate against middle and rich peasants. He also followed Shanghai Comintern representatives' advice not to support the Fujian People's government led by Guomindang (GMD) rebel generals Chen Mingxu and Li Jishen. It was subsequently crushed by Jiang Jieshi.

In January 1934, Qin convened the Fifth Plenum of the Sixth Central Committee. Qin, under the military advice of Li De, abandoned the successful guerrilla tactics and decided to defend every inch of the Central Soviet Region against **Jiang Jieshi**'s Fifth Encirclement and Suppression Campaign. The Red Army lost one-fifth of its troops in the battle of Guangchang and was eventually forced to take the Long March. The Long March was led by the "military troike" (Bo Gu, Li De, and Zhou Enlai). Because of these military defeats, Qin was replaced by **Zhang Wentian** as the head of the Party in the Zunyi conference (January 15–17, 1935). In August, Qin was put in charge of propaganda in the Politburo and became the Chairman of the Chinese Soviet Republic Provisional Executive Committee after the Red Army reached Yan'an.

In December 1936, Qin accompanied Zhou Enlai to Xi'an to persuade **Zhang Xueliang** and Yang Hucheng to release Jiang Jieshi and to force Jiang to resist Japan's invasion. After the peaceful resolution of the Xi'an incident, Qin was sent to Nanjing as a delegate to negotiate anti-Japanese cooperation with the GMD. In Nanjing, he rebuilt the CCP organizations in the southern provinces. He also helped to reorganize the New Fourth Route Army. In the CCP Politburo in December 1937, Zhou Enlai, Qin Bangxian, Xiang Ying, and **Dong Biwu** were assigned to establish the Changjiang Bureau to lead the Party organizations in the southern provinces. The Changjiang Bureau was later merged with the CCP delegation to the nationalist government and Wang Ming became the secretary of the Bureau.

In 1941, Qin Bangxian became the head of the New China News Agency and the editor-in-chief of the *Liberation Daily*, upon their establishment. In 1945, Qin was elected into the Central Committee in the Seventh National Congress of the CCP in Yan'an.

Qin Bangxian went to Chongqing in January 1946 to participate in negotiations with the GMD. On his way back to Yan'an on April 8, he was killed in a plane crash.

REFERENCES: Marilyn Levine, "Po Ku (Ch'in Pang-hsien)," in Edwin Pak-wah Leung, ed., *Historical Dictionary of Revolutionary China, 1839–1979* (Westport, CT, 1992), 325–327; Li Zhiying, *Bo Gu zhuan* [A Biography of Bo Gu] (Beijing, 1994).

CHIU-YEE CHEUNG

# C

CHAN, ANSON. *See* CHEN, ANSON.

CHEN, ANSON (Anson Chan Fang On-sang, January 17, 1940–   ). Chief secretary of the former British Hong Kong government from 1993 to 1997; chief secretary for administration of the Hong Kong Special Administrative Region government from 1997 to 2001.

Born in Shanghai, Anson Chen (better known as Anson Chan) moved with her family to Hong Kong when she was eight years old. She received her education in Hong Kong and graduated from the University of Hong Kong in 1962 with a Bachelor of Arts degree in English and English literature. Upon graduation, she was the first woman to enter the former British Hong Kong government as administrative officer. She was married to Archie Chan Tai-wing, who was a former executive of the Caltex oil company. From 1962 to 1984, Anson Chen held a number of senior posts, and in the 1970s she organized other female administrative officers in the fight for equal rights and opportunities for both sexes in the civil service. From 1984 to 1987, she was director of Social Welfare, the first woman to rise to such a position. It was during her directorship in 1986 that the Kwok Ah-nui incident happened. The media criticized her as a "heartless bureaucrat," as she ordered officers to break into Kwok Ah-nui's home and took the six-year-old girl away from her mentally unstable mother. Many years later, Chen described the event as an unforgettable experience. From 1987 to 1993, Chen was secretary for Economic Services, and was the first woman to lead a policy branch. In 1993, she became the chief secretary of the British Hong Kong government, and was the first Chinese and the first woman to head the civil service. In the same year, Chinese mainland officials attacked her in the Container Terminal 9 dispute.

The popularity ratings of Chen were high. In May 1996, the local *South China Morning Post* conducted an opinion poll and more than one half of the respondents supported Chen to be the chief executive of the future Special Administrative Region (SAR) government. Later on, rumors spread that Beijing decided on a "dream team" for the SAR, comprising Tung Chee Hwa (**Dong Jianhua**) and Chief Secretary Anson Chen. Interviewed by CNN, Chen refused to say whether she would join the election, but indicated her willingness to work for the SAR government no matter who became its head. In October, Chen announced that she would not run for chief executive. After Tung Chee Hwa became the chief executive designate in December 1996, he sought the cooperation of Chen so as to ensure the smooth transfer of the civil service after the turnover. Since 1997, the approval ratings of Chen remained high, ranging from over 60% to about 70% in opinion polls conducted by the University of Hong Kong. She enjoyed high popularity, which Tung was unable to achieve. In a *Newsweek* interview, Chen claimed that she would resign if she had to accept policies contradictory to her own principles. The foreign media often called her the "iron lady" of Hong Kong or "the conscience of Hong Kong."

Anson Chen became the chief secretary for administration of the Hong Kong SAR. There were always rumors that the "Tung-Chen partnership" did not work, because Tung and Chen had different working styles. While the chief executive laid his hands on every government policy and preferred a more personal administration, Chen upheld the traditional practice of the civil service of following established and well-defined rules. In order to remove public anxieties, Tung invited Chen to stay as the chief secretary for administration for three more years in March 1999. In 1998, Chen faced two criticisms. First, legislative council members charged that she was responsible for the chaos of the new Chek Lap Kok Airport as she had been the head of the Airport Development Steering Committee. Second, the Public Accounts Committee report blamed her for failing to clearly inform the executive council of the construction of a power plant when she was serving as secretary for Economic Services.

In January 2001, Chen announced her resignation as the chief secretary. After 39 years in civil service, she explained her retirement due to personal reasons. Speculators linked her resignation to conflicts with Tung, and to an earlier incident in which Chinese Vice-Premier **Qian Qichen** allegedly told her to provide the chief executive with better support. While Chen denied any problems in her relations with Tung, she admitted that there were people who tried to sow discord in their partnership. In addition, Chen claimed that she had no desire to run for chief executive though Tung's term would expire in 2002. She believed that her successor should be a current senior official, who could continue the best traditions of the civil service.

REFERENCES: Wang Gungwu and John Wong, eds., *Hong Kong in China: The Challenges of Transition* (Singapore, 1999); James C. Hsiung, ed., *Hong Kong the Super Paradox: Life after Return to China* (New York, 2000).

CINDY YIK-YI CHU

**CHEN BAOCHEN** (October 19, 1848–March 5, 1935). Qing loyalist; tutor to **Puyi**.

A native of Minhou, Fujian, Chen Baochen passed the *jinshi* examination and became a Hanlin academician at the age of eighteen. He soon distinguished himself in the imperial court for his fervid attacks on the weaknesses of his colleagues. In foreign affairs, he advocated a patriotic and militant policy. Together with **Zhang Zhidong** and Zhang Peilun, they constituted the *qingliudang* (purist party) in the government during the 1870s and 1880s.

When the Sino-French War broke out in 1884, Chen Baochen was sent to Jiangsu to assist Zeng Guoquan in the strenthening of coastal defenses. He was Zeng's assistant in the negotiation with Jules Patenotre, French minister to China, for terms of peace at Shanghai. War resumed as both sides failed to reach an agreement. The next year Zeng successfully concluded a peace treaty with the French. Chen's insistence on war antagonized Zeng Guoquan and other senior officials. For his severe criticism of the establishment, he was demoted five ranks in 1891, and went into retirement shortly after.

As a retired official, Chen Baochen enthusiastically promoted educational development in his home province. In 1895 he was one of the founding members of the Qiangxuehui (Society for the Study of National Strengthening) in Shanghai, an organization sponsored by Zhang Zhidong for the promotion of reform through lectures and publications. In the following years, he founded the Dongwen Academy at Fuzhou and the Fujian Normal School.

Under the recommendation of Zhang Zhidong, Chen Baochen was recalled to service in 1908. The next year he was appointed to a seat reserved for eminent scholars in the National Assembly. In the first session of the National Assembly from October 1910 to January 1911, Chen took the lead in the controversy over the draft of a new criminal code because he thought that some of the provisions disregarded traditional Chinese values. On the eve of the 1911 Revolution, he became the Chinese tutor of Puyi, Emperor Xuantong.

After the emperor's abdication in 1912, Chen Baochen continued to serve Puyi as his tutor and adviser until 1931. According to Puyi, "of all the Qing Dynasty officials, he was considered one of the most stable and cautious."

To him, Chen was the most loyal man he ever knew. For his loyalty, Chen Baochen was awarded the title of Grand Guardian in 1916. In the abortive restoration of 1917, he helped arrange the enthronement of Puyi, and was made a member of the Regency Board. On the occasion of the deposed emperor's marriage in 1922, he was honored with the title of Grand Tutor.

In 1924 Chen Baochen stayed with Puyi in the Japanese embassy after their expulsion from the Forbidden City. Later they moved to the Japanese concession in Tianjin. Chen, Zheng Xiaoxu, and Luo Zhenyu were the three advisers whom Puyi saw daily. While Zheng and Luo were seeking Japanese help for restoration, Chen opposed it. Puyi soon felt that Chen was a hindrance to his restoration. In November 1931, he went with Zheng Xiaoxu to Manchuria to plot for the establishment of Manchukuo. Chen paid a visit to Puyi at Port Arthur the next January. Disappointed, he returned to Beiping (Beijing) and died there in 1935, at the age of eighty-seven.

REFERENCES: Henry Pu Yi, *The Last Manchu: The Autobiography of Henry Pu Yi, Last Emperor of China*, trans. Kuo Ying Paul Tsai (New York, 1967); Jia Yijun, *Zhonghua minguo mingren zhuan* [Eminent Chinese of the Republic of China], 2 vols. (Beiping, 1933); *Zhongguo jinxiandaishi dadian* [A Dictionary of Modern and Contemporary Chinese History], 2 vols. (Beijing, 1992).

HENRY Y.S. CHAN

**CHEN BODA** (1904–September 20, 1989). Mao Zedong's "political secretary" (*zhengzhi mishu*) and research assistant at Yan'an; radical ideologist and chief editor of the Chinese Communist Party theoretical journal *Red Flag* upon its founding in 1958; developer of Marxist rationales to justify the harsh Party rectification of the early 1940s, the quick collectivization of the mid-1950s, the political defense of the Great Leap, and the Cultural Revolution; chief Party monitor of the Chinese Academy of Sciences; by 1966, head of the Cultural Revolution Small Group, from which he was purged for "ultraleftism" in 1970.

Chen Boda was born in Huian County, Fujian, as Chen Shangyu. His parents, who are identified as poor peasants, moved in his childhood southwest to Jimei, at the mainland end of the causeway from Xiamen (Amoy) Island. One of their motives was probably to facilitate their son's attendance at the Jimei (Chip Bee) Normal School, which had been financed by Singapore tycoon Chen Jiageng (Tan Kah Kee). Upon graduation, Chen traveled briefly to Guangzhou. By 1925, he enrolled at Shanghai Labor University, a project of the First United Front of the Nationalist (GMD) and Chinese Communist parties. The university's faculty included the leftist writer **Qu Qiubai**. Chen also befriended the future political commissar Rao Shushi, and he joined the Chinese Communist Party (CCP) in 1927.

Returning to Fujian, Chen was hired to work as the private secretary of GMD General Zhang Zhen, doing editorial and clerical preparation for the Northern Expedition as a CCP member of the First United Front. When the

Front collapsed he fled to Shanghai, was arrested in Nanjing, jailed for a month, and then released on General Zhang's recommendation. He soon renewed contacts with the Party and was chosen to depart for Moscow to attend **Sun Yat-sen** University. In three years of study there, he became an expert on Marxist theory.

He was afflicted with a stammer, and had a heavy Fujian accent. He was short, and his personality was bookish. In Moscow he was affiliated with the minority "branch faction" of CCP students, rather than with the main "international faction" that was more loyal to Soviet leaders. He was therefore excluded from most politics there—and in comparison with others, he learned more Marxist Leninism.

Returning to China in 1931, he married another Moscow student, Zhu Yuren of Sichuan (sister of CCP martyr and Politburo member Luo Yinong, who came from Mao's hometown). Chen taught ancient Chinese history in Beijing, making his name because of articles written under the pen names Chen Zhimei and Chen Boda. He also did underground Party work at Tianjin. Chen wrote articles to mediate a long-running dispute between revolutionary "national defense literature" writers who stressed class struggle and were associated with **Lu Xun** (toward whom Chen himself inclined), and other writers who emphasized nationalism and insisted that literature should serve current popular needs. When the Sino-Japanese War expanded in 1937, Chen went to Yan'an, lecturing at the Central Party School and heading its China Problems Research Office. He soon became Mao's research assistant and private secretary, finding apt quotations and helping to express Mao's ideas in Marxist terms. His calligraphy, reportedly taught by his elder brother Dunyu, was reportedly "very beautiful," which raised his prestige.

Chen claimed that dialectical materialism was the world's greatest cultural achievement, and that it came in Chinese as well as Western forms. Modern "plain speech" (*baihua*), containing some Western loan words, could be made accessible to the Chinese masses and become "common speech" (*putonghua*)—and similarly, Marxism could be sinicized. Chen relied not just on texts by Marx and Engels, but also on dialectical elements in ancient Chou philosophy. He particularly liked Mo Zi, whose notions on "appearance and reality" and "knowledge and action" (*ming shi, zhi xing*) seemed useful for contemporary problems. Chen was a Chinese academic, while Mao was an activist who often attacked Chinese traditions more broadly than did his secretary. But Chen could phrase Mao's ideas dialectically, as a Chinese national form of Marxist Leninism, and his writing talents were a complement to Mao's own.

A few months after coming to Yan'an in 1937, Chen published the first collection of Mao's writings (*Mao Zedong lun*). In the July 1, 1938, first anniversary issue of *Liberation Daily*, his article represented the Maoist faction, and it was set beside another essay from a student who had returned from the USSR. Chen participated in the Rectification Campaign after 1942. In 1944–1945 he drafted an official history of the Party, stressing that Mao had consistently evolved the correct line from 1921 onward. (This official history was revised and published in the early 1950s.) Chen joined the Central Committee in 1945, becoming a full member in 1946. By this time, he was Mao's most prominent and steady hagiographer.

After 1949, Chen's administrative duties broadened, and he published less. For example, he joined the Party's Rural Work Department in 1955 and the Politburo as an alternate member in 1956. His ideological policy portfolio included defining China's position vis-à-vis Soviet "revisionism," especially after Khrushchev's criticisms of Stalin. Chen was the only high leader to accompany Mao on both the 1949 and 1957 journeys to Moscow. He first suggested the slogan "Let one hundred schools of thought contend." The first public use of the term "people's commune" (*renmin gongshe*) appeared in his July 1, 1958, *Red Flag* inaugural article as editor. China's expanded cooperatives bore scant resemblance to the 1871 Paris Commune, but Chen had long been fascinated with the Paris precedent. In the fall of 1958, he proposed abolishing the use of Chinese currency—an idea from which even **Mao Zedong** distanced himself. Along with Mao and **Zhang Chunqiao**, Chen visited a Hebei commune that experimented with the "free supply system." In 1962, when a plenum was called to reverse post–Leap market policies, Chen was chosen to give the report on rural work, perhaps because Mao trusted his in-house radical muse at this time.

By August 1966, Chen became head of the Cultural Revolution (CR) Small Group, surely at Mao's direction. In this capacity he presided over many Red Guard rallies in Beijing that autumn. By mid-1967, however, Mao needed to mend fences with rebellious soldiers at Wuhan—and this meant a break with radicals who had long been Chen's colleagues. The autumn of 1967 saw a purge of the "ultraleft May 16 corps," removing Qi Benyu, Guan Feng, Mu Xin, Lin Jie, and Wang Li—all members of the Cultural Revolution Small Group, and all on the staff of *Red Flag*. Chen survived to help draft Lin Biao's political report to the 1969 Party congress. When Mao and **Zhou Enlai** apparently insisted on a less radical version, Chen resisted with Lin's support. The congress elected Chen one of the five Politburo Standing Committee members; this was the highest position in his career. At the August 1970 Lushan Plenum, Chen again sided with Lin to propose that Mao, contrary to the chairman's own wishes, be made head of state. To buttress this cause, Chen collected quotations on "the theory of genius." Mao, now wary of Marshal Lin, was not amused; and about a month later, Chen was purged.

In 1980, when other top leftists in the Gang of Four were tried, a court sentenced Chen to 18 years in jail. Because of sickness, he was released from prison at age eighty-four in October 1988, in a period of deradicalization of the kind he had always opposed. Chen may have been heartened by the repressions surrounding Tiananmen, but he died of heart failure at home on September 20, 1989.

REFERENCES: Parris Chang, *Radicals and Radical Ideology in the Cultural Revolution* (orig. title: "The Role of Chen Boda in the Cultural Revolution") (New York, 1972); Roderick MacFarquhar, *The Origins of the Cultural Revolution*, 3 vols. (New York, 1974, 1983, 1997); Raymond F. Wylie, *The Emergence of Maoism: Mao Zedong, Chen Boda, and the Search for Chinese Theory, 1935–1945* (Stanford, CA, 1980).

LYNN T. WHITE III

**CHEN CHENG** (Ch'en Ch'eng, January 4, 1897–March 5, 1965). Nationalist general; governor of Taiwan; vice-president of the Republic of China on Taiwan; architect of Taiwan's land reform.

Born in Gaoshi village, Qingtian county, Zhejiang province, to a modest landlord's household, Chen Cheng attended the Eleventh Normal School at Lishui. In 1917 he graduated and entered the Hangzhou provincial school of physical education, graduating in 1918. He then entered the eighth class of the Baoding Military Academy where he specialized in artillery.

He joined the Guomindang in July 1920, and in June 1922 graduated from the Baoding Military Academy. In June 1924 he became an artillery instructor at the Huangpu (Whampoa) Military Academy, where he formed what would become a lifelong friendship with Jiang Jieshi and an adversarial relationship with the academy's commandant, He Yingqin.

In January 1926 Chen Cheng became commander of the Huangpu Specialist Corps and was promoted to staff officer with the rank of lieutenant colonel when the Northern Expedition began. In the spring of 1927, he was promoted to brigadier general; that July, he received command of the Twenty-first Division.

After participating in the final stage of the Northern Expedition, Chen Cheng was assigned to the campaigns against Communist forces in Jiangxi province. In Jiangxi he not only distinguished himself militarily but collected many Chinese Communist documents; those documents describing Chinese Red Army history, organization and tactics, were reprinted in six volumes in Taiwan in 1960.

In March 1935 Chen Cheng reorganized cavalry, artillery, and engineering units throughout China. In 1936 he served in Shanxi province, curbing Communist forces in the northwest and strengthening Nationalist government control over Shanxi.

With Jiang Jieshi's full trust, Chen continued to serve in various posts. On June 14, 1938, he was made commanding officer of the Ninth War Area, governor of Hubei province, secretary-general of the San Min Zhu Yi Youth Corp, and dean of the central training corps, all at the same time.

As the Nationalist government's war of resistance against Japan worsened, Chen Cheng's responsibilities increased. Promoted to the rank of general second grade, Chen undertook the defense of Chongqing city and Hubei province and commanded the Sixth War Area. In February 1943, Jiang appointed Chen Cheng to command the new Expeditionary Army which was being created with American military aid and advisory help to spearhead the campaign to recover Burma. Rivalry with General He Yingzin complicated Chen Cheng's organizational efforts.

When the Japanese launched Operation Ichigo in mid-April 1994, Chen Cheng's task was to contain Chinese communist forces in the northwest as well as their growing influence in north China. In December 1944 Chen Cheng was made minister of war; his tasks were to upgrade the Chinese army with American military aid and to oversee military affairs in rear areas.

After Japan's defeat, Chen Cheng began fighting the Communists again, this time in Manchuria. Jiang appointed Chen director of the Northeast Headquarters. But by the time Chen took control of his troops, the Communists had infiltrated and taken the initiative in Manchuria by pushing their land reform and isolating the cities.

In January 1948, when the Communists launched their full military campaign against the Nationalist forces, Chen Cheng asked to be relieved for surgery to remove his stomach ulcers. After his recovery he was appointed chairman of the Taiwan provincial government and, on July 19, 1949, commander of the office of a new headquarters for southeast China at Taibei. On March 1, 1950, Chen Cheng became president of the Executive Yuan at Taibei. In 1952 he implemented Taiwan's land reform program.

In March 1954 and again in March 1960 the National Assembly elected Chen Cheng vice-president of the Republic of China. In July–August 1961 he paid an official visit to the United States to build goodwill between the two nation states. As Jiang Jieshi's son rose in power and influence, Chen Cheng was unable to formally succeed Jiang Jieshi as president. On March 1965 Chen Cheng died in Taibei from cancer of the liver.

REFERENCES: Howard L. Boorman and Richard C. Howard, eds., *Biographical Dictionary of Republican China*, vol. 1 (New York, 1970), 152–160; *Land Reform in Taiwan* (Taibei, 1961).

RAMON H. MYERS

**CHEN DUXIU** (October 8, 1879–May 27, 1942). Founder of the *New Youth* magazine; cofounder of the Chinese Communist Party.

A champion of revolution and leader of the Chinese Communist movement, Chen Duxiu's life and career represented the profound dilemma many Chinese intellectuals faced in their effort to save China in the first half of the twentieth century.

A native of Anhui province in central China, Chen received solid training in Confucian classics in his youth and passed the first level of the civil service examination at the age of seventeen. But he soon became critical of the system for its obsolete contents and corrupt administration. In 1898, Chen supported the abortive reform led by **Kang Youwei**. Between 1902 and 1906 Chen made two trips to Japan in search for new ideas. In 1907 he traveled to France and came under the influence of the revolutionary tradition of that country. He returned home in 1910 and established a network of Chinese patriots, many of whom became members of the Tongmenhui (Chinese United League) that was instrumental in the Republican Revolution of 1911.

In the New Culture Movement of 1915–1927, Chen Duxiu established himself as the spokesman for a generation of Chinese intelligentsia who wanted to fundamentally change Chinese society by adopting Western ideology. In 1915, he founded the *Youth Magazine*, a magazine that was almost synonymous with cultural iconoclasm of the May Fourth era. It was renamed *New Youth* the following year. In 1917, Chen Duxiu was invited by Cai Yuanpei, chancellor of Beijing University to take charge of the university's School of Letters. In 1918 he cofounded and coedited the *Weekly Review* (Meizhou pinglun), a forum for social reform and nationalist revolution.

Disappointed by the lack of progress and concerned about the continuous national crisis in China, Chen sought to save his country by changing its culture. In his writings, he loudly championed an intellectual revolution spearheaded by a new literature. Such a revolution, Chen claimed, was aimed at the destruction of the "aristocratic literature" that was "nothing but literary chiseling and flattery" and the creation of "a simple, expressive literature of the people." It was also intended to smash the "outmoded, showy, classical literature" and to construct a "fresh and sincere literature of realism."

Out of frustration by the stultifying political system in the 1910s and 1920s, Chen became increasingly radical in his world outlook. In his articles on contemporary politics, he vehemently exposed the sham of the republicanism in the Beijing government and evil doings of China's social and political establishment. Under Chen's auspices, contributors to *New Youth* placed faith in democracy and science as the keys to China's rebirth and called for a wholesale liquidation of the foot-dragging elements in China's traditional culture. They also saw individualism as the starting point of a social revolution and promoted free thinking and expression as preconditions for the development of a new citizenry. Chen's view of life was positive and optimistic. In an article published in 1918, Chen Duxiu gave the following definition of the ultimate purpose of life: "During his lifetime, an individual should devote his efforts to create happiness and to enjoy it, and also to keep it in store in society so that individuals of the future may also enjoy it, one generation doing the same for the next and so on unto infinity."

As a patriot, Chen was angered by the power politics at the Paris Peace Conference in 1919. He immediately condemned the hypocrisy of Western allies and pointed out the dangers in the peace settlement. In an article in the *New Youth*, he wrote, "Each country in the Paris Peace Conference is merely interested in the promotion of its own interests. Justice, eternal peace, and President Wilson's 'Fourteen Points' are all empty talks, not worth even one penny. . . . The Paris Peace Conference is miles away from eternal peace and human happiness. The people of the world have to stand up to solve the problem of peace themselves."

In the same period, Chen Duxiu became interested in Marxism and came to see Marxism and the Russian Revolution of 1917 as the gospel for the Chinese people. With assistance from the Third Communist International or Comintern, he began to organize Chinese communists and socialists into a cohesive movement. Even though Chen Duxiu did not attend the First Congress of the Chinese Communist Party (CCP) in July 1921, he was elected the general secretary of the Party and remained at the top of the CCP until 1927. During the First United Front between the CCP and the Nationalist Party (Guomindang or GMD) between 1923 and 1927, Chen repeatedly proposed the withdrawal of the CCP from the alliance because of the animosity of the GMD's right wing. Each time, he was overruled by the Comintern.

A believer in orthodox Marxism, however, Chen believed that the predominantly rural Chinese society was not ready for a socialist revolution in the 1920s. Thus when faced with growing violence in the mass movement during the Northern Expedition in 1926–1928, Chen cautioned his party against excessive radicalism in the hope of avoiding unnecessary loss of lives. After **Jiang Jieshi**'s coup in Shanghai in April 1927, the Communist Party was forced to go underground and Chen thereafter lost control of the Chinese Communist movement.

In 1929, Chen Duxiu came under the ideological influence of the Russian Communist leader Leon Trotsky and became a caustic critic of the Comintern. He asked the CCP to free itself from foreign control and focus on the struggle for workers' power in a parliamentary democracy and unionist movement. At the same time, he asked the CCP to give up armed struggle in the countryside. In 1931, Chen Duxiu and some Trotskyites in the Communist Party organized the CCP Left Wing Opposition in Shanghai and advocated orthodox Marxism in its official publication *Sparks*.

In 1932, Chen was arrested by the Nationalist government and remained in prison until 1937. In 1938 he left the CCP, apparently tired of the factional struggle in the party and shocked by the political purges in the Soviet Union. He condemned Stalin's tyranny and theoretically forsook proletarian dictatorship as the path toward socialism. He finally realized that neither Leninism nor Trotskyism was a solution to China's problems. Instead, he came to see Western parliamentary democracy and constitutionalism as China's new hope.

Chen died on May 27, 1942, in Baisha, Jiangjin county, Sichuan province.

REFERENCES: John K. Fairbank and Albert Feuerwerker, eds., *The Cambridge History of China, Vol. 13: Republican China, 1912–1949* (New York, 1986); Thomas C. Kuo, *Chen Tu-hsiu (1879–1942) and the Chinese Communist Movement* (South Orange, NJ, 1975); Benjamin Schwartz, "Chen Tu-hsiu and the Acceptance of the Modern West," *Journal of the History of Ideas*, 12 (1951): 61–72; Hu Shen, ed., *Zhongguo gongchandang de qishi nian* [Seventy Years of the CCP] (Beijing, 1991).

PENG DENG

**CHEN GONGBO** (October 19, 1892–June 3, 1946). Founding member of the Chinese Communist Party; leader of the Left Guomindang; collaborator during the Sino-Japanese War.

The only son of a disaffected military official in the Qing government, Chen as a teenager followed his father and participated in anti-Manchu activities in his home province of Guangdong. After the arrest and imprisonment of his father by the government in 1906, Chen managed to continue his education while working to support his family. The demise of the Qing in 1912 improved the condition of Chen's family, and in 1917 he entered the prestigious Beijing University.

At the university, Chen was influenced by the new ideological currents of the time, although not actively involved in the May Fourth Movement of 1919. Upon his graduation in 1920, Chen returned to Guangdong and helped establish one of the earliest Communist organizations there. The following year he attended the founding meeting (i.e., the First National Congress) of the Chinese Communist Party (CCP) in Shanghai. Chen, however, was troubled by both the disputes at the meeting and the harassment from local police, and left Shanghai before the meeting was concluded. In 1922, in the wake of **Chen Jiongming**'s coup d'état against **Sun Yat-sen**'s Guangzhou regime, Chen was criticized by the CCP leadership, which supported Sun, for his connections with Chen Jiongming. Angered by this accusation, and dissatisfied with the CCP's interference in his personal plans, Chen withdrew from the Party later that year and left for the United States for graduate studies.

Chen received an M.A. in economics at Columbia University in 1924, upon the completion of a thesis on "The Communist Movement in China." At the invitation of his friend Liao Zhongkai, he returned to China in early 1925 to work for the reorganized Guomindang and its new Guangzhou regime. He was soon appointed to a number of important positions in the GMD and in the provincial government of Guangdong. When Liao was assassinated in August 1926, amidst the intense power struggle following the death of Sun Yat-sen, Chen succeeded Liao as head of the Party's Peasant Department.

In the months that followed, Chen developed close ties to **Wang Jingwei**, then leader of the GMD and the Guangzhou regime. Wang, however, was soon ousted by **Jiang Jieshi** in March 1926. During the Northern Expedition, Chen played a major role in the Wuhan regime headed by Wang. After the collapse of that regime, he helped Wang in an abortive attempt to recapture Guangzhou as their new base. From 1928 to 1930, while Wang was in exile in France, Chen led Wang's supporters in China to oppose the Nanjing government established by Jiang. Their criticism of Jiang's conservative leadership won them the title the "Left GMD." In late 1928 Chen founded the "Society for the Reorganization of the GMD" (known as the "Reorganizationists") in Shanghai, which called for a return to the radicalism of the Party's 1924 reorganization and supported Wang as its leader. So critical were Chen's propagandist and organizational skills to the Society, however, that his own influence in it competed with that of Wang's. In 1929 Chen went to France to meet with Wang for a discussion of future plans. Both of them soon returned to China and organized a series of political and military revolts against Nanjing. All of the revolts failed. In early 1931, Chen consented to Wang's decision to disband the society and went in exile in Europe.

A year later, Wang decided to cooperate with Jiang and organize a new government in Nanjing. Chen returned from Europe and followed Wang into the Nanjing government, serving as minister of industry under Wang's premiership. Although frustrated by the continuous loss of power by Wang's faction to Jiang and his men in Nanjing, Chen stayed loyally at Wang's side and assisted Wang in the difficult and unpopular task of negotiating with Japan. In late 1935, after Wang was wounded by an assailant's bullets, Chen left the government with Wang. Shortly after the outbreak of the Sino-Japanese War in 1937, Chen toured Europe as a special envoy of the government and sought international assistance to China's war effort. He returned home in early 1938 and was appointed head of the GMD's provincial branch in Sichuan.

Later that year, Wang decided to leave Chongqing and launch a "peace initiative" with the Japanese. Chen was said to have been opposed to it at first. He nevertheless followed Wang to Hanoi in December and assisted him in announcing the peace plan. When Wang moved from Hanoi to Shanghai and negotiated a separate peace agreement with Japan, however, Chen refused to go along. After staying in Hong Kong for more than a year, Chen at last joined Wang's collaborationist regime in Nanjing in March 1940, largely due to his personal loyalty to Wang. For the next four years, he served as head of the regime's Legislative Yuan and, from 1941 to 1944, as its mayor of Shanghai. Upon Wang's death in late 1944, Chen succeeded him as head of the Nanjing regime, but his actual power in the regime was constantly overshadowed by that of **Zhou Fohai**, the real architect of Wang's "peace movement" and regime. Following Japan's surrender in

1945, Chen briefly sought refuge in Japan but was brought back to China for trial. He was convicted of high treason and executed in Suzhou in 1946.
REFERENCES: N. Lee, W.S.K. Waung, and L.Y. Chin, eds., *Kuxiaolu* [Bitter Smile: Memoirs of Chen Gongbo] (Hong Kong, 1979); Wai-chor So, *The Kuomintang Left in the National Revolution, 1924–1931* (Hong Kong, 1991); C. Martin Wilbur, "The Variegated Career of Ch'en Kung-po," in Chün-tu Hsueh, ed., *Revolutionary Leaders of Modern China* (Oxford, 1971).

WANG KE-WEN

**CHEN JIONGMING** (January 13, 1878–September 22, 1933). Governor of Guangdong; army minister and interior minister; champion of the movement for a Chinese federal republic.

Born in Haifeng, Guangdong, Chen Jiongming received both training in Chinese classics and modern education. Having attained a *xiucai* degree in the civil service examination, he attended and successfully completed studies at both the Haifeng Normal School and Guangdong Institute of Law and Politics, respectively, in 1905 and 1908. At the turn of the twentieth century, Chen had become keenly aware of China's critical condition resulting from both internal crises and foreign aggression. China's defeat by Japan, the abortive attempt at rejuvenation in the summer of 1898, together with the armed uprisings under **Sun Yat-sen**'s general leadership led Chen to search for ways of saving China from further decline. He plunged himself into activities like organizing forums on political reform, social improvement, as well as launching a successful campaign for removal of the atrocious prefect of Huizhou.

In 1909 Chen was elected to the provisional provincial assembly of Guangdong, as a result of Qing court's introduction of constitutional reform. He addressed social, economic, administrative, and judicial issues, and was instrumental in enacting pertinent laws on education, railroad construction, anticorruption and local autonomy. Chen's determination for China's rejuvenation and Qing court's half-hearted constitutional reform and ambition to hanging onto political power through centralization finally pushed him into joining the United League in November 1909. He was subsequently involved in the two Guangzhou uprisings of 1910 and 1911. After the Wuchang uprising in October 1911, he captured Huizhou and the adjacent region to the east of Guangzhou. For his contribution and military strength on which Guangdong revolutionary region counted for stabilizing the province, Chen was appointed deputy military governor of the province.

Together with the efforts of fellow revolutionary leaders like Hu Hanmin, Liao Zhongkai, Zhu Zhixin, and others, Chen held Guangdong firmly in control. Educational reform and new industries were promoted and armed forces were consolidated. However, their endeavors to modernize the province were cut short as Provisional President **Yuan Shikai** usurped his power and attempted to restore the monarchy. This drove Chen and others to rise up against Yuan, who summarily crushed the so-called Second Revolution and Chen fled overseas.

Meanwhile, Chen pondered upon the best way out for China, and in March 1916 he made known his ideal form of government for China: the model of a federal republic, when embarking on launching his military campaign against Yuan. After Yuan's demise, Chen rallied support for the Sun-led *Hufa yundong*, or movement for protection for the Provisional Constitution. In December 1917, Sun appointed Chen commander of the Guangdong Army, the only troops loyal to Sun's cause. Chen subsequently headed the army into south Fujian lending support to the *Hufa* movement there. The Guangdong troops soon established themselves in the Zhangzhou region, and for two years (1918–1920) Chen turned it into a model by introducing reform there.

In 1920 Sun was able to found a revolutionary regime in Guangzhou with support of the Guangdong Army under Chen's command, who led the troops back to Guangdong at Sun's instruction. Sun subsequently launched the Northern Expedition against the warlords then in control of most parts of China. However, Chen was determined to turn Guangdong into a model province, eager to see his model government for China, *Liangsheng zizhi*, or a union of autonomous provinces. Soon they were locked in serious conflicts over the best way to rid China of political turmoil and social economic ills. Sun opted for unification of China through military campaigns, while Chen opted for a federal republic through peaceful evolution. On June 16, 1922, Chen's lieutenants bombarded Sun's presidential office in Guangzhou forcing Sun out of the province. During the subsequent year, Chen ruled Guangdong hoping to turn it into a model province for eventual formation of a federal republic. However, he was driven out of Guangzhou in early 1923 and from Guangdong two years later by the forcers loyal to Sun. He fled to Hong Kong where for the remaining years of his life he continued to promote his federal model for China and published a systematic and detailed essay on it in 1927.

REFERENCES: Chen Dinyan and Gao Zhonglu, *An Inner History of Relationships among Chen Jiongming, Sun Yat-sen and Jiang Jieshi* (Hong Kong, 1997); Duan Yunzhang and Ni Junming, eds., *Collected Works of Chen Jiongming*, 2 vols. (Guangzhou, 1998); Duan Yunzhang et al., *The Life of Chen Jiongming* (Henan, 1989).

YEE-CHEUNG LAU

**CHEN SHAOYU.** *See* WANG MING.

**CHEN YUN** (1905–1995). Long-time economic planner and expert in economic development policies; chairman for the Party's discipline and inspection under economic reform.

Prior to his retirement in 1985, Chen Yun had held, at various times since 1949, a number of pivotal positions in the hierarchy of the Chinese Communist Party (CCP) and the central government in Beijing. He was vice-premier in charge of financial and economic affairs, state planning commission, vice-chairman of the National People's Congress (NPC), vice-chairman of the CCP, and a Politburo member. In 1987 he headed the Party's central advisory commission for Party discipline. Most notably, Chen Yun had been regarded by many as a theorist on the relationship between planning and market economy once **Deng Xiaoping** had embarked on economic reform for post–Mao China.

Chen Yun was born in a town near Shanghai in 1905. We know very little about his family background and education except that he reportedly had a primary school education. At age fifteen he was employed by the Shanghai Commercial Press, a known publishing firm in modern China, as a typesetter and sales person. In 1921 he became active in the trade union movement in Shanghai and in 1925 joined the CCP. With **Liu Shaoqi**, the Chinese Peoples Republic's president who was purged during the Cultural Revolution, he took an active part in the 1925 anti–British May 30th demonstration.

During 1927–1928, Chen Yun visited Moscow, but returned shortly afterward to join the guerrilla-based Jiangxi Soviet, with chief responsibility for organizing industrial workers and craftsmen. In 1934 he was elected to the Party's central committee. Chen Yun took part in the Long March (1934–1935) but did not complete the march. Instead he went to Moscow and returned to China in 1937 by way of Xinjiang in the northwest to work in economic affairs with the help of Soviet technicians loaned to Xinjiang's warlord Sheng Shicai.

From 1938 to 1943 Chen Yun headed the Party's central organization work and wrote a key treatise on Party cadres' training and discipline while giving lectures on Party affairs in Yan'an. In 1940 Chen Yun was elected to the Politburo and was put in charge of economic/financial work for the northwest border region. For five years, from 1940–1945, Chen Yun established his reputation as a thinker-doer in economics. After **Lin Biao**'s forces entered the northeast region during the civil war, Chen Yun went to Shenyang in 1945 and was put in charge of managing the heavy industries.

He joined the Chinese delegation to Moscow in 1952 to negotiate with the Soviet Union for the return of the Manchurian railroad and naval base in Dairen under the arrangement of the Sino-Soviet Treaty of Alliance. For the period 1953–1957 Chen Yun was a member of the State Planning Commission which had the responsibility for carrying out the First Five-Year Plan (1953–1957). By then Chen Yun had become a key player in China's economic affairs.

By 1958 his influence had begun to decline for he was considered to be a "conservative" and a "gradualist" against Mao's mass mobilization and

"Great Leap" approach for rapid economic development. From 1958 to the time of the Cultural Revolution, Chen Yun was on the sidelines as a party leader in economic affairs, even though he still held central committee membership. In 1978 Chen Yun returned to power as an elected member to the Party's Politburo and its standing committee, the apex of power. In 1979 Chen Yun, then a participant in Deng Xiaoping's "grand coalition" for economic reform, served as the head of the powerful state economic and financial commission as Deng consolidated his power.

Although Chen Yun was an early supporter of Deng's economic reform, he nevertheless adopted a rather cautious attitude toward it. Chen Yun's view of economic reform raised questions about the speed and extent of Deng's eagerness to move ahead. In that sense Chen Yun was a critic to Deng's reform. In 1981–1982 Chen Yun postulated the "bird-cage" thesis that the proper relationship between the planned and market economy is that of a "bird in a cage," meaning the planned economy was the "cage" that confined the "bird" in the market. He argued that planning must still play an important role, just as in the capitalist economy, in making rational decisions about questions such as markets for products and the sources of raw material. He also urged that there must be "readjustment" or cuts in spending for heavy industries such as steel, as well as improvements in the people's living standards. He wholeheartedly supported opening to the outside world for advanced technology and expertise. Also, toward the end of 1993, he cautioned about less "heat" in economic development policies and asked for some "cooling off." He insisted that in order to avoid stifling the market, planning must not be rigid.

Chen Yun, in his capacity as the first chairman of the central commission for discipline inspection, created by the 1982 Party constitution, insisted on upholding Party discipline for the cadres and correcting their work style based on Party rules that governed the behavior of Party members. He also addressed the problem of special privileges for the cadres—by criticizing the fact that they had access to material goods not available to ordinary citizens and that the children of high-ranking leaders were the first ones to study abroad.

Chen Yun died in Beijing on April 10, 1995, at age ninety.

REFERENCES: David Bachman, "Differing Visions of China's Post-Mao Economy," *Asian Survey* (March 1986), 293–330; Wolfgang Bartke, *Who's Who in the People's Republic of China* (New York, 1981), 37–38; Donald W. Klein and Anne B. Clark, *Biographic Dictionary of Chinese Communism, 1921–1965*, vol. 1 (Cambridge, MA, 1971), 149–153; James C.F. Wang, *Contemporary Chinese Politics*, 6th ed. (Upper Saddle River, NJ, 1999).

JAMES C.F. WANG

**CHIANG CHING-KUO.** *See* JIANG JINGGUO.

**CHIANG KAI-SHEK.** *See* JIANG JIESHI.

**CHU TEH.** *See* ZHU DE.

**CIXI, EMPRESS DOWAGER** (November 19, 1835–November 15, 1908). Wife of Emperor Xianfeng (r. 1850–1861); power figure in late Qing politics.

Empress Dowager Cixi was China's de facto ruler during the second half of the nineteenth century and one of the most powerful women in Chinese history. She was born Yehonala, daughter of Huizheng of the Manchu Bordered Blue Banner in 1835, and was chosen as a concubine to Emperor Xianfeng to enter the imperial court in 1851. Cixi was not the emperor's senior consort at this time, yet using her beauty, intelligence, and ability to manipulate power, she drew herself closer to him. She eventually became the emperor's favorite concubine and gave birth to his only son, Zaichun in 1856. Thereafter Cixi became a very influential member of the Qing court in Beijing.

In 1861, Cixi's son was enthroned as **Emperor Tongzhi** at the age of five following the death of Emperor Xianfeng. Empresses Cixi and Cian (who was Emperor Xianfeng's senior consort) were both appointed to be the young emperor's coregents. Naturally, Cixi was the more powerful regent; and for the first time in her life she was able to experience the sweet taste of power in the court. However, Cixi knew that if she wanted more control of the court, she had to cooperate closely with her brother-in-law Prince Gong, who was popular, influential, and powerful in Beijing.

The coup d'état of 1861 made Cixi a close political ally with Prince Gong, in which Cixi helped Prince Gong oust his ultraconservative enemies, such as Suxun, Prince Yi, and Prince Zheng. The power balance between Cixi and Prince Gong in the 1860s and 1870s seemed to have brought new strength to China, known as the Tongzhi Restoration, with Prince Gong as the leader in the Qing court to support the self-strengthening programs for the industrialization and modernization of China. It, however, would mean that China had to open its door more widely to the West. Empress Dowager Cixi, with the support of the conservative faction leader, Woren, opposed these changes. A power struggle thus developed between Cixi and Prince Gong.

In 1872, Cixi's son Emperor Tongzhi came of age and would assume his power as the emperor. Yet, Cixi remained strong and became even more ambitious in control of the court and the government after 1873. When Emperor Tongzhi died suddenly in 1875, Cixi was able to place, through her vicious nature and court manipulation, her four-year-old nephew Zaitian on the throne as **Emperor Guangxu**. This arrangement would guarantee Cixi's continued control over the emperor and the court.

Emperor Dowager Cixi's domination of the government after 1875 weakened China considerably. The rampant corruption under her reign virtually paralyzed many modernization programs initiated by Prince Gong and such

Han Chinese leaders as **Zeng Guofan**. In 1884, Cixi was able to eliminate her arch enemy, Prince Gong, from the government. In 1898, even her nephew Emperor Guangxu rebelled against Cixi by recruiting the young and reform-minded scholar **Kang Youwei** to launch the Hundred Day Reform (June 11 to September 20, 1898). The reform failed and Cixi resumed her regency by the end of 1898.

Empress Dowager Cixi's conservatism also worried foreign powers in China. As foreign encroachments on China reached new heights (such as the Sino-French War of 1884–1885, the Sino-Japanese War of 1894–1895, and the territory-lease treaties with Germany, France, Russia, and Great Britain in 1898 and 1899), Cixi became even more antiforeign. Her frustration over the government's inability to resist foreign intrusion led her to support the Boxer Uprising of 1900, which in the end not only humiliated China but also bankrupted Chinese finances. This alienated the Han Chinese leaders and stimulated such political activists as **Sun Yat-sen** to engage in anti–Manchu revolutionary movements.

It was only after the Boxer Uprising that Cixi gave in and approved a series of belated reforms in education, the military, and the restructuring of the government. They were fruitless and, at this time, her health deteriorated considerably. She died on November 15, 1908, just one day after Emperor Guangxu had died.

REFERENCES: Charlottee Haldane, *The Last Great Empress of China* (Indianapolis, 1967); Harry Hussey, *Venerable Ancestor: The Life and Times of Tz'u Hsi, Empress of China* (New York, 1970); Sterling Seagrave, *Dragon Lady: The Life and Legend of the Last Empress of China* (New York, 1992).

ANTHONY Y. TENG

# D

**DAOGUANG, EMPEROR** (September 16, 1782–February 25, 1850). First emperor to suffer humiliation at the hands of the West.

Interpretations of Qing history often revert to the theory of dynastic cycle. The concept holds that the first few emperors of a new dynasty are outstanding leaders. They reduce taxes, improve the irrigation system, and engage in other public works to benefit the people. The middle emperors are average. They basically carry on the work of their predecessors. The last few emperors are inept and/or corrupt. This leads to rebellion, which turns into revolution, and a new dynasty is founded. The cycle then begins anew.

The fifth emperor of the Qing, Emperor Daoguang's father, is usually presented as the emperor who is in power when the decline of the Qing begins. He was confronted with several problems. One was the continuing web of corruption surrounding Heshen. Other difficulties involved economic constraints, demographic pressure, and the concomitant local unrest, as expressed in numerous rebellions. These are the standard indices of dynastic decline.

When Emperor Daoguang came to the throne in 1821, he faced the same problems. In addition, his reign coincided with China's first clash with the West.

The initial years of rule were spent on internal issues. While the usual evaluation of Emperor Daoguang's handling of these matters, and in fact his entire reign, is that he was weak, indecisive, and miserly, one recent work has challenged this characterization. Jane Kate Leonard's book on the Emperor Daoguang's handling of the Grand Canal Crisis of 1824–1826 renders a much more favorable judgment. The emperor is presented as one who displayed skill, wisdom, and determination when confronted with the crisis. The conclusion Leonard offers is that the decline of the Qing dynasty came from overpopulation and fiscal shortages, rather than defective leadership at the top.

No matter which portrait of the emperor's early years one accepts, there is little question that he was overwhelmed by the confrontation with the West. Opium was at the heart of this clash. Used medicinally since the Tang Dynasty, opium consumption began to increase when the Portuguese started importing the drug into Taiwan in the early 1600s. In 1729 the Qing prohibited opium imports, to little avail. By 1820 the opium trade was booming. In that year some two million *taels* of silver flowed out of China, mostly into the pockets of British opium dealers.

The emperor became aware that this drain was damaging the national economy. By the early 1830s, the annual outflow rose to nine million *taels*. Finally, in 1838, after listening to various proposals, Emperor Daoguang decided to act. He commissioned **Lin Zexu** to stop the opium trade.

When Lin acted to carry out his orders, the British sent an expeditionary force to attack China. Once the war began going badly for China, the emperor's confidence in Lin faltered. This initial quavering then gave way to stern rebuke. The emperor made Lin Zexu the scapegoat for the humiliation the emperor suffered at the hands of the British. In reality, while nothing short of divine intervention could have prevented China's loss in the Opium War, the emperor's wavering between war and peace made matters worse.

The Treaty of Nanjing (1842), which ended the Opium War, cost the emperor's control over vital elements of his commercial, social, and foreign policies. To make matters worse, in 1848 he was advised of a substantial shortage in the vaults of the board of revenue. One year later, the Grand Canal became impassable. The unrest generated by all of these problems grew into the Taiping Rebellion.

Fortunately for him, Emperor Daoguang did not live to witness this deadly and protracted rebellion. He died in early 1850, leaving a humiliated and bankrupt empire.

REFERENCES: Arthur W. Hummel, *Eminent Chinese of the Ch'ing Period* (Washington, DC, 1943); Jane Kate Leonard, *Controlling from Afar: The Daoguang Emperor's Management of the Grand Canal Crisis, 1824–1826* (Ann Arbor, 1996).

GERALD W. BERKLEY-COATS

**DENG XIAOPING** (August 20, 1904–February 19, 1997). Informal "core," or "paramount," leader; Chinese Communist Party (CCP) general secretary; CCP military affairs committee chair; CCP Politburo standing committee member; state council vice-premier.

Born Deng Xixian to an educated landlord family in Paifang village, Xiexing township, Guang'an county, Sichuan, he was tutored, enrolled in a modern primary school and middle school, was graduated from the Chongqing Preparatory School (at age 16), worked more than studied during six work-study years in France, and then for a year in Moscow read Marxism-Leninism at **Sun Yat-sen** University (at 23). His bumpy but irrepressibly upward career in Party organization work culminated in 20 years as China's real top leader even while others held top offices. Richard Holbrooke, U.S. Assistant Secretary of State for East Asian Affairs when Washington restored full diplomatic relations with China in 1979, commented, "There is no other leader in the world who is doing anything even remotely in Deng's league."

During the early civil war years Deng, despite lack of formal military training, was active in military campaigns. In 1929, at age twenty-five, he helped Commander Zhang Yunyi establish the Seventh Red Army and Right River Soviet in the Guangxi-Yunnan border region (and during that time may have linked up with the young Vietnamese rebellion against French rule). By late 1930, in Jiangxi, he had been made chief-of-staff of the Third Army Corps under Peng Dehuai, and first met **Mao Zedong** about this time. In 1933 in Ruijin, the Communist capital, he edited a Red Army newspaper and lectured on Party history at the Red Army academy. He participated in the Long March as a political commissar; when Edgar Snow interviewed him in 1936, he had become Deputy Political Commissar of the First Army Corps under **Lin Biao**. In 1938 U.S. Military Observer Evans Carlson wrote that Deng's mind was "as keen as mustard" and his grasp of foreign affairs broad.

For the remainder of the civil war years (from age 35–45), he served as political commissar of Liu Bocheng's 129th Division, one of three major components of the Eighth Route Army operating mostly in the Taihang Mountains. The Seventh Party Congress in 1945 elected him to the Central Committee (CC). In the Huai-Hai campaign of 1948–1949, Deng stood out as secretary of the general front committee formed to coordinate the strategy of participating Communist armies. Afterward he followed Liu's columns, and redesignated the Second Field Army, into Sichuan. From 1949–1952 the three top leaders in the southwest were Deng, who was political commissar and commanders Liu Bocheng and He Long.

In mid-1952 he was transferred to Beijing and helicoptered into the inner circle. The next year, Deng was appointed to one committee to draft a constitution (chaired by Mao Zedong), another to draft an election law (chaired by **Zhou Enlai**), and a third to supervise national elections (chaired by **Liu Shaoqi**)—the sole member of all three. In April 1955 he was elevated to the Politburo, and at the Eighth Party Congress in September 1956 elected to the Politburo standing committee and chosen as the first Party general secretary (*zong shuji*). At age fifty-two he had become China's sixth ranking leader.

Deng survived the political tumult of the Great Leap Forward but not that of the later Cultural Revolution. His essential support for internal Party adjustments to policies gone awry led Mao in May 1958 to embrace him as a special "close comrade in arms." In 1957 Deng proposed measured responses to Party problems, and in 1959 to commune excesses (fortuitously possibly he was absent from the tension-filled Lushan Plenum with a ping pong injury). But his calls for "seeking truth from facts," for rehabilitating some cadres punished as "rightists," and for other corrective steps in the 1960s to meet the deepening rural crisis opened a gap between him and Mao. Deng was as visibly active in foreign affairs as in domestic matters during this period, notably joining or leading several delegations to Moscow and upholding Chinese positions as Sino-Soviet relations deteriorated.

In October 1966 Mao turned the radicalizing Cultural Revolution against Deng, now under house arrest, as the "number-two Party person in authority taking the capitalist road." This opened two long years of virulent and relentless verbal attacks, though Mao did shield him from worse. Deng finally lost his CC membership in April 1969, after which he was sent by the new leadership of Marshal Lin Biao to a tractor repair station in Xinjian County, Jiangxi, where he worked as a fitter, the trade he had learned in France as a youth. From age sixty-five to sixty-eight he cleaned the room, chopped wood, and broke up coal, and solely supported himself, his often-ill wife, his aged stepmother, and later his crippled son. He read widely during this interlude.

In 1973, after Lin Biao's downfall and subsequent military purges, Mao (now 80 and faltering) along with Zhou Enlai (75 and slowed by cancer) restored Deng as vice-premier, and by January 1975 added three more posts—vice-chairman of the Central Committee, vice-chairman of the Central Military Commission, and chief of the general staff of the People's Liberation Army (PLA). Deng took charge until Premier Zhou died a year later. Suspicious anew of Deng's agenda and abilities, however, Mao instead tapped Hua Guofeng as the new premier and three months later as Party chairman-designate. Deng was relieved of all official posts in April 1976.

When he surged once more after Mao's death, none could withstand his veteran assault, and in December 1978 the 20-year "Deng Era" began. Now seventy-four, he presided over a diverse coalition of bold reformers aligned against extreme Mao policies. He faced a cautious formation of ideologists, senior military leaders, and planners, all more apprehensive about markets and chaos, not to mention their elite status. Deng tried strategically for years to advance the reform agenda that took China away from Marxism and closer to the international economy. Notable reversals included abandoning his first two preferred successors, **Hu Yaobang** in 1986 and **Zhao Ziyang** in 1989, and consenting to orders for army units to fire on democracy protesters near Tiananmen Square on June 4, 1989.

Deng, now eighty-three and several senior leaders resigned from the Politburo in 1987. He was unable for three more years to shed his last formal position, chairman of the Party military affairs commission. Even though he finally maneuvered his third preferred successor, **Jiang Zemin**, into the post, in reality he continued to control the key commission. In fact for the next seven years, until his death at age ninety-two—despite difficulty speaking and standing, and despite increasingly rare public or media appearances—Deng remained China's "core" leader in an ever-fluid governing structure.

REFERENCES: Richard Baum, *Burying Mao* (Princeton, NJ, 1994); Richard Evans, *Deng Xiaoping and the Making of Modern China* (New York, 1997); David S. Goodman, *Deng Xiaoping and the Chinese Revolution: A Political Biography* (New York, 1995); Donald W. Klein and Anne B. Clark, *Biographic Dictionary of Chinese Communism, 1921–1965*, vol. 2 (Cambridge, MA, 1971), 819–826; Roderick MacFarquhar, ed., *The Politics of China 1949–1989* (New York, 1993); Benjamin Yang and Ross Terrill, *Deng: A Political Biography* (Armonk, NY, 1997).

GORDON BENNETT

**DENG YINGCHAO** (1904–July 11, 1992). Member, Central Committee and Politburo; vice-chairman, National People's Congress; chairman, national committee of the Chinese People's Political Consultative Conference; and honorary president, National Women's Federation of China.

Deng Yingchao was born in 1904 in Guangshan County, Henan province. Her widowed schoolteacher mother sent Deng to study successively in Beijing and Tianjin. By the time she graduated from middle school in Tianjin in 1920, she was heavily involved in the May Fourth movement. She helped found the Tianjin students' union, and was a leading participant in the Tianjin Women's Patriotic Association. She was said to have met her future husband, **Zhou Enlai,** during a street demonstration, but both were members and perhaps cofounders among others of the Awakening Society in Tianjin. Like Zhou, she was a contributor to the first radical journals that were published at the time. She was jailed at least once for her activism.

During the five years that Zhou Enlai was in Europe, Deng remained in Tianjin for the most part where she taught primary school and was a leader in women's rights activities. This included the founding of a society for progressive women and the publication of a newspaper. In 1924 she joined the Socialist Youth League and in the following year she became a member of the Chinese Communist Party (CCP) and was made the head of its Women's Department in Tianjin. She also joined the Guomindang (GMD) during this initial period of collaboration between the two new political parties. In late 1925 she went to Guangzhou where she married Zhou Enlai who had just returned to China.

In January 1926, Deng was elected to the GMD Central Executive Committee as its only woman member. She moved to Wuhan with the GMD government when that urban center was secured, and served as vice-chairman of the woman's department under Liao Zhongkai's widow, He Xiangning. But when the Left GMD turned on the CCP in July 1927, Deng moved to Shanghai where she worked underground. She attended the Sixth CCP Congress in Moscow in mid-1928, at which time she was appointed head of the Party's women's department.

In 1932, Deng went to the Chinese Soviet Republic that had been established in November of the preceding year in Ruijin, Jiangxi, where she continued to be very active, sometimes taking positions, along with her husband, opposed to **Mao Zedong**. She was reportedly made an alternate member of the Central Committee (CC), and soon thereafter became a member of the Soviet Republic's Central Executive Committee. However, that autumn the Communists were forced out of their Jiangxi base, and Deng was one of very few women who took part in the Long March and survived. She stayed in Shaanxi, the terminus of the Long March, for only a short time, but the stay was interrupted by a trip in 1937 to Japanese-occupied Beijing for medical attention. The famous American correspondent Edgar Snow facilitated her safe departure from Beijing.

In 1938 Deng was sent with Zhou Enlai to Hankou, the temporary provisional capital, to serve as CCP representatives to the Nationalist government in the new (second) United Front. A short while later, they were both evacuated with the government to Chongqing. Here she was a representative of the Eighth Route Army (the designation of the Red Army during the Second United Front period). Aside from another trip to Moscow in 1939, Deng resided for the most part in Chongqing until 1943. However, following the New Fourth Army incident in January 1941, in which the Nationalists killed thousands of Communist troops who were attempting to relocate north of the Yellow River, Deng boycotted most of the meetings of the People's Political Council. She returned to Yan'an in 1943, where she was active in women's organizing work. She was named an alternate member of the CC in 1945.

After the war of resistance against Japan, Deng was again sent to Chongqing as a delegate to the Chinese People's Political Consultative Conference (CPPCC), a new body agreed upon by Mao Zedong and **Jiang Jieshi**, and then moved to Nanjing when the Nationalist government returned to its prewar capital. However, as the situation deteriorated into outright civil war, Deng and Zhou returned together to Yan'an in late 1946. During the civil war she remained active in women's organizational work and in the land reform program. She was elected a vice-chairman of the All-China Federation of Democratic Women (renamed the National Women's Federation of China in 1957) in April 1949, a position she held for many years, becoming its honorary president in September 1978.

Deng was quite active in the work of establishing the new government and had an impressively active career for many years. In October 1949, she was appointed a member of the Committee of Political and Legal Affairs in the government administration council and served until October 1954. She was very much involved in the drafting and the exceedingly difficult implementation of the Marriage Law, the PRC's first major legislation and in many ways a capstone of her years of women's rights work. The law was adopted on May 1, 1950. She was elected as a delegate from Henan to the first National People's Congress (NPC) in August 1954 and reelected in subsequent elections. She was elected to the NPC Standing Committee in September 1954 and in subsequent elections. She was appointed vice-chairman of the NPC Standing Committee in December 1976, a post she held until June 1983, when she was elected chairman of the National Committee of the CPPCC, the leading united front organization of the PRC. In this role, her call at the 1984 New Year's tea party for reunification with Taiwan was briefly publicized.

She delivered the major report to the Second Women's Congress in April 1953. She became a full member of the CCP Central Committee sometime prior to the Eighth Party Congress in 1956, during which she gave a speech outlining the achievements and shortcomings in women's work.

Deng was a member of Guo Morou's delegation to the Second World Peace Congress in Warsaw in November 1950, and in March 1961, she led a delegation to Hanoi to attend a women's congress. She was elected to the Politburo in December 1978, and again in September 1982. But in September 1985, along with 130 other elderly Party veterans, she resigned from her positions, including membership on the CC and Politburo.

Deng died of illness in Beijing on July 11, 1992 at the age of eighty-eight. In a letter written to the CC a decade earlier, on June 17, 1982, she asked that no memorial meeting should be held after her death and requested that her ashes be scattered. Furthermore, she asked that houses in which she or Zhou Enlai had lived should not be turned into memorials but should be returned to the state. Finally, she asked that no special treatment be accorded their relatives.

REFERENCES: *Beijing Review* (July 20–26, 1992), 7; Donald W. Klein and Anne B. Clark, *Biographic Dictionary of Chinese Communism*, vol. 2 (Cambridge, MA, 1971), 838–843.

STEPHEN UHALLEY, JR.

**DING RICHANG** (1823–1882). Official of late Qing dynasty; Restoration leader, reformer, modernizer, and book collector.

Born in backward Fengshun in northeastern Guangdong, Ding, determined to rise above the limitations set by an unfavorable environment, developed early in life character traits that were at once admirable and abrasive. Son of a pharmacist with a modest income, Ding began his education at a temple school. When he was about twelve years of age, his father died, and the family had to eke out a living on his mother's meager earnings from weaving. Despite adversity, Ding earned the *xiucai* degree before he was twenty. He soon confirmed his newly earned gentry status by passing the annual examination, which gave him the rank of stipendiary student (*lingsheng*).

A talented essayist, Ding soon caught the attention of local officials. A patron financed his journey to Guangzhou for the provincial examinations in 1845. Unsuccessful at the examinations, Ding, perhaps with the help of this same patron, purchased the title of a student of the Imperial Academy (*gongsheng*). After having taught at a local school (1845–1848), thanks to his essay-writing skills, he found employment as the personal secretary (*mu-you*) to a succession of local officials. Then, in 1850, he failed the provincial examinations a second time and was never to try again. The failure to master the archaic subject matter or the eight-legged essay (*baguwen*) of the examinations—reasons for his failure—may have fueled his zeal for reform of the traditional civil service examinations.

Though he was to succeed later as an official, Ding, without a higher degree, always felt like an "outsider" on the "inside." His Hakka ("guest settler") origins further added to his sense of estrangement.

Ding earned his first office in 1857 for his leadership in suppressing a group of bandits allied to the Taipings in the Chaozhou area. He was sent to Chiongzhou prefecture on Hainan Island as a subdirector of schools, but was promoted within a year to the magistracy of Wan'an in Jiangxi province. In the mid-1850s, large parts of the province had fallen under the Taipings. Therefore, on arrival, Ding found not only a devastated Wan'an, but also one plagued by lawlessness. Many of the perpetrators were civil servants and military men. They set up illegal *lijin* (likin) stations, extorted contributions from commoners, and linked up with bandits to plunder the people. Ding quickly put a stop to these abuses. He paid special attention to legal matters. By fairly and expeditiously settling huge numbers of back-logged cases, he effectively thwarted pettifoggery, and deprived *yamen* (government) underlings of the opportunities for pretrial extortion. To restore the community to normalcy, Ding also encouraged education and rebuilt the local academy and the city religious temple, both destroyed by the Taipings. This energy and administrative style typified his approach to government throughout his entire career.

In 1860, while serving as acting magistrate of Luling, Ding committed a strategic error and lost both his county seat as well as his rank and job. But by this time, his administrative skills had already been noted by Li Hanzhang and his brother, **Hongzhang**. The latter recommended him to **Zeng Guofan**, who made him a member of his personal staff in late 1861.

For his meritorious service, the throne restored Ding to his former status in early 1862 at Zeng's recommendation. The latter then sent him in a nine-man team to Guangdong to manage the province's *lijin* and thus insure support for his anti–Taiping campaign. While in Guangdong, Ding made guns for the local commanders.

In December 1863 Li Hongzhang secured Ding's services for his antirebel campaign in Jiangsu and for directing one of Li's newly founded arsenals at Shanghai. As the rebels' defeat became evident, Ding was also put in charge of the delicate mission to disband the Ever Victorious Army, a corps of mercenaries.

Ding's successes led to a series of promotions. In mid-1864, he was made acting Intendant of the Su-Song-Tai Circuit. During his 15-month incumbency, he dealt severely with oppressive officials and military officers, improved Shanghai's public safety, and started the Longmen Academy to promote the study of current affairs among examination candidates. In foreign affairs, he disciplined rapacious officials of the foreign-run Imperial Maritime Customs Service, and regained overall control over the military training camp at Fenghuangshan, hitherto dominated by British officers. But in all matters he administered treaty provisions in a manner fair to both sides. To recapture lost economic interests, he also advocated the creation of a Chinese commercial steamship company, an idea that was not realized until 1872. In 1865 he effected the purchase of a foreign factory, which he combined with two of Li Hongzhang's arsenals to form the Jiangnan Arsenal.

Because of his growing expertise on foreign matters (*yangwu*), Ding enjoyed a series of rapid promotions: Liang-Huai Salt Controller in September 1865, Jiangsu Finance Commissioner in early 1867, and the Governor of Jiangsu in January 1868. He then retired in January 1871 to mourn his mother's death.

In Jiangsu, Ding introduced numerous measures to improve the government. "Self-strengthening" (*ziqiang*) had become the slogan of many forward-looking officials of the Restoration. Ding, like **Shen Baozhen**, saw the restoration of good government and military modernization as part and parcel of the drive toward self-strengthening, and attended to both with rigor. He clamped down on official corruption and oppression, made taxes more equitable, and promoted water conservancy and agriculture.

In foreign matters, Ding insured the continued growth of the Jiangnan Arsenal, expanding its shipbuilding program, and helped the establishment of the Tianjin Arsenal. He supported the training of future generations of modernizers both at home and abroad. In 1870 he helped settle the dispute over the Tianjin Massacre. Despite his short tenure in Jiangsu, Ding was regarded as its best governor since **Lin Zexu**, although his persistence in eradicating corruption had earned him many political enemies.

In 1871–1873, Ding mourned his mother's death in his native Fengshun. In late 1875, after helping Li Hongzhang settle the Margary Affair, he succeeded Shen Baozhen as director-general of the Fuzhou Navy Yard, a job he held only briefly as he was made governor of Fujian six months later. Other than his strong administration, his governorship was noted for his development of Taiwan both as a frontier region and as a major center for China's maritime defense. Two telegraph lines and a mechanized coal mine, begun by Shen Baozhen, were completed under him. Both were firsts in China's history.

Ill health and frustration with insufficient imperial support for defense modernization led to a decision to retire in May 1878. But even in retirement, he continued to serve the government on special missions, such as the settlement of the Wushishan antimissionary case of Fuzhou, and wrote an impassioned memorial to the throne and letters to former colleagues calling for major overhauls of China's maritime defense efforts in light of the new international environment. He died in 1882.

REFERENCES: Jonathan K. Ocko, *Bureaucratic Reform in Provincial China: Ting Jih-ch'ang in Restoration Kiangsu, 1867–1870* (Cambridge, MA, 1983); Lu Shiqiang, *Ding Richang yu ziqiang yundong* [Ding Richang and the Self-strengthening Movement] (Taibei, 1972).

DAVID PONG

**DONG BIWU** (1886–April 2, 1975). Party "elder"; vice-chairman, People's Republic of China; member, standing committee of the Politburo of the Central Committee; secretary, Chinese Communist Party Central Control Commission.

Dong Biwu was born in Huangan County, Hebei, in 1886. His family was regarded as "landless gentry" because his father was a degree-holder in the late Qing period. Dong also studied the Confucian classics, earning the *Xiucai* degree when he was fifteen, following which he pursued a modern education, initially at a middle school in Wuchang. He began a teaching career in 1911, but switched to what would be a life-long revolutionary career when he enlisted in the revolutionary army at the outset of the revolution. In 1911, he joined the *Tongmenghui*, but fled to Japan two years later when **Yuan Shikai** suppressed the revolutionary organization. While studying law in Tokyo in 1914, he joined **Sun Yat-sen**'s newly organized *Zhonghua geming dang* (Chinese Revolutionary Party). The next year, 1915, Dong returned to Hubei at Sun Yat-sen's request. He undertook secret work in the Chinese military, which resulted in his arrest and incarceration for several months. Upon his release in 1916, Dong returned to Japan in order to complete his studies. Back in China, for a time in 1917–1918, he performed propaganda work in western Hubei. But in the spring of 1919 he went to Shanghai where he began studying Marxism. He was converted to Marxism later that year or in early 1920.

Dong returned to Wuhan and opened a middle school, which, along with a bookstore founded by his friend Yun Taiying became a gathering place for left-oriented intellectuals. He founded a Communist group in Hubei, and in July 1921 found himself one of two delegates from Hubei to attend the First Congress of the Chinese Communist Party (CCP) in Shanghai, thus becoming one of its founding members. Dong returned to Hubei and continued to develop party organizations, although he is said to have spent a year in Sichuan working on tactics within the military. During the period of cooperation with the Nationalists, Dong served in a GMD branch in Hubei. In 1924, he went to Jinchai county with two colleagues to initiate a peasant movement, apparently the first such effort in this area. In early 1925, he traveled both in the northwest and northeast of China looking for recruits. In January 1926, he attended the Second Guomindang (GMD) Congress in Guangzhou and was elected an alternate member of the Central Executive Committee. Dong, along with other colleagues, succeeded in persuading Tang Shengji, who was in Hunan at the time, to side with the revolutionaries just before the Northern Expedition was launched. Dong claims to have helped in the capture of Wuhan by the Northern Expeditionary forces. He remained in Wuhan during the turbulent period of CCP–GMD cooperation until mid-1927, narrowly escaping after the termination of the alliance. He made his way to the French Concession in Shanghai and then again to Japan where he stayed for eight months. From Japan he traveled to Moscow, arriving there in September 1928. Here he attended either Sun Yat-sen University or the University of the Toilers of the East or the Comintern-run Lenin School (the latter is recorded in his own account as given to Nym Wales). He completed his studies in Russia in 1931 and returned to China the following year.

During the period of the Agrarian Revolutionary War Dong Biwu served as president of the Party school, secretary of the Party Affairs Commission, member of the Soviet Republic's Central Executive Committee, president of the Supreme Court, and vice-chairman of the Workers' and Peasants' Procuratorial Committee in the Jiangxi Central Revolutionary Base. He participated in the Long March from Jiangxi to Shaanxi in 1934–1935. In Shaanxi he continued as president of the Party School and served as acting chairman of the Shaanxi-Gansu-Ningxia Border Regional Government. Dong helped **Zhou Enlai** in negotiations with **Jiang Jieshi** and his captors during the Xi'an Incident of December 1936. Beginning in September 1937 Dong again went to Xi'an to work as a liaison officer with the GMD during the Second United Front. This assignment consumed much of the following decade and he moved as circumstances demanded to Hankou, Chongqing, and Nanjing. After Zhou Enlai returned to Yan'an in June 1943, Dong represented the Communists in Chongqing for most of the rest of the war against Japan. In March 1945, Dong was appointed by the Nationalists as the only Communist on the ten-member delegation sent by China to establish the UN organization in San Francisco. Afterward, Dong toured the United States for several months, returning to China in December 1945. He served as Zhou Enlai's top assistant in negotiating with the GMD during General George C. Marshall's mission to China in 1946–1947. After the Marshall mission failed, Dong returned to Yan'an just as it was about to fall into Nationalist hands in the resumed civil war.

Before the People's Republic of China (PRC) was established in 1949, Dong also served as a member of the secretariat of the party's North China

Bureau, director of the North China Commission of Finance and Economy, and chairman of the North China People's Government.

After the PRC was established, Dong served as director of the Central Commission of Finance and Economy, vice-premier of the Administration Council of the Central People's Government, director of the Committee of Political and Legal Affairs, president of the Supreme People's Court, vice-chairman of the Second National Committee of the Chinese People's Political Consultative Conference (CPPCC), secretary of the Party's Control Commission, vice-chairman and acting chairman of the PRC itself, and vice-chairman of the Standing Committee of the National People's Congress (NPC). In the early 1950s the super-active Dong attended numerous public functions and produced a steady flow of reports for various government organs and national conferences. He traveled abroad again only in 1954 and 1958, respectively leading delegations to Sofia on both occasions, but also visiting Prague and East Berlin on the second trip.

Dong appears to have played an important role in Mao's purge of Gao Gang and **Rao Shushi** in 1954–1955. He was named chairman of the new Central Control Commission that was established in 1955 in order to prevent a recurrence, it was said, of a Gao–Rao "anti–Party plot."

He was elected a member of the Party's Central Committee at the sixth, seventh, eighth, ninth, and tenth national Party congresses. He had been a member of the Politburo from the Sixth Plenary Session of the Sixth Central Committee and was elected to the Politburo's Standing Committee at the First Session of the Tenth Central Committee in August 1973.

Dong died on April 2, 1975 at the age of ninety. Marshall **Ye Jianying** gave the eulogy at the memorial ceremony held in the Great Hall of the People in Beijing on April 7. His ashes were interred at Babaoshan Cemetery. He was survived by his third (or fourth) wife, He Lianji, and three children.

REFERENCES: Donald W. Klein and Anne B. Clark, *Biographic Dictionary of Chinese Communism, 1921–1965*, vol. 2 (Cambridge, MA, 1971), 874–880; Yeh Chien-ying, "Memorial Ceremony Speech," *Peking Review* (April 11, 1975), 7–8.

STEPHEN UHALLEY, JR.

**DONG JIANHUA** (Tung Chee Hwa, May 29, 1937–   ). Son of a shipping tycoon, took hold of the family business, and has been the chief executive of the Hong Kong Special Administrative Region since 1997.

Born in Shanghai in 1937, Dong Jianhua or better known as Tung Chee Hwa, was the first child of Tung Chao Yung and Koo Lee Ching. Having dreamed of owning an international Chinese merchant fleet, Tung Chao Yung established his shipping business in Hong Kong in the 1940s, and later moved the two companies to Taiwan. Tung Chee Hwa received his secondary education in Hong Kong, and continued university education in England. In 1960, he graduated from the University of Liverpool with a Bachelor of

Science degree in marine engineering. He then worked at General Electric in the United States. In 1969, he returned to Hong Kong and entered the family business. Gradually, Tung Chee Hwa took over the leadership of the family enterprise, the Orient Overseas (International) Limited (OOIL). In 1982, his father died. There were rumors that China helped Tung's company when it encountered serious financial difficulties in the 1980s.

In control of a shipping enterprise, Tung Chee Hwa had multiple connections. As a Shanghainese, he was well acquainted with President **Jiang Zemin,** who headed the Beijing government, and spoke with the latter in their local dialect. Tung also took advantage of his father's connections in Taiwan. He was active in influential circles overseas, and among his friends were former American President George Bush and Assistant Secretary of State Winston Lord. From 1983 to 1997, he was international councillor of the Center for Strategic and International Studies in Washington, DC. From 1995 to 1997, he was adviser to the Institute for International Studies of Stanford University in California and the Council on Foreign Relations in New York. In Hong Kong, he maintained a low profile in politics. The media knew very little about him until 1996, even though he had served at the executive council of the British Hong Kong Government from 1992 to 1996 and the Basic Law Consultative Committee from 1985 to 1990.

In January 1996, Jiang Zemin met with members of the National People's Congress (NPC) Preparatory Committee for the establishment of the Special Administrative Region (SAR) in the Great Hall of the People. When he was about to leave the room, he suddenly approached Tung Chee Hwa in the front row and shook hands with him. From then on, the Hong Kong media speculated that Beijing had chosen Tung to be the chief executive, and the fifty-nine-year-old shipping magnate received growing attention. The subsequent developments seemed to confirm the speculation resulting from this famous handshaking incident. In his election campaign, Tung employed three "isms" to explain his vision for Hong Kong, namely Confucianism, elitism, and nationalism. In 1996, the media described the process as "the selection of the chief executive" rather than "his election" as the 400-person selection committee was responsible for casting the votes. An official candidate of the election needs to secure at least 50 votes from the selection committee to be considered nominated for the post. When Tung obtained 206 votes on November 15, he emerged as the winner even before the chief executive election on December 11. As expected, he got an overwhelming majority of votes of 320 on the day of election, and beat his opponents Sir Yang Ti-liang (42 votes) and Peter Woo (36 votes).

Tung Chee Hwa was able to enjoy public consent for a short period after the election. In an opinion poll released on election day, it recorded a 70% approval rating for Tung. Nevertheless, his popularity was short lived and soon faced serious setbacks. Even before the handover on July 1, 1997, the chief executive–designate faced the problems of the legality of the provisional legislature, the revision of civil liberties law, and his relations with key government officials. When Hong Kong suffered from the effect of the Asian financial crisis in late 1997, the approval ratings for Tung continued to drop. In late 1998, less than one half of the respondents to an opinion poll believed that Tung had the ability to solve Hong Kong's economic problems. During his administration, he always had plans to reshuffle his team of top government officials, and laid his hands on every aspect of government reform. The SAR government was an executive-led administration, and Tung relied on his executive council members. Throughout the years, Hong Kong debated about education and civil service reforms, the close relations between big business and the government, and the vulnerable real estate market. In his annual policy addresses, Tung emphasized that the local economy should transform and concentrate on the development of information technology. He also raised the concerns of environmental pollution and the improvement of the tourist industry. He was elected to a second term in 2002.

REFERENCES: Wang Gungwu and John Wong, eds., *Hong Kong in China: The Challenges of Transition* (Singapore, 1999); James C. Hsiung, ed., *Hong Kong the Super Paradox: Life after Return to China* (New York, 2000); Chu Yik-yi, "Tung Chee-Hwa and His Challenges: A Look at Hong Kong's Last Colonial Days, December 1996–June 1997," *Asian Perspective*, vol. 22, no. 2 (1998), 169–191.

CINDY YIK-YI CHU

# F

FENG YUNSHAN (1822?–June 1852). One of the key leaders of the Taiping Uprising (1851–1864).

Born in Huaxian, Guandong province, Feng Yunshan was a neighbor, a schoolmate, and remote relative of **Hong Xiuquan**, a self-baptized Christian who started the Taiping Rebellion. A frustrated Hakka scholar himself, Feng was an educated and aspiring young man when he first met Hong Xiuquan and soon became one of his earliest converts to Christianity in 1843. He shared Hong's religious conviction that their God-given mission was to rid China of all demons, including the deeply entrenched Confucianism and other existing evil social customs. Feng devoted himself to the study of the religious tracts, and joined Hong on his preaching missions to Guangxi province in 1844. Feng was the one who stayed behind and organized the God Worshipping Society (*Bai Shangdi Hui*) in the Thistle Mountain (Zijin Shan) in Guangxi, a place far removed from urban centers and Confucian influences.

The economic hardships in that area following the end of the first Opium War (1839–1842) fostered strong discontent and resentment among the local residents, who were thus receptive to Feng's message of redemption. He managed to enlist a significant number of converts, many of whom were poverty-stricken, to the God Worshipping Society with its promise of salvation. Feng also joined Hong, when the latter came to the Thistle Mountain in 1847, in smashing the idols in the villages in an effort to save the local people from the "demons," because in their minds those idols were equated to demons. Feng was captured by the local militia, which was organized by several wealthy families that were disturbed by the God Worshippers' actions. Feng defended himself with the argument that he was simply preaching God's words with no intention of causing havoc in the local community, and that freedom to worship had been decreed by the Manchu emperor after the Opium War.

Feng Yunshan was praised for his selflessness, for he devoted over three years to the God Worshippers' cause, away from his wife and children. Regarded as God's third son, Feng received the title of "South King" from Hong Xiuquan, who proclaimed himself as the "Heavenly King." After the Taiping Rebellion officially started in 1851, Feng became one of the primary generals of the Taiping army. He also helped devise the new Taiping calendar, which contained 366 days in a year, attributing 30 days to even-numbered months and 31 days to odd-numbered months. The new calendar, supposedly determined by God to ensure peace for the Taipings, also reserved Sundays for the Sabbath.

Feng Yunshan's role in the Taiping Rebellion came to an unexpected early end when he was fatally wounded in May 1852 when the Taipings were hunted by the imperial forces on their northward march from Guangxi to Nanjing. He died a month later in Quanzhou, Guangxi province.

REFERENCES: J.C. Cheng, *Chinese Sources for the Taiping Rebellion, 1850–1864* (Hong Kong, 1963); Vincent Y.C. Shih, *The Taiping Ideology: Its Source, Interpretations and Influences* (Seattle, 1967); Jonathan D. Spence, *God's Chinese Son: The Taiping Heavenly Kingdom of Hong Xiuquan* (New York, 1996).

YI SUN

**FENG YUXIANG** (1882–1948). Revolutionary warlord.

Feng Yuxiang, popularly known as Christian General in the West, though born in Xingji, Hebei in 1882, was a native of Caoxian, Anhui. His father was a low-ranking army officer in the late Qing dynasty and his mother gave birth to seven children with Feng Yuxiang being the second. The family was so poor that Feng went to regular school for only one and a half years and, at the age of fourteen, he joined the army in 1896. Because of his giant physical structure and his incessant self-taught efforts, he was promoted to battalion commander on the eve of the 1911 revolution. Together with Wang Jinming, Shi Congyun (both battalion commanders), and Shi Jingting, a company commander, in response to the Wuchang Uprising of October 10, 1911, Feng staged an unsuccessful uprising at Lanzhou, Hebei on January 3, 1912. This event caused the death of Wang and Shi Congyun and also Feng's dismissal from the army.

With the founding of the Chinese Republic, Feng started his military career anew. He found a patron in Lu Jianzhang, then minister of the Ministry of the Army. In 1914, Feng was promoted to regiment commander stationed outside Beijing; by then he had already distinguished himself in training troops and in accepting Christianity. Soon his regiment was expanded to a brigade, and Feng was assigned to move to Shaanxi to suppress banditry there.

In 1915, when President **Yuan Shikai** indulged himself in an imperial adventure, Feng secretly opposed it. In 1917, when Zhang Xun launched the imperial restoration, Feng took an active role in suppressing it. He was so bold and independent that in 1918, in defiance of Duan Qijui's Beijing government, he issued a manifesto advocating peace with **Sun Yat-sen**'s Guangzhou government, for which he paid dearly. The desperate plight of his army was only relieved in 1921 when the Beijing government, now under the control of the Hebei clique headed by Cao Kun and Wu Peifu, sent Feng's brigade to Shaanxi to suppress Chen Shufan of the Anhui clique. Feng's successful campaign against Chen was handsomely regarded, as his brigade was expanded into a division, while he was promoted to governor-general of Shaanxi. Feng seems to have been destined to be the ruler of northwest China, from which his army derived its name Xibeijun (Northwestern Army).

In answer to the call of **Wu Peifu** in the First Zhi(-li)-Feng(-tian) War in 1922, Feng's army poured out of the strategic Tongguan and marched eastward in time to save Wu from being defeated by Zhang Zuolin. However, Wu failed to bestow the reward due to Feng, but allowed his 30,000-man army to be settled at Beijing, thus inadvertently making Feng the protector of the capital. At the outbreak of the Second Zhi-Feng War in 1924, Feng had the best-trained, if not the best-equipped, troops of 34,000 men. While the battle was raging in the front, Feng's emissary made a deal with Young Marshal **Zhang Xueliang**, son of Zhong Zuolin; then Feng staged the Capital Revolution. Wu's failure to judge the man caused his downfall. What ensued was an invitation to Sun Yat-sen to come north in order to consult with the newly formed triumvirate, Zhang Zuolin, Duan Qijui, and Feng. One of Feng's revolutionary deeds was to drive **Puyi**, the "last emperor," out of the Beijing Palace in November 1924. Rumors ciculated that, in staging the coup against Wu, Feng was inspired by the Japanese and that he had stolen treasures from the imperial palace. Both rumors should be dismissed, as there is no evidence to support them, nor does reason account for them.

Sun died in Beijing on March 12, 1925 without seeing the unification of China. After his death, relations among the trio deteriorated, chiefly because the Manchurian warlord wanted not only to dominate north China but even to extend his influence in the Yangzi Valley. One of the major generals, Guo Songling, who had worked under Sun at Canton and then became a confidant of the Young Marshal, after having reached a secret agreement with Feng Yuxiang, revolted against Zhang Zuolin on November 22, 1925. December 24, the day when Feng's army successfully captured Tianjin, also brought the news that Guo's forces collapsed with Guo and with his wife being captured and executed. What followed was the Feng-Zhang War, which was intermittently fought until the defeat of Feng's army at Nankou in late August 1926.

Feng had been on good terms with the Soviets at Beijing since 1923. With the establishment of the Guominjun (People's Army) after the Capital Revolution, he got even closer to the Russians and the Guomindang (Nationalist Party). From 1925 to June 1926, Feng had received Soviet aid amounting to eleven million rubles, while 60 Soviet advisers were attached to his army. Out of desperation, Feng made a trip to Moscow and in the meantime joined the Guomindang. At Moscow he was received by Stalin who promised him massive military aid in arms and ammunition which would be delivered at Urga, Mongolia. The sudden collapse of his army forced Feng to cut his trip short and immediately return to China. Within a few weeks after his arrival at Wuyuan, Suiyuan in September 1926, Feng was able to rally his scattered forces into a strong army to coordinate with the National Revolutionary Army of the Northern Expedition launched from Guangzhou in July 1926. In the intraparty struggle of the Guomindang, Feng sided with **Jiang Jieshi**, which precipitated the fall of the Wuhan Leftist government and its purge of the Chinese Communists. Nevertheless, Feng did join Jiang to bring the Northern Expedition to fruition, thereby forcing Zhang Zuolin to return home in June 1928, when he was killed by the Japanese. A few months earlier in February 1928, Jiang Jieshi and Feng Yuxiang were made sworn brothers in a written contract, a document with their handwritings that has survived.

In 1930, Feng allied himself with **Wang Jingwei** and **Yan Xishan** to fight against Jiang Jieshi. This "great central plain" war was probably the bloodiest civil war ever fought up to that time. Now Zhang Xueliang became the arbitrator, as his support for Jiang not only brought the war to an end but also virtually terminated Feng's glorious career. Except for a brief episode of establishing an anti-Japanese allied army in Chahar in early 1933, Feng served as a titular vice-chairman of the military council of the Nationalist government, of which Jiang was the chairman, but maintained some degree of popularity by voicing, sometimes vociferously, dissenting opinions from Jiang and the government, particularly during the war. After V-J Day, he was granted by Jiang to be a special envoy on inspecting hydrodynamic engineering abroad. He left China on September 2, 1946 and spent almost two years in the United States. Before long, he began to openly criticize Jiang, for which Jiang rescinded Feng's appointment. Finally he decided to cast his lot with the Chinese Communists and returned to China via the Soviet Union. Just before landing at Odessa in the Black Sea, he was killed by a fire in a movie theater aboard the Russian freighter *Pobeda* on September 1, 1948. However, Feng's close friend Robert Payne, the novelist, in his *Torment* spells out that he does not believe that Feng died from running a movie projector as reported by the Soviets.

REFERENCES: James E. Sheridan, *Chinese Warlord: The Career of Feng Yü-hsiang* (Stanford, CA, 1966); Li Taifen, ed., *Guominjun shi gao* [Documentary History of the People's Army] (Beijing, 1930); Tao Yinghui, "Newly-edited Letters between Jiang Jieshi and Feng Yuxiang," *Zhuanji wenxue* [Biographical Literature], nos. 439, 440 (December 1998–January 1999); Jian Youwen, *Feng Yuxiang zhuan* [Biography of Feng Yuxiang], 2 vols. (Taibei, 1982).

TIEN-WEI WU

**FU ZUOYI** (June 27, 1895–April 19, 1974). Commander-in-chief of the Guomindang North China Bandit Suppression general headquarters; key figure in the "Beiping pattern"; minister of water conservancy and electric power in the People's Republic of China.

Born in Ronghe County, Shanxi province, in 1895, Fu Zuoyi was educated at the Baoding Military Academy. He served under **Yan Xishan**, warlord of Shanxi, from 1918 until the collapse of the latter's anti–**Jiang Jieshi**'s coalition in 1930. The following year Fu began to serve the Nationalist government in Nanjing, and was appointed governor of Suiyuan. In 1933 he joined the anti–Japanese campaigns in the Great Wall region. In 1935 he became a member of the Guomindang (GMD) Central Executive Committee. His great victory at Bailingmiao in Suiyuan in November 1936 cleared the province of Japanese and their Mongolian puppet armies and catapulted Fu to national fame and the attention of the Chinese Communist Party (CCP). During the Sino-Japanese War (1937–1945), Fu, a senior commander in the Second, Eighth, and Twelfth War Zones, was involved in a united-front diplomacy, and had contacts with the Eighth Route Army and other Communist organizations. In June 1945, he was elected a GMD Central Committee member.

After the Japanese surrender, Fu was charged with fighting the Communists in Suiyuan, Chahar, and Rehe. After the failure of the peace talks at Chongqing and the Political Consultative Conference, both the GMD and the CCP started a full-scale civil war in June 1946. By mid-1947 the GMD offensive failed, and Fu's policy of "20 percent military, 30 percent political, 50 percent economics" was unable to knock the Communists out of North China, which was their power base.

On December 3, 1947, Jiang Jieshi appointed Fu, a regional leader who did not graduate from the Huangpu (Whampoa) Military Academy, as the commander-in-chief of the North China Bandit Suppression general headquarters in Beiping. Fu became the de facto political leader of GMD North China, except for Yan Xishan's Shanxi province. In 1948, underground CCP members carried out united-front activities within Fu's headquarters and family. In particular, his daughter Fu Dongju was assigned by the CCP to work on her father. After the destruction of most of his armies in the Battle of Beiping-Tianjin which started in November 1948, Fu decided to surrender to the CCP in late December 1948.

On January 22, 1949, a peace agreement was announced, and Beiping fell into Communist hands. In September 1949, Fu asked his subordinate generals in Suiyuan to surrender to the Communists. Fu, whom Jiang trusted so much, betrayed the GMD. **Mao Zedong,** however, glorified the uprising or peaceful surrender of Fu and the capture of Beiping as the "Beiping pattern." It remained the first model of "peaceful liberation" in the Chinese Civil War (1945–1949), and paved the way for similar conquests in Hunan, Sichuan, Xikang, Yunnan, and Xinjiang. Besides, Fu's uprising ended the Battle of Beiping-Tianjin and sealed the fate of GMD North China. Fu's surrender of Beiping with more than 200,000 troops was the most important example of the Communist united-front activities among GMD officers and soldiers. In short, the "Beiping pattern" demonstrated the political solution for the conclusion of the civil war in China.

Mao was so pleased with Fu's surrender that he personally met the latter in Beiping on February 22, 1949. In September 1955, Mao granted Fu the Liberation Medal, first class. In 1958 Fu was appointed as minister of water conservancy and electric power but resigned the post in 1972. Protected by **Zhou Enlai** and approved by Mao, Fu survived the bloody chaos in the Cultural Revolution, and died in Beijing in 1974.

REFERENCES: Jiang Shuchen, *Fu Zuoyi zhuanlue* [A Brief Biography of Fu Zuoyi] (Beijing, 1990); *Minguo gaoji jiangling liezhuan* [Biographies of High-Level Generals in Republican China], vol. 2 (Beijing, 1988), 506–543; Joseph K.S. Yick, "Fu Tso-yi," in Edwin P.W. Leung, ed., *Historical Dictionary of Revolutionary China, 1839–1976* (Westport, CT, 1992), 131–133; Zhang Xinwu, *Fu Zuoyi yisheng* [The Life of Fu Zuoyi] (Beijing, 1995).

JOSEPH K.S. YICK

# G

GAO GANG (1905–August 17, 1954). Chinese Communist leader in Shaanxi; "Czar of Manchuria"; key figure purged in the "Gao Gang–Rao Shushi Affair."

Born in Hengshan County, Shaanxi Province, Gao Gang joined the Chinese Communist Party (CCP) in 1926. In 1928 Gao and his mentor Liu Zhidan were assigned by the Party to spread propaganda and to infiltrate Nationalist units in Shaanxi and Gansu. In 1932 Gao served as a political commissar in the Twenty-Sixth Red Army in the region. By the spring of 1935, a Shaanxi-Gansu soviet regime had been established, and Gao had become political commissar of the General Front Command.

In the summer of 1935, Gao was appointed as director of the political department of the Fifteenth Army Group. Soon after the arrival of some CCP Central Committee members in Shaanxi, a power struggle erupted. Liu Zhidan and Gao, the top local leaders, were imprisoned and charged with deviation from the Party line. In late 1935 after they reached Shaanxi, **Mao Zedong** and the central leadership ordered Liu's and Gao's release. Mao and his exhausted survivors of the Long March needed Gao's local support, and Gao was then made political commissar of the army group.

After Liu's death in combat in April 1936, Gao emerged as the leading Shaanxi Communist when he became secretary of the North Shaanxi Provincial Committee. During the Sino-Japanese War (1937–1945), Gao was secretary of the Party Committee for the Shaan-Gan-Ning Border Region and of the CCP Northwest Bureau. In that period Gao, an important ally of Mao, purged **Wang Ming**'s associates in the region.

At the Seventh Party Congress in 1945, Gao was elected a Central Committee (CC) and Politburo member. By the end of the Chinese Civil War

(1945–1949), Gao had served as secretary of the CCP Northeast Bureau, chairman of the Northeast People's Government, and political commissar of the Northeast Military Region. He was nicknamed the "Czar of Manchuria."

After the establishment of the People's Republic, Mao rewarded Gao with the vice-chairmanship of the Central People's Government while allowing him to maintain control over northeast China. Gao was the only regional leader to be granted such a joint honor and privilege. But soon his close relationship with the Soviet Union, whose influence in the northeast was strong, aroused suspicion within the CCP's top leadership in Beijing. Indeed, even before the People's Republic was founded, Gao visited the Soviet Union and concluded economic agreements. In the early 1950s, he was also the chief advocate of Soviet-style industrial development in China. Ultimately, some central leaders, including Mao, charged that Gao attempted to create an "independent kingdom" for himself in the northeast by maneuvering between Beijing and the Soviet Union.

In order to undermine Gao's growing power, Mao in November 1952 transferred him to Beijing to take the new post of chairman of the State Planning Commission. In 1953 Gao was accused of "engaging in activities aimed at splitting up the Party and usurping state leadership," and plotting to replace **Liu Shaoqi** and **Zhou Enlai. Rao Shushi**, a regional leader in east China, was charged to be the co-conspirator. At the Fourth Plenum of the Seventh CCP Central Committee in February 1954, the "Gao Gang–Rao Shushi Antiparty Clique" fell from power. Gao denied the accusations and killed himself as a form of protest in August 1954. He was posthumously expelled from the CCP in March 1955.

The purge of Gao Gang, known succinctly as the "Gao–Rao Affair," marked the first major intraparty strife of the CCP in the history of the People's Republic. It remains unclear, however, why Gao dared to challenge the undisputed power of Liu Shaoqi and Zhou Enlai.

REFERENCES: Frederick C. Teiwes, *Politics at Mao's Court: Gao Gang and Party Factionalism in the Early 1950s* (Armonk, NY, 1990); Ke-wan Wang, "Gao Gang," in Ke-wan Wang, *Modern China: An Encyclopedia of History, Culture, and Nationalism* (New York, 1998), 122–123; Joseph K.S. Yick, "Kao Kang," in Edwin P.W. Leung, ed., *Historical Dictionary of Revolutionary China, 1839–1976* (Westport, CT, 1992), 189–191; *Zhongguo gongchandang lishi dacidian: Zonglu, renwu* [A Large Dictionary of CCP History: General Discussion, Personalities] (Beijing, 1991), 481.

JOSEPH K.S. YICK

**GONG, PRINCE** (Gong Wang or Yisin, January 11, 1833–May 29, 1898). Statesman and leader in late Qing; head of the Zongli Yamen.

Prince Gong, or Yisin, was one of the key leaders of the Qing government during the Tongzhi Restoration and the Self-Strengthening Movement

(1860s–1890s). He was born in 1833, the sixth son of **Emperor Daoguang**. He had eight brothers and ten sisters, of whom only he and princess Shouan were born to Empress Xiaojingzheng, a concubine of Emperor Daoguang. For reasons unknown, the empress also took care of Daoguang's fourth son, Yiju (the heir prince), along with her own children after Yiju's own mother died in 1840. Yiju and Yisin were thus brought up together and established a very close relationship.

Following Prince Yiju's enthronement as Emperor Xianfeng in 1851, Yisin was granted a special imperial title, that of Gong Zhong Qing Wang (or "Respectfully Loyal Prince"), popularly known as Gong Wang, or Prince Gong. As the highest ranking prince in the Qing court, Prince Gong was entitled to direct access to the emperor on court and state affairs. Prince Gong's growing power at court and occasional arrogance toward his emperor brother soon bred rifts betweem them. In 1855, under the pretext that Prince Gong had mismanaged the funeral service for Empress Dowager Xiaojingzheng, Emperor Xianfeng deprived Prince Gong of all his posts in the government and ordered him to return to study in the Palace School for Princes, a gesture showing the Emperor's disfavor.

However, the Qing government at this time faced internal and external crises. Internally, the Taiping Rebellion was on the rise and threatened the survival of the Qing dynasty. Externally, the Western powers were dissatisfied with the implementation of the Treaty of Nanjing (1842) and demanded more open ports in south China. Emperor Xianfeng desperately needed Prince Gong's advice and support. In 1857, Prince Gong was recalled and appointed commanding general of the palace guards and director of the Grand Council. In 1859, he also assumed his position as senior chamberlain of the imperial forces in Beijing.

Even with Prince Gong in control of state affairs, China was too weak to cope with these crises. The British–French Joint Expeditionary Forces pressed aggressively into Tianjin and Beijing in the summer of 1860. Emperor Xianfeng had to flee the city and take refuge in Jehol. Prince Gong, left alone in Beijing to deal with the allied forces under Lord Elgin of Great Britain and Baron Gras of France, secured a peace treaty (i.e., The Beijing Convention) in November 1860. The treaty opened China to the West diplomatically, and also liberated the conservative mind of Prince Gong. He became the highest Manchu prince to adopt a realistic attitude toward the West and seek realistic policy changes to cope with the military superiority of the Western powers.

Right at that time in Jehol, Emperor Xianfeng died. Prince Gong's life had always been surrounded by ultraconservative officials, such as Sushun, who detested Prince Gong's "pro-Barbarian" policy. They prepared to challenge the new treaty upon their return to Beijing. The politically ambitious Empress Dowager Cixi, mother of the new infant Emperor Tongzhi, exploited the power struggle between Prince Gong and the ultraconservatives to enhance her own power. In late 1861, she sided with Prince Gong and launched a coup d'état, which successfully ousted all ultraconservatives from the government.

The cooperation and alliance of Prince Gong and Empress Dowager Cixi created an atmosphere of openness in the 1860s and 1870s that brought new strength to China. Prince Gong recruited Han Chinese leaders, such as **Zeng Guofan, Zuo Zongtang,** and **Li Hongzhang,** and supported their self-strengthening programs in south China. The outstanding results included the Fuzhou Shipyard, the Jiangnan Arsenal, the Tongwenguan, the appointment of Robert Hart as Inspector–General of Chinese Maritime Customs, and the establishment of the Zongli Yamen. With the help and support of Zeng, Zuo, and Li, the Taiping Rebellion was finally suppressed in 1864, and the Muslim uprisings quelled by 1873. Prince Gong's prestige and power, however, were short-lived. **Empress Dowager Cixi** began to suspect that Prince Gong had become too pro–Han Chinese and "pro–Barbarian" in his policies, and questioned his loyalty to the Manchu imperial household.

Allied with Woren, a powerful Manchu conservative at court, Cixi harshly attacked Prince Gong's alleged mishandling of the crises in 1871 and 1879. Some Han-Chinese officials, such as **Zhang Zhidong** and Zhang Peilun, who belonged to the conservative faction called *Qingyi* at this time, also criticized Prince Gong's leadership. Thus, Prince Gong became increasingly timid and unsure of himself, which further eroded his political power in Beijing. Finally in 1884, he was forced to retire to private life and left the Empress Dowager Cixi to rule the Qing court and government. Prince Gong's defeat seriously weakened China's self-strengthening movement. He died reproachfully in 1898.

REFERENCES: John K. Fairbank, *The I.G. in Beijing: Letters of Robert Hart* (Cambridge, MA, 1975); John King Fairbank, ed., *The Cambridge History of China, Vol. 10: Late Qing, 1800–1911, Part 1* (Cambridge, 1978); John King Fairbank and Kwang-Ching Liu, eds., *The Cambridge History of China, Vol. 11: Late Qing, 1800–1911, Part 2* (Cambridge, 1980); Mary C. Wright, *The Last Stand of Chinese Conservatism: The T'ung-chih Restoration, 1862–1874* (Stanford, CA, 1957).

ANTHONY Y. TENG

**GUANGXU, EMPEROR** (August 14, 1871–November 14, 1908). Ninth emperor of the Qing dynasty (r. 1875–1908).

Guangxu was the ninth emperor of the Qing dynasty. His personal name was Zaitian and he was the second son of Prince Yihuan. He was chosen in 1875, at the age of four, to succeed **Emperor Tongzhi** (who died without an heir) by his aunt, **Empress Dowager Cixi,** because Zaitian was the prince closest to Cixi by blood. This would guarantee Cixi's control over the infant emperor. Meanwhile, on January 15, 1875, Cixi officially assumed the position as coregent (with Empress Dowager Xiaozhen, the natural mother of Zaitian) of the throne until Guangxu was of age. The act seemed to have violated the dynastic laws of succession, yet it was carried out without objection.

Emperor Guangxu was therefore raised under the total domination of Cixi, who maintained full influence over him. When Guangxu came of age in 1887, Cixi continued her control of the court and the government through political manipulation, even though she had been "retired" to her summer palace near Beijing. All important state papers and key government appointments reportedly still went to Cixi for final approval.

However weak as an emperor, Guangxu was inquisitive and possessed a keen and open mind about national and international affairs. He was interested in new ideas introduced to China at this time by Westerners, and particularly concerned about the national identity and survival of China in the midst of the menace of invasion from the West.

Moreover, the defeat and humiliation suffered by China after the Sino-Japanese War of 1894–1895 shocked Guangxu in such a way that he became immensely worried about China's survival and wanted to seek his own way to avert its demise. **Kang Youwei,** a young and active scholar, who had similar concerns about China as Guangxu did, attracted the emperor's attention. Since 1890, Kang Youwei had repeatedly sent memorials to Guangxu expressing his ideas for urgent reform of the Chinese government. When Guangxu's imperial tutor **Weng Tonghe** supported Kang's advocacies in early 1898, Guangxu became more eager to pursue the new reforms. After January 29, 1898, Kang was granted a special right to have direct access to Emperor Guangxu for closer consultation on the reform. In May 1898, Kang presented his formal reform proposal to Guangxu, which included (1) a national polity under Emperor Guangxu's leadership modeled after Peter the Great of Russia and Emperor Meiji of Japan, (2) reorganization of the national government based on the new ideas under the leadership of the new reform-minded intellectuals, and (3) provincial governments to be given authority to initiate changes according to national needs.

Emperor Guangxu agreed with Kang's reform proposals and, on June 11, 1898, officially issued an imperial decree for the general government reform (known as the Hundred Day Reform) which lasted until September 20, when Empress Dowager Cixi unleashed her power and put an immediate stop to it. Guangxu was placed under house arrest and Kang Youwei fled to Japan. Cixi thereafter resumed her control of the government. Guangxu once again became nothing more than a puppet emperor under the shadow of his aunt until his death on November 14, 1908. He was succeeded by his nephew, Emperor Xuantong (or **Puyi**) in December 1908.

REFERENCES: John King Fairbank, ed., *The Cambridge History of China, Vol. 10: Late Qing, 1800–1911, Part 1* (Cambridge, 1978); John King Fairbank and Kwang-Ching Liu, eds., *The Cambridge History of China, Vol. 11: Late Qing, 1800–1911, Part 2* (Cambridge, 1980); Immanuel C.Y. Hsu, *The Rise of Modern China*, 6th ed. (New York, 2000); Evelyn Rawski, *The Last Emperors, A Social History of Qing Imperial Institutions* (Berkeley, CA, 1998).

ANTHONY Y. TENG

# H

HONG XIUQUAN (January 1, 1814–June 1, 1864). Religious and political leader of the historic Taiping Uprising (1851–1864).

Born in Huaxian, Guangdong Province, Hong Xiuquan was the third of four children of a farming Hakka family. As a young man, he was bright, confident, and somewhat impatient. His education not only enabled him to teach at a village school, but also gave him ambition to excel in the traditional Confucian civil service examinations. Hong's scholarly promise earned him support, encouragement, and even admiration from his family, friends, and fellow villagers. Hard as he tried, however, he failed four times to pass the civil service exams in 1828, 1836, 1837, and 1843, respectively. The disappointment and distress that resulted from his third failure were largely responsible for his serious illness in 1837. During a long-lasting delirium, Hong, as he later revealed upon gaining consciousness, had several visions in which he was introduced to a golden-bearded old man and his middle-aged son in heaven. More important, he was given a sword with which he was to "slay the demons" in the world. Although people around him felt dubious about Hong's claim of visions, they nevertheless found him a changed person both physically and spiritually as he emerged from the coma, seemingly taller and more amiable. While continuing to work as a school teacher, he made his fourth and last attempt at the civil service exam, but again failed.

At this juncture Hong happened to be reading through some religious tracts that he had obtained during one of his earlier exam trips to Guangzhou, and became convinced that the golden-bearded old man in his visions was in fact God, and the middle-aged man whom he had called his Elder Brother was Jesus. Furthermore, Hong believed that he himself was also

God's son whose mission was to destroy all the demons in China. After this revelation, Hong Xiuquan and several of his early converts set out on their missions to preach God's words, as interpreted by Hong, in the local communities and the neighboring Guangxi province. He proceeded to baptize himself and proclaimed to be a Christian. While studying and interpreting the Bible, Hong also went on to attack the idols in the temples and rid local schools of the Confucian templates, which he equated with the demons that he had been instructed to exterminate.

In 1847 Hong traveled to Thistle Mountain in Guangxi where **Feng Yunshan,** one of his earliest converts and friend, had organized the God Worshipping Society, which preached egalitarianism and promised salvation. In the Thistle Mountain villages, the peasants and miners were suffering from the economic dislocation that resulted from China's defeat in the Opium War (1839–1842); consequently, the anti–Manchu sentiment was running high. This kind of local climate made it possible for Hong Xiuquan and Feng Yunshan to attract thousands of followers by the summer of 1850. The religious aura that Hong projected and his personal charisma lent a great deal of credence and force to the Taiping movement. He was accepted as the leader of the God Worshipping Society with his self-composed Ten Commandments and his promise of an "Earthly Paradise." On January 1, 1851, he celebrated his 37th birthday by officially declaring the Taiping Revolution in Jintian village, Guangxi, with himself as the "Heavenly King" of the newly established "Heavenly Kingdom of Great Peace."

After a number of initial victories against the imperial army and the local militia, the Taipings were hunted by government troops, and had to march northward from Guangxi to find another base. Eventually they settled in Nanjing in March 1853, having attracted more followers along the way. The Taiping ranks swelled to over a million. Hong Xiuquan, with his nucleus of leaders, implemented a wide range of reforms, including abolition of private land ownership and redistribution of land among both men and women over sixteen years of age, and elimination of practices such as opium-smoking, gambling, concubinage, and prostitution. The Taiping government under Hong's leadership also adopted a new calendar and held Sunday church services. Some more puritanical and radical measures included the eradication of private property and the division of both men and women soldiers into different camps while banning any contact between them. Hong and the other Taiping leaders, however, excluded themselves from these stringent regulations, as Hong himself had over 80 concubines.

The initial military victories gave way to increasing internal dissention. In 1856, Hong Xiuquan was challenged by **Yang Xiuqing,** the East King, whose ambition propelled his desire to replace Hong as the paramount leader of the Taipings. In response, Hong secretly ordered two of his generals, the North King Wei Changhui and Assistant King Shi Dakai, to annihilate Yang and his entire family in the fall of 1856. Shi lost the lives of his entire family for having voiced doubts about the necessity of the massacre, though he himself barely managed to escaped. Hong then ordered the execution of the North King. From that time on the Taiping valor showed clear signs of decline.

Despite the brilliant military leadership of a young general, **Li Xiucheng**, and his several successful campaigns, eventually the Taipings fell under the unrelenting attack by government troops, with the support of foreign intervention. The Taipings were a tattered force by early 1864. Hong Xiuquan died, most probably by his own hand, on June 1, 1864, followed by the imminent collapse of his "Heavenly Kingdom."

REFERENCES: Michael Franz, *The Taiping Rebellion: History and Documents* (Seattle, 1971); Vincent Y.C. Shih, *The Taiping Ideology: Its Source, Interpretations and Influences* (Seattle, 1967); Jonathan D. Spence, *God's Chinese Son: The Taiping Heavenly Kingdom of Hong Xiuquan* (New York, 1996); Walter E.A. van Beek, ed., *The Quest for Purity: Dynamics of Puritan Movements* (New York, 1988); Rudolf G. Wagner, *Reenacting the Heavenly Vision: The Role of Religion in the Taiping Rebellion* (Berkeley, CA, 1984).

YI SUN

**HU HANMIN** (December 9, 1879–May 12, 1936). Republican revolutionary; military governor of Guangdong; president of the legislature; chairman of the Guomindang.

Born to a semiofficial family in Panyu near Guangzhou, Guangdong, Hu Hanmin mastered the Chinese classics at a relatively young age. For four years from 1898 to 1902 he worked as a reporter for Guangzhou's *Linghai Daily*. During this period, he sadly watched China's worsening social, economic, and political conditions. The Hundred Day Reform and the coup that annulled it, foreign powers' carving out their respective spheres of influence, the Boxer debacle, and China's further humiliation by the 1901 Protocol signed between China and eight invading powers further sent China to the pit of suffering. In 1902 and again in 1904 Hu traveled to Japan to seek new learning and to make contacts with like-minded people for bringing his country out of turmoil.

It was during his second sojourn in Japan when Hu launched his 30-plus years of a revolutionary career. In 1905 he joined the Chinese United League serving as an editor for its publication *People Journal*. As the chief of both Southeast Asia and South China divisions of the Chinese United League, Hu was actively involved in fund-raising and strategic planning for a series of armed uprisings aimed at toppling the Qing regime from 1907 to 1911. In November 1911 he was instrumental in securing Guangdong for the revolutionary camp and was subsequently elected the first military governor of the province. He occupied the post until mid-1913, except for the months he served as the chief of staff of the office of Provisional President **Sun Yat-**

sen. Together with Chen Jiongming, the deputy governor, Hu wanted to
turn Guangdong into a model province by introducing various reform programs. However, their goal was denied as **Yuan Shikai**, Sun's successor,
betrayed the republic. In the summer of 1913 Yuan ruthlessly suppressed
the former revolutionaries when the latter decided to take up arms against
him.

After Yuan's fall from disgrace in June 1916, China came under warlords'
control and Hu rallied to Sun Yat-sen's support for the campaign against
power usurpers. He voted for Sun's proposal to accept members of the
Chinese Communist Party (CCP) into the Sun-led Guomindang (GMD) and
to collaborate with the Communist International (Comintern). However,
Hu later realized the gulf of difference between the two parties with regards
to revolutionary objectives and ultimate goals, and became convinced that
the CCP was a tool of the Moscow-controlled Comintern that wanted to
influence the Chinese revolution. Together with **Jiang Jieshi** and GMD old
guards, Hu dealt a severe blow to the Communists then considered insurgents and rebels by the Nanjing government founded in April 1927 for
which he served as chairman.

Subsequent to the completion of the Northern Expedition in December
1928, the Nanjing regime installed the five-branch government in accordance with Sun's design. As the first president of the legislative branch, or
*Lifa yuan*, Hu vigorously pushed for legislative reform bringing China's law
in line with international practice. He was especially concerned with extra-
territoriality enjoyed by foreign powers and wanted to bring an end to it
by enacting and amending Chinese law wherever necessary, for foreign powers insisted on China's legal reform before they would relinquish the privilege.

Meanwhile, Hu and Jiang developed serious disagreements over a number
of issues including adoption of a provisional constitution during the stage
of political tutelage of the GMD rule of China. In introducing a constitution
Jiang hoped to attain greater popular support for the Nanjing regime and
his leadership. Hu was opposed to the move for he considered its adoption
against Sun's teachings on the process of revolution. He insisted on GMD
dictatorship during the period of political tutelary power that would last
for six years. In February 1931 Jiang had Hu placed under house detention.
Shortly after the outbreak of the Mukden Incident in September of the same
year, Hu was set free for the sake of national solidarity in the face of the
Japanese invasion.

During the subsequent years Hu took up residence in Hong Kong where
he headed an anti–Jiang coalition that blamed Jiang for China's continual
loss of territory to Japan and people's bitter livelihood. Hu networked with
prominent leaders who shared his stand for an immediate war of resistance
against Japan and an attack on Jiang's "nonresistance policy." Hu covertly
founded a new party, also named the GMD, aimed at replacing the existing

one, considered deviating far from Sun's teachings and under Jiang's control. For the new organization Hu was able to build up a network throughout major cities in China and among overseas Chinese communities. However, the ever-growing Japanese threat and aggression in the 1930s pulled various factions together. This was evidenced by a Hu–Jiang reconciliation and Hu's election as chairman of the GMD, with Jiang as his deputy, by the party's fifth congress that convened in December 1935. Before traveling north to Nanjing to assume the post, Hu died suddenly from a cerebral hemorrhage in May 1936.

REFERENCES: Chen Hongmin, "Hu Hanmin-Jiang Jieshi Relationship, 1932–1936," *Twenty-First Century Bimonthly*, no. 57 (The Institute of Chinese Studies, The Chinese University of Hong Kong, February 2000), 68–77; Yee-cheung Lau, *Hu Hanmin: A Scholar-Revolutionary in Contemporary China* (doctoral dissertation, University of California, Santa Barbara, 1986).

YEE-CHEUNG LAU

**HU LINYI** (July 14, 1812–September 30, 1861). Qing general, strategist, and statesman.

A native of Yiyang, Hunan, Hu Linyi was the son of a very successful scholar who came third in the 1819 *juren* examinations. Hu was also a brilliant student. He earned the *jinshi* degree in 1836, and became a compiler of the Hanlin Academy in 1838. His career was interrupted in 1841 when he returned to Hunan to mourn his father's death. In 1847 he purchased the substantive rank of prefect and was assigned to the province of Guizhou, where he held office in several prefectures until 1854. He soon distinguished himself by his efficient organization of militia and knowledge of military science in the suppression of bandits and secret societies. His manuals for *baojia* (system of mutual security) and the militia were particularly effective. The governors of Hunan, Hubei, and Guizhou, all vied for his service.

In 1854 he was promoted to the intendancy of Guidong, whence he dealt effectively with insurgents in neighboring Hunan and Hubei, and checked the advance of the Taiping rebels. For his accomplishments, he was successively appointed provincial judge of Sichuan and Hubei in the summer of 1854, but continued his military activities in the area. In early 1855 he was dispatched to help **Zeng Guofan** in the siege of Jiujiang in Jiangxi province. But as Wuchang fell into rebel hands in April, he was sent to recapture that city. To facilitate his mission, he was appointed acting governor of Hubei. In the next year and a half, there were many hard-fought battles. Funds were scarce at times until Hu introduced the *lijin* (likin) to Hubei late in 1855. He also raised the morale of his troops with Confucian exhortations of loyalty and faithful service. Eventually, with help from both within and outside the province, and with the deployment of smart tactics, he captured

Wuchang in December 1856. As a result, he was formally installed as the governor of Hubei and awarded the button of the first rank.

Hu saw the recovery of Wuchang and Hubei province in broad geopolitical terms. The security of Hubei, in his thinking, was critical to the pacification of the Taipings in the lower reaches of the Yangzi. And the safety of Hubei, in turn, depended on the government's ability to hold Hanyang, the city across the river from Wuchang. With Hanyang secured, the rebels would be denied the option of escaping or causing trouble upstream, while government forces could use it as a base for an eastward drive, particularly for the recapture of the strategic town of Jiujiang. In addition to shoring up the defense of Hanyang, Hu also attended to the rehabilitation of the entire province. He was disturbed by the shifting loyalties of the common people. To regain their faith in government, Hu took pains to clean up the bureaucracy. Many unscrupulous officials had taken advantage of the chaos created by war and continued to collect taxes in areas where taxes had been forgiven. As for areas where taxes were collected, surcharges were added until they doubled or tripled the original amounts. Yet the revenue remitted to the government invariably fell short. Hu quickly put a stop to the malpractice, thereby reducing the people's tax burden while increasing the government's revenue. At the same time, dozens of incompetent or negligent officials were impeached, while the virtuous and meritorious were rewarded. The revival of the salt monopoly also helped to restore the financial health of the province. It has been said that he laid the foundation for the modern development of Hubei.

With the provincial government put on a stronger footing, Hu was able to push the rebels eastward, out of the province by the end of 1857, paving the way for the eventual recapture of Jiujiang in June 1858. For his role in this major victory, he was given the title Junior Guardian of the Heir Apparent.

The capture of Jiujiang called for a review of the overall strategy against the Taipings. On Hu's suggestion, a four-pronged campaign was to be conducted under him, Duolongya, Li Suyi, and **Zeng Guofan**—the last had earlier been recalled from mourning for military service on Hu's urgings. An intermediate objective was the capture of Anqing, capital of Anhui. Seeing that his colleagues were wanting in tactical knowledge, he, in collaboration with others, compiled a handbook on the subject. This was the *Dushi binglue* (Military Tactics as Learned from History), published in 1861.

Although Hu, Zeng, and others enjoyed some initial successes, the dynastic cause suffered a major setback in early 1860, culminating in the collapse of the imperial troops at the Great Camp just outside Nanjing in early May. In desperation, the court appointed Zeng governor-general of the Liang Jiang provinces, giving him the authority to take over the main anti–Taiping campaign. Meanwhile, however, the rebels, who had broken the siege of Nanjing, wreaked havoc in numerous directions. A counterattack on Hubei forced Hu to return to defend his province. Hu nevertheless insisted that Zeng continue the siege of Anqing, giving him all the aid he could, even including a part of his salary. Anqing was finally taken more than a year later, in September 1861.

But the victory at Anqing was only a part of a grand plan, one that owed a great deal to Hu's strategic thinking. Back in May and June 1860, while visiting Zeng Guofan at Susong, Hu, Zeng, and others had a series of meetings on strategy. The upshot was to assign major tasks to Li Yuandu, **Zuo Zongtang, Li Hongzhang,** and **Shen Baozhen.** As history would have it, this turned out to have been the formula for success. The merit of Hu's grand plan was already evident as Zeng's forces took Anqing, and Zeng duly gave Hu the main credit for the success. In consequence, Hu was given the title Grand Guardian of the Heir Apparent, and the hereditary title, *Qi duyu.* But because of his exertions over a long period of time, his health collapsed as he had been spitting blood for four months. He died within a month of the capture of Anqing, at age forty-nine.

An astute commander who knew how to control his generals, and a brilliant student of military lore, Hu was a man made for an age of civil war. In forming his own army (*qinbing*) when serving as prefect, he was effective in restoring order to his territory. But in creating the army, he had taken the lead in the militarization of the traditional elite, though he, his colleagues, and successors remained loyal to the throne. His thoughts on military affairs, highly esteemed, were selected along with those by Zeng Guofan for publication in a volume, *Zeng Hu zhibing yulu* (Collected Sayings on Military Affairs by Zeng Guofan and Hu Linyi). Hu, Zeng Guofan, Zuo Zongtang, and Peng Yulin are often regarded as the four outstanding leaders of the period.

REFERENCES: Wang Ermin, *Huai jun zhi* [The History of the Huai Army] (Taibei, 1967); Wang Ermin, *Qing-ji junshishi lunji* [Essays on Late Qing Military History] (Taibei, 1980); Philip A. Kuhn, *Rebellion and Its Enemies in Late Imperial China: Militarization and Social Structure, 1796–1864* (Cambridge, MA, 1970).

DAVID PONG

**HU YAOBANG** (1915–April 15, 1989). Communist Youth League first secretary; Chinese Communist Party general secretary.

Born to a poor peasant family in Liuyang, Hunan, Hu was formally uneducated, outside a stint in his twenties at the Anti-Japanese Military and Political Academy, though by one report he had taught himself to read. Small in stature (under five feet), independent minded, and impetuous, Hu left home at age twelve to join the Children's Corps in the 1927 Autumn Harvest Uprising. His early career centered on all-important New Democratic (after 1957 Communist) Youth League (YL) work. These "youth," more numerous than Party members (which they aspired to become), performed similar functions and significantly strengthened the Party's organizational presence in rural areas. Capable and energetic, Hu was tapped as day-to-day manager of **Deng Xiaoping's** revival of pragmatism and reform after Mao's passing in 1976. Conservatives pushed him out of the inner circle during the political backswing of 1986–1987.

During the civil war years, Hu caught Deng's attention as a talented young organizer. At age nineteen to twenty he completed the whole 6,000-mile Long March crucible (only 10–20% of those who started survived), and later was a political commissar (Party leader in an army unit) in Liu Bocheng's Second Field Army where Deng was chief commissar. He became vice-chairman of the Taiyuan Military Control Commission after units of Liu's army under General Xu Xiangqian split off to Shansi and captured its capital. From 1949–1952, in his mid-thirties, he rejoined Deng and Liu to assert control of Sichuan, serving there in several political capacities.

In late 1952 Deng brought Hu to Beijing to head the YL. Hu's tenure there was unique until he, with Deng, joined the Cultural Revolution. No other leader so totally dominated one organizational sector. In 1956, Hu addressed the Eighth Party Congress on the status of YL work, and at age forty-one he was elected to the Party Central Committee.

During the Cultural Revolution, in his fifties, Hu suffered along with Deng and other leaders. Red Guard groups sent him to tend livestock in the countryside, and reportedly made him sleep with horses and sheep. In the 1970s he swiftly rose again as his patron's political fortunes gradually revived. One year into the post–Mao era, Deng secured his appointment as head of the Party's Organization Department, from where Hu energetically returned to power the Party leaders purged in the Cultural Revolution. In December 1978 he was named head of the Party's Propaganda Department as well, and elevated to the Politburo (Hu was 63 then, Deng 74).

Deng proceeded to push Hu to the center of his reform coalition, culminating in February 1980 in his appointments as Chinese Communist Party (CCP) Central Committee Standing Committee member and as general secretary, the post that replaced the chairman at the top of the Party hierarchy. Hu eagerly took up the cause of lowering the pedestal under Mao and **Mao Zedong** thought. In an early speech as Party leader, Hu asserted that Marxism should be not rigid dogma but only a guide. A favorite theme became the need to adapt outdated theories to fit new conditions, which left in doubt whether any Marxist or Maoist ideas had continued meaning in China. These themes were not original with Hu, but he gave them prominence from his platform as Party chief.

Hu was very much the reform coalition's political liberal. He variously favored more freedom of expression for intellectuals and artists, more latitude of economic decision for localities and enterprise managers, and stronger censure of corrupt behavior by Party leaders and their families. But as objections to liberal reform ideas strengthened, and factional lines accordingly hardened, Hu came into the conservatives' crosshairs. In 1986 when Deng (82) made known his wish to retire as informal top leader and Hu (71) bid to succeed him, conservatives and military leaders rallied to defeat him. He was deposed as general secretary, ostensibly for softness in handling student demonstrators, and in January 1987 he retired into seclusion.

Among young reform-minded intellectuals, Hu's reputation is as a man who gave up power rather than compromise principle. His death in 1989 brought forth an outpouring of commemorative expressions that catalyzed the spring's democracy movement.

REFERENCES: Richard Baum, *Burying Mao* (Princeton, NJ, 1994); Donald W. Klein and Anne B. Clark, *Biographic Dictionary of Chinese Communism, 1921–1965*, vol. 1 (Cambridge, MA, 1971), 383–385; Yang Zhongmei (trans.), *Hu Yaobang: A Chinese Biography* (Armonk, NY, 1988).

GORDON BENNETT

**HUA GUOFENG** (1921– ). Premier of the People's Republic of China (1976–1980); chairman of the Chinese Communist Party (1976–1980); immediate "successor" to Mao Zedong.

Born in Jiaocheng county, Shanxi province in 1921 (under the name of Su Zhu), Hua Guofeng began his political career in the "Chinese People's Resist-Japan and Save-the-Nation Vanguard" in 1938, the same year he became a member of the Chinese Communist Party (CCP). Throughout the war against Japan, Hua mobilized and conducted propaganda for Communist forces in Shanxi, and carried this work into the period of the Third Revolutionary Civil War (1945–1949), rising to head the propaganda department of the CCP in the No. 1 Central Shanxi District in early 1949. That summer, Hua went to Hunan to carry out political organizational work for the advancing Red Army. Thereafter Hunan became the primary location of Hua's political activities and career until the early-1970s.

In the early years of the People's Republic of China (PRC), Hua vigorously promoted land reform and agricultural cooperativization campaigns in Hunan. In 1954–1955, Hua, as CCP Secretary of Xiangtan district (**Mao Zedong**'s home district), implemented policies that accelerated the pace of rural collectivization and escalated the level of cooperativization in Hunan. Hua most likely attracted the attention of "the Chairman" for his political leadership in Hunan at this time. In 1957, Hua became an alternate Party secretary of the United Front department of the Hunan CCP committee. In July 1958, he became the vice-chairman of the Hunan Provincial People's Government.

Hua strengthened his position as a Maoist in Hunan politics through the Great Leap Forward period and in the *Sanmian honggi* (Three Red Banners) campaign, and brought these credentials into the political struggle "between the two lines" and the Cultural Revolution which erupted in the 1960s. Hua was instrumental in organizing Hunan's Cultural Revolutionary Committee and became its deputy chief in 1968. In October of that year, at the Twelfth Plenum of the Eighth Central Committee (CC) of the CCP, Hua was given the task of reading the "investigative report" on **Liu Shaoqi**, Mao's nemesis in the Cultural Revolution. In 1969, Hua entered the arena of national politics as a member of the Ninth CC of the CCP. Reelected to the Tenth CC in August 1973, he became a member of the Politburo. In January 1975, Hua attained the position of a vice-premier of the state council and was appointed minister of Public Security.

In early 1975, in the aftermath of the Cultural Revolution, it appeared as if the political climate in China could return to a semblance of stability, which seemed to be the desire of the top-ranking leadership of the CCP— Premier **Zhou Enlai** and other "elders" of the Party and state structure, and even, ostensibly, even Mao Zedong himself. In January 1975 **Deng Xiaoping**, a Zhou protégé who had been branded as "the No. 2 capitalist roader" in the Cultural Revolution but who had been reinstated in 1973, took over running the day-to-day affairs of the Chinese government as the ranking vice-premier as Zhou began to succumb to cancer. Nonetheless, even though Mao himself publicly endorsed Deng's leadership, a Maoist-ultra-Leftist faction, led by what would come to be known as the Gang of Four, continued throughout 1975 to attack Deng and his policies for undermining Mao's ideology and subverting the revolution. In these political struggles, Hua Guofeng, loyal Maoist, generally aligned himself with the tide of anti–Deng criticism that brought down Deng's leadership toward the end of 1975. In November 1975, Hua was appointed to read a summary of a Mao speech in which Deng was implicitly assaulted for "attempts to reverse the verdicts of the Cultural Revolution."

On Zhou's death on January 8, 1976, Mao intimated to the Politburo that Hua should be made acting premier and take over from Deng. In March, in an outpouring of popular sentiment for the "much-beloved former premier," thousands of protestors laid wreaths of mourning for Zhou at Tiananmen Square. In early April, the Politburo, with the Gang of Four in control, condemned the protest at Tiananmen as a "counterrevolutionary incident." Hua Guofeng joined in this condemnation, though less vociferously than the members of the Gang of Four. On April 7, Deng was relieved of his posts and Mao ordered that Hua assume the premiership and the position of first vice-chairman of the CCP immediately. On April 30, Mao gave his blessing to Hua's leadership with the words, "With you in charge, I am at ease."

Ironically, it was the Gang of Four, even more than Deng, that was taken by surprise and angry with dismay at Mao's choice of Hua to succeed to Zhou's mantle as premier. With Mao's own health rapidly failing, the Gang, as well as its opponents, quickly mobilized forces, political as well as military, for an eventual show-down that would be precipitated by Mao's demise on September 9, 1976. Hua was, at first, indecisively caught in the middle. His Maoist ideological leaning would have put him in a closer alignment with the Gang, and yet it was also clear that the Gang of Four considered him an upstart and denied his mandate for leadership. When the Gang pressed their own claim to succeed Mao at two Politburo meetings on September 19 and 29, Hua was finally moved to throw his lot in with the Gang's opponents. On October 6, under Hua's orders, the members of the Gang of Four (Mao's wife **Jiang Qing, Yao Wenyuan, Zhang Chunqiao, Wang Hongwen**) and their principal supporters were arrested. Hua assumed the position of chairman of the CCP and of its Military Affairs Commission (to go along with his premiership) on the following day.

With the Gang of Four incarcerated, Hua began forming a platform for his leadership of Chinese politics. In line with his deep-seated Maoist ideological position, and in light of the fact that his primary—perhaps even only—claim to legitimacy had rested with Mao's blessing, Hua formulated what he believed would ensure for himself the mandate of Mao's legacy. Among other things Hua coined a slogan that was intended to perpetuate the legacy of Mao and Mao Zedong thought: "Whatever policy Chairman Mao had decided we must defend with determination; Whatever directives Chairman Mao had issued we must firmly obey."

Hua's stubborn adherence to the Maoist legacy may have legitimated his leadership for a while, but in the end it would spell his downfall. In March 1977, at a Central Work Conference, Hua reaffirmed the "Two Whatevers," repeated Maoist formulas for China's "continuous revolutionary" future, reiterated the condemnation of the 1976 Tiananmen incident as counterrevolutionary, and repudiated any "attempt to reverse the verdicts of the Cultural Revolution." For a while, the old guard of the CCP, who had rallied to Hua in the struggle against the Gang of Four, gave Hua a modicum of support in the interest of stability and a calm transition. They did not, however, see Hua as one who could lead China into the future. For this, they were already turning their sights to the twice-fallen Deng Xiaoping, who, although ostensibly willing to support Hua, had been openly, if still tactfully, critical of the Maoist ideological rigidity expressed in the "Two Whatevers" formula, and called for a more pragmatic assessment of Mao's legacy and Mao Zedong thought. The same Central Work Conference in March 1977 paved the way for the third reinstatement of Deng, while continuing the acknowledgment of Hua's "supreme leadership."

Aside from the ill-fated "Two Whatevers," Hua's brief tenure at the helm of Chinese politics was also characterized by the launching of the so-called Ten Year Plan of social and economic reconstruction in February–March 1978. While on the surface the plan was to realize the Four Modernizations program which had been broached under Zhou Enlai's (and Deng's) leadership in 1975, the ideological underpinnings of the plan were still inflexibly Maoist, and in real substance repeated the unrealistic visions of Mao in the late 1950s. The plan never got off the ground and its failings only served to underscore that a successful post–Cultural Revolution, post–Mao reconstruction of Chinese society and economy simply could not be built upon the sand of ideological rigidity. The failure of the aborted Ten Year Plan precipitated a wave of criticism in the second half of 1978 which reopened the issue of the legitimacy of the Cultural Revolution and the wrongs that had been done to CCP cadres who had been victimized by Mao and the Cultural Revolution. At a Central Work Conference in November 1978, Hua made several concessions, including a reassessment of the 1976 Tiananmen incident, but it was too little, too late. At the same time, a brief but crucial expression of sentiments among the populace in November (the "Democracy Wall" Movement) in which criticism of Mao and support for Deng were openly manifested also helped to pave the way for the denouement of the Hua–Deng struggle. At the Third Plenum of the Eleventh CC of the CCP in December 1978, in a decisive swing away from Maoist Leftism, Hua's "Two Whatevers" was criticized and the Maoist theory of "continuous revolution" was repudiated. While the plenum stopped short of rendering a decisive overall "reappraisal" of the Cultural Revolution and Mao's legacy, it indicated an irreversible trend toward Dengist pragmatism. With a large number of Deng allies returning to the highest echelons of political leadership, including membership in the Politburo, as a result of the actions of the third and subsequent plenums (the Fourth Plenum in September 1979 and the Fifth Plenum in February 1980), Deng's control was strengthened and the elimination of Hua's faction became inevitable. A Politburo meeting in August 1980 resolved that Hua should relinquish his position as premier, and at another Politburo meeting in November and December, Hua was censured for grievous errors, his tenure in leadership was subject to merciless criticism and he asked to be relieved of all his posts. That decision, however, was not formalized until the Sixth Plenum of the Eleventh CC of the CCP in June 1981.

Hua's spectacular, if flimsy, rise to power and his equally spectacular fall from grace betrays the fate of a political leader who had little creativity and no independent vision to call his own. While his adherence to Mao Zedong thought may have resulted from his loyalty to the man who elevated him out of relative obscurity as well as his own deep-seated Maoist past, it debilitated a man who stood at one of the most critical crossroads of post–1949 Chinese history—the end of the Cultural Revolution and the Maoist period—with a wealth of opportunity in his hands. Unable to transcend an ideological obstinacy that was obsolete in a Chinese society that had emerged from the ravages of turmoil which ideological rigidity had caused and equally unable to claim any mastery of the opportunities of change, Hua remains on the annals of Chinese history as an example of failed political leadership.

REFERENCES: Wolfgang Bartke and Peter Schier, *China's New Party Leadership: Biographies and Analysis of the Twelfth Central Committee of the Chinese Communist Party* (Armonk, NY, 1985), 120–121; Ting Wang, *Chairman Hua: Leader of the Chinese Communists* (Montreal, 1980).

JOHN KONG-CHEONG LEUNG

**HUANG XING** (October 28, 1874–October 31, 1916). Founder of Huaxinghui (1903–1905); leader of the 1911 revolution.

Changsha, Hunan, was the birthplace of Huang Xing. Son of an educator, Huang passed the *shengyuan* degree examination in 1892. Instead of pursuing the advanced degree of *jinshi*, he enrolled at the Academy of Hunan and Hubei, an institution founded by **Zhang Zhidong** for a practical education. After his graduation from the academy in 1902, he won an official scholarship for further studies in Japan.

It was in Japan when Huang Xing was converted to revolution. While studying at the Kobun Institute in Tokyo, he cooperated with Yang Du and Yang Shouren to start a monthly, *Youxue yibian* (Overseas Students Translations), on Western political ideas. In 1903 he joined the Anti–Russia Volunteer Army (*JuE yiyongjun*), a militia formed by Chinese students in Japan to protest the occupation of Manchuria by Russian troops since the Boxer Uprising in 1900. Convinced of the weakness of the Qing regime, he returned with other radicals to China to overthrow the government through propaganda, uprising, and assassination.

In 1903 Huang Xing taught for some months at the Mingde School in Changsha. The next year he founded a revolutionary society, the Huaxinghui (China Arise Society). But their plot to stage a regional uprising in central China was uncovered by the local authorities before it was carried out. Consequently, Huang Xing fled to Japan. Through the introduction of Miyazaki Torazo, Huang and other Huaxinghui members met with **Sun Yat-sen** to review the situation in China. They agreed that it was imperative to unify various anti–Manchu groups to overthrow the Qing regime. In 1905 a united revolutionary society, the Tongmenghui (Chinese United League) came into formation.

The organization of the Tongmenghui signified a new stage in the development of the revolutionary movement. The subsequent years witnessed an intensification of subversive activities in China. While Sun Yat-sen actively promoted the revolution through propaganda and fund-raising abroad, Huang Xing and the other leaders organized a series of unsuccessful armed revolts in southern China, including the Guangzhou Uprising on April 27, 1911. In a period of failure and frustration, Zhang Binglin, Song Jiaoren, and others were critical of Sun's leadership. Huang, however, remained supportive to the party leader.

When the Wuchang mutiny broke out on October 10, 1911, the revolutionary forces were poorly led. Huang Xing hurriedly went to Wuhan to take command. After the fall of Hanyang, he retreated to Shanghai. The next year, Sun Yat-sen returned to become provisional president of the Republic of China, while Huang was appointed minister of war. As a result of the peace negotiations between the Qing government and the revolutionaries, Sun offered the provisional presidency to **Yuan Shikai**. Huang was at first made resident general at Nanking, and later director general of the Hankow-Canton railways. He resigned from all the positions by January 1913.

The assassination of Song Jiaoren in March 1913 fully exposed the ambition of Yuan Shikai. Under the command of Huang Xing, the revolutionary forces started the Second Revolution to remove him from power. Yuan's superior army easily suppressed the revolution, which sent the revolutionary leaders into exile. In Japan, Huang Xing disagreed with Sun Yat-sen on his terms in reorganizing the revolutionary party. He left China for the United States in 1914 and remained there for almost two years. In June 1916, Huang Xing returned to Shanghai, and reconciled his differences with Sun. On October 31, 1916, he died in Shanghai at the age of forty-two.

REFERENCES: Henry Y.S. Chan, "China Arise Society (Huaxinghui)," in Wang Ke-wen, ed., *Modern China: An Encyclopedia of History, Culture, and Nationalism* (New York, 1998), 53–54; Chun-tu Hsueh, *Huang Hsing and the Chinese Revolution* (Stanford, CA, 1961); Chun-tu Hsueh, ed., *The Chinese Revolution of 1911: New Perspectives* (Hong Kong, 1986).

HENRY Y.S. CHAN

# J

JIANG JIESHI (Chiang Kai-shek, October 31, 1887–April 5, 1975, also known as Jiang Zhongzheng in China). Military general; statesman; Guomindang party leader; and president of the Republic of China.

Jiang Jieshi was born into a merchant family in Fenghua, Zhejiang province, on October 31, 1887. After some training at the National Military Academy in Baoding, he went to Tokyo in 1907. There he attended the Military Staff College and met **Sun Yat-sen**, a revolutionary leader opposing the reigning Manchu Qing Dynasty. Jiang joined Sun's Chinese United League (Tongmeng Hui), a secret revolutionary organization and the forerunner of the Guomindang (GMD). When the 1911 uprising broke out in China, Jiang returned to Shanghai and became involved in the overthrow of the imperial government and the establishment of the Republic of China (ROC) (1912). He also participated in the subsequent Second Revolution (1913) and the campaign against President **Yuan Shikai** in 1915–1916. In 1923, at the request of Sun, Jiang went to the Soviet Union as a result of the GMD's new policy of alliance with the Communists. After a brief stay, Jiang returned to become the superintendent of the newly founded Huangpu (Whampoa) Military Academy.

Internal struggles soon troubled the GMD after Sun's death in 1925. Military power, however, remained in the hands of Jiang, who by then emerged as a powerful GMD leader and commander-in-chief of the National Revolutionary Army (NRA) whose goal was to unify China by eliminating the warlords in the north. In 1927, while on his Northern Expedition, Jiang ordered the liquidation of the Communists. This marked his first total break with the Chinese Communists. In the same year, he married his second wife, the American-educated **Song Meiling** (Soong May-ling).

By 1928, with the successful completion of the Northern Expedition, China was temporarily unified under the GMD headed by Jiang. In the early 1930s, however, Jiang launched a series of military campaigns against the Communists, despite the Japanese invasion of Manchuria. The Chinese Communists were thus forced to leave their base in Jiangxi in 1934 to embark on their historic Long March to Yan'an. Jiang ordered the reluctant General **Zhang Xueliang**'s Manchurian army to fight the Communists instead of the Japanese. This resulted in Zhang's kidnapping of Jiang in Xi'an in 1936, known as the Xi'an Incident. Through the mediation of a Communist delegation headed by **Zhou Enlai**, however, Jiang was later released. After his release, a national united front (also known as the Second GMD–CCP United Front) against Japan began to emerge.

One year after the Xi'an Incident, an all-out war with Japan broke out. The war years with Japan (1937–1945) witnessed the emergence of Jiang as a national and world leader. While continuing his effort to contain the Communists, he mobilized China's national resources in an effort to resist the Japanese invasion. In 1942, he became the supreme commander of the allied forces in the China theater and later participated in the Cairo Conference. After the war ended in 1945, he was immediately confronted with the Communist challenge for supremacy, and the civil war erupted again. A meeting in Chongqing between Jiang and Communist leader **Mao Zedong**, arranged through U.S. Ambassador Patrick Hurley, failed to bring peace to China. The United States offered to mediate by sending General George C. Marshall to China. Both Jiang and Mao considered Marshall an obstacle to their victory, and the American mission eventually failed.

Jiang opted to resolve the Communist problem by military means, since the GMD enjoyed a significant military superiority. From July to December 1946, the Nationalist army under Jiang captured 165 towns and 174,000 square kilometers of territories from the Chinese Communists. In early 1947, when the Communist capital of Yan'an was seized, Jiang confidently predicted that the Chinese Communists would be totally defeated or driven to the hinterland by the end of the year. But the Chinese Communists had been expanding steadily, reaching 1.95 million in June 1947, as compared with GMD's 3.73 million. In the second half of 1947, the Communist army conducted a general offensive, scoring victories in Henan and northern Hebei. The severest blow to Jiang came in late 1948 in Manchuria, where he lost almost half a million troops. The battle of Huai-Hai (1948–1949) was another disaster for Jiang as he lost another 200,000 men. But the Nationalist forces did not actually collapse until General **Fu Zuoyi**, the commander of the Beijing–Tianjin region, surrendered to the Communists in early 1949. Jiang's position was further weakened by China's rapidly deteriorating economic situation. He was thus forced by the peace faction within the GMD to resign the presidency in January 1949, and Vice President **Li Zongren** took over the government as acting president. In April, the Communist forces occupied Nanjing, driving the Nationalist government to seek asylum in Guangzhou, and eventually, in late 1949, in Taiwan by way of Chongqing and Chengdu.

During his exile on Taiwan, Jiang adopted some reforms needed to strengthen his rule and to resist the Communist attempt to take the island by force. The outbreak of the Korean War in 1950 led to the American decision to protect Taiwan against Communist invasion. Jiang was thus able to stabilize the situation on the island and carry out an ambitious economic development program. He broadened his political base by injecting some native Taiwanese talent into his regime. Under his leadership and with American aid, Taiwan began to modernize its agriculture and industry and became highly competitive in foreign trade. In 1954, he signed a mutual defense treaty with the United States, which provided American protection against Communist action. In the late 1960s, he began to groom his son **Jiang Jingguo** (Chiang Ching-kuo) to be his successor. Even though he never abandoned his dream of an eventual return to the mainland, he made no serious effort to achieve his objective. Jiang's dream was not totally shattered, however, until 1972, when U.S. President Richard Nixon began an effort to normalize relations with the Communist government on the mainland. Abandoned by the United States, Jiang died embittered on April 5, 1975, after a prolonged illness.

REFERENCES: Hsi-sheng Ch'i, *Nationalist China at War: Military Defeats and Political Collapse, 1937–45* (Ann Arbor, 1982); Parks M. Coble, Jr., "Chiang Kai-shek," in Ainslie T. Embree, ed., *Encyclopedia of Asian History*, vol. 1 (New York, 1988), 259–262; Edwin Leung, "Chiang Kai-shek, 1887–1975," in *Read More About It: An Encyclopedia of Information Sources on Historical Figures and Events* (Ann Arbor, 1989).

EDWIN PAK-WAH LEUNG


**JIANG JINGGUO** (Chiang Ching-kuo, March 18, 1910–January 13, 1988). Chairman of Guomindang; president of the Republic of China; architect of Taiwan's democratization.

Born in Fenghua county, Zhejiang province, Jiang Jingguo was the son of **Jiang Jieshi,** a stern taskmaster and his first wife, Madam Mao (Fuk-mei). His paternal grandmother influenced him to become a Buddhist. He was sent to Shanghai for better schooling.

Jingguo received a scholarship to study in the Soviet Union. On October 19, 1925, at the age of fifteen, he sailed from Shanghai by cargo ship, eventually arriving in Moscow. He remained in the USSR until March 1937, when, with Faina Epatcheva Vahaleva, whom he married in March 1935, and his two-year-old son, Alan, he returned to China. Reconciled with his father and disillusioned with socialism, Jingguo read the Chinese classics and rediscovered his Confucian roots.

Under his father's tutelage, Jiang became a deputy chief of the provincial security bureau in southern Jiangxi province, where he went on to hold various posts including serving on diplomatic missions to the Soviet Union and participating in negotiations with Soviet military commanders for the return of Manchuria to the Republic of China (ROC).

In 1949 he accompanied his father to Taiwan to help him restructure and reform the Guomindang (GMD). In 1954 Jingguo became deputy secretary-general of the National Defense Council. Holding leading positions in the GMD, military, and youth corp, he carved out a significant sphere of power and influence.

On April 1975 he became chairman of the GMD, succeeding his father, and on March 25, 1978, he was elected as the sixth president of the ROC on Taiwan by the National Assembly. As president, he publicly justified his government's use of martial law as preserving ROC security and promoting the rule of law. He supported gradually increasing supplementary elections for national government representatives. By expanding Taiwan's electoral process, President Jiang hoped that Taiwan's example of democracy would take root in mainland China, preparing the way for China's unification.

In 1982 Jingguo astonished his party (they expected him to choose a mainlander) by selecting the Taiwanese **Li Denghui** (Lee Teng-hui) to be his vice-president. On March 24, 1984, the National Assembly elected them as president and vice-president, respectively. President Jiang began training Li in the art of presidential politics and the supervision of Taiwan's democratization.

Because of an unforeseen financial scandal and the slaying of the journalist Jiang Nan on October 15, 1984, which required his efforts to resolve, President Jiang delayed political reform for two years. Deeply committed to political reform, however, he believed that by democratizing Taiwan, the moral example of Taiwan's modernization and democracy could induce mainland China to follow suit. On March 29, 1986, Guomindang chairman Jiang informed standing committee members that he had hand-picked a committee of 12 to plan, study, and recommend expanding elections and constitutional reform.

On September 28, 1986, when opposition politicians illegally established Taiwan's first opposition party, the Democratic Progressive Party, President Jiang told his vice-president that, "We should try to adopt a calm attitude and consider the nation's stability and the people's security." Pressing for his party's reforms, President Jiang lifted martial law on July 15, 1987, and initiated a policy, which became law on October 15, 1987, that allowed retired military personnel to visit their relatives on the mainland, setting the stage for the first cross–Taiwan Strait exchanges. Obsessed with speeding up democratization, he continued to meet with top party and government leaders.

By late 1987, he was confined to his residence where he continued to meet with his advisers. He quietly passed away on the afternoon of January 13, 1988, in his residence.

REFERENCES: Government Information Office, *Jiang Jingguo xiansheng quanji* [Collected Works of Mr. Jiang Jingguo], comp. Jiang Jingguo xiansheng zhuangji bianji weiyuanhue [Editorial Committee for the collected works of Mr. Jiang Jingguo] (Taibei, 1991); Jiang Nan, *Jiang Jingguo zhuan* [A Biography of Jiang Jingguo] (Monte Bello, CA, 1985).

RAMON H. MYERS

**JIANG QING** (1913–May 14, 1991). Member of the Politburo of the Chinese Communist Party; wife of Mao Zedong; one of the Gang of Four.

Jiang Qing (other names Li Yunhe, Li Jin; stage name Lan Ping) was born in the town of Zhucheng, Shandong province. She joined the Chinese Communist Party (CCP) in 1933, while a member of the Seaside Drama Society in Qingdao. Later the same year she moved to Shanghai, where she joined the city's community of leftist artists, literateurs, and bohemians. In Shanghai, she acted in a number of films and plays, including Ibsen's *A Doll's House*.

In 1937, Jiang left Shanghai for Communist-controlled Yan'an. Here she met with **Mao Zedong**, whom she married in 1939. Because Jiang's political and personal past were regarded as somewhat murky (she was rumored to have been on intimate terms with members of the Guomindang while in Shanghai, and to have betrayed the CCP in order to get out of jail), the CCP leadership approved of the marriage only on the condition that Jiang refrained from involving herself in any kind of political work for the next 30 years. Aside from occasionally acting as Mao Zedong's personal secretary, and playing a minor role in the Ministry of Culture's Film Guidance Committee in the early 1950s, Jiang played no significant role in Chinese politics or culture until the early 1960s, when she launched an attempt to reform Chinese opera along revolutionary lines.

Jiang's efforts to instill the traditional form of the Beijing opera with a modern, socialist revolutionary content met with strong opposition from the CCP's cultural establishment in Beijing. It did, however, win the support of the Party apparatus in Shanghai, where Jiang established a working relationship with the Propaganda Department Director **Zhang Chunqiao** and the literary critic and essayist **Yao Wenyuan**. Another supporter of Jiang's at this time was Minister of Defense **Lin Biao**, who in 1966 made her a consultant to the People's Liberation Army in matters related to literature and the arts. For the next ten years, the Chinese media referred to Jiang's eight so-called "Revolutionary Model Operas" as the pinnacle of revolutionary proletarian art.

At the beginning of the Cultural Revolution, Jiang became deputy head of the Central Cultural Revolution Group, a powerful ad hoc organization charged with leading and monitoring the progress of the movement on behalf of the CCP Politburo. Even more important, she also became a leading member of the Central Case Examination Group—Mao's inquisition—and in this capacity she mercilessly persecuted, among others, people who knew the truth about her life as a young actress in Shanghai, Party leaders who in the 1930s had opposed her marriage to Mao, and cultural figures and officials who in the early 1960s had opposed her attempts to reform Beijing opera. At the National Day celebrations in Beijing in 1968, she ranked number six among the Party and government leaders present. In April 1969, the Ninth CCP Central Committee elected her onto its Politburo. She retained this position in August 1973, when the Tenth CCP Central Committee held its first plenary session.

In the early 1970s, Jiang became deeply embroiled in factional politics within the highest echelon of the CCP. Together with Zhang Chunqiao, Yao Wenyuan, and **Wang Hongwen**, she formed a clique (given the name Gang of Four by her husband) whose political program centered around the continuation of the Maoist policies and practices developed since the beginning of the Cultural Revolution. The Gang of Four's opposition consisted of a group of older politicians headed by **Deng Xiaoping**, who deeply resented everything the Cultural Revolution stood for. Jiang's main problem at this time would appear to have been her lack of a broad base of support within the Party. The fact the she was surviving in politics was largely due to the tacit support given her by Mao Zedong.

On October 6, 1976, four weeks after the death of her husband, Jiang was arrested together with the other members of the Gang of Four. The political enemies she had made over the past decade now accused her of having attempted to use the Cultural Revolution to destroy the CCP and to usurp power for herself and her "counterrevolutionary clique." On January 23, 1981, at a major show trial in Beijing, she was branded an enemy of the state and sentenced to death with a two-year reprieve (a sentence subsequently commuted to life imprisonment). According to the official Chinese news agency Xinhua, she committed suicide on May 14, 1991.

REFERENCES: Ross Terrill, *The Whiteboned Demon: A Biography of Madame Mao Zedong* (New York, 1984); Roxane Witke, *Comrade Jiang Qing* (Boston, 1977); Ye Yonglie, *Jiang Qing zhuan* [Biography of Jiang Qing] (Changchun, 1993).

MICHAEL L. SCHOENHALS

**JIANG ZEMIN** (1926–    ). Replaced **Zhao Ziyang** as Chinese Communist Party chief after the 1989 Tiananmen Square incident; president of People's Republic of China.

In the views of several biographic writers and analysts, Jiang Zemin's rise to become the most powerful leader in China after **Deng Xiaoping**'s death and for China's entry into the twenty-first century may be attributed to a number of background factors. First and foremost, Jiang had been a member of the third generation leadership corps, the background and training of which has been characterized as technocratic. He was born into a family of intellectuals in 1926 in Yangzhou in east China. He graduated with an electrical engineering degree in 1947 from Qiaotong University in Shanghai, a prestigious higher educational institution noted for technical training in eastern China. Then he worked for a firm in Shanghai which had some connection with American business in China. At the same time Jiang Zemin was operating underground for the Chinese Communist Party (CCP). When liberation came to Shanghai, Jiang had been promoted from engineer to operations director and deputy plant manager and party secretary within the firm. He was sent to Moscow in 1955 for a year's training at the Stalin auto factory. In 1956 Jiang returned to Shanghai serving, after numerous promotions, until 1962 to be in charge of the electrical research institute for the First Machine ministry.

The second factor was his family background. There is scanty information about Jiang's father except he was the eldest son of a shipping executive who had many children. However, Jiang was adopted by his uncle who in 1929 joined the CCP while a student at an art academy in Shanghai. When the anti-Japanese war broke out in 1937, the uncle was dispatched to his ancestral province of Anhui where he was the special Party (CCP) secretary working closely with the then new Fourth Route Army under Marshal Chen Yi in Anhui.

Jiang's uncle was executed in 1939 by the landlord armed band. To this day the uncle has been remembered as a revolutionary martyr in the CCP. As the adopted son of the revolutionary martyr, Jiang Zemin has the necessary family background to be considered for high positions in the party, in addition to the family's connections, through the uncle, with many top level leaders of the party since the founding of the People's Republic in 1949. This family background of revolutionary lineage certainly was a factor in Deng Xiaoping's choice of Jiang Zemin as Party chief after sacking Zhao Ziyang during the Tiananmen student demonstration in June 1989.

The third possible contributing factor in Deng Xiaoping's selection of Jiang Zemin to replace the embattled Zhao Ziyang was the manner in which Jiang, as Party secretary for Shanghai, and **Zhu Rongji**, as the city's mayor, handled the massive student demonstration in Shanghai in the spring of 1989. Jiang's decision to ban the publication of a more liberal economic journal and the joint agreement with Zhu Rongji to organize and dispatch a worker-picket brigade to maintain street order and control student demonstrations in Shanghai without using force won praise from Deng Xiaoping. Also, Deng seemed to have been impressed by Jiang's plan for developing Shanghai as China's premier industrial metropolis.

Although Jiang lacked wide-based support from the Party-government bureaucracy and from the military establishment in the initial years of his ascendancy as the head of the "third-generation leadership core," he had the consistent and firm backing of Deng Xiaoping, who made firm appeals to the Party-government military top leaders to pledge their allegiance to Jiang Zemin. By 1992–1993 when the Fourteenth Party Congress and the Eighth National People's Congress convened, Jiang had been named, for the first time since Mao, not only the Party chief and chairman of the powerful Military Affairs Committee, but also the president of the republic.

It was really no surprise to many that Jiang chose to elevate Zhu Rongji, a knowledgeable and proven economic manager, to vice-premier in 1992, for Jiang had realized by then that his role as Deng's successor depended to a large extent on how well economic reforms and growth policies were to be implemented. Jiang must have reasoned that China's future well being after Deng rested on economic stability and progress. Reforms that involved the overhauling of the inefficient state-owned enterprises, the debt-ridden banking system, the vast bureaucracy with rampant corruption, and the burdensome government subsidies, all of these were not easy tasks to accomplish. From that point of view Jiang needed a capable chief administrator like Zhu Rongji to provide not only continued economic growth, but social stability as well.

The paramount mission for Jiang Zemin is to provide continued economic growth in order to deter possible social unrest as more people become unemployed and lose their traditional social security nets, such as state pension and housing.

Jiang Zemin is married and has two grown sons—one has a doctorate from the University of Texas and the other is a computer specialist. Jiang has a working knowledge of Russian and a good command of English. It has been reported that Jiang can recite verbatim, in English, Lincoln's Gettysburg Address. He is an avid reader whose readings include works of Tolstoy and Mark Twain. While in college at Shanghai's Qiaotong University, he acquired a fondness for music and learned to play the piano. He can also play the traditional Chinese two-string instrument known as the *erhu*. On occasion he sings popular, as well as Russian, folk songs.

REFERENCES: Seth Faison, "Beijing's New Face," *New York Times*, November 3, 1997, A-1, A-11; Matt Forney, "Hoist with His Own Petard," *Far Eastern Economic Review* (November 13, 1997), 16–20; Kevin Platt, "China's Man-of-Many Colors Tours US," *Christian Science Monitor* (October 24, 1997), 1–7; James C.F. Wang, *Contemporary Chinese Politics*, 6th ed. (Upper Saddle River, NJ, 1999).

JAMES C.F. WANG

# K

KANG YOUWEI (1858–1927). Scholar, Hundred Day reformer, and writer.

Kang Youwei was born in 1858 in Nanhai, Guangdong. While he greatly exaggerated his kinsmen's scholarly accomplishments, it is also clear that he was born into a locally prominent gentry family which aspired after scholarly pursuit. A man with self-confidence, Kang did not shy away from expressing his desire to become a Confucian sage whose mission was to save humanity. And like many educated Chinese of his own time, he dedicated himself to the task of saving the Chinese nation, which was besieged by internal decay and imperialist powers.

To contribute to China's self-strengthening, Kang sought out information about foreign countries. Not only did he read Chinese publications about the West, but he also made firsthand observations of Western culture in Shanghai and Hong Kong. He went to Beijing to take the civil service examination in 1888, and at the same time to try to maneuver into the political stage. Although his effort was fruitless, upon his return to Guangdong he successfully attracted a small number of young scholars, who were interested in his political activities and intellectual power. At his academy, in addition to teaching traditional subjects and Western learning, Kang also contemplated the social relevance of scholarship. He was drawn to the New Text tradition of Confucianism, which viewed Confucius as a religious leader, and an action-oriented reformer. Before Kang scholars like Wei Yuan and Gong Zizhen had used the New Text tradition to advocate institutional reform, scholarly exploration of foreign cultures, and greater attention to the people's economic welfare. In 1891, Kang Youwei wrote *A Study of the Forged Classics of the Xin Period*, in which he represented the Old Text as

Liu Xin's forgeries. Five years later, he wrote *A Study of Confucius as a Reformer* to point up that reform and change were basic ideas in the Confucian tradition. For his radical and rather arbitrary interpretation of Confucianism, he was called a "wild-fox meditator."

Kang's reinterpretation of Confucianism was accompanied by his continuous endeavor to influence politics. After the Sino-Japanese war (1894–1895), Kang gained national attention as he, together with his students, led over one thousand candidates for the metropolitan examination to submit a memorial to the emperor protesting the terms of the Treaty of Shimonoseki and calling for reform. A man of action, he established study groups to advocate his views on reform, founded newspapers to inform the public, and submitted memorials repeatedly to the emperor.

In 1898 **Emperor Guangxu** issued an edict on June 11 to declare his commitment to reform. Kang was granted an audience with the emperor on June 16. While Kang is generally hailed as a leader of the reform movement, his influence on the reform was in fact limited. Although Professor Lo Jung-pang calls Kang "one of the prime movers of the movement," he also admits that Kang was successful only in his effort to abolish the practice of the "eight-legged essay" in the civil service examination system, and to "widen the channels for the expression of popular opinion." Professor Luke Kwong even argues that Kang did not play any significant role in imperial decision making. But as the **Empress Dowager Cixi** and her supporters staged their coup d'état, **Kang Youwei** was identified as a leading reformer. While the conservative faction of the government detained the emperor and executed six of the reformers, including Kang's only brother Guangren, Kang Youwei escaped and was in exile in foreign lands for 16 years.

He did not give up his struggle for China's self-strengthening. He founded the China Reform Society (*Zhongguo wenxinhui*), more popularly known as the Restore the Emperor Association (*Baohuanghui*). But the armed uprising, which was sponsored by the organization and took place in 1900, was suppressed. Kang then embarked on other ventures. He published books, and founded newspapers and magazines to promote his political ideas; he established schools in China and abroad; he toured around Asia, Europe, and America to rally overseas Chinese support for his program. A versatile man, he was active not only as a thinker-writer but also as a businessman. To raise funds for his activities, in 1903 he, together with his followers, planned to found an international commercial corporation which encompassed various lines of business from banks to mines to streetcar lines. His investments in Mexico seemed to be particularly successful. While he disapproved of the Qing state under the control of the Empress Dowager, he also fought the revolutionaries who wanted to overthrow the Manchu dynasty. His most immediate political goal always remained the establishment of a limited monarchy, which departed from absolutist monarchy and thus prepared the Chinese nation for democracy.

But as far as modern Chinese intellectual history is concerned, what makes Kang's overseas life most interesting is that he finished *The Book of Great Community (Datongshu)*, a project he had worked on before the Hundred Day Reform. Envisioning a utopia in his book, as Professor Hsiao Kung-chuan rightly observes, Kang Youwei wrote with "a certain degree of philosophical detachment from the immediate situation." Aside from being a nationalist, he was also a universalist, devoted to the mission of seeking a way of life for humankind which would be both individually gratifying and morally legitimate. Combining, evaluating, and appropriating traditional and Western cultures, he attempted to construct a blueprint for future society which is based on the premise of hedonism. To imagine a "perfect" society, he attacked various types of existing social institutions, condemned social stratification, blasted racial discrimination, and criticized the practice of private property—all this, he believed, caused human suffering. His onslaught on the family as a social institution proved to be shockingly unconventional: family, a site which bred selfishness and evils, and perpetuated inequality, was detrimental to the progress of humankind. The institution of marriage would find no place in his Great Community. Kang's vision of a utopia, it seems, foreshadowed the rise of May Fourth antitraditionalism, an intellectual-emotional trend that identified the pursuit of personal happiness as one of its basic tenets.

The revolutionaries overthrew the Qing dynasty in 1912. Upon his return to China in the winter of 1913, Kang worked to curb **Yuan Shikai**'s ambition, and supported the campaign aimed at restoring the Qing monarch, which turned out to be an abortive attempt. Seeing what he considered to be the rise of materialism, Kang was eager to reshape Confucianism and use it to maintain the Chinese people's spiritual integrity. It is far from surprising, however, that his efforts were not appreciated by the radical intellectual leaders who declared Confucianism to be despotic. Frustrated repeatedly by his own endeavors to save China and to rejuvenate Chinese culture, Kang increasingly turned to philosophy, one thing that he had been interested in, for consolation.

He created the doctrine of "celestial peregrination" not only to free himself from suffering but also to emancipate others from earthly afflictions. He died in 1927, as he "roamed the heavens" to transcend the human world.

REFERENCES: Kung-chuan Hsiao, *A Modern China and a New World* (Seattle, 1973); Joan Judge, *Print and Politics: "Shibao' and the Culture of Reform in Late Qing China* (Stanford, CA, 1996); Luke S.K. Kwong, *A Mosaic of the Hundred Days: Personalities, Politics, and Ideas of 1898* (Cambridge, 1984); Jung-pang Lo, *K'ang Yu-wei: A Biography and a Symposium* (Tucson, 1967).

HUNG-YOK IP

**KONG XIANGXI, CHAUNCEY** (better known as H.H. Kung, 1880–August 15, 1967). Financier; minister of industry, commerce, and labor; finance minister and vice-premier of the Republic of China.

Born into a pawnbroker family on the downturn in the late Qing dynasty, Kong Xiangxi allegedly claimed direct descent from Confucius by falsifying the genealogy after getting rich. Kong's career falls into two periods—as an educator, merchant, missionary, and revolutionary before 1926, and as a conservative statesman thereafter. Kong attended a missionary school before studying at the North China Union College in 1895. In 1899, he set up a branch of the Xingzhonghui. During the Boxer Uprising, he saved some missionaries and afterward helped **Li Hongzhang** settle religious atrocities in Shanxi. In 1901, he entered Oberlin College in Ohio and obtained his B.A. in 1905. Inspired by **Sun Yat-sen,** he opted for mining instead of social work at Yale. He tried his hands in business by importing tea from China. In 1907 he obtained his M.A. and returned to China to set up the Oberlin Memorial School.

Kong was skillful in shifting between business, politics, and educational enterprises. During the 1911 Revolution, he set up local militia to defend the local township against disbanded Qing troops. Following the failure of the Second Revolution, he went to Japan to continue missionary work and joined Dr. Sun's China Revolutionary Party, helping to solicit donations. He married Sun's secretary, Song Ailing in 1914. In 1915, Sun married her sister, Qingling. In 1915, Kong returned to China to manage Oberlin Junior University, formerly Oberlin Memorial School. In 1919, he built roads to facilitate relief work in Shanxi. Meanwhile, he started a trading company and a bank, exporting iron to the United States and importing soap, matches, candles, and kerosene into China. Soon he also invested in Shanghai property and diversified into textiles and herbal medicine. In 1922, he helped arrange the return of Qingdao to China, thereby establishing relations with the warlords, father and son—Zhang Zuolin and **Zhang Xueliang,** acting as their go-between with Sun. Kong maintained good relations with other warlords like **Yan Xishan** and **Wu Peifu** in north China. Then in 1924, as Sun's envoy, he recruited warlord **Feng Yuxiang** into the revolutionary camp. In 1926, he became the finance minister of Guangdong, giving financial backup to the Northern Expedition.

In 1927, he became minister of industry, commerce, and labor at Nanjing. He helped **Jiang Jieshi** to win over **Wang Jingwei** and **Song Ziwen,** convincing the latter to be finance minister. He also persuaded Feng to abandon his sympathy for the Communists and to accept Jiang's leadership instead of allying with Wuhan. The Kong couple were matchmakers for Jiang and their sister Meiling, convincing their mother and brother Ziwen to give consent. In 1928, his conservatism was revealed in the promulgation of the Trade Union Law to subdue frequent strikes. He worked with Song Ziwen to issue government bonds worth six million yuan to support the silk industry. The resumption of stability in the Yangzi estuary attracted sizable foreign investment, so China was relatively unaffected by the world depression of 1931.

Kong stepped down with Jiang temporarily in 1927 and 1931. In April 1932, he replaced Ziwen as president of the Central Bank. Jiang also transferred arms purchase from Ziwen to Kong on his mission to the West. Upon return, he convinced Jiang to start an air force academy. In 1933, he replaced Song as finance minister and vice-premier. Jiang preferred him to Song because he was diplomatic and amiable while Song was temperamental. Kong also supported his anti–communist campaigns and consented to all his requests for funds. To do so, Kong had to appease Japan and to tighten government control of the banks and taxes. He increased the Central Bank's holding of government bonds from 13 million to 1.73 billion in 1934. He set up tax offices in 17 provinces by 1936 and initiated income tax and profits tax in 1937. To divert popular support for the Communists, he reduced taxes for farmers and small businesses and abolished levies in rural areas. He won over the warlords by giving them a 40% rebate from tobacco and liquor taxes, stamp duty, and business registration. To appease Japan, he reduced the import duty on some textiles in 1934, to the detriment of Chinese manufacturers. In 1934, Kong passed the saving banks law, requiring banks to invest a quarter of their capital in public bonds, to be held in trust by the Central Bank. Then in 1935, the government seized control of the Bank of Communications and Bank of China by appointing directors to the banks, among whom were the Song brothers and triad boss Du Yuesheng. Other banks were to follow suit. The "banking coup" effectively put 66% to 70% of the banking sector under government control.

When the United States abandoned the gold standard in 1933, raising the price of silver in China and effecting an outflow, Kong imposed an embargo, only to push silver export underground. Facing currency depreciation and inflation, he dropped the silver standard and issued the *fabi*, but inflation worsened as the *fabi* in circulation tripled from late 1935 to mid-1937. His ministry of finance reports did not feature payments and receipts for 1936 and 1937. Moreover, his belated announcement of foreign-currency exchange control in March 1938 allowed an outflow of foreign currency. Allegedly, he manipulated the bonds market, utilized treasury funds for personal speculation, and collaborated with Du Yuesheng in opium trafficking. His banks re-lent capital from the Central Bank to the ministry of finance at a higher rate. He was attacked by the Central Committee clique, the Zhengxue clique, and Professor Ma Yinchu for speculation.

During the Xi'an Incident of 1936, he favored arbitration with Zhang Xueliang, negotiated with Yan Xishan and others to save Jiang, and consoled the financial circle in Shanghai. He asked for a pardon of Zhang from Jiang but to no avail. To reinforce defense against Japan, Kong purchased arms from Europe and arranged German officers to train the Chinese army. He also obtained a loan of ten million dollars from the United States in 1937. Upon return to China, he took over as head of the united office of four banks from Song Ziwen, widening their rift. In preparation for Japanese invasion, he moved factories and iron smelting and mining equipment inland. To facilitate trade and transportation of supplies, he built railways and roads there. In 1938, he lent government support to the industrial co-operative movement initiated by Song Meiling. As a result, government expenditure rose one third from 1937 to 1939.

In response to poor harvests and runaway inflation in 1940, the government monopolized the selling of salt, sugar, tobacco, and matches in 1941, with Kong chairing the commission in charge. Starting from 1941, newspapers launched attacks on Kong and his family. In 1942, his protégé, Lin Shiliang, was convicted of corruption and executed. Other cases involving his protégés followed in 1943. Still, he became president of the Bank of China in 1944. Meanwhile, Ailing, Meiling and his son Lingkan visited Brazil, reportedly to transfer assets there. Accusing him of corruption, President Franklin D. Roosevelt demanded his removal. Kong resigned as finance minister. Then in 1945, Song Ziwen replaced him as vice-premier.

Amid demands to investigate his crimes, he transferred his assets to Hong Kong and overseas in 1947. In 1953, he was on top of the GMD's list of expelled members but in 1963, he visited Taiwan at Jiang's invitation. In 1966, Kong finally resigned as director of the Bank of China, giving up all official posts. He lived in the United States till he died in 1967.

REFERENCES: Shen Guoyi, *Kong Xiangxi zhuan* [Biography of Kong Xiangxi] (Taibei, 1996); Sterling Seagrave, *The Soong Dynasty* (London, 1985); Arthur N. Young, *China's Nation-Building Effort, 1927–1937: The Financial and Economic Record* (Stanford, CA, 1971).

TERENCE PANG TIM TIM

# L

LEE TENG-HUI. *See* LI DENGHUI.

LI DAZHAO (October 6, 1888–April 28, 1927). Propagandist of Marxism-Leninism; librarian of Beijing University; and cofounder of the Chinese Communist Party.

A prophet of revolution, Li Dazhao was Marxism's first convert in China and one of the founders of the Chinese Communist Party (CCP).

A native of Hebei province in north China, Li Dazhao entered the North Sea College of Law and Political Science in Tianjin in 1907. There he came under the influence of some members of the Tongmenhui (Chinese United League), which was instrumental in overthrowing the Manchu Dynasty in 1911. In 1913, Li went to Japan to study political science at Waseda University in Tokyo. In 1916, he returned home to join the struggle against **Yuan Shikai** who was trying to restore monarchy in China. During this time, however, Li also maintained a close tie with the Progressive Party that advocated conservative reformism and constitutional monarchy. For a brief period of time, he edited *The Morning Bell*, a newspaper sponsored by the Party. In late 1916, he broke with the Progressive Party and resigned as editor of *The Morning Bell*. In the following year, Li became closely associated with some radical intellectuals in Beijing, especially **Chen Duxiu**, dean of the School of Letters at Beijing University and the most eloquent spokesman for the New Culture movement.

In 1918, Li Daozhao joined the faculty of Beijing University and became the head of the school's library. Thereafter, he became Chen Duxiu's close ally in championing the New Culture movement. He not only edited the *New Youth*, then a forum for China's most restless youth, but also founded and cofounded radical publications such as the *Weekly Review* and *Young China Monthly*. In these periodicals, Li published a series of articles advocating revolutionary changes. Unhappy about the anarchy under the sham of republicanism of his time, Li found hope in the Russian Bolshevik Revolution of 1917. In "The Victory of Bolshevism," published in the November 15, 1918 issue of the *New Youth*, Li hailed the Russian Revolution as a crusade of the downtrodden against the evil system of capitalism and as a model for the Chinese people in their fight against Western imperialism for modern nationhood. "In the course of such a world mass movement," he wrote, "all those dregs of history which can impede the progress of the new movement—such as emperors, nobles, warlords, bureaucrats, militarism, capitalism—will certainly be destroyed as though struck by a thunderbolt." By the same token, he rejected the political gradualism advocated by Western educated intellectuals such as Hu Shi.

Using his office at the Beijing University library as a base, Li Dazhao established an informal study group, where a dozen or so professors and students met frequently to exchange their views on various political and philosophical issues. His study group, together with other groups of Chinese socialists, laid the foundation for the CCP.

After the founding of the CCP in 1921, Li served on the executive committee of the CCP in the Beijing area and was elected to the Central Committee of the Third and Fourth Congresses of the Party. As the regional director of the Chinese Labor Movement (Zhongguo Laodong zuhe shujibu) in north China, Li also organized strikes in Kailuan Coal Mines, Beijing–Shuiyuan Railroad, and Beijing–Hankou Railroad. In 1922–1923, he facilitated the First United Front between the CCP and the Nationalist Party (Guomindang or GMD). In 1924, Li joined the GMD and was elected to the executive committee of the GMD. In June, Li led a delegation of the CCP to attend the Fifth Congress of the Third Communist International or the Comintern in Moscow.

While imbibing Marxism Leninism, Li Dazhao was apparently aware of the obvious gap between the Western philosophy of proletarian revolution and China's social realities. China was a rural nation and the vast majority of its population was peasants. For Li, the liberation of the peasants was an integral part of China's national revolution and prerequisite for China's national rebirth. The mainstay of the Chinese revolution was, by necessity, the peasant masses. Because of this, the future of the Chinese revolution hinged on whether the revolutionary intelligentsia could awaken the largely illiterate masses with a revolutionary ideology. He said passionately that the task facing Chinese revolutionaries was to reach out to the peasants and help them to know that "they should demand revolution, to speak out about their sufferings, to throw their ignorance and be people who will themselves plan their own lives." By merging with the peasants, Li reasoned, the Chinese intelligentsia would also achieve their own social and political salvation. His ideas, while indicating the difficulty in adapting Marxist theory to Chinese circumstances, apparently influenced many younger Chinese Marxists, including **Mao Zedong** and **Qu Qiubai,** both of whom later became leaders of the CCP.

In 1926, Li Dazhao was forced to go underground because of the pro-Japanese policy of the Beijing government under warlord Zhang Zuolin. In April 1927, the police of the Beijing government arrested Li who was taking refuge in the Russian embassy. After a speedy trial, Li was sentenced to death for alleged treason. He was executed on April 28.

REFERENCE: John King Fairbank and Albert Feuerwerker, eds., *The Cambridge History of China, Vol. 13: Republican China, 1912–1949* (Cambridge, 1986); Maurice Meisner, *Li Ta-chao and the Origins of Chinese Marxism* (Cambridge, MA, 1967); Benjamin Schwartz, *Chinese Communism and the Rise of Mao* (Cambridge, MA, 1980); Hu Shen, ed., *Zhongguo gongchandang de qishi nian* (Seventy Years of the CCP) (Beijing, 1991).

PENG DENG

**LI DENGHUI** (Lee Teng-Hui, 1923–   ). Leader in Taiwan; president of the Republic of China on Taiwan; chairman of the Guomindang but expelled from the Party in 2001.

Li Denghui was born in the town of Sanchi near Taibei city during the period of Japanese colonial rule on Taiwan (from 1895 to 1945), a period that saw the rise of a self-defined and self-conscious Taiwanese elite. His father (a Hakka) served in the Japanese administration as a manager of the local irrigation service. He came from a Presbyterian family and remains to this day a devout Presbyterian and a member of the island's influential Presbyterian Church of Taiwan.

Li seems to have had a normal youth but was one of those few who did attend Tamsui High School, an educational facility established by the pioneering Presbyterian Missionary, George Leslie MacKay. This school was one of the few places that Taiwanese could attend and receive the education they needed to go on to Japan to attend one of the major universities. Li followed this path and the final years of World War II saw him attending the Kyoto Imperial University. The end of the war forced him to cut short his education. He returned to a Taiwan badly damaged by the U.S. bombing and being ransacked by Guomindang (GMD) officials and mainland business. However, he was able to return to his studies, graduating from Taiwan National University in 1949. Later on he studied in the United States and received a Ph.D. from Cornell University. He then returned to Taiwan and to his steadily advancing career as a scholar and bureaucrat.

From 1972 to 1978 he served in the cabinet as Minister-Without-Portfolio. He specialized in his field of expertise, agricultural policy. He was appointed mayor of Taibei City and served during the critical months and years of the Meilidao Movement and its aftermath.

In 1981 Li was chosen to be the governor of Taiwan province, serving until 1984. During these years he began once again to work on Taiwan's rural irrigation system. In 1984 President **Jiang Jingguo** (son of **Jiang Jieshi**) took the next step by making Li the vice-president of the Republic of China (ROC). This can be seen as one more example of Jiang's wish to show that Taiwanization was real. Jiang and Li won the National Assembly election. In 1986 the state under Jiang legalized the *tangwai* and the DPP (Democratic Progressive Party) officially came into being.

Jiang died in January 1988 and Li Denghui took his place. His years as president can be broken down into a number of distinct stages. The first period began in early 1988 and lasted until the spring 1990. During this period he created a base of power and defined the faction that would support him. He also began to define his foreign policy, one that was based on a dual strategy of reaching out to the mainland even as he developed economic and political ties with the major states of Southeast Asia.

The second period began with student demonstrations in the spring of 1990 and ended with the Legislative Yuan election of 1992. During demonstrations students demanded major governmental reforms. This led to the convening of the National Consultative Conference. Held in early July 1990, it brought together a wide number of individuals representing vastly different agendas. In the end, a set of proposals—a blueprint of sorts—was drawn up and agreed upon. In the years that followed Li used this document as the formal or theoretical basis for his wide-scale reform program.

In 1992 the National Assembly convened and began its efforts at putting the GMD list of proposed amendments in place to change the nature of the 1947 Constitution and make it more responsive. The rise of the DPP, and the perceived failure of the premier to gain more seats for the GMD, gave Li the rationale he needed to push Premier Hau aside and pick his own man as premier, **Lian Zhan**. He was another Taiwanese educated in the West and had earned a Ph.D. from the University of Chicago.

Li put Lian into the center of the political arena as the third period in his presidency began in early 1993. That period would end with another step toward democratization, the first election of Taiwan's provincial governor in late fall 1994.

A number of issues took center stage in 1994. One was a scandal in the navy, which dominated debates in the first part of the legislative year. A second was a conflict over the construction of Atomic Power Plant Number Four, which would rage during the summer and fall with little resolution.

The next six years were a dramatic whirlwind for Li and Taiwan. The campaign for the presidency began in 1995 and ended with Li's landslide victory in the election of March 1996. Li had gained so much influence and prestige that he was almost invulnerable and he won a victory that made him his nation's most powerful man.

After the first few easy months since Li's inauguration, however, a combination of natural disasters and bad political mistakes made the presidency more difficult than it might have been. The floods in the summer of 1996 were the prelude and the government's failure to deal with key issues presaged the problems that would come. Li and Lian created their own nightmare in their attempts to decrease the size of the provincial government and undercut another GMD leader, James Song's, power. Song did not go quietly and gave notice he would remain a thorn in Lian and Li's sides thereafter. The early phases of the 1999 presidential campaign demonstrated how fractured GMD politics had become. Song left the Party. The New Party showed it was still in the game, and Lian and Li spent the summer making the best of a difficult situation.

By the time the campaign was well under way, with all the dire predictions of a divided Party coming true, yet another natural disaster, the great earthquake of September 21, struck. The government's response to this disaster was not as quick nor effective as it might have been. Lian's popularity was thus greatly affected.

Li became deeply involved and used his own influence and considerable skill to campaign for his friend but Lian's image and personality were not as attractive as those of the other men ahead in the race. Chen Shuibian, the charismatic DPP candidate, won the day and the GMD expressed their bitterness about Li, Lian Zhan, and their parties' great failure in demonstrations near GMD Party headquarters. For Li, the man of unity and the would-be-messiah, these final days were the most bitter medicine one could imagine. It was a sad end to his long, effective, oft-times dramatic, and precedent-shattering career as government official and as political leader.
REFERENCES: James Carman, "Lee Teng-hui: A Man of the Country," *Cornell Magazine* (1995); http.www.news.cornell.edu/campus/Lee/Cornell_Magazine_ Profile.hmtl; Murray A. Rubinstein, "Political Taiwanization and Pragmatic Diplomacy," in Murray A. Rubinstein, ed., *Taiwan: A New History* (Armonk, NY, 1999), 436–480; Lee Teng-hui, *The Road to Democracy: Taiwan's Pursuit of Identity* (Tokyo, 1999); Lee Teng-hui, "Understanding Taiwan: Bridging the Perception Gap," *Foreign Affairs* (November–December 1999).

MURRAY A. RUBINSTEIN

**LI HONGZHANG** (posthumous title Wenzhong, February 15, 1823– November 7, 1901). Statesman and diplomat in late imperial China.

Li Hongzhang was one of the most important modernizers, reformers, and diplomats of the late Qing dynasty. He was born in 1823 in Hefei, Anhui, to a gentry family. His father, Li Wenan, was a *jinshi* degree holder. Thus, Li Hongzhang received a good education and passed the provincial examination in 1844. He too became a *jinshi* degree holder in 1847 and was appointed to the Hanlin Academy in 1850 as a compiler, a prestigious academic position for a scholar in China.

The Taiping Rebellion (1851–1864) brought Li Hongzhang into government service when he was asked to participate in the suppression of the rebellion in 1853 in his home province of Anhui. In 1858, Li joined the staff of Governor **Zeng Guofan** and began a long association with him, as his mentor and friend. Because of his excellent performance, Li was named acting governor of Jiangsu in 1862. It was during this assignment that Li began his lifelong interest in reforms and Westernization of China. Shanghai, the capital of Jiangsu, had become the center of European activities in China. And Li's effort in hiring foreign mercenaries such as the Ever Victorious Army to defend the city from the Taiping forces began also his long association with foreigners in China.

In 1864, after the defeat of the Taipings, Li Hongzhang was appointed acting governor general of Nanjing. The Nian Rebellions (1851–1868) in South and Southwest China also prompted Li's participation in the many successful suppressions of these uprisings. In 1867, Li was promoted and appointed as the governor general of Hubei and Hunan. Even though Li admired the West for its technology, he distrusted the foreign encroachment in China. He repeatedly rejected foreign requests to build railways in China.

However, it was in the position as High Commissioner of Trade in North Ocean, appointed by the emperor in 1879, that provided Li the opportunity to engage himself in the promotion of modernization and industrialization in China. Throughout his government career, Li implemented many key industrialization projects that benefited China immensely in its future modernization programs. They included the Hubei Coal Mining Company (1875), the Jiangnan Shipyard (1876), the Jiangnan Arsenal (1876), the Kaiping Mining Company (1877), the Shanghai Cotton Cloth Mill (1878), the Tianjin Military Academy (1885), and the China Merchant's Line (1872).

Li Hongzhang's diplomatic career started in 1870 when the Emperor appointed him to investigate the Tianjin Massacre and then to negotiate with France for the compensation of those involved in the incident. Five years later, Li was asked to bargain with Sir Thomas Wade, the British minister in China, over the Margary Affair of 1875, which ended satisfactorily between the two countries by signing the Chefoo Convention in 1876.

Li Hongzhang thus received numerous honors and promotions by the Emperor because of his distinguished performances. Li's diplomatic skills earned him as "the most experienced diplomat" in China, yet his involvement and signing of the 1885 Treaty of Tianjin and the 1895 Treaty of Shimonoseki depressed him and discredited his abilities as a diplomat. For, in dealing with the French over the Treaty of Tianjin, China lost control of Indochina; and in the signing of the Treaty of Shimonoseki with Japan, China lost Taiwan and the Pescadores totally. Li took the blame on both occasions. Li was relieved of most of his governmental positions shortly afterward and sent into semiretirement by the emperor.

The last few diplomatic services that Li Hongzhang provided for the Qing court were all honorary ones. In 1896, Li was China's emissary at the coronation of Tsar Nicholas II of Russia. He was, however, the first Chinese high official who ever visited Europe. Aged and physically weak, Li was summoned in 1900 by **Empress Dowager Cixi** to represent China in the negotiations of the Boxer Protocol with the West, which was finally signed on September 7, 1901. By then, Li seemed to have reached the lowest point in his life, as did the Qing dynasty. Li Hongzhang died on November 7, 1901, only two months after the signing of the Boxer Protocol.

REFERENCES: Immanuel C.Y. Hsü, *The Rise of Modern China*, 6th ed. (New York, 2000); Kwang-ching Liu and Samuel Chu, eds., *Li Hung-Chang: Diplomat and Modernizer*, special issues of *Chinese Studies in History*, Fall 1990 and Summer 1991, also published under the title *Li Hung-chang and China's Early Modernization* (Armonk, NY, 1994).

ANTHONY Y. TENG

**LI LISAN** (1899–June 1967). Early Chinese Communist leader educated in France; led the Chinese Communist Party from 1928–1930 with what came to be known as the Li Lisan Line.

Li Lisan was a native of Liling, Hunan province in central China. As a young man, Li was concerned about China's national crisis and anxious to find a remedy for China's social and political problems. In 1919, Li went to France on work-study programs, where he came under the influence of European socialist ideology. Upon his return to China in 1921, he joined the infant Chinese Communist Party (CCP).

A Chinese Marxist and leader of the Chinese labor movement, Li Lisan is often associated with the Comintern's blunder in the Chinese revolution.

A superb orator and organizer, Li became actively involved in China's labor movement. He orchestrated the famous strike of the Anyuan Coal Miners in Hunan province in 1922 and the May 30th demonstration of 1925 in Shanghai. In 1927, Li was elected to the Central Committee of the CCP at the Party's Fifth Congress. In the summer of this year, when the First United Front between the Chinese Communists and Nationalists (Guomindang or GMD) was laid in ruins, Li participated in the Nanchang Uprising which marked the birth of the CCP's partisan army. At the CCP's Sixth Congress held in Moscow, Li Lisan was elected the general secretary of the Party. Under the new leadership, the CCP became a branch of the Comintern and Li used his connection with Moscow to strengthen his own position in the CCP and the Jiangxi Soviet Republic.

In 1929, Li Lisan felt encouraged by the financial crisis in Western countries and disunity of the Nanjing government under the GMD. As the general secretary of the CCP, he predicted the arrival of a high tide in the Chinese revolution and advocated a shift of strategic focus from rural areas back to the cities. At the same time, he became increasingly impatient with what he saw as the "rightist opportunism" in the CCP that was manifested by an excessive interest in the peasantry and guerrilla warfare in rural areas. Out of his orthodox Marxist belief, Li distrusted peasants and saw them as "petty bourgeoisie" who were opportunistic by nature and therefore unable to assume the task of the Chinese revolution. He believed that a proletarian revolution had to be carried out by the working class.

Following the policy of the Comintern, Li urged his party to instigate armed uprisings in urban areas, regardless of China's social and economic conditions. Workers' uprisings, Li insisted, marked the "maturity of the revolutionary movement." At a meeting of the Politburo of the CCP in June 1930, Li pushed through a resolution that demanded military actions for the victory of the Chinese revolution in several important provinces and industrial centers. Under his leadership, the small and poor-equipped Chinese Red Army came out of its rural bases in an attempt to seize some cities in central China.

Ironically, neither Li Lisan nor the Comintern behind him had a well-defined strategy for the campaigns. Blind leadership at the top of the CCP inevitably led to military disasters. The campaigns in the summer of 1930 failed miserably. Luckily for the Red Army, its leaders like **Zhu De** and **Mao Zedong** were not totally under Li's control and pulled their troops back in time to avoid total annihilation. The ill-fated military campaigns ended Li's leadership in the CCP. In November 1930, he was stripped of all his positions in the Central Committee of the Party and at the top of the Jiangxi Soviet Republic. All his allies in the CCP fell from power with him. His brief dominance of the Chinese revolution is often known as the Li Lisan Line, which is equivalent to revolutionary dogmatism.

Mao Zedong, who rivaled Li Lisan for leadership in the CCP in 1930, called Li's strategic plan as an "illusory story." To Mao, armed struggle in the countryside remained the most sensible strategy for the Red Army and the CCP. He urged his party to focus on the rural area and to seize small urban areas only when conditions were ripe.

After his fall from power, Li Lisan went into semiretirement between 1931 and 1946 in the Soviet Union. After returning to China in 1946, he first worked in the northeast region during the civil war. After the founding of the People's Republic of China (PRC) in 1949, he served successively as the vice-president of the All China Workers Federation, Minister of Labor, General Secretary of the CCP's North China Regional Bureau, and so on.

Li died in June 1967, during the Great Proletarian Cultural Revolution. REFERENCES: John King Fairbank and Albert Feuerwerker, eds., *The Cambridge History of China, Vol. 13: Republican China, 1912–1949, Part 2* (Cambridge, 1986); Hu Shen, ed., *Zhongguo gongchandang de qishi nian* [Seventy Years of the Chinese Communist Party] (Beijing, 1991).

PENG DENG

**LI PENG** (1928–   ). Premier; member of the Standing Committee of Politburo and Chairman of the National People's Congress.

Li Peng was born in 1928 in a small town near the city of Chengdu in Sichuan province. His father was an early leader in the Chinese Communist Party and a close associate of **Zhou Enlai**. Li Peng is one of many symbolically adopted sons of the late premier Zhou Enlai and his wife. Li's father, an upper-middle-level Party cadre, was captured and put to death by the Nationalists in 1931. As a youngster Li went to Hong Kong to live with his mother, who was then a Party member working underground. In 1939 Li returned to wartime Sichuan, his native province. He became a Party member in 1945 and was one of the privileged few to go to the Soviet Union for further training. Li attended the Moscow Power Institute from 1948 to 1954 and graduated with an electrical engineering degree. Li speaks fluent Russian and some English.

Before he became prominent, at the age of fifty-four, Li was in charge of China's hydroelectric and nuclear energy development. Until recently, most of his work had been concerned with the technical aspects of electrical power and hydroelectric development projects in Beijing. He became concurrently the minister for the State Education Commission before he was promoted to the post of one of the five vice-premiers in the State Council in 1983. In the 1985 reshuffle of top echelon leaders, Li was elected to the Politburo. Long before he was appointed as acting premier at the end of the Thirteenth Party Congress in November 1987, Li was considered by many as the likely successor to **Zhao Ziyang** because of his training, education, and executive experience, in addition to his good connections with the old veterans by virtue of being an adopted son of Zhou Enlai.

When Li was designated in late November 1987 as the acting premier, several questions were raised about his elevation to succeed Zhao at the State Council. These questions or concerns seemed to fall into two major areas. One was his Soviet connection. His training as an engineer at the Moscow Power Institute in the 1950s placed him in the "pro-Soviet" camp. At an unusual press conference of China's vice-premiers in April 1987, Li defended his position by saying that, "The second question seems to ask whether I favor a pro-Soviet policy. Here I formally declare that I am a member of the Chinese government, and also a new young member of the Communist Party's Central Committee. I'll faithfully carry out the policies of the Central Committee and the government." Thus, it may not be fair to have labeled Li as "pro-Soviet" on the grounds that he received technical training in the Soviet Union. A number of Soviet-trained technocrats have supported **Deng Xiaoping** and Zhao Ziyang and the reform programs; they have been given important positions in the Party and government.

A second question raised about Li concerned the degree of his support for economic reforms, particularly urban reform and the open door policy. Li was said to be under the influence of the late **Chen Yun**, who championed centralized planning and issued cautions on economic reforms. Li's selection to succeed Zhao as premier was one of the compromises struck just prior to the Thirteenth Party Congress between Deng and the conservative hardliners at Beidaihe in the summer of 1987. Apparently Zhao's opposition to Li was based on two main considerations: their disagreements on some reform measures, and Zhao's fear that Li's elevation to the premiership in time could lead to a takeover by the conservative hard-liners. There is little evidence to document Li's open opposition to any of the economic reforms. On the day when he was designated the acting premier, Li pledged to carry on both the economic reform and the open-door policies. However, at a general staff meeting of the State Council, he stated that the speed of economic reform might be "too fast."

Li disagreed with Zhao over the issue of how to handle the Tiananmen student demonstrations. Aligning himself with the hardliners on the Politburo and Yang Shangkun, the People's Republic of China president and the then permanent secretary for the Military Affairs Committee, Li proclaimed martial law on May 20, 1989. Since then, Li has emerged as one of the spokesmen for the hard-liners and as a target of attack and criticism by students, intellectuals, and those who have been sympathetic toward political and economic reforms. Li Peng suffered humiliation at the 1993 National People's Congress (NPC) session when more than 11% of the deputies voted against or abstained from his reelection as premier. Li Peng's power has been weakened considerably since 1993, and there have been signs suggesting his gradual political decline. Then in the March 1995 session of the NPC, delegates from several provinces registered their criticism of Li Peng for his unwillingness to assume responsibility for the inflation and the rampant corruption in the officialdom.

However, in September 1997 the departure of Qiao Shi from the Politburo made Li Peng the second highest-ranking member in the Politburo's Standing Committee. The arrangement agreed to by the top leaders in their informal meetings in the summer at Beidaihe resort was to "promote" Li Peng to be the incoming chairman of the NPC at its next session, which convened in the spring of 1998. Thus, Li Peng has survived in spite of his health and his past unpopularity among NPC delegates. By moving Li Peng to the NPC slot, **Jiang Zemin** and his leadership core have been freed to designate **Zhu Rongji** as the new premier of the State Council, a position that has been occupied by Li Peng since November 1987.

Under the present top leadership lineup, Li Peng ranks as number two in the hierarchy and outranks Zhu Rongji, the premier for the State Council. Although there is some reduction in Li's power, he is now chairman of the Standing Committee for the NPC, and he could still wield his influence in promoting the hard-line stance and views.

REFERENCES: Li Kuocheng, *CCP's Top Leadership Group* (Hong Kong, 1990, in Chinese); James C.F. Wang, *Contemporary Chinese Politics*, 6th ed. (Upper Saddle River, NJ, 1999); Gao Xin and He Pin, *The Most Powerful People of CPC* (Hong Kong, 1998, in Chinese).

JAMES C.F. WANG

**LI XIANNIAN** (June 23, 1909–June 21, 1992). Top-ranking cadre of the Chinese Communist Party in military and economic affairs; president of the People's Republic of China, 1983–1988.

Born on June 23, 1909 in Huangan *xian*, Hubei province, Li Xiannian began his military career as a soldier in Guomindang (GMD) forces in the Northern Expedition in 1926. In 1927, as the United Front between the GMD and the Chinese Communist Party (CCP) broke up and Communists were driven underground, Li returned to Huangan as an operative in the Communist Youth Pioneers. Later that year he took part in leading peasant guerrillas in the Huangan–Macheng uprising, and in December 1927 became a member of the CCP. He joined the Worker-Peasant Red Army in 1928, and subsequently became chairman of the Soviet government of Huangan. After serving several years in local Communist regimes, Li joined the newly formed Fourth Front Army in late 1931 as political commissar of the Thirty-third Regiment (11th Division), and began a long-term relationship with its commander, Xu Xiangqian. Later he became political commissar of the Eleventh Division, and of the Thirtieth Army. He also became a member of the CCP's Northwest Revolutionary Military Affairs Committee in December 1932 and a member of the Central Executive Committee of the Chinese Soviet Republic in 1934.

In 1932 and early 1933, the Fourth Front Army broke out of **Jiang Jieshi**'s "Fourth Encirclement and Suppression Campaign" blockade of the Communist forces in the Oyuwan revolutionary base and went into Sichuan province. After much fighting in the region it joined, in the summer of 1935, the CCP forces under **Mao Zedong** and **Zhu De**, which had broken out of Jiang's "encirclement" of the Central Soviet in the Hunan-Jiangxi area the previous year. Afterward, the CCP's Long March forces split up, with troops led by **Zhang Guotao** heading westward into Gansu and Xinjiang, and the smaller force, led by Mao, slogging through dangerous terrain northward toward Shaanxi. With a remnant of his Thirtieth Army, Li was sent in a deep foray into Western Sichuan to clear the path for the bulk of the Red Army. In October 1936, Li's troops were ordered to cross the Yellow River into Ningxia and in the spring of 1937, with barely 700 troops left under his command, he reached the Gansu–Xinjiang border. In these various maneuvers, Li's forces played a major role in protecting the Red Army's Western flank in and subsequent to the Long March and experienced much bitter fighting. In December 1937, Li and what remained of his troops were transported to Yan'an, in northern Shaanxi, which by this time had become the CCP's strongest base. Li then entered the Anti-Japanese Military and Political University at Yan'an.

In 1937, with the GMD and CCP forming a Second United Front, national war against Japan was declared. In late 1938, Li was sent back to Hubei to organize and command CCP guerrilla forces on the Hubei-Henan border. During the war against Japan, he played an important role in the formation of the New Fourth Army and in its reorganization after the Southern Anhui Incident in 1941. He served as the commander and political commissar of the Fifth Division of the New Fourth Army and of the Hubei-Henan-Anhui-Hunan-Jiangxi Military District, as well as CCP secretary of the Hubei-Henan Border region. In June 1945, Li was elected to the Central Committee (CC) of the CCP, and at the end of the war against Japan, he held the posts of commander of the Central Plains Military District and Deputy Secretary of the Central Plains Bureau of the CCP.

In June 1946, as the Third Revolutionary Civil War broke out, Li was faced with overwhelming five to one odds against a more well-equipped GMD army that was mustered against the CCP forces in the Central Plains liberation area. Li's ability to withstand these odds and defend the region against numerous GMD attacks and finally break out of the siege was a major turning point in the early phase of the war. As the war neared its end in 1949, Li was CCP secretary of Hubei province and chairman of the Hubei Provincial People's Government, as well as commander and political commissar of the Hubei Military District. At the founding of the People's Republic of China (PRC) in October 1949, Li was elected to the Revolutionary Military Affairs Commission of the Central People's Government Council (CPGC) and in December he became a member of the Central-South China Military-Administrative Committee, for which he became a vice-chairman in 1952.

In the first five years of the PRC, when China's governmental structure was dominated by a system of regional division, Li continued to hold top posts in the Hubei region, in the Central-South Military-Administrative Committee and in the CCP's Central-South Bureau. Then with the promulgation of the PRC Constitution in 1954 and the reorganizing of the government structure and the formation of the State Council that followed, Li was transferred to Beijing, where he began a second career as an economic administrator in the national government. He became a vice-premier of the State Council, Minister of Finance, and director of the Fifth Staff Office of the State Council, in charge of trade and finance, while also holding membership on the National Defense Council. He was a member of the CC of the CCP, and was elected to the Politburo for the first time in September 1956 at the Eighth Congress of the CCP. In 1958 he became a secretary of the CCP's Central Secretariat, and, in 1962, became the chairman of the State Council's State Planning Commission, the main body for long-term strategic national planning in the Chinese government.

Ironically, Li's involvement in financial administration and state and economic planning put him in a vulnerable position as China plunged into the Cultural Revolution in the mid-1960s. Although for the most part he was able to survive the criticism of the radical faction and the attack of the Red Guards through retaining the trust of Mao Zedong and protection by Premier **Zhou Enlai**, he was criticized for his role in the post–Great Leap

Forward economic reconstruction period which had been dominated by a **Liu Shaoqi–Deng Xiaoping** leadership, and especially for his part in the drafting of the Six Articles on Finance in 1961, at the so-called Xilou Conference of 1962 and at the Tenth Plenum of the Eighth CC in September 1962. In early 1967, in the aftermath of the Red Guard movement which had severely undermined the work of crucial state and economic institutions, a number of senior government officials and CCP cadres criticized the direction of the Cultural Revolution and its continued and intensifying radicalization. The radical faction, whose leadership would eventually gel as the so-called Gang of Four, seized on this criticism, which it labeled as a "February Reversal" of the Cultural Revolution and of Maoism, to counterattack, and, despite Zhou's protection, Li was sent down to a lumber mill in Beijing's outskirts for "correction by labor." He was not rehabilitated until April 1969, when at the First Plenum of the Ninth CC, he was reinstated as a member of the Central Committee.

In 1975, as Zhou Enlai's health began to fail, Deng Xiaoping was reinstated as first vice-premier and ran the nation's affairs. Li was clearly in Deng's corner, and when Deng fell to the criticism of the Gang of Four late that year, Li was once again implicated. When Zhou died on January 8, 1976, **Hua Guofeng** was chosen by Mao to succeed Zhou as premier, and Li, together with other senior officials, threw their support to Hua in the political struggle of that year between Hua and the Gang of Four, who were unable to disguise their contempt for Hua—whom they considered an upstart—and who also attacked Zhou's legacy increasingly blatantly. As Mao's own demise, which would come on September 9, 1976 drew near, the battle lines of an inevitable show-down in the power struggle were drawn. On Mao's death, the Gang of Four immediately pressed for their own claim to succession and attempted to exclude Li and **Ye Jianying**, who were the most senior members of the Politburo (and both had strong ties to the People's Liberation Army command) from the decision-making. In early October, as rumors of an impending military coup being staged by the Gang of Four flew around Beijing, Ye, in consultation with Li and Hua, acted swiftly and decisively to bring about the arrest of the Gang of Four on October 6.

With the purge of the Gang, Hua assumed command as chairman of the CCP and of its Military Affairs Commission as well as premier, which he had been since early 1976. Li became a member of the Standing Committee of the Politburo and ranking vice-chairman of the Central Committee of the CCP in August 1977, as well as member of the Standing Committee of the Military Affairs Commission. However, Hua's brief tenure at the helm (1976–1980) was handicapped by his far-too-obstinate adherence to Maoist ideology and to the legitimacy of the Cultural Revolution. Hua was also faced with rising sentiment both in the Party and in the nation at large for the return of Deng Xiaoping to office. While Li and Ye, the elder statesman, had some ambivalence toward Deng's return to power, they (and in particular Li) accepted its inevitability. Li, having played a major role in finance and economic planning in the past, was particularly disillusioned by Hua's grandiose and rigidly Maoist vision of the so-called Ten Year Plan of economic reconstruction. In the Hua–Deng struggle which unfolded in 1978–1980, Li, who had reclaimed a major role as deputy director of the Finance and Economics Commission of the State Council in March 1979, began to throw his still considerable political weight into Deng's corner. When Hua was subjected to humiliating criticism in late-1980, which led to his being relieved of his positions in early 1981 and the return of Deng to full leadership in the Chinese government, Li was considered a major Deng sponsor. In June 1983 Li became president of the PRC—the highest, though in fact a titular, post in Li's political career. Li held this position until March 1988. He died on June 21, 1992.

Through its vicissitudes, Li's political leadership in the history of the CCP and the PRC was a remarkable one. His military exploits in the Long March and in the civil war era remain the stuff of legend, and yet he also managed to turn himself into a major force in financial and economic matters in the Chinese government after 1949. His continued influence in the People's Liberation Army (PLA) and the ability to use such influence to affect political outcomes in characteristic of PRC politics. Albeit that by the time he attained his highest government position it had already turned into a titular post rather than one of true leadership, Li nonetheless did provide leadership in major decision-making junctures that affected the course of PRC history. This demonstrated to the very end his uncanny ability to back the right person in the turbulent and dangerous currents of Chinese politics.

REFERENCES: Wolfgang Bartke and Peter Schier, *China's New Party Leadership: Biographies and Analysis of the Twelfth Central Committee of the Chinese Communist Party* (Armonk, NY, 1985), 139–140; *Weida de remmin gongpu—Huainian Li Xiannian tongzhi* [A Great Public Servant of the People: In Memory of Comrade Li Xiannian] (Beijing, 1993).

JOHN KONG-CHEONG LEUNG


**LI XIUCHENG** (d. August 7, 1864). One of the finest generals and key leaders of the Taiping Uprising.

An educated Hakka and spectacled farm worker when he joined the Taiping troops in 1851, Li Xiucheng demonstrated his talent and excellent leadership as a military commander and strategist, for which he was rewarded the title "Loyal King" in 1858 by **Hong Xiuquan**, the supreme leader of the Taiping Uprising. After the 1856 internal strife, which resulted in the killing of two top Taiping leaders, it was Li who saved the Taiping cause from immediate collapse through both his military campaigns and administrative skills. For almost eight years he exerted his uttermost efforts at managing the Taiping affairs. His troops were able to retake Jiangsu province despite the setback that they suffered from foreign intervention during their assault on Shanghai. Ironically Li Xiucheng, who was more willing than most of his countrymen to believe in the rationality of the Westerners in China, ended up inviting the latter to abandon their neutrality by posing a threat to their economic interests in Shanghai.

Meanwhile, his military endeavor to tackle the Qing forces west of Nanjing in 1863 did not fare well. With the food supply cut off by the government troops, Li Xiucheng tried to implement a futile plan to stockpile weapons in Nanjing. Li, though remaining loyal to Hong Xiuquan, grew increasingly suspicious of the latter's lofty religious hyperbole. Upon Hong's death on June 1, 1864, it fell upon the Loyal King to assist Hong's successor, his sixteen-year-old son. On July 19, 1864, a destitute Taiping capital fell to the Qing forces.

Li's last act of loyalty was to give his own horse to Hong Xiuquan's son while helping the young king to escape at the risk of his own life. In captivity from July 30 to August 7, Li was instructed to write an autobiographical deposition by **Zeng Guofan**, his captor who was instrumental in defeating the Taipings. He finished a voluminous account of the Taiping movement before being executed in Nanjing on August 7, 1864. It is worth noting that Li Xiucheng at the very end of his life admitted that he did not completely understand Hong Xiuquan, the religious mystic and leader of the Taiping, and he went so far as to advise the Qing authority to purchase the best ammunition from Western powers in its efforts at strengthening China.

REFERENCES: J.C. Cheng, *Chinese Sources of the Taiping Rebellion 1850–1864* (Hong Kong, 1963); C.A. Curwen, *Taiping Rebel: The Deposition of Li Hsiu-ch'eng* (Cambridge, 1977); Immanuel C.Y. Hsü, *The Rise of Modern China*, 6th ed. (New York, 2000); Jonathan D. Spence, *God's Chinese Son: The Taiping Heavenly Kingdom of Hong Xiuquan* (New York, 1996).

YI SUN


**LI YUANHONG** (1864–1928). Army officer who rose quickly to prominence in the early days of the republic; twice served as president during the period of warlordism.

Li Yuanhong was born in 1864 in Huangpi, Hubei province, in central China, not far from Wuchang, the site of the 1911 Revolution, in which he was forced to become a reluctant leader. His father was an army officer who took part in the suppression of the Taiping Rebellion and young Li apparently aspired to a military career as well. After finishing classical preparatory school in his hometown, he was sent to northern China to attend the Naval Academy in Tianjin, where he spent six formative years of his life as a cadet. During those years, he not only went through a rigid curriculum in military science taught by Western instructors, he also became quite Westernized, versed in the English language and embracing Christianity. After graduating from the Naval Academy, he served briefly as chief engineer officer on a modern cruiser, but lost his job when his ship was sunk during the Sino–Japanese War of 1894–1895.

Soon after the war, he began to work for **Zhang Zhidong**, the viceroy (*zhongdu*) at Wuhan and one of the powerful regional leaders in China, training the new army with the aid of a German instructor. Later, he was sent to Japan for two years of further military training. He advanced quickly in the ensuing years, becoming commander of the Infantry Fourth Advance Guard in 1903 and of the Second Division in 1905. When the new army was organized in the following year, he was promoted to a colonel in command of the elitist Twenty-first Mixed Brigade, the new army unit that was heavily infiltrated by the revolutionaries. Li's attitude toward the revolutionaries was mixed: He appeared to be somewhat tolerant of them as long as they were not operating in an overt way.

When the revolution broke out in October 1911, with no leader of recognizable status on the scene, many organizers regarded Li to be the most suitable to assume command of the revolutionary forces in order to rally support from other parts of China. While Li was liberal and reform-minded compared to other military commanders, he was far from being a revolutionary. According to Edwin Dingle, a resident of Hankou who worked for the *China Press* at the time, Li did not seem to have much choice, for "above his neck glistened half a dozen narrow swords" held by the revolutionaries. After acceding to the demand of the leaders of the uprising, Li quickly rose to prominence riding the tidal wave that was to sweep the Qing dynasty from power. He became military governor (*dudu*) of the newly independent Hubei province and de facto leader of the revolution as 14 provinces (out of 18 in the nation) declared independence of the Qing dynasty in the first six weeks of the revolution. He began issuing proclamations in the name of the military government, abolishing the traditional practice of counting the year by the reign of the sitting emperor to signify the ending of the dynastic rule. He also sent out invitations to military governors of other independent provinces to come to Hankou for a meeting to organize a constitutional government of the new republic.

Meanwhile, Li began to espouse revolutionary ideals in great clarity and even tried to persuade **Yuan Shikai** to join the revolutionary side. In an interview with the *China Press* on November 20, 1911, in all probability the first extensive interview given by any revolutionary leaders, Li told of his vision for a new China. He wanted China to be a republic ruled by the Chinese with a constitutional government based on the American system, rejecting British constitutional monarchy as a model. Although he personally favored Christianity, he envisioned Confucianism as China's state ideology and he would encourage more Western investment to help open up China. All this is in substantial agreement with **Sun Yat-sen**'s views, which Li had picked up quickly. He spoke of himself as a military man with no interest in politics, but this was not true of his career in the next decade, when he was deeply involved in politics and eventually was a victim of power play.

When Sun Yat-sen was elected president of the republic in January 1912, Li became vice-president. After Sun handed over the presidency to Yuan Shikai two months later, Li continued to be vice-president. When Yuan was inaugurated in Beijing, Li first refused to leave his power base to go north. When he finally did, his suspicion came true for he was soon to find himself in a high position but with little real power in the shadow of Yuan. When Yuan died in 1916, Li became president and was still a man with no real power base. In the next seven years, he was in and out of office, depending on with which warlord he was allied at a particular time. In the spring of 1917, his dispute with his premier, the powerful warlord Duan Qirui, over China's joining World War I on the allied side degenerated into a mini–civil war in which each side called in other warlords to help. Li lost, and was forced out of office. In 1922, he resumed the presidency in a government controlled by bickering northern warlords only to find himself again forced out a year later. He lived out his last years in retirement and died in 1928, at the age of sixty-four.

REFERENCES: Howard L. Boorman and Richard Howard, eds., *Biographical Dictionary of Republican China*, vol. 2 (New York, 1968); Edwin J. Dingle, *China's Revolution, 1911–1912* (New York, 1912); Edward S.G. Li, *Life of Li Yuan-hung* (Tientsin, 1925).

TA-LING LEE

**LI ZONGREN** (1890–1969). Regional militarist; leader of the Guangxi clique; and last acting president of the Republic of China on the mainland.

Born in Guilin, Guangxi of a well-to-do family, Li received a military education in Guangdong and then attended the famous Guangxi Military Academy in Guilin. Classmates included Bai Chongxi and Huang Shaohong. Together these three would become the key members of the Guangxi clique. Li also joined the Tongmeng hui (Chinese United League) as a student and participated in the 1911 revolution. His military career began in 1916 as an officer under the overall command of Lu Rongting. Wounded twice in Guangdong and Hunan, Li was promoted to battalion commander in 1918. After the defeat in 1921 of Lu's army by the Guangdong army, he led 1,000 men into the mountains of Guangxi and began to build up an independent force. Eventually Huang Shaohong and Bai Chongxi joined him at his base camp in Yulin. By 1924 he and his army had become major contenders for power in Guangxi. By allying with one of the other pretenders, Shen Hong-ying, Li managed to occupy Nanning and soon thereafter took Guilin. He proclaimed himself "rehabilitation commissioner" of the province and was recognized by the newly reconstituted Guomindang as commander of the first Guangxi army, so that all of the province was under his control. In concert with Huang Shaohung and Bai Chongxi and the troops under their command, the Guangxi clique was duly formed. The clique and its troops were critical participants in the Northern Expedition of 1925–1927. They also played a pivotal role in supporting **Jiang Jieshi** in the handling of the Left Guomindang at Wuhan and Shanghai in 1927. The outcome left Li in control of Hunan and Hubei provinces (as well as Guangxi) and a member of the Military Affairs Commission at Nanjing. At a personal level, however, Li felt betrayed by Jiang Jieshi and the two men never again trusted one another.

The years 1928–1931 were critical of the political and military maneuver for Li Zongren and the Guangxi clique. For a while in 1929 their power extended from Guangxi to Hobei in north China. Inevitably, this brought the conflict with Jiang Jieshi out into the open. Their fortunes reversed in Guomindang backroom politics and Li and Bai were expelled from the Party in March 1929. After regrouping with Huang in Hong Kong, the three generals reestablished themselves as an independent force and the government of Guangxi. By 1932 a sort of modus vivendi with Jiang Jieshi was worked out in which the generals' authority over Guangxi was recognized as part of a new Nationalist political framework. From 1932 to 1937 Li's and Bai's reform government in Guangxi was considered a national model in the fields of industry, education, and law and order. Emphasis was put on the three selfs: self-government, self-defense, and self-sufficiency as slogans of the regime.

The next major phase in Li Zongren's career began with the formal declaration of the Sino-Japanese War in July 1937. Li was soon appointed commander of the fifth war zone, covering northern Jiangsu, northern Anhui, and southern Shandong. Under Bai Chongxi's tactical guidance, Li's Guangxi units scored the only major ground victory by Chinese troops of the war at Tairichuang, a walled town to the northeast of Li's headquarters at Xuzhou. The Japanese retreated and eventually laid seige to Xuzhou itself. An immense battle ensued, one of the most costly and largest of the war. The Japanese eventually prevailed but not without significant losses. Xuzhou and the blowing up of the dykes on the Yellow River in southern Henan slowed down the Japanese enough to delay significantly the battle and seige of Wuhan during the fall of 1938. Li's leadership at Tairichuang and Xuzhou made him a national hero in everybody but Jiang Jieshi's eyes. The two men hated each other.

After the fall of Wuhan, Li's leadership helped to prevent the Japanese from advancing further West. A stalemate on the ground remained in place until the Ichigo offensive of 1944. In the meantime Li returned to Guangxi but retained leadership of the fifth war zone until the end of the war. After 1945, with breaking out of civil war, Li moved to Beiping as head of government for the region. In 1948 Li challenged Jiang Jieshi openly by running for the vice-presidency of the Nationalist government against **Sun Ke—**

Jiang's candidate. Thus, after further losses on the battlefield, when Jiang retired from the presidency in January 1949, Li assumed the presidency. At first he proposed to defend China south of the Yangzi and then he negotiated with **Zhou Enlai** in March—refusing a position as vice-chairman in a new coalition government. After the Communists moved south in April, Li resigned and returned to Guangxi, fed up with battling both Jiang and the Communists. Eventually Li used his poor health as an excuse to avoid defense of Guangdong or Guangxi for that matter. He and his family left for the United States in December 1949. In 1954 he was impeached as president of the Republic of China and was replaced formally by Jiang Jieshi. Li remained quietly in the United States dictating his memoirs until 1965 when he returned to China with much fanfare and a warm reception. Eclipsed by the Cultural Revolution (his wife died in 1966), Li lived quietly in Beijing until he died in 1969.

In short, Li Zongren was a master warlord politician who was a better organizer and publicist than military strategist. His warm, outgoing personality made him popular with his troops and officers. Quite a contrast with his alter ego, Bai Chongxi, who was a brilliant strategist. It was Li's charisma as a leader that made him one of the most significant figures of Republican China and an effective bête noir to Jiang Jieshi.

REFERENCES: Diana Lary, *Region and Nation: The Kwangsi Clique in Chinese Politics* (London, 1974); Eugene Levich, *The Kwangsi Way in Kuomintang China, 1931–1939* (Armonk, NY, 1993); Li Zongren memoir, trans. T.K. Tong, 1960.

STEPHEN R. MACKINNON

**LIAN ZHAN** (Lien Chan, August 27, 1936–   ). Leader in Taiwan; vice-president of the Republic of China on Taiwan; Chairman of the Guomindang.

Lian Zhan is a talented man with a strong academic and governmental background who, as vice-president of the Republic of China (ROC) under **Li Denghui** (Lee Teng-hui), was deemed the heir apparent of Taiwan's first democratically elected president. Though he was the candidate of Taiwan's most powerful party, the Guomindang (GMD), he failed to win the complex multicandidate presidential race of 2000.

Lian Zhan was born in Xi'an, in Shaansi province on the Chinese mainland. The family moved back to Taiwan after 1945 and based itself in Tainan, Lian's father's ancestral home. Like many of the island's most prominent individuals, he attended National Taiwan University, entering in 1953 and graduating with a degree in political science in 1957. He was admitted to the University of Chicago, completed his M.A. in international law and diplomacy in 1961, and finished his doctorate in political science in 1965.

Lian then began a year-long teaching stint at the University of Wisconsin and the University of Connecticut. He returned to Taiwan in 1968. During his first years home he first taught at his alma mater, Taida in the department of political science. A year later he was appointed the chair of the department and also became the director of the graduate department of political science. He served for seven years at Taida and as he did so widened his network.

In 1975 he became a diplomat, serving as the ambassador to El Salvador. A year later he came back to Taiwan to serve as the GMD's director of Youth Affairs, a body that was under the Party's Central Committee (CC). Within a few months he received another promotion. He was made head of the National Youth Commission of the Executive Yuan. His career path over the course of the next politically charged decade would be fast paced. He was made minister of transportation and included among his accomplishments were the establishment of global shipping lanes and air routes and the construction of the new and modern central railway station in Taibei.

His next post was as vice-premier and in this high-level post he served on committees and task forces that dealt with issues such as environmental protection and the ROC's relationship with Hong Kong and Macao. He also was on a committee that revised the Organic Law of the Executive Yuan.

In 1988, during the first months of Li Denghui's presidency, Lian Zhan was appointed the minister of foreign affairs. Lian carried out Li's policy of "pragmatic diplomacy" by working to expand Taiwan's somewhat shaky position in the larger world. He worked hard to expand Taiwan's formal diplomatic presence in a host of smaller nations such as Belize, the Bahamas, and Grenada in Central America and the Caribbean, and with Guinea-Bissau in Africa. He restored relations with such nations as Lesotho and Liberia. In each case, Taiwan, rich nation that it was, had promises of economic aid to offer on the table. He also made Taiwan a member of the Asian Development Bank and set in motion the application process that would give Taiwan membership in the World Trade Organization.

The next step in the progression to the highest level of government was the post of governor of Taiwan. Lian became the governor in 1990 and served until 1992. Over his two years and eight months in office he worked hard to gain recognition as a hard worker, an effective initiator and implementer of policy, and a friend of the *lao bai xing*. He did accomplish much, but his lack of a personal touch and his appearance of aloofness and above the fray continued to haunt him.

He had to fight in order to gain Legislative Yuan confirmation of his appointment as premier in 1993. As premier, Lian became president Li's point man for the reform initiative. A sunshine law was drafted and, after much debate, was passed thus opening the political process and beginning a war on the notorious process of "black gold," Taiwan's version of contribution-driven politics. Lian also helped draft legislation for self-governance. One such law defined the process for the direct election of the provincial governor. Finally, Lian also involved himself in a variety of safety-net initiatives such as health care.

Lian's foreign policy experience also served him well. He visited a number of countries that the ROC had quasi-formal or formal relations with on these trips. Among the countries he visited were Honduras, Malaysia, El Salvador, Mexico, and Austria. He also participated in talks with People's Republic of China (PRC) representatives, held in Singapore, that helped to define the mechanisms of cross-the-strait relations and led to a better atmosphere in the informal—or people-to-people—facet of ROC/PRC relations.

By the middle of the 1995, presidential elections became central to Li and to his premier. An election law was formally in place and elections were scheduled for March of 1996. Lian was chosen as the GMD's candidate for the vice-presidency. When the election was over, the Li/Lian ticket had soundly beaten its Democratic Progressive Party (DPP) and New Party rivals.

The election and the inauguration in May proved to be, in retrospect, the high points in the history of the new administration. Nature and perhaps hubris combined to put land mines in the way of political and governmental success. A devastating typhoon, with its landslides—and the government's inadequate response to this natural disaster was one problem. The second was a serious political blunder on the part of the Li/Lian administration. They tried to eliminate the provincial level of government, thus virtually eliminating the role of the provincial governor. This was one reason, publicly at least, for government efficiency, but the real reasons were political for it was intended to remove James Song, a major rival for the presidency, from the scene.

The move against Song backfired in the election campaign of 1999–2000. Lian as heir apparent to Li was nominated but a difficult and painful election campaign followed. Song, driven from the GMD, became an independent and very appealing candidate. The DPP also chose an attractive candidate, Chen Shuibian.

Lian was lucky early on in gaining "positive visibility" for he led the Executive Yuan's post–September 21 earthquake relief effort. However, Song was well ahead in the polls and by the late winter the election became more a two-man race with Lian Zhan coming in third. The election vaulted Chen of the DPP to power, with Song proving his power as near frontrunner and finally spoiler. Lian was a distant third.

Yet Lian was not dead yet. By the end of 2000 he had become a reborn politician leading the GMD in their struggle against the faltering Chen, who had wandered into a severe governmental crisis that only came to an end in 2001.

Lian Zhan is in many ways an admirable man and a solid servant of the people, but his lack of a public touch conspired against him. Yet he is still active as a politician and if he can learn from his own mistakes, he may yet serve Taiwan as its president.

REFERENCES: Profile of Lian Zhan (http://th.gio.gov.tw/p2000/lien.htm); profile of Lian Zhan (http://www.channelnewsasia.com/taiwanelex/lien.htm); Murray A. Rubinstein, "Political Taiwanization and Pragmatic Diplomacy," in Murray A. Rubinstein, ed., *Taiwan: A New History* (Armonk, NY, 1999), 436–480.

MURRAY A. RUBINSTEIN

**LIANG QICHAO** (February 23, 1873–January 19, 1929). Active participant in the Hundred Day reform; writer and journalist.

Politician, political thinker, cultural critic, historian, popular writer, and journalist, Liang Qichao undoubtedly is one of the most versatile historical figures in modern China. Born in 1873 in Xinhui, Guangdong, Liang earned the reputation as a prodigy for his early success in the civil service examination. In 1890, he met **Kang Youwei**. Overwhelmed by Kang's scholarship, Liang immediately submitted himself as a disciple. This began a teacher-disciple relationship that was to cause much inspiration and frustration to Liang. Sharing the premise that Confucius was a reformer, in the 1890s they committed themselves to the project of modernizing China. In 1895, Liang supported Kang's effort to rally examination candidates in requesting the Qing government to begin some basic institutional reforms.

From 1897 to 1898, he was active in Hunan at the Academy of Current Affairs (*Shiwu xuetang*), disseminating radical ideas like popular rights among his students. After the Hundred Day reform, Liang escaped to Japan, where he led an extremely productive life. He founded *Qingyibao (The Journal of Disinterested Criticism)*, *Xinmin congbao (New Citizen Journal)*, and a short-lived journal called *Xiaoshuobao (New Novels)*. After visiting the United States in 1903, he rethought the prospects of a democratic government in China, and advocated constitutional monarchism. He also helped found *Shibao* in 1904. In 1912, he parted politically from Kang Youwei, and became active in the republican regime. Resigning his position as the minister of finance in the warlord-dominated government in 1917, he invested his energy in scholarly pursuit. In the final decade of his life, in response to what he saw and heard in his tour around postwar Europe, and still under the influence of his traditional upbringing, Liang revisited Chinese tradition from Laozi's philosophy to Confucianism. He died in 1929.

Examining his life, historians seem to share the consensus that Liang the politician was the least impressive, and concentrate on his life as an outstanding intellectual who helped shape modern Chinese culture not only through his contemplation of politics and history but also through his journalistic undertakings. In their analyses of Liang Qichao, a few scholarly themes emerge.

For Professor J.R. Levenson, Liang's life manifests the tension that marks modern Chinese intellectual history, the tension between the individual's commitment to history and intellectual commitment to "value." He was, in other words, intellectually drawn to the value of non–Chinese, Western culture while still emotionally tied to the Chinese tradition. To reconcile history with value, he embarked on his intellectual-emotional journey in search of the "equivalence of China and the West." He first attempted to integrate what he valued in the West into Confucianism, which he cherished as an important product of Chinese history. From 1899 to 1919, dispensing with "the Confucian sugar-coating," and believing that tradition could be put aside for the sake of national strengthening, he emphasized the contrasts between "the new" and "the old," but not between the West and China. But he still wrestled with the tension between history and value, for, in his brave new world which celebrated nonculturalistic or even antitraditional nationalism, he ironically strove to draw parallels between Western ideas and Chinese tradition. After the First World War, he constructed China and the West as two diametrically opposed intellectual-emotional orientations, one representing "spirit" and the other "matter." The mission of China, in the postwar world, was not only to accept Western materialism but also to resolve the problem of "spiritual famine" in the West.

While J.R. Levenson uses the theme of tension between value and history to structure the life of Liang Qichao, other scholars (such as Chang Hao and Philip Huang) contend that Liang's intellectual commitment to history—to Chinese tradition, that is—was much stronger than Levenson suggests. In his theories on the "new citizen," they point out, what Liang created was an ideal image of the Chinese individual whose personality was a mixture of traditional, Japanese, and Western attitudes toward life and morality that allowed him to be an effective modern citizen.

Experts on Liang believe that intellectual commitment, either to the West or to China, is far from sufficient in explaining Liang's political thinking. They always explain his interest in liberalism in terms of his concern for the nation. Liang was not another John Stuart Mill, who admired liberty as essentially instrumental in allowing the individual to actualize his individuality and to obtain happiness. Liberty, for Liang, was admirable because it could help unleash the individual's dynamism, which in turn would contribute to China's struggle for modernization. Some experts even argue that in modern China, intellectuals, Liang Qichao included, interpreted or rather misinterpreted liberal democracy as an effective means to national development. Thus, Chinese commitment to liberal democracy could only be weak.

Exploration of Chinese and other cultures, contemplation of the relationship between the individual and the nation, and immense interest in modernity and its ramifications—all this, according to the scholarship of the 1990s, in addition to molding Liang into a political thinker and cultural critic, also made him a historian. Liang's historical thinking evolved substantially from 1889 to 1920. It first appeared to be a historical discourse marked Liang's temporality oriented belief in nationalist history as the tool for a people to understand the path of progress, the path to modernity. But his tour around the United States and his trip to Russia allowed him to be more sensitive to historicized differences between nations and thus to localized manifestations of modernity. In the postwar period, through his discovery of the spatial coexistence of various cultural systems in the world, he freed himself from the temporalization of history which celebrated the Western modernist notion of progress.

It should be noted, last but not least, that Liang not only engaged in intellectual activities which were integral parts of and helped shape modern Chinese intellectual history, he also took part in the creation of a "middle realm" in his capacity as a great journalist, founding, writing, and publishing a journal, *The New Citizen*, in turn-of-the-century China. He was one of those who mediated between social groups—between the official elite and the nonelite, or between people who held opposite views—to advance political opposition vis-à-vis in the existing system of authority. By linking print and politics, Liang belonged to a collective of people who invented a new mode of politics in which newspapers appeared to be a significant institution enhancing the political stature of Chinese citizens vis-à-vis the state.

REFERENCES: Hao Chang, *Liang Ch'i-ch'ao and Intellectual Transition in China, 1890–1907* (Cambridge, MA, 1971); Philip Huang, *Liang Ch'i-ch'ao and Modern Chinese Liberalism* (Seattle, 1972); Joan Judge, *Print and Politics: "Shibao" and the Culture of Reform in Late Qing China* (Stanford, CA, 1996); J.R. Levenson, *Liang Ch'i-ch'ao and the Mind of Modern China* (Cambridge, MA, 1959); Andrew Nathan, *Chinese Democracy* (Berkeley, CA, 1986); Don Price, *Russia and the Roots of the Chinese Revolution, 1896–1911* (Cambridge, MA, 1974); Xiaobing Tang, *Global Space and the Nationalist Discourse of Modernity: The Historical Thinking of Liang Qichao* (Stanford, CA, 1996); John Willis, *Mountain of Fame: Portraits in Chinese History* (Princeton, NJ, 1994).

HUNG-YOK IP

**LIEN CHAN.** *See* LIAN ZHAN.

**LIN BIAO** (1907–September 13, 1971). Defense minister; designated successor to Mao Zedong; died in an aborted coup against Mao.

Lin Biao was born into a well-to-do merchant family at Huanggang, Hubei in 1907. While attending high school at Wuchang, the provincial capital of Hubei, Lin joined a satellite organization of the Chinese Communist Party (CCP) and took part in the Thirtieth Movement in 1925, primarily a movement against Japanese imperialists. That October he entered the fourth class of the Huangpu (Whampoa) Military Academy, from which he was graduated in 1926, just in time to join the Northern Expedition launched

was over. At the Lushan Conference, **Chen Boda**, Mao's long-time secretary and chairman of the Cultural Revolution group supported Lin in his bid for chairmanship of the state, a position vacated by **Liu Shaoqi**. Lin's ambition was blocked by Mao himself, for fear that Lin might become a threat to his power. Failing to come to terms with defeat at Lushan, Lin, encouraged by his insatiably ambitious wife Ye Qun and son Lin Liguo, acceded to conspiratorial activities as evidenced by a document known as the Outline of Project 571 engineered by his son and his followers.

Mao was not idle either, as he set out to have an inspecting tour to Wuhan and Shanghai to rally support from top military leaders. By the time Mao returned to Beijing on September 12, 1971, the attempted armed coup d'état and assassination of Mao had aborted or failed. Then Lin and his family stayed at the sea resort Beitaihe near Shanhai Pass, the starting point of the Great Wall. In the nick of time, Lin with his wife and son took off in a military transport to flee from the country. However, when on the way to the airport, Lin's own daughter Lin Liheng (Dou Dou) telephoned Wang Dongxing who, in turn, told **Zhou Enlai** and Mao Zedong of Lin's flight. While Zhou and Mao made preparations for the worse to happen, the news of Lin's airplane crashing near Undur Khan, Outer Mongolia on the morning of September 13 arrived at the Great Hall of the People at Beijing, which gave Mao and Zhou a sigh of relief.

The melodrama of Lin Biao did not come to an end with his death, for he had been Chairman Mao's comrade-in-arms for nearly half a century and had been designated his successor. His conspiracy against Mao and his failure not only constituted a disgrace of Lin himself, but also revealed Mao's failure. Hence, a rectification movement (a communist movement to correct the party line) was needed to criticize Lin's thought and deeds. The so-called Criticizing Lin and Confucius Movement was one phase of the Cultural Revolution that went far beyond what its title implied. Aside from criticizing Lin, the movement turned to be an innuendo attack on Zhou Enlai, Deng Xiaoping, and even Hua Guofeng and was not concluded until the death of Mao on September 9, 1976.

REFERENCES: Zhang Ning, *Chen jie* [The Dust of Havoc] (New York, 1999); Li Wen-pu, "Bu te bu shuo" ["[I] Cannot but Speak Out"], *Qiao bao zhou mo* (*The China Press: Weekend*), March 7, 1999; Tien-wei Wu, *Lin Biao and the Gang of Four: Contra-Confucianism in Historical and Intellectual Perspective* (Carbondale, IL, 1983).

TIEN-WEI WU

**LIN ZEXU** (August 30, 1785–November 22, 1850). Morally impeccable official who became the scapegoat for China's defeat in the Opium War.

Lin Zexu received his first degree at the age of nineteen. By twenty-six he had passed the highest level of the Chinese civil service examination and was on track for an outstanding career as a public servant. His initial appointment was as a bachelor of the prestigious Hanlin Academy. While in Beijing, Lin moved in that city's most dazzling cultural circles and attracted a following of like-minded individuals. He went on to serve as a provincial examiner, censor, circuit intendant, salt commissioner, provincial judge, provincial treasurer, and governor. By 1837 Lin Zexu was governor general of Hubei and Hunan. The following year he sent his fateful memorial regarding the opium problem to **Emperor Daoguang.**

Used medicinally since the Tang dynasty, opium consumption began to increase when the Portuguese started importing the drug into Taiwan in the early 1600s. In 1729 the Qing prohibited opium imports, to little avail, and by 1820, the opium trade was booming. In that year some two million *taels* of silver flowed out of China, mostly into the pockets of British opium dealers. By the early 1830s, the annual outflow rose to nine million *taels*. The resulting rise in the price of silver and the cost of commodities alarmed Chinese officialdom, as did the debilitating effect the drug was having on their people.

Lin Zexu's memorial contained several suggestions for dealing with the opium problem. First, he proposed that dealers and smugglers be harshly punished. Second, he advocated the destruction of the drug and the equipment utilized in its consumption. Third, he suggested the need to "cure" those who had become addicted. Lin even went so far as to contact Dr. Peter Parker, an American medical missionary in China, to ask for a prescription for curing all opium smokers. Parker's response was that no such medicine was currently available.

The Emperor Daoguang approved Lin's plan and commissioned him to take whatever measures were necessary to stop the opium trade. On March 10, 1839 Lin Zexu arrived in Guangzhou, vowing not to quit until he had accomplished his mission. Even before he reached Guangzhou, he had issued orders for the arrest of the Chinese known to be dealing opium.

Once in Guangzhou, Lin ordered the British traders confined to their factory compound. He let it be known, however, that the Englishmen would be released once all of their opium had been turned over to him. Captain Charles Elliot, a British government representative, commanded all British traders to surrender their stocks of the drug to him. It thus became British government property. Elliot then delivered the 20,000-plus chests of opium to Lin Zexu, who immediately began to have it destroyed.

Once the British community had evacuated Guangzhou, Elliot urged London to redress the affront to English pride and profit. A British expeditionary force was dispatched to do just that. Upon arrival, the Opium War began.

Once the war reached the northern coast of China, the emperor needed a scapegoat. He blamed Lin Zexu for creating complications without resolving the opium problems. Lin's response was that if he had been provided with the military force needed to confront the British, he would have been able to end the opium trade. Lin's argument was, of course, found unacceptable.

In September 1840, Lin Zexu was dismissed from office and ordered to Beijing to await punishment. In July 1841 he was condemned to exile in Yili, near the Russian border in Central Asia. Lin remained there for three years. In 1844 he was put in charge of colonization affairs in Xinjiang province. Because of the skill he displayed in this task, he was ordered back to Beijing in 1845.

Lin Zexu's rehabilitation completed, he was appointed as acting governor general of Shaanxi and Ningxia. Two years later he was named governor general of Yunnan and Guizhou. His success in this appointment was such that in 1848 Lin Zexu was awarded the title of Grand Guardian of the Heir Apparent. One year later Lin attempted retirement, but was called back when the Taipings became active in Guangxi. Appointed imperial commissioner yet again, this time to suppress rebels rather than the opium trade, Lin Zexu died while on route to Guangxi.

REFERENCES: Hsin-pao Chang, *Commissioner Lin and the Opium War* (New York, 1970); Peter Ward Fay, *The Opium War, 1840–1842* (New York, 1976); Arthur W. Hummel, *Eminent Chinese of the Ch'ing Period* (Washington, DC, 1943).

GERALD W. BERKLEY-COATS

**LIU KUNYI** (January 21, 1830–October 6, 1902). Militia leader and longtime Qing official.

A native of Xinning, Hunan, Liu Kunyi rose to high office primarily because of the conditions created by the Taiping Rebellion and the patronage of Liu Changyou, the son of a distant cousin who was eleven years older than he.

Liu's career can be divided into three stages: (1) as a military leader in 1855–1865; (2) as governor and governor general in 1865–1882; and (3) as governor general of Liang Jiang in 1891–1902.

Not much is known about Liu's early years, except that he earned his *lingsheng* (senior licentiate) status before joining Liu Changyou's mercenary (*yong*) forces in 1855. In the war against the Taipings, he quickly gained recognition for his bravery. Victories in Jiangxi soon led to a succession of rewards, culminating in the brevet of a circuit intendant in 1857. For the next two years, he followed Changyou in pursuit of the Taipings from Jiangxi to Hunan, and then into Guangxi. As Changyou was rewarded with the governorship of Guangxi in 1860 and Liu the title of provincial treasurer, Changyou gave him the command of his entire army, and stationed him at Liuzhou. Continued military success brought him first the judgeship of Guangdong in May 1862 and the treasurership of Guangxi in October, the same time when Changyou was made viceroy of the Liang Guang provinces. In Guangxi, Liu Kunyi finally put an end to the Dachengguo (Kingdom of Ultimate Accomplishment) of the rebellious Heaven and Earth Society, whose leaders and their relatives he executed with telling brutality. In mid-1865 he was rewarded with the governorship of Jiangxi as **Shen Baozhen** retired to his native Fuzhou.

During his nine years in Jiangxi, Liu attempted to restore peace and order through conservative means. In contrast to Shen's energetic and hands-on approach to government, Liu believed in the virtue of less government. Rather, he relied on the self-interests of the gentry to achieve the goals of postrebellion rehabilitation. He was equally indulgent toward the "good' and the "bad" gentry. Even the punishment of his provincial officials was partly to appease the gentry, as were his efforts to seek greater civil service examination quotas for Jiangxi's candidates. In financial management, Liu always made sure that the demands of the central government and the imperial court were met first. To cover Jiangxi's needs, he reduced expenses by demobilizing large numbers of *yong* mercenaries, eliminated the less profitable *lijin* stations, and increased the land and poll taxes by collecting them in silver rather than in copper cash. The last measure did provoke instances of tax resistance, but the disorder was quickly suppressed. By his overall ability to maintain peace and to meet the revenue demands of the throne, Liu's administration was viewed favorably in Beijing.

He was promoted to acting governor general of Liang Jiang in early 1875. Yet his long tenure in Jiangxi was distinctly lacking in reformist drive. Nor was there any attempt to modernize the weapons or training of the troops he kept after demobilization. In 1875, following the Japanese invasion of Taiwan, when a number of high-ranking officials were asked to submit proposals for improving the empire's defense, all Liu could offer was some half-hearted support for the building of steam-powered warships and Western-style guns. Secretly, he confided to a colleague that "self-strengthening" did not depend on ships and guns. Further, he was deadly opposed to the telegraph and the railway, which he thought would turn China's civilization into barbarism.

In the next several years, Liu was governor general first of Liang Guang (1875–1880) and then of Liang Jiang (1880–1882). His administration of Liang Guang was effective. He brought stability to provincial government by cutting the number of acting appointments and frequent changes of office. He increased revenue by way of setting a uniform rate for the opium *lijin*. He combated salt smuggling by using steam patrol boats and by allocating surplus salt to commercial dealers. He curbed gambling and, by deployment of military force, maintained peace and order.

In his last year in Liang Guang, the Japanese annexed the Liuqiu Islands while the dispute with the Russians over the Yili region also came to a head. In weighing the relative importance of the issues, Liu took the safe, traditional position—the northwest must be defended, whereas Liuqiu could be sacrificed. In this, he failed to rise above the age-old dispute between frontier and maritime defense. And when the settlement with Russia turned out to be far too conciliatory, leading to a death sentence for Chonghou, who negotiated the treaty, Liu, fearful of British and French opposition, opposed the execution. This "about face" drew the ire of the war party, among whose vociferous proponents were members of the Qingliu group. In an attempt to ingratiate himself with some of the Qingliu scholars, however, Liu further gave them cause for criticism. He was soon relieved of his duties.

Since the early 1860s, the Liang Jiang provinces had been largely put in the hands of Hunanese to counterbalance the power of **Li Hongzhang** in the north. In late 1889, with the death of Zeng Guoquan, the Liang Jiang viceroyalty became vacant. As Liu was now a leading Hunanese, he was recalled from retirement and put back in his old office at Nanjing.

In the spring of 1891, a series of antimissionary riots broke out along the Grand Canal and the Yangzi River. Concerned with maintaining good relations with the Western powers, Liu cooperated with **Zhang Zhidong** in protecting the Christians and putting down the rioters. Liu's decisiveness in crushing the riots stood in stark contrast to his wavering during the Sino-Japanese War of 1894–1895. When the throne appointed him imperial commissioner and put him in charge of the forces on either side of Shanhaiguan in late 1894, he repeatedly delayed his departure on flimsy excuses. Yet, when the terms of the Treaty of Shimonoseki became known, he joined Zhang Zhidong in denouncing Li Hongzhang of selling out China. He advocated continuing the war effort, and sent support to the resistance movement on Taiwan. But, within a month, when the situation changed, he condemned the resistance movement and demanded their return to the mainland.

Three events at the end of his long career showed him in a much more favorable light and regained for him a place among the notable officials of the Qing. First, following the suppression of the Hundred Day reform, when the **Empress Dowager Cixi** plotted to dethrone the **Guangxu Emperor**, Liu was almost alone in opposing Cixi. As a result, his stature rose significantly. Second, during the Boxer Uprising, Liu and Zhang Zhidong repeatedly warned the Empress Dowager of the suicidal policy she was pursuing. And when she declared war on the foreign powers on June 21, 1900, Liu, Zhang, and Li Hongzhang disobeyed imperial orders and declared their provinces neutral. They thus helped restrict the Boxers to the north, and saved China from even greater disasters at the hands of the imperialist powers. Finally, in the wake of the Boxer catastrophe, Liu and Zhang jointly submitted three memorials on reform. Despite their rather conservative hue, they became the basis for the Empress Dowager to launch a series of reform in the next several years. The reforms, which were remarkably similar to those the Empress Dowager had opposed in 1898, provided opportunities for the emergent social groups to express their grievance and demonstrate their newfound power. They thus ironically helped hasten the demise of the Qing dynasty. Liu died in office the following year, aged seventy.

REFERENCES: Li Guoqi, "Tongzhi zhongxing shiqi Liu Kunyi zai Jiangxi xunfu rennei di biaoxian" [Liu Kunyi's Performance as Governor of Jiangxi during the Tongzhi Restoration Period], *Lishi xuebao*, vol. 1 (January 1973), 241–269.

DAVID PONG

**LIU SHAOQI** (November 24, 1898–November 12, 1969). The Chinese Communist Party's most important administrator; chairman of the People's Republic of China from 1959 to 1967, when he became the highest-ranking victim of the Cultural Revolution.

From the mid-1940s until August 1966, Liu Shaoqi ranked directly after **Mao Zedong** in the Party. He gained a reputation for being the stable top commissar of the Party's daily business during its whole period of revolutionary consolidation. Colleagues described Liu as a lonely and taciturn man, highly disciplined, always sacrificing himself to work for Communist ideals. His organizational ethos stressed "self-cultivation" to produce reliable cadres, and this emphasis on education melded Chinese with Leninist traditions. The Cultural Revolution cast him as the chief symbol (followed by **Deng Xiaoping**) of Party bureaucratism. Zealots of this movement purged him as "China's Khrushchev" and over a period of three years hounded him to his death.

Liu was born the son of a landowner who was also a primary school teacher, on November 24, 1898 at Yinshan, Ningxiang County, Hunan. This place is near the provincial capital, Changsha and also near the hometown of Mao Zedong (who was five years older). After receiving an elementary education, almost surely from his father, Liu entered the local school in 1913. He was already active in politics by 1915, when he joined a movement against **Yuan Shikai**'s partial acceptance of Japan's "Twenty-one Demands." By mid-1916, Liu went to the Teacher's College in Changsha, where Mao was also a student. Liu soon joined a "military study society," which Hunan's warlord of that time forced to dissolve. So Liu returned home for further reading on his own. After several other attempts to join Hunan political clubs that were repressed, Liu in 1920 traveled to Shanghai, where in 1921 he became a member of the China Socialist Youth League, a forerunner of the Chinese Communist Party (CCP). He was selected by his Russian teacher, a Comintern agent, as one of the first Chinese to study at the University of the Toilers of the East in Moscow. By the winter of 1921, while in Russia, he became a member of the new CCP.

Liu's time in formal university classes was brief, but he was a studious person, reading and writing often. In early 1922, he returned to organize Shanghai workers under **Zhang Guotao**, and then to assist Mao Zedong in their native Hunan and in adjacent Jiangxi among miners at Pingxiang Coal

Mine, where Liu helped to plan a strike that brought better conditions for those workers. In 1925–1926, he organized labor unions in Shanghai, Guangzhou, and Hong Kong, and he worked as a cadre of the Northern Expedition in Wuhan. In 1927, **Jiang Jieshi**'s (Chiang Kai-shek's) attack on the First United Front sent Liu into hiding and then to Moscow for the CCP's Sixth Congress. He soon returned to Shanghai, where he led the workers' movement that Jiang had decimated; and by late 1932 went to Ruijin, seat of the Jiangxi Soviet guerrilla base. There Liu opposed the political claims of other students who had returned from Russia, and this stance made him a political ally of Mao. When the Nationalist government's "encirclement campaigns" finally destroyed the Jiangxi Soviet, Liu joined the Long March northward and was again Mao's political ally at the Zunyi Conference in 1935.

Established at the North China guerrilla headquarters at Yan'an, Liu sometimes lived in a cave next to Mao's. He gave lectures on "How to Be a Good Communist," which appeared as a pamphlet in 1939 and became the standard manual for teaching Party discipline. When the cult of Mao grew in Yan'an, Liu reportedly stressed that a Communist's obedience was to the Party, not to any individual—even though Mao's wise policies entitled him to allegiance. In 1942, when Mao's title as Party chairman was much publicized, Liu remarked, "What is a chairman? I have never heard people in the Soviet Union calling Lenin Chairman Lenin." He told a 1947 meeting, "There is no perfect leader in the world." He trusted the cultivation of large numbers of ethical loyalists more than short-term leadership tactics as the key to Communist success. Mao and Liu nonetheless often praised each other in public, perhaps because Mao's organizing expertise was mostly rural and Liu's was mostly urban. Their abilities were mutually complementary.

Yet Liu agreed with Mao on most specific policies and largely administered several 1940s purges (rectification campaigns), even while his personal manner remained more self-effacing and detached than Mao's. He was Mao's first deputy in the party from 1945 to 1966. (See Dittmer and MacFarquhar in the references below for more on the enigmatic Liu-Mao relationship.) Liu believed that procedures and education could create an effective Party. Liu's organizational policies stressed the need to separate leftist dissident leaders from their constituencies, sending them away for correction but then restoring them to lower positions.

As the People's Liberation Army swept into Chinese cities during the late 1940s, Liu led meetings to teach techniques of building support for the Party among urban workers and entrepreneurs. Although Liu seldom advertised his personal opinions after collective decisions had been taken in Party councils, he was less radical than other top leaders about fast collectivization. In October 1955, he criticized himself for this reticence. Liu gave the longest speech at the Party Congress of 1956, a watershed time as the Party assumed more administrative work after the transition to socialism. His government counterpart, Premier **Zhou Enlai,** spoke then about the need for more efficiency—a theme Liu downplayed, perhaps because he was more hopeful that planning could effectively replace markets. Liu thought of bureaucratism as a common fault in the government, but not in the Party because of its members' training. Thus ordinary people might legitimately criticize the state, whereas the Party did not need to subject itself to this check.

Liu reportedly originated the idea that urbanites should, at least in some periods, be "sent down" (*xiafang*) to do rural work. This policy was applied in the mid-1950s to large numbers of urban technicians, and later to many school graduates. Liu applied the same policy to himself and his family, who sometimes left cities for brief stints of agricultural labor.

The Great Leap Forward was formally launched at a Party congress in early May 1958, with full support from both Liu and Mao. As the Leap faltered and Mao moved into quasi-retirement, Liu headed the "first line of leadership." In April 1959, he presided at a National People's Congress that elected him chairman of the Republic (and of the National Defense Committee, which met in the next month). Although Mao and other civilian leaders supported Liu's succession as head of state, Defense Minister Peng Dehuai apparently felt Marshal **Zhu De** deserved the job instead. After Peng was dismissed in 1959, Liu (along with **Lin Biao** and others) made speeches implicitly defending Mao's prestige. The Party Propaganda Department mandated that newspapers print Liu's and Mao's pictures, equal in size and side by side, on national day.

Toward the end of 1959, a painful inflammation of Liu's shoulder and elbow forced a month's sick leave in warm Hainan, where he called a conference to study China's troubled economy. Liu worked collegially with Zhou and Mao for many years. He also cooperated with Deng Xiaoping and especially with Peng Zhen, who may have been his only close personal friend among the leaders. Liu's virtues of reliability, loyalty, and hard work served the Party as a whole in the early 1960s, when his career peaked. In 1962, "How to Be a Good Communist" was serialized in the *People's Daily* and was republished as a book. Liu's life remained famous for asceticism, and he was known to scold his children when theirs was not stoic enough.

When radicals associated with Mao and Lin stepped up their critique of Liu's administered revolution during the mid-1960s, Liu apparently accepted their long-term goals and was slow to perceive their interest in political confrontation. By early June 1966, Liu and Deng sent work groups to lead the Cultural Revolution in Beijing universities and middle schools. In early August, Liu was criticized at a plenum that reorganized the Party's leading organs and demoted him from second to eighth place on public rosters. Attacks against him, often from supporters of Lin Biao, continued at a work conference in October as Red Guard posters excoriated his policies and followers. By the end of 1966, Liu's position became nearly irrelevant, as the Party he treasured was destroyed at all levels by social forces broader than his immediate followers or rivals.

On July 18, 1967, while Mao was outside Beijing, **Jiang Qing**, Kang Sheng, and **Chen Boda** organized a struggle meeting against **Liu Shaoqi** and his wife Wang Guangmei. Liu's health and spirit were severely weakened by harangues throughout 1968. The Twelfth Plenum, in October, received a "Criminal Investigation Report on the Renegade, Traitor, and Strike-breaker Liu Shaoqi." It passed a resolution that "forever expelled" Liu from the Party to which he had devoted his life. Although he was severely ill, Liu was transferred to a jail in Kaifeng on October 17, 1969. He had pneumonia, as well as diabetes and open skin sores, was denied medical care, and died on November 12. Two of Liu's sons were also hounded to death during the Cultural Revolution.

Liu's posthumous long-rumored rehabilitation was official only on February 29, 1980, when the Central Committee reinstated his name. On May 17, a memorial service was held in Beijing's Great Hall of the People. Numerous exhibits then honored Liu, and his *Selected Works* were published. Some Chinese liberals also hold him in esteem, despite his administration of manipulative campaigns, simply because he was victimized by Mao. Footage of his family spreading his ashes on the sea is seen in the last episode of the famous 1988 documentary, *River Elegy*. In 1997, his widow attended the ceremony to start production of a China Central Television documentary about Liu. The 100th anniversary of his birth was celebrated, in November 1998, by the minting of commemorative medals and a speech from President **Jiang Zemin**. Liu's life manifested a deep tension between egalitarian ideals and Party discipline.

REFERENCES: Lowell Dittmer, *Liu Shaoqi and the Chinese Cultural Revolution* (rev. ed., Armonk, NY, 1998); Xu Guansan and He Linren, eds., *Liu Shaoqi yu Liu Shaoqi luxian* [Liu Shaoqi and His Line] (Hong Kong, 1980); Roderick MacFarquhar, *The Origins of the Cultural Revolution*, 3 vols. (New York, 1974, 1983, 1997); New China News Service Correspondents' Society and CCP Central Archive, eds., *Gongheguo zhuxi Liu Shaoqi* [Liu Shaoqi, Chairman of the Republic] (Beijing, 1988); Liu Shaoqi, *Collected Works*, 3 vols. (Hong Kong, 1968–1969).

LYNN T. WHITE III


**LU XUN** (Zhou Shuren, September 25, 1881–October 19, 1936). Leader of the May Fourth Cultural Revolution and Chinese Left-wing writers; writer, scholar, and translator.

Lu Xun was Zhou Shuren's pen name. He was born in Shaoxing, Zhejiang province into a declining scholar-official family. His grandfather had been a high ranking official jailed for his part in a bribery case and his father had failed to pass any of the imperial examinations.

Due to his economic circumstances, Lu Xun enrolled in tuition-free vocational schools in Nanjing in 1898: first, the South China Naval Academy and a few months later, the School of Mining and Civil Engineering. In 1902, he went to Japan and studied in Kobun College. Two years later, he entered Sendai Provincial Medical School, but after watching a news slide in which apathetic Chinese watched the execution of their fellow countrymen in the Russo-Japanese war, he decided to give up his medical career and devote himself to literature. Lu Xun began a program of self-directed study. He learned German and studied Chinese philology under Zhang Tai-yan for a few months in 1908. It is probable that he joined the Restoration Society in Japan.

In the essays "On the Extremities of Cultures" and "On the Power of Mara Poetry" (1908), Lu Xun criticized the common belief that parliamentary democracy was the solution for China's problems. He argued that "national character" was the root of all the problems and could only be addressed through literature. Influenced by romanticism and Nietzschean individualism, he believed that China could only be rescued by a revolution and a literary movement, with Nietzschean revolutionary poets ("fighters in the spiritual world") as their agents. He wanted a revolution to overthrow the Manchu regime to liberate the Han people from slavery. He also wanted a literary movement, including cultural criticism and creative writing (especially poetry), to provoke a revolution and at the same time to remould the Chinese "national character." Resorting to literature and cultural criticism to solve social and political problems, Lu Xun's literary movement was essentially antipolitical.

In order to promote this literary movement, he planned to publish a magazine *New Birth (Xinsheng)* in 1907 but failed to obtain any financial support. Some of his preparatory works, his translations of short stories of the "oppressed peoples," were published in the collection *Stories from Other Lands* but only 20 copies were sold. He virtually stopped publishing after returning to China in 1909. He taught sciences in Shaoxing and Hangzhou but he also became a member of the Yue Society (*Yue she*), a branch of the Nan Society (*Nan she*). The Nan Society was purportedly an organization of revolutionary poets and many of their members died in the 1911 revolution. Lu Xun was nevertheless dissatisfied with it. In the 1930s, he commented that the Nan Society had failed to continue its literary activities after the 1911 revolution. It would seem that he had expected the poets in the Nan Society to become "fighters in the spiritual world" and to bring about an effective literary movement. After the 1911 Revolution, he was invited by Cai Yuanpei to join the education ministry in Nanjing. He later followed the ministry to Beijing in 1912.

When the May Fourth cultural revolution began, Lu Xun was skeptical about its consequences. He was nevertheless persuaded by Qian Xuantong to contribute to *New Youth*. Between 1918 and 1925, he produced two volumes of short stories and many essays, or *zawen*. Among them, "Diary of a Madman" and "The True Story of Ah Q" were the most successful in promoting iconoclasm and spiritual reform. The success of the cultural revolution rekindled his desire to form a literary movement aimed at remolding Chinese "national character." (He did not want to promote radical social and political changes at this stage.) He tried to influence one of the May Fourth student leaders Fu Sinian, but failed.

Between 1920 and 1926 and while serving in the education ministry, Lu Xun taught in National Beijing University and National Beijing Women's Teachers College. He was involved in the campus unrest in the Women's Teachers College supporting a dozen rebel students against a conservative principal backed by Chen Xiying, Xu Zhimo, and Zhang Shizhao, the Minister of Education of the Duan Qirui government. Xu Guangping was one of the rebel student representatives. She later became Lu Xun's lover.

In 1925, he published his own magazine *The Wilderness (Mangyuan)* and gathered a small group of young rebels around him. Under the influence of Nietzschean evolutionism, Lu Xun dedicated himself to helping talented young rebels in his literary movement. Among his disciples, Gao Changhong was the leader of a small group called the Storm Society (*Kuangbiao she*). Gao later turned against Lu Xun because of some trifle quarrels with other Lu Xun disciples of the Not-Yet-Named Society (*Wei ming she*). The fatal blow to his literary movement, however, was the "3.18" Incident in 1926, in which several of his promising students were killed in a demonstration. He realized that a literary movement alone was not enough for China's reform and that the Chinese needed a social revolution.

In 1926, Lu Xun left Beijing with Xu Guangping, who had become a member of the Guomindang (GMD). Xu went to Guangzhou and Lu Xun took up an appointment at Xiamen University. Due to ideological and personal conflicts, Lu Xun only stayed a few months in Xiamen before leaving for Guangzhou. At that time, a few young radicals of the Creation Society planned to form a united front with Lu Xun in Guangzhou but the plan did not go forward because of objections by other leftists under the influence of the Japanese Marxist Fukumoto Kazuo. In Guangzhou, Lu Xun was unimpressed by the revolutionary government, although he found genuine revolutionary endeavor in a few Communists he met. He felt that the revolutionary atmosphere in Guangzhou was mostly artificial. In 1927, he was shocked by the massacre of young radicals in the "4.12" coup d'état. He witnessed young people killing each other no less brutally than old people. His belief in evolutionism was shattered. Moreover, the GMD was not bringing about a social revolution as Lu Xun had expected. Lu Xun left Guangzhou for Shanghai, where he spent the rest of his life.

Although Lu Xun was sympathetic to the leftists, he was, ironically, attacked during the revolutionary literature debate between 1928 and 1930 by the Creation Society and the Sun Society (founded in 1928). Both groups were influenced by **Li Lisan**'s "left opportunism" and **Wang Ming** and **Bo Gu**'s left "closed-doorism." The debate prompted him to study Marxism.

He read Trotsky's *Revolution and Literature* and transformed some of Trotsky's arguments in the course of the debate. Although Lu Xun appreciated Trotsky's open-mindedness in literary issues, he found his theory too "idealistic." Lu Xun became interested in Marxism, but he was against the CCP's "left opportunism." In May 1930, Li Lisan met Lu Xun and asked him to denounce the GMD regime publicly. Lu Xun refused.

The campaign against Lu Xun created such bad publicity that the CCP leadership decided to intervene, allegedly at the initiation of **Zhou Enlai**. The Creation Society and the Sun Society were ordered to stop their attacks and to seek cooperation with Lu Xun. They invited him to form the Chinese League of Left-Wing Writers in 1930. In January 1931, shortly after the founding of the league, five left-wing writers were executed by the GMD. The execution enraged Lu Xun and made him more determined in his support of the CCP. Obviously he did not know that the execution was related to factional conflicts within the CCP. The five writers were in a secret meeting against Wang Ming and Wang Ming did not attempt to rescue them after their arrest. Around the same time, Lu Xun also joined a few anti-GMD and pro-Communist organizations such as the League for Freedom in China (1930), the China League of Civil Rights (1932), and the International League for Anti-Imperialism and Anti-Aggressive War (1932).

In 1931, **Qu Qiubai** stayed in Shanghai after being excluded from the Politburo by Wang Ming and Pavel Mif. Qu turned his attention to the cultural and literary arena in Shanghai and made contact with Mao Dun and Feng Xuefeng, the Party secretary of the communists within the League. Lu Xun met Qu in 1932 and they became close friends. Lu Xun was impressed by Qu's knowledge of Marxist literary theory and Russian language. They had high regard for each other and cooperated in criticizing the GMD's "cultural encirclement campaigns" against the Communists, the "nationalist" literature, "the third category," and the left "closed-doorism" in the league. In 1933, Qu wrote a preface to a collection of Lu Xun's essays. The preface was the first appraisal of Lu Xun by a Communist leader and made Lu Xun an irrefutable spiritual leader of left-wing writers. Although the Communist revolution seems to be the social revolution that Lu Xun had wanted, the League of Left-Wing Writers was just a modification of his previous plan of a literary movement to rescue China. The "fighters of the spiritual world" and the young rebel critics and writers were now replaced by left-wing writers.

However, because of ideological differences within the CCP, Lu Xun's opinions were always unorthodox in the eyes of some Communists under the influence of Wang Ming's policies. Immediately after Qu Qiubai and Feng Xuefeng left for Ruijin in 1934, Lu Xun lost the support of the CCP within the league and was anonymously attacked by Tian Han, a Communist and member of the league, for political ambivalence.

In 1936, Feng Xuefeng, now a self-claimed Maoist, was sent back to

Shanghai after taking the Long March to Shaanxi. He was ordered to contact Lu Xun and then to spread the message of the CCP's new anti-Japanese United Front policy now led by **Mao Zedong**. The return of Feng was not welcome by the league headed by Zhou Yang since 1933. Zhou Yang had no contact with Yan'an and his policy was based on publications of the Comintern and Wang Ming. Feng's return ignited the CCP's internal political conflicts in the literary arena in Shanghai. The political differences resulted in a heated debate between the two camps and their slogans in 1935 and 1936: "the national defense literature" camp (Zhou Yang and his followers) and "the literature of the masses in a national revolutionary war" camp (Lu Xun, Feng Xuefeng, and their followers). In June 1936, a Chinese Trotskyist, Chen Zhongshan, interpreted the debate as Lu Xun's denunciation of the Chinese Stalinists and wrote a letter seeking his support. In an open reply letter, Lu Xun expressed his unequivocal support for the CCP, claiming that he was proud to be a comrade of the CCP and criticized Trotskyism as unrealistic. In August, Lu Xun published an open letter to Xu Maoyong about the slogan debate and criticized Zhou Yang's factionalism. Due to Lu Xun's fame and influence, the debate virtually stopped after the publication of this letter. To show his support for the United Front, Lu Xun signed two anti-Japanese declarations by Chinese writers. Without consulting Lu Xun, the League of Left-Wing Writers was secretly disbanded in 1936 in accordance of Wang Ming's instructions.

Although Lu Xun supported the CCP, he was never a member. He once told Feng Xuefeng that it was possible that he could be executed in the future Communist society. This was because he believed that literary creation is rebellious while politics maintains the status quo. The two are in nature diametrically opposed to each other. In this sense, he was only a "fellow traveller." Or from his perspective, the CCP was only a "fellow traveller" of his literary movement.

REFERENCES: Lu Xun Bowuguan and Lu Xun yanjiushi, eds., *Lu Xun nianpu* [Chronology of Lu Xun], 4 vols. (Beijing, 1981–1984); Chiu-yee Cheung, "Lu Hsün and Nietzsche: Influence and Affinity after 1927," *The Journal of the Oriental Society of Australia*, 18/19 (1986–1987), 3–25; Chiu-yee Cheung, "Lu Xun yu Nicai fan 'xiandaixing' de qihe" [The Anti-Modernity Affinities between Lu Xun and Nietzsche], *Ershi-yi shiji* (June 1995), 91–96; *Lu Xun quanji* [Collected Works of Lu Xun] (Beijing, 1981).

CHIU-YEE CHEUNG

**LUO FU** (Zhang Wentian, August 30, 1900–July 1, 1976). Russian-trained Chinese Communist Party leader; one of the Twenty-Eight Bolsheviks; general secretary in 1934; vice-minister in foreign affairs, 1954–1959; writer and translator.

Luo Fu was Zhang Wentian's pen name. It was taken from the Chinese transliteration of two syllables of his adopted Russian name. Zhang Wentian was born in Nanhui (now Chuansha, Shanghai), Jiangsu province into a rich peasant family.

In 1919, under the influence of Zuo Shunsheng, Zhang Wentian joined the Young China Association. In 1920, Zhang Wentian went with Shen Zemin to Japan to study for a year. When he returned to China, Zuo Shunsheng found him work in the Zhonghua Bookshop, where he met the Marxist theorist Li Da. In 1922, he sailed for the United States and worked for a local Chinese newspaper, *Datong Daily*, in San Francisco while continuing his self-directed study using the library of the University of California at Berkeley. He returned to China in early 1924 and taught in Sichuan. He also edited the weekly *Nanhong*, which was banned after publishing six issues.

Before he joined the Chinese Communist Party (CCP), Zhang Wentian was a prolific writer. His publications include plays, poems, essays, translations of, and commentaries on modern Western authors. His most acclaimed works were the novel *Journey* (*Lütu*, 1924) and a three-act play *Dream of Youth* (*Qingchun de meng*, 1924).

Zhang Wentian's literary career ended after he joined the CCP in May 1925. In October, he was among approximately 100 young Chinese Communists, including **Wang Ming** and **Jiang Jingguo** (Chiang Ching-kuo), sent by the CCP to study in the **Sun Yat-sen** University in the Soviet Union. In 1928, he took up further studies at Red Professors' College in Moscow.

In January 1931, Zhang Wentian left his Russian wife and one-year-old son and returned to Shanghai with **Yang Shangkun**. They failed to contact the Party until February and missed the Fourth Plenum of the Sixth Central Committee, which was held on January 7, and chaired by the Comintern representative Pavel Mif. **Qu Qiubai** and **Li Lisan** were removed from the Politburo. Wang Ming entered the Politburo and took control of the Party. Russian-trained Communists were quickly appointed to key positions in the Party. Zhang Wentian became head of the organization department of the Central Committee and later took over the positions of minister of propaganda and the editor-in-chief of *Red Flag* and *Struggle*. After Wang Ming left for Russia in October, he was nominated by the Comintern to join the CCP Central Committee Provisional Politburo in Shanghai headed by **Bo Gu**.

Although Zhang was known as one of the Twenty-Eight Bolsheviks, he did not always agree with Wang Ming and the Comintern policies. His article "On Closed-Doorism on the Literature and Art Front" (1932, under the pen name "Gete") is a criticism of policies of Bo Gu and Wang Ming. On October 27, 1932, Zhang Wentian also openly criticized the Provisional Politburo in a meeting.

The Provisional Politburo in Shanghai was forced to move to Ruijin in 1933. In the following year, Zhang was elected central secretary in the Fifth Plenum of the Sixth Central Committee. However, he was reluctant to support Bo Gu's campaign against "Luo Ming's opportunism" and opposed the removal of **Deng Xiaoping** and other experienced cadres from their posts. He was then excluded from the Party decision-making body and became the chairman of the People's Committee of the Chinese Soviet Republic. In Ruijin, Zhang met **Mao Zedong** and was impressed by Mao.

The Chinese Red Army, under the leadership of Bo Gu and Li De (Otto Braun), was defeated by the Guomindang (GMD) and the CCP had to abandon the Central Soviet Region in 1934. The military catastrophe intensified the political conflicts between the Military Council led by the "military troike" (Bo Gu, Li De, and **Zhou Enlai**) and the so-called "Central Triad" (Mao Zedong, Zhang Wentian, and Wang Jiaxiang). Between January 7–8, 1935, an enlarged session of the Politburo of the Central Committee was convened in Zunyi to remove Bo Gu and Li De from leadership. Zhang Wentian replaced Bo Gu as the head of the Party and Mao Zedong secured his leading position in the Red Army. In 1935, Zhang Wentian supported Mao's anti-Japanese national United Front at the "Wayaobao Conference," and further supported Mao at the "Luochuan Conference" in his stand against Wang Ming's "capitulationism" in 1937. In 1936, he was appointed president of the Marx-Lenin Academy.

Although Zhang Wentian supported Mao, he gradually lost influence in the Party after the Yan'an Rectification Movement between 1942 and 1944 because of his past association with Bo Gu and the Comintern. From then on, and especially after 1949, he was appointed to less senior Party and government positions. Between 1945 and 1949, he worked under **Chen Yun** and **Gao Gang** in the northeastern region. In 1950, he was the chief delegate from the People's Republic of China (PRC) to the UN, and in the following year succeeded Wang Jiaxiang as the Chinese ambassador to the USSR. In 1955, he was appointed vice-minister of Foreign Affairs.

Zhang Wentian was reelected to the Central Committee and the Politburo in 1959. In the same year, he was stripped of all Party and government positions after criticizing Mao Zedong's "Great Leap Forward" policies in the CCP's Lushan Conference. He was accused of supporting Peng Dehuai's anti-Party "military club." In 1960, he worked as a special researcher in the Institute of Economic Research. He was further persecuted during the Cultural Revolution and died of a heart attack in 1979. Zhang Wentian was posthumously rehabilitated in 1979.

REFERENCES: Jin Shengxian, *Zhang Wentian de zuji* [The Footsteps of Zhang Wentian] (Shanghai, 1995); *Zhang Wentian wenji* [Collected Works of Zhang Wentian], vols. 1–2 (Beijing, 1990–1992).

CHIU-YEE CHEUNG

# M

MAO TSE-TUNG. *See* MAO ZEDONG.

MAO ZEDONG (Mao Tse-tung, December 26, 1893–September 9, 1976). One of the founders of the Chinese Communist Party (CCP); leader of the CCP for more than 40 years, from 1935 to his death in 1976.

Mao Zedong was one of the most important leaders in Chinese history. He achieved many remarkable successes in the face of formidable obstacles, but his ideology, willful behavior, and grave mistakes brought horrific calamities upon China.

Mao was born December 26, 1893 in Shaoshan, Hunan province, to parents who became rich peasants by the time he was in his teens. He received a traditional primary education, but left home in order to continue into middle school. By 1911 he moved to Changsha and after a half year in the army and some independent study, enrolled at age nineteen in what would soon become the Hunan First Normal School. An irrepressible student activist, Mao was immersed in the excitement of this early May Fourth period. He taught in a night school for illiterate workers and, with a friend, helped establish the *Xinmin xuehui* (New People's Study Society), which later became one of the nuclei of the Chinese Communist Party (CCP). Following his graduation in 1918, Mao took a position in Peking University's library, where he became involved with other activist students and was influenced by **Li Dazhao**, the university librarian and radical historian. During this period, although Mao was an ardent Nationalist, he was still open to various ideas and schools of thought from abroad. He went to Shanghai in early 1919, and then returned to Changsha soon after the May Fourth Incident. He helped organize a Hunan student organization, but his two publication ventures, successively the *Xiangjiang pinglun* (*Hsiang River Review*) and the student newspaper, *Xin Hunan* (*New Hunan*), were closed down by the authorities. Mao was forced to flee Hunan after participating in a student strike aimed at the provincial governor. He went to Beijing and then to Shanghai, where he met with the leading intellectual **Chen Duxiu**, who was to become the first chairman of the CCP. Mao returned to Hunan later in the summer of 1920 and became head of the primary school attached to the Hunan First Normal School. He married Yang Kaihui, the daughter of progressive Professor Yang Changqi with whom Mao had a close relationship. Mao opened a radical bookstore and soon after the arrival of Comintern agent Gregory Voitinsky in China he established both a Communist cell and a Socialist Youth League branch in Changsha.

Mao was one of the founders of the CCP in July 1921 in Shanghai and returned to Changsha as secretary of the newly formed CCP Hunan Committee. Among other activities, Mao helped establish the Self-Education College in Changsha, which was to train many people who would become Communists, and he helped organize workers at the Anyuan mines in Jiangxi province. Mao was elected to the Party Central Committee for the first time at the Third Party Congress in Guangzhou in June 1923 and was given direction of the Party's organization department. In accord with the CCP-GMD (Guomindang) policy of cooperation, Mao attended the GMD's First Congress in January 1924 in Guangzhou. He was given various posts in the GMD organization, including secretary of its organization department and alternate member of its Central Executive Committee, eliciting criticism from some of his own Party comrades that he was too cooperative with the GMD.

In late 1924 Mao recuperated from an illness in Hunan, after which he spent some months investigating the situation in the countryside, an interlude that ended in late 1925 when he had to flee to Guangzhou. Mao continued for sometime to retain influential positions within the GMD, including service on the credentials committee for the Second GMD Congress and de facto leadership of the GMD propaganda department. After losing the latter position following the Zhongshan Incident in March 1926, Mao became director of the sixth class of the Peasant Movement Training Institute in Guangzhou. In December 1926, in defiance of Party Chairman Chen Duxiu's directive, Mao told a conference of peasant delegates in Changsha of the importance of the peasant issue, exhorting them to intensified revolutionary action.

Following further rural investigation near Changsha, Mao wrote one of his best-known reports in March 1927, in which he called the peasant movement "a colossal event." Mao was convinced that the Party needed to harness this rural social force. But most of his comrades disagreed, hence Mao departed from the Party's Fifth Congress before it concluded. That meeting was held after **Jiang Jieshi**'s coup against the CCP in Shanghai in early April

1927, but within three months what remained of the CCP-GMD alliance, in Wuhan, came to an end too. This experience and the military engagements in the months and years afterward confirmed Mao's conviction that "political power grows out of the barrel of a gun." He himself was partly responsible for the ill-fated Autumn Harvest Uprising in September–October 1927 after which he led some of the survivors to the mountainous terrain between Hunan and Jiangxi provinces. In the spring of 1928 he was joined at Jinggangshan by reinforcements led by **Zhu De**. The merged Zhu-Mao forces eventually established a base centered on Ruijin in southeast Jiangxi. Mao assiduously politicized his troops and improved their relations with the civilian population. His counsel in this regard was best articulated at the Gutian Conference in December 1929.

Mao avoided cooperating fully in the costly ill-conceived initiatives of **Li Lisan** who sought to occupy major cities in 1930. Instead, he continued to preside over Communist forces in the countryside where the power of the movement had clearly shifted. Following the establishment of the Chinese Soviet Republic in late 1931, Mao occupied two of the top positions in government and had an influential role in the military. However, he did not have influence in the Party apparatus which was dominated by the returned students faction (or Twenty-Eight Bolsheviks). Consequently, his over-all position steadily eroded. Mao was replaced by **Zhou Enlai** as chief army political commissar. Mao disagreed with many policies that were implemented during this period and seems to have lost almost all authority by the time of the collapse of the Soviet Republic under the onslaughts of Jiang Jieshi's final encirclement campaigns.

However, during the flight of the Communists from Jiangxi, at a conference in Zunyi, Guizhou, Mao gained effective leadership of what would come to be known as the Long March. Through brilliant maneuvers he turned what had been a debacle into an orderly campaign that traveled over 6,000 miles, much of it over exceedingly tortuous terrain. Although the personnel losses were tremendous by the time the remnants of the retreat reached Shaanxi a year after the breakout in Jiangxi, the feat was a notable symbolic achievement.

Mao profitably used the years in Yan'an, where his new headquarters were established in 1936. A new United Front with the GMD was agreed to in 1937, facilitated by the Xi'an Incident of December 1936 and necessitated by Japan's massive invasion of North China in July 1937. But this cooperation for the most part ended by late 1938 when Japanese offensive operations ceased and the Nationalist army reimposed a blockade on the Communists. However, despite opposition from both Nationalists and Japanese, the Communists managed to expand control over desperate territorial bases and their populations. Mao also used these years to consolidate his political position. The *zhengfeng* or rectification campaign of 1942–1944 served this purpose, indoctrinating the Party with his ideas. In this way Mao triumphed over the political challenge of the returned students faction and cajoled the CCP into accepting his objective to adjust Marxism-Leninism to meet the circumstances and needs of the people in China. Mao's victory within the Party was confirmed at the Seventh Party Congress held between April and June of 1945. In 1939 Mao married a former Shanghai actress, Lan Ping, whom he renamed **Jiang Qing**. In order to do so, he had to set aside his second wife, Ho Zuzhen, whom he married in 1931, sometime after Yang Kaihui's death. This headstrong act elicited a long-lasting, if subdued, resentment among many of Mao's comrades.

By the end of the War of Resistance against Japan in August 1945, the Communist forces had expanded tremendously since their arrival in Yan'an some eight years earlier and they enjoyed good morale and discipline. But Mao's military forces were still overwhelmingly outnumbered so that he was amenable to suggestions of a political settlement with the Nationalist government. Hence, Mao was at this point more willing than was Jiang Jieshi to talk and later to cooperate with the Marshall Mission in 1946 that sought to prevent renewed civil war in China. However, mediation proved unavailing and war broke out in earnest in 1946. As it turned out, the war followed the three stages that Mao himself predicted, and the third stage—that of positional warfare with large armies—came to a conclusion even more quickly than he, or anyone, anticipated.

Mao proclaimed the establishment of the People's Republic of China in Beijing on October 1, 1949. He visited the Soviet Union from late December 1949 until March 1950, the visit culminating, after hard bargaining, in a Sino-Soviet Treaty on February 14, 1950. The new government restored the economy with some success by 1952. The initial policies of the new regime were intended to be moderate, at least apparently so under the banner of New Democracy. But any pretense of moderation was eventually abandoned partly as a result of China's entry in late 1950 into the Korean War during which Mao lost a son.

In September 1956, the Eighth Party Congress celebrated the Party's apparent success in many undertakings, including the amazingly rapid collectivization of agriculture and socialization of industry and commerce throughout the country. But rifts began to appear among the leaders. Mao insisted on programs such as the Hundred Flowers thaw of 1956–1957 and the 1957 Rectification Campaign, which elicited outside criticism of the Party, against the wishes of the majority of Party leaders. His initiatives culminated in the notorious 1957 Anti-Rightist Campaign that would cause great suffering for many intellectuals for decades and detract from Mao's credibility among both Party members and intellectuals. Then in 1958 Mao instigated the Great Leap Forward and the radical communization of agriculture that resulted in incredible losses of life (as many as 30 million people) and untold suffering. As the situation worsened, in the fall of 1958

Mao decided not to continue as state chairman. In July 1959 at a Party plenum in Lushan, he survived a serious challenge inspired by the forthright criticism of his policies by Peng Dehuai. Mao's radical policies contributed to the further deterioration of relations with the Soviet Union which finally terminated its aid programs in 1960.

Mao's policies were now systematically reversed and China gradually recovered somewhat from the disastrous post–Great Leap depression. Mao became increasingly frustrated as a result of his diminishing power, critical of the recovery policies, and resentful because he was being ignored and even ridiculed by Party intellectuals. In 1962 he again began to emphasize the need for class struggle. He insisted upon a Socialist Education Program that in the end yielded considerable opposition and little results. Neutralized by his opponents, Mao countered by reforming the PLA to his taste. This maneuver was facilitated by Peng Dehuai's replacement as defense minister in 1959 by Mao's trusted lieutenant, **Lin Biao.**

Unable to prevail in the "watertight kingdom" of Beijing, Mao went to Shanghai where in November 1965 he initiated the opening gambit of what would become the Great Proletarian Cultural Revolution by authorizing the publication of a critical review of a play that had been used earlier to criticize him. By the following summer, at the Eleventh Plenum of the Eighth Central Committee, this ill-fated campaign was formally underway, the purpose of which was to criticize those in authority alleged to be revisionists and capitalist-roaders. Following Mao's own "Bombard the Headquarters" wall poster, Chinese youth, organized now as Red Guards, traveled about the country at will, generally creating havoc. By the end of 1996, they participated in huge rallies in Beijing at which Mao appeared. By the end of 1966, their attention was shifted to the provinces and chaos was spread throughout the country. Beginning in early 1967 government bodies everywhere were gradually displaced in "power seizures" by revolutionary committees, comprised of cadres ostensibly loyal to Mao, representatives of new revolutionary mass organizations and military representatives. The military had to be called in to support Mao's leftists in these struggles, but in the confusion did so only selectively as it simultaneously tried to restore and maintain order. Mao's principal antagonist, Liu Shaoqi, was persecuted to death. The Cultural Revolution was exhausted by the time of the Ninth Party Congress in April 1969, although later it officially would be held to have lasted for the entire decade that encompassed Mao's death.

In the early 1970s, Mao radically shifted China's foreign policy, ending the country's isolation and improving relations first with the United States, and subsequently with most other countries around the world. Ironically dubbed "Mao's Revolutionary Line in Diplomacy," the change was brought about largely as a consequence of China's perceived threat from the Soviet Union. Its success was partly marred for Mao by the Lin Biao incident of

September 1971, when Lin, previously Mao's chosen and constitutionally designated successor, allegedly attempted to assassinate Mao. This still mysterious development further damaged Mao's credibility.

While the rehabilitated government sought to regularize governance once again by the early 1970s, Mao continued to insist upon radical mobilization campaigns to assure the continuity of his revolutionary ideals, although fewer and fewer Chinese any longer understood what it was that he sought to achieve.

Mao died on September 9, 1976. A mausoleum was subsequently erected on Tiananmen Square where his deteriorating remains are periodically on public display. Revelations subsequent to Mao's death about his scandalous personal behavior over the years, jarringly contradictory to his moralistic pronouncements for public consumption, and further reservations about his failed ideology and its consequences have greatly detracted from his reputation.

REFERENCES: Donald W. Klein and Anne B. Clark, *Biographic Dictionary of Chinese Communism*, vol. 2 (Cambridge, MA, 1971), 676–688; Li Zhisui, *The Private Life of Chairman Mao: The Memoirs of Mao's Personal Physician* (New York, 1994); Ross Terrill, *Mao* (New York, 1980 and 1993, and rev., Stanford, CA, 1999); Stephen Uhalley, Jr., *Mao Tse-tung: A Critical Biography* (New York, 1975).

STEPHEN UHALLEY, JR.

# P

PUYI (Aisin Gioro Puyi, Henry Puyi, 1906–October 17, 1967). Last Qing emperor (1908–1912); figurehead of Manchukuo (1932–1945).

Nephew of **Emperor Guangxu**, Puyi was selected successor to the ailing emperor by the **Empress Dowager Cixi**. Barely three years old when he was crowned as Emperor Xuantong in 1908, his father, Prince Chun, acted as the regent. The 1911 Revolution soon ended the Qing dynasty. Puyi abdicated on February 12, 1912, at the age of six. According to the agreement arranged by **Yuan Shikai**, the deposed emperor was allowed to live temporarily in the Forbidden City, with an annual subsidy from the republican government.

Puyi continued to live in the Forbidden City during the warlord years. It was in June 1917 when the loyalist warlord, Zhang Xun, restored the former Manchu emperor to the throne. Challenged by other warlords, Zhang and his army quickly left the capital. The abortive restoration lasted only 12 days. In 1924 during the second Zhili-Fengtian War, **Feng Yuxiang** drove the imperial family out of the Forbidden City. For half a year, Puyi and his entourage temporarily took residence in the Japanese embassy. In 1925 they quietly moved to the Japanese concession in Tianjin.

In Tianjin, Puyi's advisers were divided on the prospect of a restoration. **Chen Baochen**, whom Puyi considered the most loyal man he ever knew, was pessimistic. A patriotic loyalist, Chen objected to seeking foreign help. Both Zheng Xiaoxu and Luo Zhenyu were ambitious. They were ready to enlist outside support for the restoration cause. Through different channels, Zheng and Luo had been making contacts with the Japanese. After the Manchurian Incident in September 1931, Doihara Kenji, head of the secret service of the Japanese Kwantung Army, paid a visit to Puyi and discussed the possibility of establishing a Manchurian state under his leadership. Chen Baochen opposed the proposal, while Zheng Xiaoxu favored it. Puyi decided to cast his lot with the Japanese and left for Port Arthur in November.

On March 7, 1932, Puyi became the chief executive of Manchukuo under the reign title of Datong. Two years later, he was installed as Emperor Kangde. His role as Japanese puppet ended with the defeat of Japan in 1945. Captured by Soviet troops, Puyi was imprisoned in Khabarovsk for five years, during which he served as a witness at the war crimes trial in Tokyo. In 1950 the Soviet government returned him to the People's Republic of China. The former Manchukuo emperor spent nine more years in a reform prison in Harbin before his release. Living a new life as gardener in the Beijing botanical garden, Puyi died on October 17, 1967. His memoirs, drafted in the Harbin prison, were edited and published in Beijing in 1964 under the title of *Wodi qian bansheng* (*The First Half of My Life*).

REFERENCES: Brian Power, *The Puppet Emperor: The Life of Pu Yi, The Last Emperor of China* (New York, 1988); Henry Pu Yi, *The Last Manchu: The Autobiography of Henry Pu Yi, Last Emperor of China*, trans. Kuo Ying Paul Tsai (New York, 1967).

HENRY Y.S. CHAN

# Q

**QIAN QICHEN** (1928–   ). People's Republic of China foreign minister; Politburo member and vice-premier in charge of foreign affairs and Hong Kong and Macao affairs.

Qian Qichen was born in 1928 in Tianjin in north China. He joined the Chinese Communist Party (CCP) in 1942 when he was fourteen, participated actively in the student movement in Shanghai, and rose to be a leader in the underground movement. In 1945 Qian worked for the Shanghai *Da Gong Bao* and continued his underground student activities. When Shanghai fell during the civil war in May 1949, Qian was working within the CCP youth corps as one of its branch secretaries. In 1952 Qian was assigned to youth corps national headquarters in Beijing. Two years later Qian was sent to study at the Soviet youth corps special training school in Moscow.

From 1955 to 1963 Qian was employed as the second secretary at the Chinese embassy to the Soviet Union. This marked his debut in the Chinese diplomatic service. During this period he acquired a working knowledge of several languages: English, French, and Russian. His knowledge of Russian is of a high proficiency. He returned to China in 1963 and was given a state council assignment in charge of the overseas higher-learning section of the central government.

During the turbulent years of the Cultural Revolution, Qian Qichen spent time at a May Seventh Cadre School in rural Anhui province doing physical labor as part of the "downward transfer" movement waged by Mao's radicals. He was rehabilitated in 1972 and was given an assignment as a councilor at the Chinese embassy in Moscow. After a brief stint as ambassador to an African nation, he returned to Beijing as the spokesman for the foreign affairs ministry. By 1982 Qian had risen to his position as the deputy foreign minister responsible for Soviet Union and Eastern European affairs in the foreign ministry in Beijing.

In that capacity, plus the fact that Qian was fluent in Russian and knowledgeable about Soviet affairs, in 1982–1983 he was thrust into the task of key Chinese negotiator in the Sino-Soviet bilateral border talks, which paved the way for the subsequent Soviet initiative by Mikhail Gorbachev in his 1986 Vladivostok speech for rapprochement. Qian Qichen led the Chinese delegation in a dozen rounds of bilateral talks that centered on the border demarkation of the disputed boundaries and water system of the Amur and Ussuri rivers, the scene of Sino-Soviet clashes in 1969. At these bilateral talks Qian Qichen's proposal that the middle channel of the rivers should serve as the borderline between the two nations was finally accepted.

In 1988 Qian Qichen succeeded Wu Xueqian as China's seventh foreign minister when **Li Peng**, another leader trained in the Soviet Union, became the prime minister. However, that elevation to foreign affairs minister also might possibly be attributed to Qian's long-time association with his predecessor, Wu Xueqian, who in the early 1940s was the Party's overall secretary for the Shanghai youth corps underground operation and a supervisor of Qian's early revolutionary student activities.

Qian Qichen was elected to the party's Politburo in 1992 and reelected at the CCP's Fifteenth Party Congress held in September 1997. He vacated the foreign minister position to Tang Jiaxuan at the Ninth National People's Congress (March 1998), but remained as one of the vice-premiers of the state council, charged with the responsibility of supervising foreign and international affairs in the central government under **Zhu Rongji**, the new premier.

Qian Qichen was married in 1952 and has two grown children. His son, Qian Ning, graduated with a master's degree in Chinese literature from People's University in Beijing and later attended the University of Michigan for further graduate work. He has written a popular best-seller book in Chinese recounting his experiences in the United States.

REFERENCES: "Election to CCP Politburo," *Beijing Review*, no. 43 (October 26–November 11, 1992), 7; Li Kuocheng, *CCP's Top Leadership Group* (Hong Kong, 1990, in Chinese), 461–465; James C.F. Wang, *Contemporary Chinese Politics*, 6th ed. (Upper Saddle River, NJ, 1999); Gao Xin and Ho Pin, *The Most Powerful People of CPC* (Hong Kong, 1998, in Chinese), 170–198.

JAMES C.F. WANG

## QIN BANGXIAN. *See* BO GU.

**QU QIUBAI** (January 29, 1899–June 18, 1935). Russian-trained Chinese Communist Party leader; head of the provisional Politburo in 1927; writer, translator, and Marxist literary critic.

Born in Changzhou, Jiangsu province, Qu Qiubai was influenced by

Zhang Tailei while studying at the Changzhou Middle School. When Qu was twelve, his family lost all means of income, and eventually his family debts led his mother to commit suicide. Qu Qiubai was unable to finish his high school education.

Qu went to Beijing in 1917 and studied at the tuition-free Russian Language Institute, an affiliate of the Ministry of Foreign Affairs. During the May Fourth Movement, Qu Qiubai was head of the institute's student union and was elected representative of the Beijing Student Union. In March 1920, he joined the Marxist Theory Study Group organized by **Li Dazhao**. In October, Qu went to Russia as a correspondent for the *Beijing Morning Post* (*Beijing chen bao*) and *Current Events* (*Shishi xin bao*). He joined the Chinese Communist Party (CCP) in Russia in 1922, through the introduction of Zhang Tailei and **Zhang Guotao**.

Qu was **Chen Duxiu**'s interpreter when Chen attended the Fourth Congress of the Comintern in Moscow in November–December 1922. Upon Chen Duxiu's request, Qu Qiubai returned to China the following year and was elected to the Central Committee in the Third National Congress of the CCP. He joined the Guomindang (GMD) in accordance with the Comintern policy of forming a United Front with the reorganized GMD. In 1924, he was elected as an alternate member of the Central Executive Committee of the GMD. He also became the chief editor of the CCP journal and newspaper *New Youth* (*Xin qingnian*) and *Hot Blood Daily* (*Rexue ribao*). In 1925, he became the vice-chairman of the Propaganda Department of the CCP. He published a series of articles in 1925 and 1926 criticizing the right-wing faction of the GMD represented by Dai Jitao. He was also the head of the department of sociology at Shanghai University during the same period.

In February 1927, Qu Qiubai participated in leading the second workers' uprising in Shanghai. The uprising failed. In April, he supported the publication of **Mao Zedong**'s "Report of an Investigation into the Peasant Movement in Hunan," which was rejected by Chen Duxiu's personal assistant Peng Shuzhi because the report could upset the GMD. In the same month, the GMD launched a coup d'état against the Communists. The split between the GMD and the CCP coincided with the change of leadership in the Comintern. The political and policy changes turned Qu Qiubai against Chen Duxiu, and Qu became an opposition faction leader in the Party. The CCP convened the Fifth National Congress in Wuhan, in which Qu criticized Chen Duxiu's "right opportunism." After receiving instructions from the Comintern representative Lominadze, Qu chaired the August 7th meeting, which elected a new provisional Politburo headed by Qu himself. The meeting marked the end of Chen Duxiu's "right opportunism," but also the beginning of Qu's "left putschism." Under Qu Qiubai's leadership, the CCP hastily organized an armed uprising in Guangzhou. The uprising was quickly suppressed and its organizer Zhang Tailei was killed.

In June 1928, the Sixth National Congress of the CCP was convened in Moscow. Qu Qiubai's "left opportunism" was criticized and Qu himself was replaced by Xiang Zhongfa. Qu remained in the Politburo and was elected to the Comintern's executive committee in the Sixth Congress of the Comintern in July. During his stay in Moscow, he devised a Chinese romanization system. In 1929, he was involved in the factional conflicts in the Communist University for Chinese Laborers (formerly **Sun Yat-sen** University). He criticized Wang Ming's group which was supported by P. Mif, the president of the university and head of the Chinese section of the eastern department of the Comintern. In autumn, when the Russian Communist Party started a party purge, Mif and Wang Ming took the opportunity to suppress their opponents at the university (all Chinese students were required to join the Russian CP). Qu Qiubai was criticized and his younger brother Qu Jingbai disappeared during the purge.

In July 1930, Qu was sent by the Comintern back to China to correct **Li Lisan's** "left opportunism," but the Comintern was dissatisfied with his work and accused him of political ambivalence. In 1931, Wang Ming and Mif convened an enlarged session of the Fourth Plenum of the Sixth Central Committee and removed Qu from the Politburo. Qu Qiubai turned his attention to the literary arena in Shanghai. He met Mao Dun and Feng Xuefeng, the Party secretary for the Communist writers in the Chinese League of Left-Wing Writers, and helped the league in establishing its direction. Qu also established contact with **Lu Xun** but they did not meet until 1932. At one stage, he was in charge of the Committee of Cultural Activities.

Qu Qiubai and Lu Xun became close friends. Between 1932 and 1934, they cooperated in criticizing the GMD's "cultural encirclement campaigns" against the Communists, the "nationalist" literature, "the third category," and the left "closed-doorism" of the league. In 1933, Qu wrote a preface to a collection of Lu Xun's essays, which was the first positive appraisal of Lu Xun by a Communist leader and made Lu Xun an irrefutable spiritual leader of the Left-Wing Writers. Qu also continued to contribute to party journals such as *Struggle* (*douzheng*), but his views were criticized by the Party as "right opportunism" in 1933.

While he was still in Shanghai, he was appointed as the People's Education Commissar in the Central Soviet Government in Ruijin. He was summoned to Ruijin in January 1934. When the Chinese Red Army left Ruijin, he was ordered to stay and was later captured by the GMD troops. He was executed on June 8, 1935 in Changting, Fujian province, but before the execution, he wrote his famous and controversial self-analysis, "Redundant Words."

REFERENCES: *Qu Qiubai wenji* [Collected Works of Qu Qiubai], 6 vols. (Beijing, 1985–1988); Zhou Yongxiang, *Qu Qiubai nianpu xin bian* (rev. ed. of Qu Qiubai Chronology) (Shanghai, 1992).

CHIU-YEE CHEUNG

# R

RAO SHUSHI (1901–March 2, 1975). Political commissar of the New Fourth Army; a leading Communist official in east China and Shanghai; director of the Chinese Communist Party's organization department.

Born in Linchuan County, Jiangxi, in 1901, Rao Shushi graduated from the Nanchang First Provincial School, where his father taught. Rao joined the Socialist Youth League (YL) in 1924, and the Chinese Communist Party (CCP) in 1925. He was active in the May 30th movement and organized workers in Shanghai. In the spring of 1927, he operated under **Chen Yun** and **Zhou Enlai** in organizing the workers' uprising that facilitated the entry of **Jiang Jieshi**'s army into Shanghai.

In 1928 he served as secretary of the YL in Zhejiang, and the following year he became secretary of the league in Manchuria. In 1930 he was arrested by the GMD authorities and released the following year. He was a leading Communist labor organizer in Shanghai during 1932–1933. In 1935 he lived in Moscow for a time as the representative of the All-China General Labor Union to the Red Labor International. In 1936 he worked on the staff of a Chinese-language newspaper in New York and was assigned to work under **Liu Shaoqi** in the Communist political mobilization programs in North China.

After the outbreak of the Sino-Japanese War (1937–1945), Rao worked in Yan'an. In 1940 he served as deputy secretary of the CCP southeast bureau. In March 1941, he worked under Liu Shaoqi and became deputy secretary of the CCP Central China Bureau and director of its propaganda department. Soon he also was appointed as director of the political department of the New Fourth Army.

After the New Fourth Army Incident of January 1941, Rao became deputy commissar of the New Fourth Army. In the spring of 1942, he succeeded Liu as secretary of the Central China Bureau and acting political commissar of the army. Since the New Fourth Army performed well behind the Japanese lines from 1943–1945, Rao was rewarded for his wartime service. At the Seventh CCP Congress in 1945, he became a Central Committee (CC) member. In August 1945, he served as political commissar of the New Fourth Army.

After the end of the war, the Marshall Mission was mediated between the CCP and the Guomindang. A truce agreement was signed by the Communists and the Nationalists in January 1946. An executive headquarters for the implementation of the agreement was established at Beiping. **Ye Jianying** served as the Communist representative to the headquarters, and Rao was assigned to Ye's staff as political adviser. Before they returned to Yan'an after the outbreak of the large-scale CCP-GMD civil war in mid-1946, Rao once served as the Communist representative to the advance section of the executive headquarters in Changchun. In January 1947, he became political commissar to the CCP East China Military Region. He was one of the first Communist leaders to enter Shanghai after its capture in May 1949.

After the establishment of the People's Republic, Rao became a member of the government council and the military council. He also served as first secretary of the CCP East China Bureau, chairman of the East China Military and Administrative Committee, political commissar of the East China Military Region, and secretary of the CCP Shanghai municipal committee.

In October 1952, Rao and Liu Shaoqi attended the Soviet Communist Party's Nineteenth Congress in Moscow. At the end of the year, Rao resigned from most of his posts in East China and went to Beijing, where he became a member of the State Planning Commission, led by Gao Gang. In the spring of 1953, Rao was appointed as director of the CCP Central Organization Department.

Rao's promising political career came to a sudden halt in the **Gao Gang–Rao Shushi Affair** of 1953–1954. At the Fourth Plenum of the Seventh CCP Central Committee in February 1954, Rao was accused of being the co-conspirator to split the Party and usurp state leadership. Gao committed suicide. Rao refused to confess to alleged anti-Party crimes. He was expelled from the CCP in March 1955. He passed away in March 1975. What exactly he did for the two decades before his death is unclear.

REFERENCES: Howard L. Boorman and Richard Howard, eds., *Biographical Dictionary of Republican China*, vol. 2 (New York, 1968), 215–216; Frederick C. Teiwes, *Politics at Mao's Court: Gao Gang and Party Factionalism in the Early 1950s* (Armonk, NY, 1990); *Zhongguo gongchandang lishi dacidian: Zonglu, renwu* [A Large Dictionary of CCP History: General Discussion, Personalities] (Beijing, 1991), 445.

JOSEPH K.S. YICK

# S

SHEN BAOZHEN (March 20, 1820–December 18, 1879). Confucian, patriot, administrator, reformer, modernizer, and high official.

Born into a scholar-gentry family of modest means in Fuzhou, Fujian, Shen Baozhen was brought up by his parents and teachers to abide by the noblest of Confucian principles and to apply them in the tradition of the School of Practical Statecraft (*jingshi*). Impressed by the qualities of the young Shen, **Lin Zexu** promised him the hand of his second daughter, Puqing. The couple married in 1839, the year Shen passed his provincial (*juren*) examinations. Shen eventually earned his metropolitan (*jinshi*) degree in 1847, entered the Hanlin Academy, and received a series of appointments in the imperial capital. In 1854 he was made a supervisory censor for Jiangsu and Anhui, which were being bitterly contested between the Taiping rebels and government forces. His censorial memorials, incisive and critical of the government's management of military affairs and the wartime economy, betrayed a strong reformist bent as well as courage borne out of loyalty to the throne.

During his early years, Shen was influenced not only by the poignant anti-British sentiments of one of his teachers but also by his father-in-law, who played a central role in the Opium War (1839–1842). Lin's continued dedication to the dynasty after his exile in 1841 may also have left a deep imprint on Shen. Shen's loyalty to the throne and the dynasty was exhibited in 1856 when he and his wife, with only a small number of troops at their disposal, refused to abandon his prefectural seat of Guangxin, Jiangxi, in the face of a strong rebel onslaught. After the siege was raised by the arrival of reinforcements, **Zeng Guofan** commended Shen for his loyalty and unswerving adherence to Confucian principles, and Shen became a legend in his own time.

Rapid promotions followed, and in early 1862, at the age of forty-one, he became the governor of Jiangxi. Though the province was often threatened by the Taipings, Shen, along with his superior, Zeng Guofan, now governor general of the Liang Jiang provinces, introduced a series of tax rate reductions. Shen himself also started Jiangxi on the road to rehabilitation. As a result his province was able to contribute substantial material aid to Zeng's military efforts. But Zeng's demands were great and Shen, having to defend his own province as well, was unable to meet Zeng's needs in full. Zeng was greatly displeased. When Nanjing, the Taiping capital, fell in mid-1864, Shen's forces tracked down **Hong Xiuquan**'s heir, Hong Fu, and captured him. Zeng, who earlier had mistakenly reported that Hong Fu was killed in battle, was embarrassed and became further estranged from Shen. Still, the throne rewarded Shen for his services in the Taiping war with the button of the first rank and the hereditary title *Qingche duyu* of the first class.

As governor of Jiangxi, Shen was exposed for the first time to the presence of the West. One unfortunate encounter involved the destruction of properties of the Roman Catholic Church and its Chinese followers by the local population. That the antimissionary riots were allowed to take place was often attributed to Shen's antiforeignism. But if his handling of foreign affairs is examined as a whole, it becomes evident that his overriding concern was with China's territorial and administrative integrity. In fact, he was generally fair-minded in adhering to the provisions of the treaties, and was ready to acknowledge the advantages of such Western inventions as the telegraph and the steamship.

Shen was an able governor, but just as conditions began to improve after the defeat of the Taipings, he, in 1865, had to retire to his native Fuzhou to mourn his mother's death. It was there, in 1866, that **Zuo Zongtang** persuaded him to accept the director generalship of the Fuzhou Navy Yard, which was being planned. Out of a sense of patriotism and the need to tend to his aging father at Fuzhou, Shen sacrificed a promising career and took a post that was viewed by many as unworthy.

In the next eight years (1867–1875) Shen headed China's first full-scaled naval dockyard and academy. Despite the stigma attached to this transplant of Western technology, made even less appealing by the presence of a large contingent of French engineers and technicians, Shen directed the Navy Yard with unusual vigor and dedication. He encouraged his gentry-staff to acquaint themselves with modern science and technology, and created opportunities for job specialization among them. Schools were established to train young Chinese in modern naval warfare, construction, and navigation. Chinese workers and apprentices were also given instruction in modern shipbuilding. The vessels built were used to suppress pirates, rescue merchant ships in distress, and, in 1874–1875, help defend Taiwan during a Japanese invasion. Initially designed to build only fully-rigged, steam-powered wooden vessels, the Navy Yard, under Shen's leadership, quickly moved to building the next generation of warships—composite gunboats with compound engines—immediately after the contract with the Europeans expired in 1874. Graduates of the Navy Yard school were also sent to Europe for advanced studies. Though successful in building warships and training naval personnel, Shen, without strong support from either the throne or the provinces, made little headway in the creation of a "national" or even regional naval service.

The Japanese invasion of Taiwan jolted the Qing court to reexamine its policy of defense modernization. One result was the appointment of Shen to the all-important post of governor general of the Liang Jiang provinces, and the concurrent office of imperial commissioner for the southern ports. Shen was thus charged with not only the administration of the provinces of Jiangsu, Anhui, and Jiangxi, but also the foreign affairs and defense of the southern coastal provinces. For a time, it appeared that he could have worked in tandem with **Li Hongzhang**, his counterpart in the north. But Shen's efforts were repeatedly frustrated by the shortage of funds and, again, by the lack of central planning and decisive leadership from Beijing. So, despite his larger powers, he was unable to implement most of the reforms he had been advocating since the mid-1860s: modernizing the curriculum of the civil service examinations, encouragement of the scholar-gentry to study science, centralized budgeting, and the creation of a modern naval force. Under these circumstances, Shen, to defend China's territorial and administrative integrity, had to resort to the rather negative approach of curbing further Western incursions. His purchase and destruction of the Wusong (Woosung) Railway, often misunderstood, is a case in point. He was not opposed to the railway per se, but only to an unauthorized, foreign-owned railway in China. (His subsequent attempt to use the materials for a railway on Taiwan had to be abandoned for lack of funds.)

Shen's administration of the Liang Jiang provinces began most promisingly. He worked hard at restoring the quality of government, applying the strictest standards in the periodic examination of his subordinates. He also made substantial progress in the reconstruction of the post–Taiping economy. But before the full benefits of his efforts could be felt, the provinces were devastated by successive years of locust plagues which, in turn, were aggravated by the prolonged drought and famine in north China. His own failing health also adversely affected his administration, which finally came to an abrupt end with his death in December 1879.

Shen was an administrator of unimpeachable probity and dedication. He combined Confucian principles with practicality. His patriotism led him to an unusual career path. As a modernizer, he not only gave the Fuzhou Navy Yard the most successful period in its entire history, he also used his position in it to acquaint himself with Western technology, and to introduce the first modern coal mine and telegraph lines in China. Throughout his career, however, his reforms and modernizing efforts were frequently thwarted by imperial indecision and conservative obstruction. Then, toward the end, his poor health and untimely death also prevented him from leaving a stronger legacy for modern China.

REFERENCES: David Pong, "Confucian Patriotism and the Destruction of the Woosung Railway, 1877," *Modern Asian Studies*, 7(4) (1973), 647–676; David Pong, "Li [Hung-chang] and Shen Pao-chen: The Politics of Modernization," in Kwang-ching Liu and Samuel Chu, eds., *Li Hung-chang and China's Early Modernization* (Armonk, NY, 1994); David Pong, *Shen Pao-chen and China's Modernization in the Nineteenth Century* (Cambridge, 1994); David Pong, "The Vocabulary of Change: Reformist Ideas of the 1860s and 1870s," in David Pong and Edmund S.K. Fung, eds., *Ideal and Reality: Social and Political Change in Modern China, 1860–1949* (Lanham, MD, 1985), 25–61.

DAVID PONG

**SHENG XUANHUAI** (November 4, 1844–April 27, 1916). Industrial officer; promoter of the *guandu shangban* (official supervision and merchant management) policy in the late Qing.

Born in Wujin, Jiangsu, to a scholar-gentry family, Sheng Xuanhuai received a traditional education. He gained the *shengyuan* title at the age of twenty-one. After failing the *jinshi* degree examination three times, Sheng joined the entourage of **Li Hongzhang** as a functionary. In 1876 he successfully negotiated with the Jardine & Matheson Company for the return of the unauthorized Shanghai-Wusong (Woosung) railroad. Li soon entrusted him with the administration of various state-sponsored enterprises, among which were the China Merchants' Steam Navigation Company, the Imperial Telegraph Administration, and the Shanghai Cotton Cloth Mill.

Li Hongzhang's fall after China's defeat in the Sino-Japanese War of 1894–1895 hardly affected Sheng Xuanhuai's career. Under the aegis of **Zhang Zhidong**, governor general of Hunan and Hubei, his industrial empire continued to expand. One of his major acquisitions in this period was the bankrupt Hanyang Ironworks, which was reorganized as a *guandu shangban* industry in 1896. He merged the Ironworks with the Daye Iron Mines in Hubei and the Pingxiang Coal Mines in Jiangxi to form the Han-Ye-Ping industrial complex under his directorship in 1908.

As an entrepreneur, Sheng Xuanhuai's interests went beyond the development of basic industries. For the training of engineers and administrators, he founded two Western educational institutions—the Beiyang College in Tianjin (1895) and the Nanyang College in Shanghai (1896). Between 1896 and 1906, he was director general of the Imperial Railway Administration, which contributed to the building of the Beijing-Hankou line. In 1897 he organized the first modern Chinese bank, the Imperial Bank of China.

During the Boxer Uprising, Sheng Xuanhuai played a leading role in designing the policy of neutralization of southeast China, which saved the area from social disturbance and economic devastation. In recognition of his contribution, he was awarded the title of Junior Guardian of the Heir-Apparent in 1901. He became vice-president of the Ministry of Public Works the next year. Between 1902 and 1907 his official career suffered a temporary eclipse as a result of the rise of **Yuan Shikai,** who aggressively took over the enterprises formerly started by Li Hongzhang.

Sheng Xuanhuai managed to regain his influence in the imperial government after Yuan Shikai's retirement in 1909. He reached the apex of his career with his appointment to the position of minister of Posts and Communications in 1911. However, his negotiation of a new loan from the Four-Power Banking Consortium and the policy of railroad nationalization led to the bitter opposition of the provincial gentry and merchants. This triggered the Railways Protection Movement in central China, which in part brought about the fall of the dynasty. Sheng was dismissed from office by the imperial court in 1911. During the 1911 Revolution, he fled to Japan. After his return to Shanghai in 1913, he resumed control of the China Merchants' Navigation Company and the Han-Ye-Ping Coal and Iron Company. In the same year, Sheng offered support to Yuan Shikai in the suppression of the Second Revolution. He died in Shanghai on April 27, 1916.

Sheng Xuanhuai's career generally epitomized China's early attempts at industrialization. Economic historians have often emphasized the limitations of the state-sponsored enterprises, and projected a negative image of the industrial officials. Based on newly available material, recent studies have shed light on the positive side of the *guandu shangban* policy. The industrial officials, particularly Sheng Xuanhuai, are credited for their pioneering role in the defense of China's commercial and national rights during the late Qing period.

REFERENCES: Wang Erh-min (Wang Ermin), "Sheng Xuanhuai yu Zhongguo shiye liquan zhi weihu" [Sheng Xuanhuai and the Defense of China's Commercial Rights], *Bulletin of the Institute of Modern History, Academia Sinica* 27 (Taibei, 1997), 1–44; Albert Feuerwerker, *China's Early Industrialization: Sheng Hsuan-huai and Mandarin Enterprise* (Cambridge, MA, 1968); Chi-kong Lai, "The Qing State and Merchant Enterprise: The China Merchants' Company, 1872–1902," in Jane Kate Leonard and John R. Watt, eds., *To Achieve Security and Wealth: The Qing Imperial State and the Economy, 1644–1911* (Ithaca, NY, 1992), 139–155.

HENRY Y.S. CHAN

**SHI DAKAI** (1831–June 1863). One of the five original leaders of the Taiping Uprising, 1851–1864.

Shi Dakai was the son of a wealthy Hakka family in Guangxi province that provided substantial financial help to the God Worshipping Society, a religious organization that precursored the outbreak of the Taiping Rebellion. Shi was educated and passionately devoted to the Taiping cause, which he joined at the age of nineteen. Granted the title of Assistant (or Wing)

King in 1851, Shi soon proved himself to be one of the finest Taiping generals. After the outbreak of the Taiping Rebellion, Shi led one of the vanguard land forces to charge toward the northeast. He was instrumental in uniting his Taiping troops with other local secret society armies in Jiangxi province, southeast of Nanjing, and in ensuring food supplies for his forces.

However, he also became embroiled in the internal strife that began to plague the Taiping leadership in 1856. Shi was recalled to Nanjing by **Hong Xiuquan,** the supreme leader of the Taiping movement, in September 1856 to eliminate **Yang Xiuqing,** the East King who attempted to usurp Hong's power. Shi's reservation about the massacre of Yang's family, relatives, and followers almost cost his own life. Though he managed to escape, his entire family and relatives fell victims to the ruthless slaughter carried out by one of his fellow generals, the North King.

After the North King, Wei Changhui, was executed on Hong Xiuquan's order, Shi Dakai was again called back to the capital. Now the only survivor of the original four kings, Shi helped with administering the Taiping affairs, but soon aroused the suspicion and resentment of Hong's two brothers. When Hong offered to raise his title from "Assistant King" to "Righteous King" together with "Lightening of the Holy Spirit," Shi, to Hong's surprise, declined the honor. With all his family massacred, Shi lived in seclusion and depression while trying to attend to administrative affairs.

After about half a year in Nanjing, a disheartened and disgruntled Shi Dakai left Nanjing in the summer of 1857 with a large loyal following. However, still determined to demonstrate his loyalty to Hong Xiuquan, Shi led another military operation to show his sincerity. After having conducted tireless campaigns in a number of provinces in the next six years, yet besieged by the imperial forces, Shi Dakai surrendered to the Qing authority in Sichuan in the hope that, in exchange for his own life, those of his 2,000 soldiers could be spared. His hopes were dashed, however, when he was executed, together with all his followers, in June 1863, a year before the ultimate failure of the Taiping movement.

REFERENCES: J.C. Cheng, *Chinese Sources for the Taiping Rebellion, 1850–1864* (Hong Kong, 1963); Michael Franz, *The Taiping Rebellion: History and Documents* (Seattle, 1971); Jonathan D. Spence, *God's Chinese Son: The Taiping Heavenly Kingdom of Hong Xiuquan* (New York, 1996).

YI SUN

**SONG MEILING** (Known in the West as Soong May-ling, March 5, 1897–   ). Wife of Jiang Jieshi.

Song came from a famous and influential family, one of the Big Four families in Republican China. The Songs were an exception in late Qing China—Americanized, entrepreneurial, Christian, and puritanical. The family derived its power from blood and marital ties. Of the three sisters, it is said that the oldest one, Ailing, who married **Kong Xiangxi,** loved money;

the second one, Qingling, who married **Sun Yat-sen**, loved the country; and the youngest one, Meiling, who married **Jiang Jieshi**, loved power. Meiling's brother, Ziwen, was a banker and at one time finance minister; her husband, Jiang Jieshi, was a military general and president of the republican government, while another brother-in-law, Kong Xiangxi, was minister of industries, finance minister, and vice premier.

When Song Meiling was five, she entered a Methodist school for rich girls, the McTyeire School in Shanghai. In 1908, with her older sister Qingling, she went to study in the United States, first at the Piedmont College of Demarest and then at Wesleyan College at Macon, Georgia, as a special student for she was under age. She transferred to Wellesley College in Massachusetts as a freshman in 1913 and graduated in 1917. The two girls were educated to be independent and pioneering. Their Christian background and American education gave them a perspective and a status very different from most of the Chinese women of the time.

Upon Song's return to Shanghai in 1918, she had become thoroughly American. She joined the YWCA, worked as a censor for the National Film Censorship Board, and was a committee member of the industrial bureau of the foreign concessions. Her marriage to Jiang Jieshi in 1927 was seen as opportunism on both sides. Song Meiling probably wished to follow her sister Qingling to become First Lady in China. Qingling objected to the marriage largely out of political considerations, for Jiang was adopting a reactionary policy. Her brother, Ziwen, also objected initially for he looked down on the old-fashioned warlord from Zhejiang with connections to the notorious Green Gang. However, her oldest sister, Ailing, and her husband, H.H. Kong, were keen matchmakers. Eager to bring the general and future president into the family, they prevailed on their mother to give consent. With Qingling away on a self-imposed exile, the wedding took place when Jiang had temporarily relinquished all his official posts. It is hard to contemplate the romance between a Western-oriented, liberal, overseas-educated woman and a conservative soldier who was non-Christian and had had two wives, but her biographer, Xu Han, believes that there was love between them. The marriage linked Jiang with the financial circle in Shanghai and opened him to the outside world, a connection he badly needed if he were to succeed as a statesman.

While Jiang was busy suppressing the Communists and resisting Japanese invasion, Song became his secretary, filing documents and receiving foreign guests. At times she visited wounded soldiers at the front. From 1929 to 1932, she sat on the Legislative Yuan. Starting from 1934, she was fully involved in the New Life Movement. Even though the orthodox philosophy of the neo-Fascist movement advocated a traditional role for women, that is, that they confine themselves to the home and the family, Song was nevertheless able to exert her influence to start a women's department and became its director. Aided by American journalists like Henry Luce, she helped boost the image of the regime by touring the nation, recruiting wives of officials and missionaries to help in the anti-opium-smoking campaign. In 1936, she became secretary general of the National Aeronautical Affairs Commission aimed at developing a modern air force in face of mounting Japanese aggression. However, most of the work was done by an American pilot, Claire Lee Chennault, her role being confined to liaisons with foreign advisers, endorsing their plans and helping to set up the Flying Tigers. She subsequently relinquished the post to her brother Ziwen in 1938. It was believed that the purchase of planes involved substantial commission, though the P-40s purchased in 1940 did score some victories in the 1941 defense of Kunming.

The Xi'an Incident of 1936 further convinced Jiang and Song that the control of the air force should not fall into any other hands. During the ensuing impasse, some of Jiang's former proteges like General He Yingqing suggested sending an expedition to Xi'an and bombing the city, which would in effect lead to the killing of Jiang, effecting a coup d'état. Song advocated caution, and went in person to Xi'an to arrange for the release of her husband. The propaganda machine of the regime was so effective that the Jiang couple was nominated "Man and Wife of the Year" by *Time* magazine. Her magnanimity is fully revealed in the visits she paid to **Zhang Xueliang** when the latter was under house arrest in Taibei.

An incident that proves Meiling's bravery was on a par with that of Qingling which occurred during the 1937 Songhu battle against Japan. During an air raid in Nanjing that accompanied the Japanese invasion of Shanghai, a bomb narrowly missed the Jiangs' house. Though Jiang asked Meiling to leave with the Kongs, she insisted on staying with him. Subsequently, she formed the Chinese National Women's War Relief Association on August 1, with the mission of tending wounded soldiers and distributing relief to the front. On one of her relief visits with Australian adviser William Donald on October 22, she was severely wounded in an air raid, suffering several broken ribs. Her other relief work was the setting up of orphanages, in cooperation with her sister Qingling. In 1938, Meiling started the National Refugee Children's Association for Orphans, supporting over 20,000 children, with aid from Qingling's China Defense League. It was also in 1938 that the three sisters were allied in their efforts to start industrial cooperatives in rural areas as a backup to the war effort, and sponsored by Ziwen and H.H. Kong who set aside five million government dollars to start the movement and became its president. The intrafamilial unity displayed stunned the nation, but the entrepreneurial spirit behind it seemed to have come from their father. The sisters overcame political differences in the wartime spirit of unity against Japan, and in 1940 they assembled in Hong Kong and subsequently in Chongqing.

Her most outstanding achievement, from which she emerged from her husband's shadow, was in diplomacy. It was also a vital part in the regime's propaganda efforts. In 1942 and 1943, she went to the United States for medical treatment at Presbyterian General Hospital in New York. Apart from staying three times at the White House as President Franklin D. Roosevelt's guest, she was also the first private citizen to address both houses of Congress in 1943. U.S. politicians and citizens alike were charmed by this Wellesley graduate with a Georgian accent. Duly impressed, the U.S. government gave huge amounts of aid to China, and Lend-Lease in particular pumped continuously to sustain China's war efforts. Her fund-raising tour secured U.S.$17 million for United China Relief. In Cairo with Jiang in 1943, she reinforced the image of China as a democracy fighting against militaristic, Fascist-oriented Japan. In November 1948, when the GMD was facing imminent defeat by the Communists, Song visited Washington once more to appeal for aid, only this time she was given a cold reception by Harry S. Truman. She retired to the Kongs' mansion in Riverdale, New York and never set foot on mainland China again.

In Taiwan, Song established the Chinese Women's Antiaggression League. She visited the United States in 1965 as the first lady of an ally, and again was given a huge reception. After Jiang's death in 1975, Song quietly left Taiwan and has been living on Long Island and on the Upper East Side in New York City. In 1995, at the age of ninety-seven, she addressed the U.S. Senate to mark the end of World War II in the Pacific. She announced, "I will always think of America as my second home, and it is good to be back home today."

REFERENCES: Xu Han, *Song Meiling: Zhongguo diyi furen zhuan* [Song Meiling: Biography of China's First Lady] (Taibei, 1994); Adam Platt, "The Talk of the Town—the Final Bow," *The New Yorker*, 71(24), 24–26; Sterling Seagrave, *The Soong Dynasty* (London, 1985); Helen Foster Snow, *Women in Modern China* (The Hague, 1967).

TERENCE PANG TIM TIM

**SONG QINGLING, ROSAMOND** (January 27, 1893–May 29, 1981). Wife of **Sun Yat-sen;** revolutionary; vice-chairman of the People's Republic of China (PRC); honorary president of the PRC.

Song was born into a rich Christian family in Shanghai. The Songs were an exception in late Qing China—Americanized, entrepreneurial, Christian, and puritanical. Her father, Charles Jones Song, educated in the United States, was a Methodist minister and a printer. His commercial press printed both bibles and revolutionary pamphlets, and financed Sun Yat-sen's revolutionary movement. Song Qingling's political life underwent three stages— as Sun's follower in the republican revolution; as a Communist supporter and a critic of **Jiang Jieshi's** government; and as a figurehead under Communism.

Qingling first studied at the McTyeire School for Girls in Shanghai, and in 1908, together with her sister Meiling, followed Ailing to study at Wesleyan College for Women at Macon, Georgia, graduating in 1913. Independent and pioneering, the sisters held perspectives beyond the reach of the bulk of Chinese women of the time.

In 1913, Song Qingling joined her family who had fled to Japan after **Yuan Shikai** took power, and there she met Dr. Sun. In 1914, she took over from Ailing as Sun's English secretary and despite family opposition, she eloped and married him in 1915. Her bravery won her great fame in warlord **Chen Jiongming**'s 1922 mutiny against Sun who was then president extraordinaire in Guangzhou (Canton). Sun intended to unify the nation while Chen favored a loose federation of warlords but intended to enlarge his base in Guangdong. During the skirmish, Song pleaded with Sun to escape first. After an arduous journey, she managed to escape, disguised as a countrywoman. The ordeal convinced Sun that the Guomindang (GMD) should turn to the Soviets instead of the warlords for support. Duly impressed by Soviet renunciation of all Tsarist gains from China through unequal treaties, she participated in negotiations with Soviet advisers Adolf Joffe and Michael Borodin in 1923. The GMD was reorganized and an alliance forged with the Chinese Communist Party (CCP). Song was identified, together with the couple Liao Zhongkai and He Xiangning, as members of the GMD Left. In 1924, she accompanied Sun to Peiping to negotiate national unification with the warlords.

It was after Dr. Sun's death in 1925 that her political stamina began to shine. She returned to Shanghai, establishing ties with the CCP elements and the student movement after the May 30th incident of 1925. It was rare for a Chinese widow to be involved in politics. Enraged at the assassination of Liao Zhongkai in 1925 and the Party purges, she showered attacks on the GMD Right. However, for her status as Sun's widow and for some semblance of unity within the GMD, she was elected in 1926 a member of the Second Central Executive Committee. (She was reelected in every subsequent congress until 1945.) Her sympathy for the Communists rendered her a one-person opposition party. She supported the Northern Expedition which started in mid-1926, and directed the Red Cross to care for wounded soldiers. With He Xiangning, she led the women's movement in 1925–1927, upholding women's rights and self-determination in marriage, but the efforts backfired when women activists were executed by village elders with the acquiescence of the GMD Right.

She helped form the Left-Wing Wuhan government with GMD leftists, Borodin and **Song Ziwen** who soon defected to Jiang at Kong Xiangsi's persuasion. When **Wang Jingwei,** alarmed by Stalin's instruction to the CCP to "lead the National Revolution to the goal of Communism," considered expelling Communists from the GMD, Song recommended prudence, maintaining that Wuhan needed Soviet support to fend off Jiang. In 1927, Wang defected to the Nanjing government. Purges of Communists and execution of feminists, unionists, and student activists followed, and Song went on exile in protest.

The political differences produced a family feud. Qingling alone openly objected to the marriage of Meiling to Jiang, which the Kongs favored. In Europe, she attended the International Antiimperialist Convention in Brussels and formed the Third Force as an alternative to the GMD and CCP with Deng Yanda, a rebel general against Jiang. Back in 1929 to attend the burial of Sun in Nanjing, Song announced her "dissociation from participation in the work of the GMD, on account of the counterrevolutionary policy of the Central Executive Committee," and ushered attacks on Jiang's White Terror and his sanctimonious resistance against Japan. Jiang's execution of Deng in 1931 led her to form the China League for Civil Rights with Cai Yuanbei in 1932, remonstrating against executions and torture of political prisoners. In 1936, she protested against the imprisonment of seven members of her National Salvation Association, which called for ending the civil war and stronger resistance against Japan.

When Shanghai fell in 1937, she moved to Hong Kong and organized the China Defense League to channel medical aid to both government and Communist areas. Amid the amicable climate of the second GMD–CCP cooperation after the Xi'an Incident of 1936, the league included high officials like Song Ziwen. She obtained aid from the China Aid Council in the United States for both the league and the industrial cooperative movement initiated by her sisters to set up factories in rural areas. To boost morale and to forge solidarity, she reconciled with her sisters. They persisted in welfare and relief work. In 1945, Qingling established the China Welfare Fund in Shanghai, with a coordinating committee in New York, the China Welfare Appeal. When Japan occupied Hong Kong in 1941, she fled for the wartime capital Chongqing. As a gesture of unity, she accepted official appointments—in 1945, member of the GMD Central Executive Committee; in 1946, member of the Standing Committee and GMD delegate to the National Assembly; in 1947, adviser to the government. Nevertheless, she kept her own agenda—she criticized Jiang, complaining about undemocratic conditions to U.S. vice-president Henry Wallace in 1944; proposed a coalition government with the CCP in 1946; and in 1948 formed a GMD revolutionary committee with dissident elements. She remained in Shanghai when the city fell to the Communists.

In 1949, she helped legitimize the Communist regime as a delegate to the Chinese People's Political Consultative Conference establishing the PRC, and became vice-chairman of the Central People's Government Council and also of the Sino-Soviet Friendship Association. She received many honorary titles. Shortly before her death in 1981, she became honorary president of PRC and a CCP member. After 1949, if she had any functions to perform, they were not in politics, but in welfare. She chaired the Chinese People's

Relief Administration in 1950; in women's work, she spoke at the Asian Women's Conference in 1949; and in peace efforts, she won the Stalin Peace Prize in 1951. She also figured in goodwill diplomatic visits, for example, she headed a delegation to India in 1955. That year, she rejoiced at the formation of nationwide agricultural and industrial cooperatives, believing naively that they were a revival of their wartime counterparts and a realization of Dr. Sun's wish. During the Cultural Revolution, she was rescued by **Zhou Enlai** from the Red Guards who ridiculed her as a bourgeois liberal. In 1998 Meiling, who survived her, asked a friend to pay tribute to their late mother but not her though their graves were close to each other.

Song's virtues were her unwavering adherence to principles, and her undefeatable vision of a great China. She continued Sun's path of alliance with the CCP and national unification. The view that she was a pliant tool of the CCP is invalid at least up to 1949. She had studied Marxism and was trained by Soviet experts. However, her historical mission was fulfilled in 1949, when Jiang and the GMD were defeated. Helen Foster Snow remarks that Song "defied the laws of Marxism by breaking away from the social class into which she was born and trained." In the eyes of the GMD she was always "Song the rebel."

REFERENCES: Israel Epstein, *Woman in World History: Life and Times of Soong Ching Ling* (Beijing, 1992); Shang Mingxuan and Tang Baolin, *Song Qingling Zhuan* [Biography of Song Qingling] (Beijing, 1990); Sterling Seagrave, *The Soong Dynasty* (London, 1985); Helen Foster Snow, *Women in Modern China* (The Hague, 1967).

TERENCE PANG TIM TIM

**SONG ZIWEN, PAUL** (better known as T.V. Soong, December 4, 1894–April, 24 1971). Banker; diplomat; premier, finance minister, and foreign minister of the Republic of China.

Song studied at St. John's University in Shanghai and at Harvard, obtaining a B.A. in Economics in 1915. After graduate studies at Columbia, he returned in 1918 to work at Hanyeping Coal and Iron Works Ltd. In 1923, recommended by his sister Qingling, he joined **Sun Yat-sen**'s government in Guangzhou becoming the Central Bank's president in 1924, and was later appointed director of commerce, then finance minister. He reformed Guangdong's taxation, simplified the taxes, abolished the antiquated *liqin*, seized revenue controlled by warlords, organized tax corps to bypass corrupt rural collectors, and set up tax offices all over Guangdong. He used the revenue to finance the Northern Expedition of 1926, and applied the experience to Wuhan, setting up the Central Bank there, restructuring debts, and raising new taxes.

To win Song Ziwen over to Nanjing, **Jiang Jieshi** declared support for his centralization effort. However, Song resented Jiang, believing he threatened civilian control of the army. To him, Wuhan carried Sun's revolutionary banner. His position gradually changed, and in July 1927, he delivered Jiang's letter to his sister Qingling in Wuhan and declined to be Wuhan's finance minister. He left for Japan after Jiang and there consented to his proposal to his sister Meiling. Jiang made him finance minister in 1928.

Song financed Jiang's antiwarlord expeditions by issuing bonds, raising taxes, and bank credits. After unification in 1928, Song unified the currency, abolishing silver, centralized taxes, recovered tariff autonomy, reformed the salt tax, and amid the global recession, balanced the budget in 1932. In the Manchurian Incident of 1931, he protested to the League of Nations about Japanese invasion. In 1932, he dispatched his Salt Protection Brigade to defend Shanghai and organized a conference at the Shanghai General Chamber of Commerce against civil war, much to Jiang's dislike. In 1933, he persuaded **Zhang Xueliang** to defend Rehe. To obtain aid, Song went on a tour to the West, obtaining a cotton and wheat loan of U.S.\$50 million from the United States. He set up the National Economic Council in October 1933, but resigned as finance minister due to resentment of Jiang's compromise with Japan in the Tanggu truce, concluded during his absence. His insistence on authorizing all expenses by the budgeting committee also contributed to his replacement by Kong. Previously, to restrain Jiang's mounting military expenditure, Song had introduced budgeting, but Jiang suggested issuing bonds and raising debts to fight Communists.

Song stayed in the National Economic Council, and established the China Development Finance Corporation, which soon reaped profits with foreign investment in railroad building and mining. In 1935, he headed the Bank of China, supporting Kong's currency reform. Song's businesses extended from banking to textile, tobacco, shipping, and through the Bank of China, to other areas, creating a form of bureaucratic capitalism. The semigovernmental China Cotton Company he headed became a large commodity trading firm. He negotiated support from the United States and Britain, but continued to complain about Jiang's conciliation toward Japan. However, in the 1936 Xi'an Incident, Song negotiated for Jiang's release, accepting Communist demands to purge anti-Communist elements and forge a GMD–CCP alliance. In 1937, during Kong's overseas visit, he formed in Shanghai a united office of the four major banks which Kong took over when he returned to China. Meanwhile, Song became chairman of a national salvation bond promotion association. Representing diverse political interests, the members included **Sun Ke**, **Song Qingling**, Du Yuesheng, and Chen Lifu. When Shanghai fell to Japan, Song went to Hong Kong and negotiated for British aid. Unity was again displayed in the China Defense League formed in 1938, with Song Ziwen as president and Qingling as chair, and Western friends and leftists like Liao Chengzhi as members. In 1941, he resigned, fearing the league had become the scene of political struggles.

In June 1940, Song visited the West. Relentless in his bargains, he obtained sizable loans from the United States and Britain. Jiang appointed him foreign minister in December 1941, following U.S. entry into the Pacific theater. Song stayed on in the United States to forge alliance with the allies, participated in the formation of the United Nations and requested more aid. He also helped Jiang to get rid of General Joseph Stilwell, U.S. adviser to China. After Kong fell from power, Song became acting premier in December 1944 and premier in May 1945. Favoring reconciliation with the Communists through General George Marshall, he conducted talks with **Zhou Enlai**, but was reproached by Jiang.

He faced the double challenge of wartime diplomacy and economic rehabilitation. Twice he visited Moscow to negotiate Soviet entry into the China theater and obtained recognition of China's sovereignty in Manchuria; but failing to prevent the secession of Outer Mongolia, he resigned as foreign minister in July 1945. With gold from the United States to support the *fabi* (Chinese dollar) he was optimistic about economic rehabilitation and the combat of inflation. His devotion to the redemption of resources from the puppet government and Japan alienated him from GMD factions intent to reap profits from them. In 1945, he announced plans for rehabilitation offering civilian enterprises technical support, rebuilding the transportation network, and increasing energy supply. Realism soon overcame his optimism. On New Year's Day 1946, he admitted that poor law and order, destruction of the transportation network, and idle factories were causing prices to surge. He blamed this on the huge military expenditure during the long drawn-out war, the previous printing press approach to inflation, poor harvests, and the struggle against the Communists. However, the real difficulty was Jiang's anti-Communist campaigns which left a deficit of 200% of the budget and huge borrowings. Otherwise, he could have achieved a balanced budget for 1946, as tax increases, especially on luxuries, and proceeds from selling the puppet regime's property, almost doubled the projected income.

Song opened the foreign exchange market, fixing the rate between the *fabi* and U.S. dollar. However, adverse confidence caused by the civil war resulted in the frantic purchase of government reserves. Soon, he had to readjust the exchange rate and restrict imports. A worse mistake was his policy to sell gold reserves. In the last years of the war, banks had accepted savings in gold. To control inflation, he resorted to selling gold, but rapid rises in black market prices drained government reserves. By February 1947, Song stopped selling gold, causing black market prices to soar and the *fabi* to plummet, triggering runaway inflation. Attacked by the Central Committee clique and the Gexin group, he resigned as premier in March.

To dispel rumors that he had amassed fortunes by illegal means, Song donated his shares in the China Development Finance Corporation, amounting to 5,000 billion *fabi*, to the state. In 1948, he returned as governor of Guangdong, hoping to build it as an anti-Communist base. He boosted the police as a force against "bandits," enforced conscription, and reformed taxes. However, in January 1949, he resigned when the government faced imminent defeat. At Jiang's request, he made an inspection tour of Taiwan and offered advice on reinforcing it as an anti-Communist stronghold.

He lived in the United States after 1949, but visited Taiwan in 1963. His policy of fusing government and private enterprises amounted to a resumption of **Li Hongzhang**'s bureaucratic capitalism, characterized by monopolies, but which failed to develop the agrarian sector.

REFERENCES: Wu Jingping, *Song Ziwen Pingzhuan* [A Critical Biography of Song Ziwen] (Fuzhou, 1992); Sterling Seagrave, *The Soong Dynasty* (London, 1985); Arthur N. Young, *China's Nation-Building Effort, 1927–1937: The Financial and Economic Record* (Stanford, CA, 1971).

TERENCE PANG TIM TIM

**SOONG CHING-LING.** *See* SONG QINGLING, ROSAMOND.

**SOONG MAY-LING.** *See* SONG MEILING.

**SOONG, T.V.** *See* SONG ZIWEN, PAUL.

**SUN KE** (Sun Fo, October 21, 1891–September 13, 1973). Son of **Sun Yat-sen**; president of the Republic of China's Legislative Yuan and Executive Yuan.

Born in Zhongshan county, Guangdong province, Sun Ke moved to Hawaii in 1896 to attend school in Honolulu. After studying in various colleges in America, he obtained a master's degree in economics from Columbia University in 1917.

After returning to China, Sun worked as a secretary in the Guangzhou city parliament and at the ministry of foreign affairs and later served as the associate editor of the English-language newspaper *Canton Times*. He then moved to Hong Kong.

When Sun Yat-sen appointed Chen Chiungming governor of Guangdong province, Chen asked Sun Ke to prepare the legal rules for governing Guangzhou's new municipal council; in 1921 Chen appointed Sun Ke mayor of Guangzhou. Sun worked energetically to expand Canton's public works, financing those expenditures by increasing Guangzhou city's property taxes. Through his efforts, Guangzhou became southern China's most modern city.

In October 1923 the Guomindang appointed Sun Ke to its provisional central executive committee, where he drafted a constitution, new Party regulations, and a manifesto. Sun Ke helped plan the Party's first congress, held in January 1924, at which he presented his draft of the constitution.

In November 1924 Sun Yat-sen went to north China to negotiate with the warlords but became ill. Sun Ke joined his father and witnessed the signing of his two wills on March 11, 1925. One of the wills became the oath whereby future Guomindang (GMD) members swore their loyalty to the Nationalist Party.

Thereafter, Sun Ke rapidly rose in the GMD. In January 1926 he became a member of the Party's central executive committee while continuing to serve as Guangzhou city's mayor as well as member of the GMD's political council.

On March 10–16, 1926, Sun joined the five-man standing committee of the government council in Wuhan city, and thus became a key player in the Wuhan government; along with his provincial colleague Hu Hanmin, Sun Ke and others toured Europe in 1928. After returning, Sun joined the Nanjing government and served in the state council and other high posts. But after President **Jiang Jieshi** illegally arrested Hu Hanmin in 1931, Sun returned to Guangdong province and joined his GMD comrades in opposing Jiang's leadership of the Party. Not until Hu was released did Sun return to Nanjing to serve as president of the Executive Yuan.

Sun continued to oppose Jiang's authoritarian rule and some of his policies, especially Jiang's moderate stance toward Japan. Both men agreed to disagree, whereupon Sun Ke resumed his career as a public servant and held many high offices. Sun participated in negotiations with the Soviet Union leading to the signing of a Sino-Soviet nonaggression pact in August 1937, and in January 1938 and April 1939 went to Moscow as a special envoy of Jiang Jieshih. While there he obtained substantial loans from the Soviet regime and signed a Sino-Soviet commercial treaty.

Sun Ke spent the war years in the Nationalist capital city of Chongqing, Sichuan province. In 1948 he was elected president of the Legislative Yuan and later headed the Executive Yuan. In early 1949 Sun Ke moved the Executive Yuan to Guangzhou because Communist military forces were rapidly moving southward. He resigned and went into retirement in March 1949 and moved to Taiwan; then he moved to France in 1951, and then finally to America in 1952. In October 1965 he settled in Taiwan, becoming a senior adviser to the Office of the President as well as president of the Executive Yuan in May 1966. He died on September 13, 1973, in Taibei.

REFERENCE: Howard L. Boorman and Richard C. Howard, eds., *Biographical Dictionary of Republican China*, vol. 3 (New York, 1970), 162–165.

RAMON H. MYERS


**SUN YAT-SEN** (Sun Yixian, November 12, 1866–March 12, 1925). Founding father and first president of the Republic of China.

Sun Yat-sen was born in 1866 in Cuiheng village, Xiangshan Xian county, Guangdong province in south China. He received classical education in China until he was thirteen, when he traveled in 1879 to Hawaii to join his older brother, who had emigrated earlier and now was the owner of a ranch there. Sun attended missionary schools, graduating from Oahu

College in 1883 before returning to China the following year. This early exposure to Western experience was to have a lasting influence on him.

His horizons much broadened, Sun now found his home village too small and backward, so he moved to Guangzhou and then to Hong Kong to study medicine. He graduated from the College of Medicine for Chinese in 1892 after a total of seven years of study. These seven years were a crucial period in the development of Sun's revolutionary ideas. As Sun said later himself, while in Hong Kong, he often discussed revolution with his best friends. Sun now increasingly saw the only way out in China was the ending of the Manchu monarchical rule in favor of a republic in the hands of the majority Chinese. After receiving his medical license, he practiced briefly in Macao while spending more time engaged in political activities.

In 1894 he traveled to Beijing, where he sought unsuccessfully an audience with the powerful viceroy **Li Hongzhang**, offering his ideas for political and economic reform. In a long memorial, he called for measures to allow for "the optimal employment of all human talents, the skillful exploitation of all natural resources, the full utilization of all goods and the free flow of all commodities." His recommendation fell on deaf ears, so he traveled to Honolulu and took the first fateful step of his revolutionary career, forming the Xing Zhong Hui (Revive China Society) in 1895. Worth noting is the fact that in its manifesto, the Xing Zhong Hui openly advocated a "federal republic" for China, a clear American influence. It also advocated the overthrow of the Manchus and the return of China to the Chinese, a nationalistic appeal which Sun later said was derived from the lesson that the Hawaiians failed to achieve self-rule after toppling the monarchy.

After founding the Xing Zhonghui, Sun returned to China and, with the help of his followers in the secret societies, launched the first uprising in a coastal city in south China, hoping to capture it as a revolutionary base from which subsequent actions could be taken against the government. This move ended in failure and Sun fled to London as a fugitive with a price on his head.

While in London, he survived a kidnap attempt by the Chinese legation officials in 1896. After regaining his freedom, he spent two years reading at the British Museum, refining his economic ideas by borrowing from socialism. He then traveled first in European capitals, then in America, trying to win followers and raise funds in the Chinese communities and among Chinese students studying abroad.

In 1905, Sun founded the Tongmenghui (Chinese United League) in Tokyo, expanding his organization by combining two other groups under his leadership. Between 1906 and 1911, Sun's party staged nine unsuccessful uprisings along the south China coast before the October 10, 1911 revolution led to the birth of Asia's first republic. Sun was inaugurated as provisional president on January 1, 1912. Two months later, political reality led to his decision to resign the presidency in favor of **Yuan Shikai**, the prime minister and military strongman in the last days of the Manchu dynasty. Ambitious and unscrupulous, Yuan soon decimated Sun's party and went on to make himself emperor. Sun launched a "second revolution" against Yuan, but without a military force of his own, he failed and once again became a "roving revolutionary."

Yuan's death in 1916 saw China sink into total political chaos, with the Beijing government alternately controlled by different warlords. In the meantime, Sun continued his campaign to restore constitutional government. Shunned by most Western nations, he finally turned to Russia and began to receive help from the Communist International (Comintern) after 1923. A military academy was set up with Soviet assistance to train many future military leaders of China.

In late 1924, a frail and sick Sun traveled to north China to talk with the leaders in Beijing for the unification of China. On March 12, 1925, he died there at the age of fifty-nine, his dream for a unified China unfulfilled. He left behind many writings on political and economic development of China, including a series of lectures he made before the cadets of the military academy in which he expounded his ideas on nationalism, democracy, and social well-being. This has come to be known as his "Three People's Principles." He is revered by all Chinese as the Founding Father of the Chinese republic.
REFERENCES: Harold Schiffrin, *Sun Yat-sen and the Origins of the Chinese Revolution* (Berkeley, CA, 1968); Lyon Sharman, *Sun Yat-sen: His Life and Its Meaning* (New York, 1934); C. Martin Wilbur, *Sun Yat-sen: Frustrated Patriot* (New York, 1976).

TA-LING LEE

**SUN YIXIAN.** *See* SUN YAT-SEN.

# T

TAN SITONG (March 10, 1865–September 28, 1898). Philosopher; appointed fourth-rank secretary in the Grand Council in 1898; one of the "six martyrs" of the Hundred Day reform (1898).

Tan Sitong was a native of Liuyang, Hunan, and his father was governor of Hubei. He lost his mother when he was twelve years old, and his father's concubine mistreated him. With an unhappy childhood, he spent his time studying. Educated in conventional teachings, Tan was fond of reading and demonstrated the potential to become an essayist. Originally, he shared the Sinocentric views of his fellow people. At the age of twenty-five, he wrote the essay "Zhi yan" ("A Treatise on Politics") and believed that the Chinese were superior to other surrounding "barbarians." For a few years, he worked at the office of the Xinjiang provincial governor.

Nevertheless, in the 1890s he changed his ideas after his devotion to "Western learning." The change came with his acquaintance with the "foreign affairs specialists" of his father's senior colleague, Governor General **Zhang Zhidong**. With the Chinese defeat in the Sino-Japanese War (1894–1895), Tan felt deeply the miseries of his country. He compared the Chinese and Western civilizations, and advocated reform through borrowing from the West. In 1896, he was an expectant prefect in Nanjing. In the same year, Tan met **Liang Qichao** and became closely acquainted with him. Liang was a political activist of the time, and later proved to be an outstanding intellectual. The meeting was a remarkable experience for Tan Sitong. From 1896 to 1897, Tan wrote *Ren xue* (*A Study of Benevolence*), which earned him a place in modern Chinese philosophy. In *Ren xue*, he combined the teachings of Confucianism, Buddhism, and Christianity with his own understanding of Western science. He aimed to break away from traditionalism and the blind worship of the past, and to provide solutions to China's problems.

Between 1897 and 1898, both Tan Sitong and Liang Qichao were in Hunan. Tan returned to Hunan province to negotiate a mining project with the government officials. As for Liang, he took up the post of chief lecturer at the newly established Shiwu Xuetang (College of Current Affairs) in Changsha, the capital city of Hunan. Tan worked as Liang's assistant. For a while, the two men participated in the reform movement of the provincial governor and the local gentry. During this time, new schools, societies, and publications appeared in Hunan.

Tan edited and published newspapers. He also chaired Nanxuehui (Southern Society) to promote modern learning. Nanxuehui started in 1898, with its headquarters in Changsha and its branches over the Hunan province. Nanxuehui provided opportunities for Tan to make his public speeches; and its many lectures included topics on politics, culture, education, geography, astronomy, and so on.

Tan Sitong had proclaimed himself student of **Kang Youwei**, and had been closely associated with Kang's group of political activists. Outraged at the Chinese defeat in the Sino-Japanese War and the resulting Treaty of Shimonoseki in 1895, Kang Youwei and Liang Qichao presented a 10,000-word memorial to the Qing court, and asked for immediate institutional reform. The event became known as "*gongche shangshu*" ("taking public transportation and presenting a memorial"), as Kang secured the signatures of hundreds of provincial graduates who traveled to Beijing by public transportation. After his eighth memorial in 1898, Kang had the opportunity to elaborate his views to **Emperor Guangxu**. Subsequently, the emperor placed Kang's group in high positions. Liang Qichao secured a sixth-rank position; and Tan together with three other people became fourth-rank secretaries in the Grand Council.

From June 11 to September 20, 1898, Emperor Guangxu and Kang Youwei embarked on their ambitious reform program known as the "Hundred Day Reform." Of the 40 to 50 reform decrees issued during this time, they included the abolition of the eight-legged essay in civil service examinations, the closing down of sinecure and unnecessary offices, and the establishment of the Imperial University at Beijing.

The reform movement soon developed into a power struggle between Emperor Guangxu and the **Empress Dowager Cixi**. Rumors spread that the Empress Dowager and her supporters were about to stage a coup d'état to remove Guangxu. Sensing the urgency of the situation, Kang's group sent Tan Sitong to Yuan Shikai, and urged the latter to deflect and to help kill Cixi. The plot never materialized, and Guangxu was under house arrest. Tan Sitong could have fled (like Kang and Liang), but he chose to die, to show that without bloodshed the hope for a new country would be in vain. Tan became one of the "six martyrs" of the Hundred Day Reform.

REFERENCES: Sin-wai Chan, *T'an Ssu-t'ung: An Annotated Bibliography* (Hong Kong, 1980); Compilation Group for the "History of Modern China" Series, *The Reform Movement of 1898* (Beijing: 1976); Luke S.K. Kwong, *A Mosaic of the Hundred Days: Personalities, Politics and Ideas of 1898* (Cambridge, MA, 1984).

CINDY YIK-YI CHU

**TONGZHI, EMPEROR** (April 27, 1856–January 12, 1875). Noteworthy for the "Restoration" that carries his imperial title.

The most significant aspect of Emperor Tongzhi's reign is that it carries with it the idea of a revival or restoration. Mary C. Wright, who wrote about the period, made the argument that during the Tongzhi era Confucian scholar officials were able to suppress the deadly and protracted Taiping Rebellion and three other major uprisings, to reestablish civil government and recapture the allegiance of the local gentry, to carry out a measure of agrarian and economic rehabilitation, and to develop a foreign affairs office that performed with distinction.

Other scholars, however, are less willing to accept the designation of restoration or even full revival. They take the position that while the decline of the Qing was stemmed for a relatively brief period, nothing was done in a sufficient degree to allow China to operate with honor in the modern world. In short, their position is that what has been labeled "the Tongzhi Restoration" was merely a superficial gesture of limited duration.

Regardless of which of these judgments one accepts, the actual role played by Emperor Tongzhi was negligible. While some have raised questions concerning paternity, Emperor Tongzhi is officially recognized as the only son of Emperor Xianfeng (r. 1851–1861). His mother was the infamous **Empress Dowager Cixi**. When Xianfeng died in August of 1861 a power struggle was sparked between two factions that wished to serve as regent for the new child emperor. With the aid of Xianfeng's younger brother, **Prince Gong**, the Empress Dowager emerged victorious, and, while there was no precedent for the imperial distaff to serve as regent, Cixi and Cian, mother of Xianfeng's only daughter, became coregents.

On November 11, 1861, at the age of five (6 *sui*), Emperor Tongzhi formally ascended to the throne. Most of his first 11 years were spent in study, during which time much happened in China. The rebellions that had racked the country were suppressed. A policy of appeasement, rather than confrontation, was adopted in dealing with the outside. This latter change was primarily the work of Prince Gong.

In 1872 Emperor Tongzhi reached his majority and was married. Cixi had selected another woman to be his wife, and she was not pleased that he went against her wishes. She reportedly made sure that their happiness was limited. According to some accounts, one way that she did this was to encourage the emperor to frequently visit outside pleasure quarters, where he supposedly engaged in bisexual debauchery and may have contracted syphilis.

In February 1873, Emperor Tongzhi began his personal rule. Unfortunately, the pet project he devoted himself to, the rebuilding of the summer palace, soon became the object of a rather notorious scandal. Shortly thereafter the nineteen-year-old emperor is said to have become infected with smallpox. Whatever the actual cause, smallpox or syphilis, Emperor Tongzhi died on January 12, 1875. Rumor has it that his wife, who was with child, was encouraged by Cixi to follow her husband in death. She did so on January 16, 1875.

REFERENCES: Arthur W. Hummel, *Eminent Chinese of the Ch'ing Period* (Washington, DC, 1843); Mary C. Wright, *The Last Stand of Chinese Conservatism: The T'ung-chih Restoration, 1862–1874* (Stanford, CA, 1957).

GERALD W. BERKLEY-COATS

**TUNG CHEE HWA.** *See* DONG JIANHUA.

# U

ULANFU (December 23, 1906–December 8, 1988). Top-ranking Mongol cadre of the Chinese Communist Party and in the government of the People's Republic of China.

Ulanfu was born on December 23, 1906 in Tabu village in Tumet Banner in what came to be known as Inner Mongolia. His initial involvement in political activity appears to have been a student demonstration in September 1921 against a Japanese-funded electrical light company in the city of Guisui (today's Hohhot) where, in 1919, Ulanfu had enrolled as a student in the Tumet Upper Primary School. In 1922, he took part in the organizing of a "work-study society for the masses," and in May of the following year, he participated in a series of demonstrations organized by the Guisui student federation to boycott Japanese goods. In Autumn 1923, Ulanfu enrolled, along with 40 other Mongol youths, in the Mongolian-Tibetan School in Beijing. It was at this school, and through the propaganda work done by **Li Dazhao**, Deng Zhongxia and Zhao Shiyan, that Ulanfu was introduced to Marxist thought and socialist theory.

In December 1923 he joined the Chinese Socialist Youth League, and soon became an active organizing member of Li Dazhao's Marxism study groups. At this time, Ulanfu became involved in debates regarding Inner Mongolia's political future, a debate which was intensified by the declaration of independence of the People's Republic of Mongolia (PRM, i.e., what used to be called "Outer Mongolia") in 1924, and one that informed, and in turn was significantly influenced by, an article, "The Mongol People's Path of Liberation," that Li Dazhao published in the *Minguo ribao* on March 20, 1925.

By this time, the still-fledgling Chinese Communist Party (CCP) had formed a United Front with the Guomindang (GMD, or Nationalist Party) on the basis of principles that **Sun Yat-sen** had articulated. Ulanfu therefore became involved in the effort to form what was in essence a socialist organization, but which appeared, formally, to be a GMD, or at least GMD-affiliated Party organization, in Inner Mongolia. In April 1925, together with several Mongol compatriots, Ulanfu launched the magazine *Menggu nongmin* (*Peasants of Mongolia*). He also took an active part in organizing student demonstrations in Beijing in reaction to the May 30th incident that occurred in Shanghai that year. In June he returned to Guisui to continue the work of organizing students and young people in anti-imperialist demonstrations and in preparation for the formation of a Nationalist Party movement. In September, Ulanfu officially became a member of the CCP (with simultaneous membership in the GMD, as provided by the terms of the United Front). Then on October 12, 1925, he attended the first congress of the Inner Mongolia Nationalist Party as a student delegate.

In late 1925, Ulanfu and four other Mongol youths (including his older brother) joined a large group of over 300 students who were sent to the Soviet Union by the GMD–CCP to further their political and ideological studies. Ulanfu enrolled in Sun Yat-sen University from which he would graduate in July 1927. After his graduation, and subsequent to a short-term military training course, he was sent to the University of the Toilers of the East to work as a classroom interpreter in early 1928. In the autumn of that year he was transferred back to Sun Yat-sen University to continue the same work. In September 1929, Ulanfu returned to Inner Mongolia.

Ulanfu was engaged for the next four years in propaganda and organizational work for the CCP, mainly in the region of Guisui and the Tumet Banner in Western Inner Mongolia. The United Front relationship between the CCP and the GMD had been broken off since April 1927, and China's CCP forces had largely been driven underground. Ulanfu's work in Inner Mongolia was therefore clandestine and extremely dangerous, operating in the shadow of warlord governments aligned with the GMD. Moreover, since there was no practical way of connecting directly with the leadership of the "Central Soviet" or the Central Committee (CC) of the CCP in Jiangxi or with other major CCP forces, Ulanfu often had to secretly cross the border into the PRM to report on his work to the Third International. In mid-1931, the CCP's "Northwest Special Work Committee," led by Wang Ruofei (whom Ulanfu had met and befriended earlier in Moscow) was dispatched from the Soviet Union to Inner Mongolia, and for a short time, Ulanfu worked under Wang's supervision. Wang was arrested by the GMD secret police on November 22, 1931, and Ulanfu went into hiding, while making repeated attempts to organize political support from the Third International to secure Wang's release from prison as well as carry on clandestine organizational work in Wang's absence.

With Japanese forces, which had begun their invasion of China in Man-

churia in 1931, penetrating Rehe (Jehol) and Chahar in 1932, Ulanfu began
to organize anti-Japanese guerrilla forces in Inner Mongolia and took part
in founding the Mongol–Han Anti-Japanese Alliance Military Committee
at Zhangjiakou in February 1933. In April and July 1934, the Mongolian
Regional Autonomy Political Council and the Inner Mongolia People's Revolutionary Alliance were formed, respectively. When the leadership of the
former of these organizations split in late 1935, with two Mongol princes,
De Wang and Yun Wang, defecting to the Japanese, Ulanfu and other leaders who remained anti-Japanese established the Suiyuan-Mongolia Political
Council to continue the defense of Mongolia against Japanese invasion. By
late-1935, the Chinese Red Army had reached northern Shaanxi after the
arduous Long March, and Ulanfu's group was able to connect with the CCP
forces at Yan'an. Also the GMD generals in the northwest, especially **Fu
Zuoyi**, had declared their intent to collaborate with the Communists in
defending northwest China against Japan; thus it was possible for Ulanfu
to "come out of hiding" and, in fact, join Fu Zuoyi's staff as a Russian
interpreter.

In the aftermath of the Xi'an incident in December 1936, a second GMD–
CCP United Front was formed in early 1937 and national war against Japan
was declared. Ulanfu became a political commissar in the Suiyuan–Mongolia Peace Preservation Corps (later reorganized as the Mongolian Brigade
of the National Army) under the command of Bai Haifeng. The relationship
between the GMD and the CCP remained tenuous, however, and Ulanfu's
activities in promoting the expansion of Communist forces put him in constant danger. In 1939 and 1940, the tide of war turned against the defensive
forces in the northwest. At the same time, the GMD authorities pressured
Bai Haifeng to pull his troops, then designated as the New Third Division,
out of the Suiyuan region and relocate to Gansu to join forces with GMD
general Hu Zongnan. In the face of this betrayal, the CCP Committee ordered Ulanfu to leave Bai and report to Yan'an, which he did in August
1941. At Yan'an, Ulanfu became the head of the Nationalities Institute of
the Anti-Japanese Military and Political University and chairman of the Na-
tionalities Affairs Committee of the Shaanxi-Gansu-Ningxia Border Region
(SGNBR) government. Toward the end of the war against Japan, in 1944,
Ulanfu returned to northern Suiyuan and organized a provisional Suiyuan–
Mongolian government under the auspices of the SGNBR. At the time of
Japan's surrender, he formed and became chairman of the Inner Mongolia
Independent Movement Association which came under the protection of
Communist forces as the GMD–CCP civil war broke out soon thereafter.
On May 1, 1947, at the Inner Mongolia People's Congress, Ulanfu was
elected chairman of the People's Government of the Inner Mongolia Au-
tonomous Region.

In 1945, Ulanfu had been elected to the Seventh Central Committee (CC)
of the CCP, as that body's only non-Han member at the time. As the civil

war drew to a close, he was named to the Standing Committee of the Preparatory Committee for the Chinese People's Political Consultative Conference (CPPCC) and in September 1949, when the CPPCC was convened, he
became a member of the Standing Committee of the Presidium of the
CPPCC. He was also a member of a committee charged with drafting the
Common Program and a member of the Central People's Government
Council (CPGC). In the early years of the People's Republic of China, a
period of transition from a largely regional structure to a centralized system
of civil and military administration, Ulanfu's unparalleled position in Inner
Mongolia placed him, at once, at the head of the Party organization, the
government and the military administration in the autonomous region (as
secretary of the Inner-Mongolia Sub-bureau of the CCP, chairman of the
IMAR People's Government from 1947, member of the North China Administrative Council in 1951, and chairman of the Suiyuan People's Government after 1952, and the commander and political commissar of the
Inner Mongolia Military Region) while holding national offices at the CC
of the CCP and in national government at the same time. In 1954, with the
promulgation of the PRC Constitution and resulting government reorganization, Ulanfu began to become more involved in politics at the national
level. He became a vice-premier of the state council, serving also as the
chairman of the State Council Nationalities Affairs Commission and a member of the National Defense Council. Within the CCP structure, having
served as a vice-chairman of the Nationalities Affairs Committee and a
member of the Political-Legal Affairs Committee, he became a secretary of
the IMAR Party (CCP) Committee (becoming First Secretary in 1956). He
was named an alternate member of the Politburo, the highest executive body
of the CCP, at the First Plenum of the Eighth CC of the CCP in 1956.

As high as his political star had risen, Ulanfu was brought down in the
Cultural Revolution. On April 13, 1967, the CC of the CCP issued a "Resolution on Dealing with the Inner Mongolia Problem," which called for the
formation of a preparatory committee for the establishment of an IMAR
Revolutionary Committee. A military force under Teng Haiqing was introduced to enforce this Cultural Revolutionary transformation of the political
structure in the IMAR, and when the IMAR Revolutionary Committee was
established in November 1967, Ulanfu, who had been labeled in a September 20 broadcast as "the agent of China's Khrushchev in Inner Mongolia,"
was excluded from its membership. Ulanfu then virtually disappeared from
the political scene until his rehabilitation in 1973, when he was elected to
the Tenth CC of the CCP in August. Although between then and his final
resignation from governmental and Party positions in 1985 Ulanfu continued to be elected to high positions both in the Party and in the state structure—he regained membership in the Politburo in 1977, for instance, and
was apparently still active as head of the CCP's United Front department
in the same year, and was vice-president of the PRC from 1983 to the time

of his death on December 8, 1988—it would appear that in the last decade and a half of his life Ulanfu was largely uninvolved in day-to-day political affairs and, especially, in the political struggles in the late-Mao and post-Mao eras. For the most part, he was even out of the politics of Inner Mongolia, and did not seem to have played any significant or active role in the 1976 struggle of **Hua Guofeng** and the "old revolutionary guard" against the Gang of Four, or in the Hua–**Deng Xiaoping** struggle in the late-1970s and early-1980s.

Ulanfu was the key Communist cadre (not to mention the highest ranking one) in Inner Mongolia throughout his long political career, and played a critical role in keeping Inner Mongolia within the PRC and the Party organizations in the IMAR within the mainstream of the CCP after 1949. He was one of the highest ranking, if not *the* highest ranking, non-Han CCP cadres, and had tremendous influence on the conducting of "nationalities affairs" in Chinese politics over the last six decades.

REFERENCES: Wolfgang Bartke, *Who's Who in the People's Republic of China* (Armonk, NY, 1981), 353–354; Wang Shusheng and Hao Yufeng, eds., *Ulanfu nianpu* [A Chronology of Ulanfu's Life] (Beijing, 1989); *Zhonggong renminglu* [Biographies of Chinese Communists] (Taibei, 1978), 495–496.

JOHN KONG-CHEONG LEUNG

# W

WAN LI (1916–   ). Governor of Anhui; architect for the rural reform; vice-premier; Politburo member; and chairman of the National People's Congress (1988).

Prior to **Deng Xiaoping**'s death in 1997, he instructed the Party leadership under **Jiang Zemin** to seek advice and consultation from senior elder statesman **Wan Li** on matters of importance which would affect the Party and the government. For at the time of retirement, before the convening of the Fourteenth Party Congress in the fall of 1992, Wan Li held a number of powerful positions in the leadership hierarchy: a regular member in the Politburo, a member of the Party's central secretariat, vice-premier in the state council, and chairman of the Standing Committee of the National People's Congress.

Wan Li was born in 1916 of a poor peasant family in Dongping county in Shandong province in north China. As a youth he struggled with meager family earnings to gain entrance to a teacher training school from which he graduated in 1933. In 1936 he joined the Chinese Communist Party and rose thereafter to become a local Party organizer. By 1946 Wan Li was the political commissar for a branch unit of the Second Field Army system commanded by Deng Xiaoping and Liu Bocheng. Deng was then the chief political commissar and thus the overall supervisor for the Second Field Army.

This was the beginning of a long close association between the two. Wan Li followed Deng/Liu's army into Nanjing in 1949 and became the city's economic construction chief after defeating the Nationalists. As Deng/Liu's army marched into southwest China, Wan Li followed and emerged as the Party leader responsible for economic reconstruction of the entire southwest

China. In 1952 Wan Li was promoted to Beijing to head the central government's urban reconstruction. By 1958–1959, he was the deputy mayor and party secretary for the city of Beijing and remained involved in the Beijing municipal government until 1966 when the Cultural Revolution was launched by **Mao Zedong** and the radicals.

From September 1966 to March 1971, Wan Li was denounced by the Red Guards as "antirevolutionary" and was forced to be removed from the Beijing municipal party office. He was banished to the countryside to do manual labor. He returned to Beijing after March 1971 when Premier **Zhou Enlai** brought back the power to the exiled veteran Party leaders, including Deng Xiaoping and Wan Li. Wan Li returned to the Beijing municipal Party secretariat. Then, in 1975, Deng Xiaoping assumed the major responsibilities of the premier's office as Zhou Enlai was hospitalized and was unable to carry on the daily central government activities. In 1975, Deng then appointed Wan Li to the position of minister for China's railroads.

As Mao became incapacitated and the radical leaders began to seize control of the central government, Deng Xiaoping was purged again in April 1976. Wan Li also lost his ministerial position.

With the arrest of the radical leaders after Mao's death in the fall of 1976, Deng Xiaoping returned to power in 1977 and Wan Li was brought back as the deputy minister for transportation. In 1977 Wan Li was named the provincial Party secretary and governor of Anhui province. It was there that Wan Li, a man from a poor peasant background, introduced experimental agricultural reform in Anhui, later known as the rural responsibility system under which peasants were permitted to manage their land and farms on the basis of fixed output quota contracts for each household. Wan Li's successful experiment in Anhui became the key to the 1978 Party decision for nationwide rural reform.

The success of the responsibility system in the countryside enabled the reformers to move a step further, to "legitimize" and "institutionalize" the widely accepted "*Baogan Daohu*," or simply "*Da Baogan*," system of leasing land owned collectively by the township under contract. This step had been termed the "second land reform" or the "decollectivization" of the communes in the countryside. Party Document No. 1 of 1984 extended the duration of household contracts from a period of 3 to 5 years to 15 years. The 15-year extension of land contracts not only signified to peasants the legitimacy of the responsibility of the system, but also gave them a sense of permanence and stability, alleviating the fear that the leased-land contracts, the "*Da Baogan*," might be subject to shifting political winds. In addition, the longer period for leased land provided the peasants with "a greater incentive to invest in the land" and to make other improvements needed to enable the land to be continuously productive. Wan Li's name became a popular household word: "If one wants to eat rice or '*mi*,' then ask for Wan Li."

In 1980 Wan Li was elected to the Party's central secretariat and became a vice-premier in the state council, responsible to the national agricultural commission and other economic reform matters. In 1982 he was elected to the Party's Politburo, the apex of political power. At the Seventh National People's Congress in 1988 he was chosen to the chairmanship of its standing committee.

Wan Li often articulated his thoughts on political structural reform, a popular topic in the mid-1980s. For instance, as vice-premier and Politburo member he spoke on the policy-making process, which he advocated based on computerized quantitative input-output analysis, rather than on an individual leader's subjective judgment. He deplored the fact that China had not yet established a policy-making procedure that included research support, consultation with experts, evaluation and feedback before a policy was adopted. Instead, Wan Li pointed out, China had a system of policy-making by intuition or osmosis. As a first step, he proposed the creation of "a political climate of democracy, equality, and consultation." He argued that policy issues must go through three stages or processes: research, decision, and implementation. He seemed to stress the need at the research stage for permitting free airing of views "within certain limits." He also carefully pointed out that these free discussions could not be allowed to deviate from the ideological guidance of Marxism.

However, Wan Li, then chairman of the National People's Congress Standing Committee, failed to play a role in the 1989 Tiananmen student demonstration. He was visiting the United States when the upheaval erupted. On May 20, 1989, at the height of the student's demonstration, the Party's Politburo Standing Committee members made the decision to declare martial law, presumably at the prodding of Deng Xiaoping. The Politburo action raised a constitutional controversy in that the standing committee of the NPC was not involved—for Article 67(20) of the 1982 state constitution stipulated that the only organ authorized to declare and enforce martial law would be the NPC's standing committee, not the Party's Politburo.

Evidently Wan Li had been receiving conflicting cables from the Chinese leaders: one from **Zhao Ziyang**, then the Party chief, ordering Wan Li to return; and another from **Li Peng**, the premier, appealing to Wan Li to continue his visits in the United States and not return to Beijing. Wan Li then decided to terminate his travels in the United States and returned to Shanghai instead of Beijing for reasons of health. By not being present in Beijing he avoided involvement in the political turmoil, for he could have invoked the state constitution by convening the NPC's standing committee with the move, as urged by many, to nullify martial law or at least to call for a review of the martial law declaration. Wan Li's return might have been motivated by his desire to not get involved in convening the NPC session for reasons of his long association with Deng Xiaoping and his desire to maintain that close relationship.

Wan Li retired in 1992 and he became one of China's elder statesmen.

REFERENCES: Li Kuocheng, *CCP's Top Leadership Group* (Hong Kong, 1990, in Chinese), 346–355; James C.F. Wang, *Contemporary Chinese Politics*, 6th ed. (Upper Saddle River, NJ, 1999); Zhang Zhi, "A Portrait of Wan Li," *Beijing Review*, no. 12 (March 23–29, 1992), 21–23.

JAMES C.F. WANG

**WANG HONGWEN** (1935–August 3, 1992). Labor leader during the Cultural Revolution; member of the Gang of Four.

Born in Changchun, Liaoning province, Wang Hongwen began his political career when he joined both the Chinese Communist Party (CCP) and the Chinese People's Volunteers in October 1950, during the Korean War. After the war, in 1956, Wang became a worker at the No. 17 National Cotton Mill in Shanghai, where he soon became a cadre in the security department and a workshop CCP Committee secretary.

At the outset of the Cultural Revolution in June 1966, in response to **Mao Zedong**'s May 16 bulletin which identified the targets of the Cultural Revolution, Wang wrote what Mao would later acclaim to be "the first significant big-character poster of the Cultural Revolution"—a denunciation of the CCP secretary at the No. 17 National Cotton Mill. He went on to attack CCP cadres in Shanghai municipality, such as Chen Pixian and Cao Diqiu. As the Maoist faction began to gain control at the Eleventh Plenum of the Eighth Central Committee (CC) of the CCP in August 1966, Wang followed the pattern of "Cultural Revolution Groups" everywhere and expanded the attack on a wide spectrum of Shanghai CCP cadres branded as loyal to the **Liu Shaoqi–Deng Xiaoping** faction. In September he organized the Shanghai Workers' Revolutionary Rebels' General Headquarters (SWRRGH) which laid siege to the CCP offices in Shanghai. Rebuffed by the Shanghai CCP organization, the SWRRGH then sent a mass petition group to Beijing, with Wang as a leader. The delegation was detained at the Anting Railroad Station outside Shanghai. The CC of the CCP, sent **Zhang Chunqiao**, a leading member of the radical Central Cultural Revolution Group, to Shanghai to mediate. Zhang promptly recognized the SWRRGH as the "legitimate revolutionary rebellious faction" in Shanghai and as the backbone of the Cultural Revolution in central-south and south China. Wang thus became Zhang's protégé and began to be recognized by the uppermost-echelon Maoists in Beijing as a major promoter of the Cultural Revolution in Shanghai.

As the power struggle in Shanghai intensified in 1967, Wang led in organizing the Provisional Committee of the Shanghai People's Commune, which was subsequently reorganized as the Shanghai Cultural Revolutionary Committee, at which point Wang became its vice-chairman. Henceforth Wang emerged as a major proponent of Mao Zedong thought, writing various essays from 1967 to 1969 that were published in the *Renmin ribao* (*People's Daily*) and the *Dagongbao* extolling Maoism and calling on the people to study Mao's writings. In April 1969, Wang was elected to the Ninth CC of the CCP. In January 1971, as the "rebellious phase" of the Cultural Revolution began to wind down and as Cultural Revolution groups around the country began to shed the label of "Cultural Revolutionary Committees" and turned, instead, to consolidate and institutionalize their political gains in a reversion to the more "normal" CCP Party Committee and secretariat structure, Wang became the No. 3 CCP Committee secretary of Shanghai municipality, with Zhang Chunqiao and **Yao Wenyuan** as the first secretary and No. 2 secretary, respectively. However, since both Zhang and Yao remained in Beijing, Wang was virtually the active head of the CCP organization in Shanghai. In July 1972, he added to his titles the position of political commissar of the Shanghai garrison of the People's Liberation Army (PLA).

In late-1971, in the aftermath of the **Lin Biao** affair, the coalition of Cultural Revolution radicals at the top of the CCP structure in Beijing became depleted. Of the original members of the Central Cultural Revolution Group, only **Jiang Qing** (Mao Zedong's wife), **Kang Sheng**, Xie Fuzhi, Yao Wenyuan, and Zhang Chunqiao were left, with Kang and Xie both in ill health. Meanwhile the question of succession to Mao Zedong loomed. Lin Biao, once called "Mao's best disciple" and tagged as Mao's most likely successor, had betrayed Mao and, fleeing from China, had died on September 13, 1971, in an airplane accident. The question of who would next emerge among the various factions as Mao's successor became a burning issue in early 1972. Among the remaining radicals, whose ideological positions remained closest to Mao's own, Jiang Qing and Zhang Chunqiao wielded the greatest influence but they were unlikely to be acceptable to the other factions and especially to the military.

In an enigmatic move, Mao reached into the ranks of the CCP organization in Shanghai to elevate Wang Hongwen to high office. Wang was transferred to Beijing in the autumn of 1972, and to the amazement of many, was given standing membership in the Politburo under Mao's personal orders in May 1973. In August, as a result of actions of the Tenth CCP Congress, Wang became not only a member, but the No. 3 ranking member, of the CC, a vice-chairman of the Party, and, most importantly, a member of the standing committee of the Politburo. Suddenly Wang, who had only six years of experience in revolutionary politics, found himself at the very apex of the Chinese government.

The abruptness of his rise to these positions was clear evidence that Mao himself was quite possibly intent on grooming Wang for the succession. As a young man (he was 38) and with his background as a worker, Wang would have brought the qualities of youth and "proletarian" credentials to rejuvenate the radical faction which had been seriously tainted by the betrayal of Lin Biao. Although he was unquestionably a "Cultural Revolutionist" he was from the periphery, not the tarnished Beijing center of

Cultural Revolution politics. Perhaps Mao also saw Wang as a potential counterpoint to the increasingly ambitious leaders of the radical faction, Jiang Qing and Zhang Chunqiao.

At the Tenth CCP Congress, Wang, together with Zhang and Yao Wen-yuan, was given the task of preparing three major documents, the political report, the draft of a new Party constitution, and a report that explained and justified the revision of the Party constitution (the last of which Wang was chosen to read to the Congress) which spelled out the still-radical Mao-ist ideological positions that had been articulated at the height of the Cultural Revolution at the Ninth Congress in 1969. These documents helped to consolidate Wang's position among the radicals.

Whatever Mao may have expected of him, Wang proved unable to emerge independent, out of the shadows of his seniors in the radical faction that would soon come to be known as the Gang of Four (*si ren bang*), a term that Mao himself would use, for the first time, at a Politburo meeting in July 1974 to describe this cabal. Wang's long-time association with Zhang Chunqiao, and perhaps his own lack of political experience and his far-too-abrupt rise to high position without any independent power or political base, rendered him a pawn to his radical colleagues. In 1974, Wang collab-orated, much as a junior partner, with Jiang Qing in formulating the "Crit-icize Lin Biao, Criticize Confucius" campaign, which, while ostensibly aimed at weeding out Lin Biao's supporters, was in fact a scarcely veiled attack on **Zhou Enlai,** the premier and the remaining bastion of moderation among the revolutionary old guard of Mao's own generation.

In 1975, as Premier Zhou began to succumb to cancer and was unable to carry out day-to-day management of the affairs of state, Deng Xiaoping, Zhou's protégé who had been labeled as the "No. 2 capitalist roader" in the Cultural Revolution but who had been reinstated in 1973, was put in charge of the state council's business as first vice-premier. The Gang of Four, furious at such a prospect, lobbied Mao ferociously to block Deng's rein-statement, and then repeatedly undermined and criticized Deng's policies and measures throughout 1975. While they succeeded in bringing Deng down in late 1975, they had also made clear their stance in opposition to Zhou himself, a most popular figure among the Chinese populace at large.

On Zhou Enlai's death on January 8, 1976, the Gang of Four began to take on a political fight on two fronts; on the one hand they were keen on bringing down Deng, and at the same time, they were disdainful of Hua Guofeng, upon whom Mao chose to confer the mantle of succession to Zhou as premier. Their all-too obvious contempt for Hua would soon bring about an ironic situation—pushing Hua, himself a staunch Maoist, into the arms of the antiradical faction. Wang and his cohorts in the Gang also made a grievous mistake of pitting themselves against the popular sentiment for Zhou Enlai, beginning with urging media attacks on Zhou's policies if not Zhou's person, especially in Shanghai's *Wenhuibao*. By late March these attacks took on an unmistakably ad hominem character and precipitated an outpouring of popular mourning for and remembrance of Zhou that took the shape of the laying of wreaths, literally in the tens of thousands, at the Monument for the People's Heroes in Tiananmen Square in late March and early April. The Gang, with Hua as a temporary ally, managed to steer the Politburo toward condemning this Tiananmen incident as a "counterrevolutionary activity" and pressed to have Deng relieved of all his positions. At this point the Gang might have benefitted from making common cause with Hua, who was then installed as premier and first vice-chairman of the CCP, and yet their hubris and their depth of disdain for him quite possibly prevented them from doing so and led them to criticize Hua throughout the summer of 1976. By August, in anticipation of Mao's impending demise, all political factions, including the Gang, were bracing themselves politically and even militarily for the contest that was to come. In his capacity as the political commissar of the Shanghai militia, Wang Hongwen put these troops on alert and in readiness for the impending struggle, even though it must have been clear to the Gang that the forces whose loyalty they could command would be no match for the far-stronger forces that their rivals in the PLA command would muster in the event of an all-out power struggle.

On Mao's death on September 9, 1976, the Gang of Four proceeded to press their claim for assuming total leadership. Wang, for instance, set up an office inside Zhongnanhai, the nerve center of the Central Government and Party power, and used the general office of the CC of the CCP's name to issue orders that the provincial CCP committees report only to him. The Gang then attempted to press the issue at Politburo meetings on September 19 and 29 at which they attempted to exclude their rivals. When these political maneuvers proved less than decisive, Mao Yuanxin (Mao Zedong's nephew, aligned with the Gang) issued an order to call up an armored division to Beijing. This prompted a swift response from the Gang's rivals—**Ye Jianying**, who countermanded Mao Yuanxin's troop orders, Li Xiannian, and Hua, who then decided on October 5 to issue orders, carried out the following day, to have the Gang and its principal supporters arrested.

Wang Hongwen was formally removed from Party membership and from all his positions in July 1977, and was sent to a state farm in Inner Mongolia for correction through labor in November 1978. In October 1979 he was put in prison, and a year later put on public trial, at the end of which (in 1981) he was given life-imprisonment and stripped of his political rights for life. On August 3, 1992, Wang died in prison of a liver ailment.

Wang Hongwen's political leadership in what is probably the most turbulent half-decade in post–1949 Chinese politics was at best ephemeral. Wang's being handpicked by Mao to rise abruptly to exceptionally high office borders on the totally inexplicable and was clearly the result of exaggerated expectations of what would turn out to be an empty vessel. Wang simply did not have the skills, experience, or even basic political acumen to provide leadership for such a political system as China's. Even in calmer times his flaws would probably have failed him, but under the harsh light of such a treacherous period as 1973–1976, Wang Hongwen was revealed, in the end, as being little more than a shadow.

REFERENCES: Wolfgang Bartke, *Who's Who in the People's Republic of China* (Armonk, NY, 1981), 586–587; Ting Wang, *Wang Hongwen, Zhang Chunqiao pingzhuan* [Critical Biographies of Wang Hongwen and Zhang Chunqiao] (Hong Kong, 1977); *Zhonggong renminglu* [Biographies of Chinese Communists] (Taibei, 1978), appendix 3-7.

JOHN KONG-CHEONG LEUNG

**WANG JINGWEI** (May 4, 1883–November 10, 1944). Leader of the Guomindang; head of the Nanjing collaborationist regime during the Sino-Japanese War (1937–1945).

Born in 1883 to a poor scholarly family in Guangdong province, Wang received classical education and passed the provincial examination with distinction before pursuing studies in Japan on a government scholarship in 1904. While in Japan, he came in contact with the emerging anti-Manchu movement among overseas Chinese students, and joined the Tongmenghui (Chinese United League), the revolutionary organization founded by **Sun Yat-sen**, in 1905. He subsequently rose to fame as a principal participant in the polemic between Tongmenghui's organ, *Minbao*, and the constitutionalist publications guided by **Liang Qichao**. In 1910 Wang led a mission to assassinate the Manchu regent prince in Beijing. The mission failed and he was arrested and sentenced to life imprisonment by the Qing government.

Released shortly after the outbreak of the 1911 Revolution, Wang, by then a national hero, was nominated by the Tongmenghui as its new leader, but he declined. Instead he worked for a compromise between the revolutionaries and the leader of the Qing military, **Yuan Shikai**. When a settlement was reached and Yuan became the first president of the new republic, Wang temporarily retired from politics and devoted his attention to cultural and educational affairs. He made two trips to Europe with his former comrade and new bride, Chen Bijun. In 1917 Wang returned to the entourage of Sun Yat-sen, who was organizing his own government in Guangzhou to challenge the warlord regime in Beijing. For the next seven years Wang served as Sun's secretary, publicist, and emissary in negotiations with various political forces in China. A gifted writer and orator, Wang quickly gained trust from Sun as well as respect from his colleagues. When Sun reorganized his Guomindang (GMD) in 1924 with Comintern support and assistance, Wang became a member of its Central Executive Committee.

Sun's death in 1925 made Wang a leading contender for the succession to GMD leadership. He was elected head of the Party and the government in July, and as such he continued Sun's policy of allying with the Soviet

Union and cooperating with the Chinese Communists. The succession struggle, however, was far from over. In March 1926 Wang was ousted by **Jiang Jieshi** in a coup d'état known as the *Zhongshan* Gunboat Incident. He left Guangzhou for France in April. In early 1927, the GMD, halfway in its northern expedition against the warlords, was paralyzed by a bitter rift within itself and with its Communist allies. Wang was welcomed back by his supporters to head the leftist Wuhan regime, which was in rivalry with Jiang Jieshi and the Party's right-wing in Nanjing. Although the two camps were reunified later that year, after both had purged the Communists from their ranks, Wang again lost to Jiang in the ensuing contest for GMD leadership.

From 1928 to 1931, while spending most of his time on another overseas exile, Wang led an intraparty opposition to Jiang's conservative Party and government leadership. He became known as the leader of the "Left GMD," which vowed to revive the Party's radical line of the 1924–1927 period. With the assistance of his personal following, known as the "Reorganizationists," as well as several anti–Jiang militarists, Wang directed a series of political and military offensives aimed at toppling Jiang's new government in Nanjing. All of these offensives, most notably the Beiping (Beijing) regime of 1930 and the Guangzhou regime of 1931, ended in failure. In early 1932, as the Japanese invasion in Manchuria alarmed the warring GMD factions, Wang decided to cooperate with Jiang and joined the Nanjing government.

During the first half of the 1930s, Wang served as China's premier (head of the Administrative Yuan) and shouldered the main responsibility of dealing with the Japanese threat. Buying time for domestic pacification and reconstruction, he insisted on a conciliatory stance toward Japan, which seriously tarnished his reputation as a nationalist and national leader. Meanwhile, Wang's share of power in Nanjing diminished as Jiang continued to expand his control over the Party and the government. In late 1935 Wang was wounded in an assassination attempt and forced to resign. He took another trip to France and did not return until early 1937.

Shortly after Wang's return the Sino-Japanese War began. In the early stage of the war, Wang was second-in-command in the GMD and its wartime government, a position reaffirmed by his election as the Party's deputy leader (with Jiang as leader) and head of the People's Political Council in 1938. Wang, however, was disappointed by his continued loss of power to Jiang, and extremely pessimistic about the possible outcome of the war. Soon he was involved in a secret effort to seek peace with Japan. In late 1938 Wang left China's wartime capital, Chongqing, and announced his "peace initiative" in Hanoi. Failing to persuade his colleagues in Chongqing to join him, he moved to Shanghai and negotiated a separate peace settlement with Japan. In March 1940, with Japanese help, Wang established a new "national government" in the Japanese-occupied Nanjing. For the next four years his regime tried, with little success, to restore Chinese rule and reduce Japanese control in the occupied territories. The regime was constantly weakened by Japanese pressure and internal strife. Wang died of illness in Japan in 1944, months before the end of the war. By then he had been regarded by most Chinese as a traitor and a Japanese puppet.

REFERENCES: Howard L. Boorman, "Wang Ching-wei: A Political Profile," in Chün-tu Hsueh, ed., *Revolutionary Leaders of Modern China* (Oxford, 1971); Gerald E. Bunker, *The Peace Conspiracy: Wang Ching-wei and the China War, 1937–1941* (Cambridge, MA, 1972); Cai Dejin, *Wang Jingwei shengping jishi* [A Chronology of the Life of Wang Jingwei] (Beijing, 1993).

WANG KE-WEN

**WANG MING** (Chen Shaoyu, April 9, 1904–March 27, 1974). Leader of the "third 'leftist' line" in Chinese Communist Party (CCP) history; head of the Twenty-Eight Bolsheviks; CCP representative on the executive committee of the Communist International (Comintern).

Born Chen Shaoyu in Jinzhai County, Anhui province, Wang Ming was active in student politics in Wuchang in the early 1920s. He joined the CCP in 1925. In November he studied at **Sun Yat-sen** University in Moscow, and represented the Hubei party branch in attendance on campus. He mastered Russian and became a protégé of Pavel Mif, the university rector who groomed him to become a leader among the Chinese students. By April 1929, when Wang returned to Shanghai to participate in Communist propaganda, he and his associates dominated the university's party branch bureau and created what their enemies dubbed a "Wang Ming dogmatic faction" within the university. In China, with the backing of Mif, Wang rose rapidly in the CCP hierarchy.

After the fall of **Li Lisan** in 1930, Wang and the Twenty-Eight Bolsheviks—a group of returned students from the Soviet Union—were able to control the CCP Central Committee. In January 1931, Wang was elected a Central Committee and Politburo member at the Fourth Plenum of the Sixth CCP Central Committee. During the period of the "third 'leftist' line" (January 1931–January 1935), the Chinese Bolsheviks dominated the CCP's policy-making and eclipsed the power of Chairman **Mao Zedong** of the Jiangxi Soviet. In November 1931, Wang Ming returned to Moscow to serve as the CCP representative to the Comintern. At the Seventh Congress of the Comintern in 1935, he was elected a member of its executive committee.

Before the Xi'an Incident of 1936, Wang promoted the United Front with the Guomindang (GMD). Loyally following the Comintern line, he was willing to cooperate with **Jiang Jieshi**. In November 1937, Wang returned to China, served as secretary of the CCP Changjiang Bureau, and helped the GMD to mobilize the masses to defend Wuhan. But the city fell into Japanese hands, and other CCP leaders did not support Wang's "rightist" idea of merging CCP and GMD troops in a United Front. At the Sixth

Plenum of the Sixth CCP Central Committee in Yan'an from September–November 1938, Wang was criticized for his "rightist capitulationism" toward the GMD, and the Changjiang Bureau was abolished. Wang nevertheless was allowed to serve as director of the CCP's United Front Work Department and stay with the Communist delegation in GMD Chongqing.

Wang Ming's power within the CCP declined after Mao's rectification movement of 1942–1944, and plummeted further after the establishment of the People's Republic of China in 1949. Although he was able to retain his Central Committee membership at the Seventh and Eighth CCP congresses, his influence was gone. In January 1956, Wang left for the Soviet Union and began to publish anti–Mao writings until his death in 1974.

Wang Ming's political support mainly stemmed from Mif, Stalin, and the Comintern. His concrete revolutionary activity within China was minor as compared with Mao's. Wang's political ideas and action nonetheless influenced the Chinese Communist concept of urban revolution, the United Front policy with the GMD, and the issue of political factions within the CCP. Being the leading Chinese Communist representative to the Comintern during the 1930s, Wang was also influential in his portrayal of Chinese political realities to the Communist International. In the end, however, Wang Ming and his Russian-returned associates were no match for Mao Zedong and his allies in pragmatic revolutionary activities and power seizure in the Communist revolution.

REFERENCES: Zhang Guoquan, Guo Dehong, and Li Mingsan, *Wang Ming pingzhuan* [A Critical Biography of Wang Ming] (Hefei, 1989); Marilyn Levine, "Wang Ming," in Edwin P.W. Leung, ed., *Historical Dictionary of Revolutionary China, 1839–1976* (New York, 1992), 454–456; Cao Zhongbin and Dai Maolin, *Wang Ming zhuan* [A Biography of Wang Ming] (Changchun, 1991); *Zhongguo gongchandang lishi dacidian: Zonglu, renwu* [Large Dictionary of CCP History: General Discussion, Personalities] (Beijing, 1991), 131.

JOSEPH K.S. YICK

**WENG TONGHE** (May 19, 1830–July 3, 1904). Tutor of Emperor Guangxu and president of the Board of Revenue.

Weng Tonghe was a native of Changshu, Jiangsu, and his father was a grand secretary of the Qing Court. In 1856, he obtained the highest honor in the metropolitan examinations. He subsequently took up a number of posts, which were in charge of provincial education and examination. He was tutor of two emperors, **Emperor Tongzhi** and **Emperor Guangxu**. Weng Tonghe presided on various boards, which included the Censorate, the Board of Punishments, and the Board of Works. He began to serve in the Grand Council in 1882. He became president of the Board of Revenue in 1886, and remained in that position for over ten years.

While Weng was tutor of Emperor Guangxu for 20 years, he obtained the trust of the **Empress Dowager Cixi**. In 1889, the Empress Dowager had retired from her position as regent, but Weng observed that she still held the reins of power. A Confucianist and a calculating politician, Weng emphasized the need for conservative reform in the late 1880s and the 1890s, and advocated the idea of Chinese learning for foundation and Western learning for supplement. As a first-rank court official, Weng advocated moderate reform especially after the Chinese defeat in the Sino-Japanese War (1894–1895). He ended his tutorship of the emperor two years before the launching of the Hundred Day Reform (1898), but he still maintained close ties with Guangxu.

In the late 1890s, Qing officials agreed to the need for reform despite their conservative outlook. In the court, there was the Northern Party led by a grand secretary and the Southern Party under the leadership of Weng Tonghe. In the power struggle, Weng sought to secure the collaboration of officials and scholars. His idea was the necessity of moderate reform.

Weng Tonghe endorsed the call for reform of **Kang Youwei**. Weng supported Kang's Qiangxuehui (Society for the Study of Self-Strengthening) for some time. While Kang was much more radical than Weng, the former imperial tutor was very concerned about his struggle with the Northern Party. Weng had mentioned Kang Youwei to the emperor and subsequently, officials at Zongli Yamen were willing to meet with Kang and listen to his reform ideals. In that incident, Weng was shocked to hear Kang's radical thoughts, and he could not accept the daring ideas of Kang and his interpretation of Confucianism. Weng's support for Kang quickly eroded as he saw him as a potentially strong competitor.

In June 1898, Emperor Guangxu received Kang and embarked on the Hundred Day Reform. At the very beginning, Weng was upset by the drastic reform program, the ascendance of Kang, and the emperor's reliance on Kang's group of reformers. Weng was dismayed when conservative scholar-officials attacked him for his earlier recommendation of Kang to the court. Subsequently, Weng urged the emperor to disassociate himself from Kang, but Emperor Guangxu was too eager for reform to listen to Weng, and the close relationship between the former tutor and the emperor collapsed. Kang's group also filed charges against Weng. While he had angered the emperor, Weng also made himself an enemy of the Empress Dowager, who blamed him for introducing Kang to the court. In June 1898, Weng lost all his official posts.

The Hundred Day Reform ended in September 1898. The Empress Dowager regarded the reform movement as an attempt of the emperor and Kang's group to seize power from her. She and her supporters planned to stage a coup d'état to remove the emperor. In order to save him and the reform, Kang's group sent **Tan Sitong** to **Yuan Shikai**, and urged the latter to deflect and to help kill Cixi. The plot of the reformers never materialized and the Empress Dowager put the emperor under arrest. The reform leaders, Kang Youwei and Liang Qichao, fled to Japan. Others were executed, and they were known as the "six martyrs" of the Hundred Day Reform. The Empress Dowager blamed Weng Tonghe for introducing Kang Youwei to the emperor and leading to the disaster. In December, he lost all his ranks and was placed under house arrest.

REFERENCES: Immanuel C.Y. Hsü, *The Rise of Modern China*, 6th ed. (New York, 2000); Luke S.K. Kwong, *A Mosaic of the Hundred Days: Personalities, Politics and Ideas of 1898* (Cambridge, MA, 1984).

CINDY YIK-YI CHU

**WU PEIFU** (April 22, 1874–December 4, 1939). Major warlord in the early Republican era and leader of the Zhili clique.

A native of Shandong, Wu Peifu passed the beginning level of civil service examinations before enrolling in the modern military academies established by the Qing government. He served under Cao Kun in a division of the Beiyang army when the Revolution of 1911 began. Both Cao and Wu provided critical assistance to **Yuan Shikai** during the Revolution and in the early years of the Republic, ensuring Yuan's control of the presidency. For their services Yuan rewarded them with repeated and generous promotions.

After Yuan's death in 1916, Wu emerged as a leading figure in the military faction, the Zhili clique. He participated in the war against Zhang Xun when Zhang attempted to restore the Qing monarchy in 1917, and then in a series of campaigns against **Sun Yat-sen**'s Guangzhou regime. As the rivalry between the Zhili clique and the ruling Anhui clique intensified, Wu denounced the policy of forcible national reunification promoted by Premier Duan Qirui, the Anhui clique leader, and proposed instead peace negotiations between Beijing and Guangzhou. In 1920, Wu and Cao Kun collaborated with the Fengtian clique and ousted Duan from the Beijing government. For the next two years the two victorious factions jointly controlled the government in Beijing while competing with each other in expanding their respective domains into the Yangzi valley. This conflict eventually led to the first Zhili-Fengtian War in 1922, in which Cao and Wu's Zhili forces triumphed.

As new national leaders, the Zhili clique initially adopted a conciliatory gesture toward other political forces in China. In an attempt to peacefully reunify the country, Wu and Cao restored the Constitution and parliament that had been abolished by Duan Qirui but had been defended by Sun Yat-sen's Guangzhou regime. The attempt was largely unsuccessful. Sun was soon ousted by his partner in Guangzhou but remained hostile toward Beijing. Moreover, the Fengtian clique was fermenting another challenge to the Zhili rule. In 1923, Wu helped elect Cao as the new president of the Republic. The election, pushed through with bribery and intimidation, further alienated other political forces from the Zhili clique. Wu himself assumed the position of commissioner of the Zhili-Henan-Shandong provinces, but in many ways he was the de facto leader of the Beijing government.

In foreign policy, the Zhili clique discontinued the pro-Japanese stance of the Anhui clique and solicited support from the Western powers. For a while Wu also maintained contacts with the Soviet Union and tolerated Communist labor unions in his territories. That tolerance, however, came to an end in 1923 when Wu suppressed the Communist-organized Beijing-Hankou Railway strike.

In 1924 Wu suffered a disastrous defeat in the second Zhili-Fengtian War after one of his commanders, **Feng Yuxiang**, defected to the Fengtian side. The Zhili rule in Beijing thus collapsed. After a year of recuperation and reorganization in Henan, Wu staged a political comeback in late 1925 and again dominated the middle and upper Yangzi regions. He then joined forces with his former rival, the Fengtian clique, in a war against Feng Yuxiang. While this conflict was still underway, the Guangzhou regime under **Jiang Jieshi** launched its Northern Expedition against Wu and other warlords. In late 1926 Wu was again defeated by Jiang's Nationalist forces and fled to Sichuan.

During the following decade of Nationalist rule, Wu retired from politics and lived quietly in Beiping (Beijing). After the Manchurian incident of 1931, he rejected repeated Japanese offers to lead a pro–Japanese separatist regime in North China. When the Sino-Japanese War broke out in 1937, however, Wu decided to stay behind the enemy lines. He died, following dental surgery, in occupied Beiping in 1939; it was rumored that he had been murdered by the Japanese.

REFERENCES: Andrew Nathan, *Peking Politics, 1918–1923: Factionalism and the Failure of Constitutionalism* (Berkeley, CA, 1976); Arthur Waldron, *From War to Nationalism: China's Turning Point, 1924–1925* (Cambridge, 1995); Odoric Y.K. Wou, *Militarism in Modern China: The Career of Wu P'ei-fu, 1916–39* (Canberra, Australia, 1978).

WANG KE-WEN

# X

XIAO CHAOGUI (1820?–September 1852). One of the military and political leaders of the Taiping Revolutionary Movement.

Xiao Chaogui was born around 1820 to a peasant family in the Wuxuan district of Guangxi province. Sources differ as to his ethnicity, whether Hakka or Zhuang. The village in which he resided was close to the home village of **Yang Xiuqing**, a follower of **Hong Xiuquan**, the leader of the Taiping Revolutionary movement. Xiao married a relative of Yang's, Yang Yunqiao, a religious zealot and visionary. Yang Yunqiao had foretold Hong Xiuquan's appearance as a divinely inspired Christian teacher and charismatic leader. Following Yang Yunqiao's death, Xiao married Hong's younger sister Hong Xuanqiao.

Xiao was baptized by Hong Xiuquan in the 1840s in the Guiping district of Guangxi. At about the same time he joined the God Worshippers, a Christian revolutionary society headed by Hong. Xiao rose quickly to a position of leadership in the society through his claim that, during a visit to earth, Christ had empowered him to speak the words of God. Hong and his deputy **Feng Yunshan** subsequently named Xiao and three others to positions in the highest echelon of the God Worshippers. In 1850 they placed Xiao in charge of field operations of the society's military forces and gave him personal command of a large army, a move seemingly designed to offset the mounting influence of Yang Xiuqing.

Military action by the God Worshippers began in early 1851 at Jintian in the Guiping district following heavy-handed measures by government forces against villages controlled by the God Worshippers. With a force of 500, Xiao vanquished a government army of 3,000 and personally decapitated the Manchu commander. Not long after this victory, on January 11,

1851, Hong disclosed his dynastic intentions by proclaiming the Taiping Tianguo (Heavenly Kingdom of Great Peace). He placed Xiao in command of the Forward Taiping Army.

After the victory at Jintian, the Taiping forces advanced westward and then backtracked to the northeast occupying the walled city Yongan (the present-day Mengshan) in September. At Yongan, Hong Xiuquan organized the Taiping government and named the members of his court. Xiao was designated West King, one of the five kings directly subordinate to Hong. An imperial army of more than 30,000 besieged Yongan during the winter of 1951–1952. The Taipings finally broke through the encirclement on the night of April 5. As their forces advanced northward toward Guilin, rear elements came under attack by an imperial army commanded by the Manchu General Wu-lan-tai. Several thousand Taiping followers, mostly women and children, perished. Flushed with victory, the imperial army followed closely as the Taiping forces disappeared into the Dadong Mountains. Taiping forces there under the direction of Xiao Chaogui ambushed the imperial army inflicting severe losses. Four general officers perished. Wu-lan-tai narrowly escaped with his life only to die a few days later from a bullet wound suffered in fighting on the outskirts of Guilin. The unsuccessful Taiping siege of Guilin lasted from April 17 until May 19, when they abandoned the city and continued northward occupying Xingan and Quanzhou in northern Guangxi. Crossing into Hunan they took the district city of Daozhou (present-day Daoxian) on June 12.

At Daozhou, East King Yang Xiuqing and West King Xiao issued three fiery proclamations appealing to the nationalist (i.e., anti-Manchu) sentiments of all Chinese, denouncing the crimes of the Manchus, and calling on all to worship God and create a kingdom of peace and prosperity. On August 17, the Taipings moved successfully against Chenzhou. From this base Xiao led a contingent of light infantry northward through eastern Hunan arriving at the provincial capital Changsha on September 11. After defeating the imperial forces in the suburbs, Xiao's troops found the city wall secured and defended by a force of 8,000 militia organized by Governor Lo Bingzhang. Xiao positioned his smaller force outside the city gates where they came under fire from towers within the city and were forced to take cover. The next day wearing the highly visible insignia of his rank, Xiao personally led his forces in an attack on the city. He was quickly defeated by enemy fire and died a few days later as a result of his wounds. He was survived by his widow and a son, Yuhe, who inherited his title.

Xiao was famed for his bravery and loyalty to the Taiping cause. His untimely death during a display of bravado seemed a pointless act of self-sacrifice. With Xiao no longer a divine spokesman, the upward path was clear for the personally ambitious East King Yang Xiuqing. The resulting leadership struggles would eventually undermine the Taiping's hopes to establish a lasting kingdom.

REFERENCES: Cai Guanluo, ed., *Qingdai qibai mingren zhuan* [Biographies of Seven Hundred Famous People of the Qing Period], vol. 3 (Beijing, 1984), 1868–1870; Yu-wen Jen, *The Taiping Revolutionary Movement* (New Haven, CT, 1973).

THOMAS L. KENNEDY

# Y

YAN JIAGAN (Yen Chia-kan, October 23, 1905–December 24, 1995). Governor of Taiwan; premier and vice-president of the Republic of China in Taiwan; architect of financial reforms in China mainland and Taiwan.

Born in Suzhou city, Jiangsu province, to a well-to-do family, Yan Jiagan was tutored in the Chinese classics at home by his grandfather and father, both scholars. After graduating from the missionary-managed Daowu Middle School in Suzhou, he attended St. John's University in Shangai, focusing on the sciences, especially chemistry. Graduating in 1926, he became the supply director of the Nanjing-Shanghai railroad bureau in Shanghai.

In the winter of 1938, after Japan's invasion of China, Yan became the commissioner of reconstruction in Fujian province. The following year Fujian's governor, Chen Yi, appointed him finance commissioner. In an effort to reform Fujian's budgetary system and efficiently collect more taxes, Yan conceived of a scheme to collect land taxes in grain instead of currency. Using Yan's plan Fujian's government collected more tax revenue than in the past and managed to reduce inflation, which was becoming a problem elsewhere in the mainland. Yan's reform ideas were soon adapted by other provinces, winning him considerable fame and respect.

Yan then began to ascend the Republic of China's (ROC) bureaucracy. In February 1945 he served as director of procurement of the war production board in Chongqing city and later became a member of the army general headquarters' planning committee and then a standing committee member of the ministry of economic affairs committee for reorganizing Japanese assets in the Japanese-occupied areas.

In December 1945 the Nationalist government dispatched Yan to Taiwan as the communication commissioner under the first Taiwan governor, Chen

Yi, a colleague of Yan's from Fujian. In April 1946 Yan became the Taiwan finance commissioner and board chairman of the Bank of Taiwan. In that position, Yan supervised the Taiwan 1946 currency reform, which insulated the island's economy from the inflation that was ravaging the mainland.

In June 1949, as the ROC government moved to Taiwan and the island's inflation worsened, Yan implemented another currency reform, pegging the value of the new Taiwan dollar to the U.S. dollar. By 1952, the government's anti-inflationary program, assisted by American military and economic aid, had checked hyperinflation and had begun restoring currency stability.

Yan then began assembling talented technocrats such as Yin Zhongrong, Yang Jizeng, Xu Boyuan, and Li Guoding to advise the government and chair review committees for economic policies. Yan continued to serve in important government posts such as governing of Taiwan in 1955 and finally became a central executive committee member of the Guomindang in 1963. In December 1963 Yan succeeded **Chen Cheng** as premier and served ten years in that position. In March 1966 the National Assembly elected him vice-president, a post he held for three years, assuming the presidency when **Jiang Jieshi** died on April 5, 1975. He was president for three years and then stepped down, recommending that Premier **Jiang Jingguo** become president.

Taiwan's leaders and elites revered Yan, judging him to be an incorruptible and dedicated official. They especially praised him for his contributions to Taiwan's economic growth and financial stability. In March 1986 Jiang Jingguo displayed his high esteem for Yan Jiagan's integrity and capabilities by appointing him chair of the Guomindang's ten-person committee for planning Taiwan's political reforms. Those reforms ultimately led to the island's becoming a democracy.

On December 16, 1986, Yan was admitted to Veteran's Hospital in Taibei after suffering a stroke. He remained hospitalized until his death on December 24, 1995.

REFERENCES: Howard L. Boorman and Richard C. Howard, eds., *Biographical Dictionary of Republican China*, vol. 3 (New York, 1970), 40–41; Yan qian zongtong Jiagan xiansheng aisi lu bianzuan xiaozu bianji [The Compilation Committee for Compiling the Record to Commemorate Former President Mr. Yan Jiagan], *Yen qian zongtong Jiagan xiansheng aisi lu* [A Record Commemorating Former President Mr. Yan Jiagan] (Taibei, 1994).

RAMON H. MYERS

**YAN XISHAN** (October 8, 1883–May 24, 1960). Provincial ruler of Shanxi and one of the most durable warlords in the Republican era.

Born to a wealthy family in Shanxi, Yan Xishan attended a military academy in his home province and then went to Japan for advanced military studies and training in 1904. The following year he joined **Sun Yat-sen's**

Revolutionary Alliance in Japan and also became a member of the anti-Manchu military group, the "Dare-to-Die Corps." Returning to China in 1909, Yan served in the Shanxi army but continued to work secretly for the revolutionary cause.

When the Revolution of 1911 broke out, Yan led his troops in an uprising in Taiyuan and was later appointed governor of Shanxi by President **Yuan Shikai**. During the early years of the Republic, he managed to survive both the dictatorship of Yuan Shikai and, after Yuan's demise, the power struggle among various military factions. While participating occasionally in the warlord wars, Yan took as his priority the security and stability of his provincial base. He also experimented in Shanxi with a new grassroots-level bureaucracy, known as the "village system" (*cunzhi*), with some success. He gradually emerged as a leading warlord in North China.

In 1927, the Northern Expeditionary Army commanded by **Jiang Jieshi** swept from South China into the Yangzi valley in an effort to reunify the country by force. Facing this threat, Yan decided to join the winning side. Together with the Northwestern warlord **Feng Yuxiang**, he declared support for Jiang's Nationalist Party and then joined forces with Jiang in completing the Northern Expedition. In return, Jiang not only recognized Yan's rule in Shanxi but also allowed him to expand his domain into the neighboring province of Hebei. In the years that followed, several remaining warlords revolted against Jiang's new national government in Nanjing. Yan demanded greater autonomy for himself in North China from Jiang in exchange for his neutrality in these conflicts. In 1930, however, fearing that Jiang might soon move against him, Yan collaborated with Feng Yuxiang and others in a major rebellion against Nanjing. They established a rival government in Beiping (Beijing), with Yan as its leader, but it was soon defeated by Jiang. Yan announced his "retirement" and took refuge in the Japanese-controlled Dairen.

On the eve of the Manchurian Incident in 1931, Yan returned to Shanxi and reached a rapprochement with Jiang. He resumed control over the province and promulgated a "Ten-Year Plan" for its reconstruction. For the next few years Yan developed industries and the infrastructure in Shanxi, relying largely on government monopolies for the funding of these projects. As a result of his efforts, the social-economic conditions in Shanxi improved, and the province came to be known as a "model province" in Nationalist China.

In 1936 the insurgent Chinese Communist Party, having established its base in neighboring Shaanxi, extended its influence into Yan's province. In an attempt to control the Communists, Yan formed an "anti-Japanese alliance" with them and organized their forces into his "New Army." Shortly thereafter the Sino-Japanese War began and eastern Shanxi fell to the invading Japanese. Yan retreated to the western part of the province and was appointed by Jiang Jieshi as commander of the Second War Zone. In 1939, alarmed by the growing external and internal threats to his power, Yan purged the Communists from his "new army" and negotiated a secret truce with the Japanese. He concluded another peace agreement with the Japanese in 1941, and for the remainder of the war shrewdly stayed out of the Sino-Japanese conflict.

After the war, Yan supported Jiang's government in its Civil War against the Communists. In March 1949, a month before the Communist forces captured Shanxi, Yan fled to Nanjing. In June he was appointed as Premier of the Nationalist government, which was then in the process of retreating to Guangzhou. His premiership did not last long. By the end of that year Yan was removed from office as the Communists took the entire Chinese mainland. He followed Jiang to their island refuge of Taiwan and spent his last years there in semiretirement.

REFERENCES: Donald G. Gillin, *Warlord: Yen Hsi-shan in Shansi Province, 1911–1949* (Princeton, NJ, 1967); James E. Sheridan, *China in Disintegration: The Republican Era in Chinese History, 1912–1949* (New York, 1975); Lyman P. Van Slyke, *Enemies and Friends: The United Front in Chinese Communist History* (Stanford, CA, 1967).

WANG KE-WEN

**YANG SHANGKUN** (1907–September 1998). Member of the famed Twenty-Eight Bolsheviks; took part in the Long March; president of People's Republic of China (1988–1993).

Yang Shangkun was born in 1907 in Sichuan of a large and well-to-do family. He attended a middle school in Chongqing where, under the influence of a cousin, he participated in underground activities for the Chinese Communist Party (CCP). In 1945 Yang went to Shanghai and joined in the Party's student activities. Then he proceeded to Moscow in 1930 and enrolled in the **Sun Yat-sen** University for working Chinese, founded in a joint venture between Russian Soviet Communists and Chinese Socialist revolutionaries, led by **Wang Ming**. Of the more than 1,000 students studying or receiving revolutionary training in Moscow, Yang was one of the famed Chinese Twenty-Eight Bolsheviks who graduated from the Sun Yat-sen University. It was in 1925 when **Deng Xiaoping** left France and moved to Moscow that the two became friends; and Yang, in later years, became one of Deng's closest advisers.

Yang Shangkun returned to China in 1931 and plunged immediately into Party affairs, serving variously as propaganda chief for the guerrilla armies and as head of the Party's training school. In 1934–1935, Yang took part in the Long March by supporting **Mao Zedong** in the power struggle at the historic enlarged Politburo meeting at Zunyi—the meeting which ushered in Mao's rise as the Party leader and marked the gradual demise of influence by Moscow-oriented Stalinist Chinese Communists. However, Yang had Mao's trust, so that in 1941 he served as secretary for the Party's central office and sat on the military affairs committee headed by Mao. For some time thereafter Yang Shangkun served as Mao's secretary for military affairs until the mid-1950s. From 1955 to 1965 Yang was elected to the Party's Central Committee. For many years he was also director of the Central Committee's general office, responsible for security and living arrangements for the top Party leaders.

Yang was purged during the Cultural Revolution and lost all of his Party positions. He spent time, as did many other prominent leaders, in the countryside doing manual labor. He was rehabilitated in 1978 together with a host of other veteran Party leaders as Deng Xiaoping returned to power. In 1981 Yang Shangkun was designated by Deng Xiaoping to serve as secretary for the Military Affairs Committee (MAC), of which Deng was chairman. Two years later Yang was elected to the Politburo and held the vice-chairmanship of the powerful Military Affairs Committee under Deng.

In 1988 Yang was elected president of the People's Republic of China (PRC) while concurrently holding the position of vice-chairman of the Military Affairs Committee. Along with Deng, he was awarded the rank of general for the military. During the 1989 student demonstration at Tiananmen, on May 19, Yang Shangkun, as the Republic's president, along with **Li Peng**, the premier, declared martial law. On June 2, Deng Xiaoping and Yang Shangkun ordered the troops to move into the square to forcefully terminate the students' demonstration.

In the aftermath of Tiananmen, one of the most significant personnel changes in the military was Deng's resignation from his long-held chairmanship of the powerful MAC. His successor to that post, tantamount to commander-in-chief for the entire armed forces, was not Yang Shangkun, who reportedly coveted the position, but the new Party general secretary, **Jiang Zemin**, who up until then had had hardly any experience with the military. However, the real power of the military rested with Yang Shangkun, who became the first vice-chairman of the MAC. In addition, Yang's brother, Yang Baibing, became permanent general secretary of the MAC. There were some complaints inside and outside the military that the Yangs had made the military their "family enterprise."

Continued discontent within the military motivated some officers from the Shenyang, Beijing, and Nanjing Military regions to produce a secret anti–Yang Shangkun circular. They accused Yang of refusing to support Jiang Zemin as party chief and of nepotism by appointing his brother as general secretary of the MAC, while concurrently serving as director of the military's General Political Department. The resentment against increasing domination and control of the military by the Yang brothers reached its height when some 20 senior retired generals confronted Jiang Zemin, the Party chief, on the eve of the August 1, 1990 Army Day to register their complaints and concerns.

Presumably, the removal of the Yang brothers from positions of power at the 1992 Party Congress assuaged the resentment against them within the military command. This was followed by a massive purge of nearly half the generals who were considered to be followers of the Yang brothers. This move was considered essential to ensure Deng's hand-picked successors' survival in case of a possible military coup in future power contests.

In March 1993, Yang Shangkun was replaced by Jiang Zemin as the Republic's president. He died in September 1998 at the age of ninety-one as the last of the Twenty-Eight Chinese Bolsheviks.

REFERENCES: Li Kuocheng, *CCP's Top Leadership Group* (Hong Kong, 1990, in Chinese), 377–385; James C.F. Wang, *Contemporary Chinese Politics*, 6th ed. (Upper Saddle River, NJ, 1999).

JAMES C.F. WANG

**YANG XIUQING** (original name Silung, 1820?–September 2, 1856). One of the political and military leaders of the Taiping Revolutionary movement.

Yang Xiuqing was born to a poor peasant family in the Guiping district of Guangxi around 1820. Both of his parents were deceased by the time he had reached the age of nine. Thereafter, he was raised by a paternal uncle whose family he assisted in farming and making charcoal. Yang had no opportunity for education and could read and write only a few simple characters. Nevertheless, his native intelligence and resourcefulness enabled him to rise to a position of leadership among the farmers and workers of the Guiping district. In 1846, he met **Hong Xiuquan** and **Feng Yunshan** who convinced him to join the God Worshippers, a Christian revolutionary society headed by Hong. His kinsmen in the Guiping district followed Yang into the God Worshippers, greatly improving the status of the organization among local people.

In early 1848, while Feng was imprisoned and Hong was absent from Guiping seeking his release, Yang claimed that he had been possessed by God, empowered to speak God's will, and to transfer the sicknesses of others to his own body. Following the return of Hong and Feng to Guiping, in the summer of 1849, they formed a blood brotherhood of seven including Jesus Christ, themselves, Yang, **Xiao Chaogui**, Wei Changhui, and **Shi Dakai**, pledging themselves to overthrow the Manchus and establish a Christian kingdom.

In May 1850, Yang claimed to have been stricken deaf and dumb. His affliction seriously disrupted the God Worshippers' mobilization of forces. A few months later when Yang claimed to have been miraculously cured by divine intervention, his status within the leadership of the society was greatly enhanced. In December of that year, he dispatched a force from the Guiping district to the adjoining Pingnan district to rescue Hong and Feng who had been held there by government forces.

Full-scale military action by the God Worshippers began in early 1851 at Jintian in the Guiping district following attacks by government forces against village strongholds of the God Worshippers. After the God Worshippers' initial victory at Jintian, Hong disclosed his dynastic intentions, proclaiming the Taiping Tianguo (Heavenly Kingdom of Great Peace) and placing Yang in command of the central Taiping army. The Taiping forces advanced westward from Jintian and then reversed course to the northeast taking the walled city of Yongan (present-day Mengshan). At Yongan, Hong organized the Taiping government and appointed the members of his court. Yang was named Central King, one of five directly subordinate to Hong, the Heavenly King. An imperial army of 30,000 besieged Yongan during the winter of 1851–1852 but the Taipings managed to slip through the imperial encirclement on April 5, 1852. They headed north toward Guilin pursued and attacked by government forces en route. Unable to force entry to Guilin, in late May the Taipings raised their siege of the city and headed north again. After a bitter battle at Quanzhou they withdrew eastward into Hunan occupying Daozhou (present-day Daoxian) in preparation for a strike northward at the provincial capital Changsha. In the summer of 1852, while at Daozhou, Yang and Xiao Chaogui issued a call to the entire nation to rise up against Manchu impotence and ineptitude to establish a God-fearing kingdom of peace and prosperity.

The Taiping attempt to subdue Changsha in the late summer of 1852 resulted in the death of Xiao Chaogui opening the way for Yang to assert greater authority. In November, however, the Taipings abandoned their campaign to take Changsha and marched north into the Yangzi valley. Advancing eastward they captured Nanjing, capital of the Liangjiang Viceroyalty, in late March 1853. There, Yang exhorted the populace to submit to God and to Hong, to defend the new kingdom, and to enjoy its benefits. Yang was named prime minister of the Taiping kingdom at Nanjing, which became its capital.

Yang directed the new government as Hong became more and more disposed to remain secluded in his palace. The numerous pronouncements on taxation, security, social reforms, the calendar and the like that defined the nature of the Taiping regime were the work of Yang. He launched two major military campaigns from Nanjing: a thrust northward to capture Beijing faltered in the suburbs of Tianjin late in 1853. Undermanned and poorly supplied, this force suffered a disastrous defeat in Shandong in late spring 1855. A westward offensive designed to take the principal Yangzi River ports upstream from Nanjing and occupy the surrounding agricultural areas, also foundered when it encountered the determined opposition of **Zeng Guofan**'s Hunan army. Nevertheless, in 1856, the Taipings held the principal river ports along a 300-mile stretch from Wuchang in the west to Jinjiang in the east. In that year, Yang directed the defense of Nanjing against a massive onslaught by imperial forces. Yang's strategy succeeded in dispersing the enemy and inflicting a crushing defeat that freed Nanjing from the threat of further attack by imperial forces. His ambition and arrogance buoyed by military success, Yang attempted to usurp Hong's royal prerogatives. Hong retaliated by inducing Yang's fellow king Wei Changhui, who was bitterly resentful of Yang's lust for power, to assassinate him. The strife that ensued among the Taiping leaders resulted in a purge that brought the movement to the brink of extinction. Much of the responsibility for these events must be laid at the feet of the brilliant but overly ambitious Yang Xiuqing.

REFERENCES: Cai Guanluo, ed., *Qingdai qibai mingren zhuan* [Biographies of Seven Hundred Famous People of the Qing Period], vol. 3 (Beijing, 1984), 1863–1868; Arthur W. Hummel, ed., *Eminent Chinese of the Ch'ing Period* (Washington, DC, 1943), 1886–1888; Yu-wen Jen, *The Taiping Revolutionary Movement* (New Haven, CT, 1973).

THOMAS L. KENNEDY

**YAO WENYUAN** (1931–    ). Literary critic and essayist; member of the Politburo of the Chinese Communist Party; one of the Gang of Four.

A native of Chuji County, Zhejiang province, Yao Wenyuan is the son of the Leftist writer Yao Pengzi. He joined the Chinese Communist Party (CCP) while attending middle school in Shanghai in 1948. After the Communist takeover of the city, he became a resident correspondent for the *Literary Gazette*, the official publication of the Chinese Writer's Union, and began a career that two decades later was to make him one of the most powerful people in Chinese cultural and literary circles.

During the CCP's 1955 campaign to denounce the prominent Left-wing writer Hu Feng, Yao emerged as a representative of a new breed of young and fierce Party polemicists and literary critics. Over the next few years, his relentless attacks on allegedly bourgeois, revisionist, or decadent writers and works of literature appeared frequently in Shanghai newspapers like the *Wenhui Bao* and *Liberation Daily* as well as in major national literary journals. By March 1957, he had attracted the attention of **Mao Zedong**, who found his essays "quite convincing."

In the early 1960s, Yao continued to publish in the fields of literary criticism, theory, and aesthetics. Many of the ideas he developed in his writings at this time later became cornerstones of Cultural Revolutionary literary orthodoxy. Around 1963, together with **Zhang Chunqiao**, he became close to Mao Zedong's wife **Jiang Qing**, who was attempting to reform traditional Beijing opera, using Shanghai as her base. With Jiang as his patron, Yao took part in some of the preparations for what eventually was to become the Cultural Revolution. On November 10, 1965, the publication of his article, "On the New Historical Play 'Hai Rui's Dismissal from Office' " in the *Wenhui Bao* triggered off a series of events that eventually led to the downfall of Beijing's mayor Peng Zhen.

In May 1966, Yao was made a member of the CCP Politburo's Central Cultural Revolution Group, of which Jiang Qing and Zhang Chunqiao were deputy heads. In February 1967, he became vice-chairman of the Shanghai

Revolutionary Committee. At the National Day celebrations in Beijing in 1968, he ranked number eight among the Party and government leaders present. With the backing of Mao Zedong, he soon became one of the Party center's chief ideological watchdogs, and it was primarily in his capacities as censor and ghostwriter for the CCP Central Committee that he was to exercise power over the following years.

In April 1969, the Ninth CCP Central Committee elected him onto its Politburo. He was reelected to this position in August 1973, when the Tenth CCP Central Committee held its first plenary session. On March 1, 1975, the *People's Daily* published his highly significant article, "On the Social Base of **Lin Biao**'s Anti-Party Clique," in which he in the ideological jargon of the time explained the correctness of the politics pursued by the CCP since the beginning of the Cultural Revolution. In the spring of 1976, together with Jiang Qing and Zhang Chunqiao, he was largely responsible for the orchestration of a nationwide media-campaign to disgrace **Deng Xiaoping**. He also attempted to use his influence over the media to mobilize public opinion against a departure from Cultural Revolution policies and practices after the death of Mao Zedong.

On October 6, 1976, four weeks after Mao's death, Yao was arrested at the orders of a coalition of senior government and military leaders opposed to the Cultural Revolution. Together with Jiang Qing, Zhang Chunqiao, and **Wang Hongwen** (known collectively as the Gang of Four), he was accused of counterrevolutionary crimes and of having attempted to usurp state power. The Party press he had once controlled now heaped abuse on him and compared him to the Nazi Propaganda Minister Joseph Goebbels. On January 23, 1981, at a major trial in Beijing, he was sentenced to 20 years in prison. In the late 1990s, rumor had it that he was living in freedom in Shanghai.

REFERENCES: Lars Ragvald, *Yao Wenyuan as a Literary Critic and Theorist: The Emergence of Chinese Zhdanovism* (Stockholm, 1978); Ye Yonglie, *Yao Wenyuan zhuan* [Biography of Yao Wenyuan] (Changchun, 1993).

MICHAEL L. SCHOENHALS


**YE JIANYING** (1897–October 1986). A top-ranking military cadre of the Chinese Communist Party; marshal of the People's Liberation Army.

Ye Jianying's long military-political career in the Chinese revolution began shortly after his graduation from the Yunnan Military School in 1920 when he returned to his home province of Guangdong to join campaigns to oust Guangxi warlords from Guangdong. Ye joined the Guomindang (GMD, or, the Nationalist Party) in 1921, and for the next few years was active in **Sun Yat-sen**'s entourage as Sun put in place the grand scheme of a Northern Expedition against the warlord system. Ye played an important military role in protecting Sun during **Chen Jiongming**'s Guangzhou rebellion against Sun in 1922 and in the 1924–1925 campaign against Chen.

Meanwhile, he had a hand in organizing the Huangpu (Whampoa) Military Academy in 1924 and became one of its chief instructors. When the Northern Expedition got underway in July 1926, Ye served as the chief-of-staff of the First Army of the National Revolutionary Army (NRA) and later commanded its Second Division in garrisoning Jian, Jiangxi province.

In April 1927, **Jiang Jieshi** (Chiang Kai-shek), who had assumed control of the NRA after Sun's death in 1925, took drastic steps to purge the ranks of the GMD of Communists who had come into the GMD under the auspices of a GMD–CCP United Front in 1923. At this time, though not yet formally a member of the Chinese Communist Party (CCP), Ye issued an anti–Jiang bulletin and joined a number of Leftist officers under his command in plotting military insurrection against Jiang. When that failed, Ye relinquished his command in Jian and went to Wuhan, where the "national government" of the GMD Center led by **Wang Jingwei** appeared for the time being to offer some protection to the Communists. In Wuhan, Ye was appointed chief-of-staff of the Fourth Army, and he also joined the CCP. In August and December 1927, Ye took part in the unsuccessful Nanchang and Guangzhou uprisings of the Communist forces. In the wake of these failures, and with Wang Jingwei turning against the Communists to achieve accommodation with Jiang's Nanjing regime, many Communist leaders left China for the Soviet Union, while others were forced underground, to re-emerge in guerrilla units in different parts of China. In late 1928 Ye went to Moscow and "enrolled" in the University of the Toilers of the East. In 1930, he secretly returned to Shanghai, and then went to Jiangxi in 1931.

When the Central Soviet Revolutionary Military Committee was established on November 15, 1931, Ye became its chief-of-staff and set about organizing the Central Soviet Red Army in various campaigns in the Jiangxi region. In late 1932, he took over from Liu Bocheng as head and political commissar of the Red Army school. Under his leadership, the ranks of cadets in the Red Army school expanded and provided leadership for CCP guerrilla forces against Jiang Jieshi's "encirclement and extermination campaigns." In May 1933, Ye also became chief-of-staff of the First Front Army (under **Zhu De**'s command). Later the same year he was named commander of the Fujian-Jiangxi Military Region, and took the fighting to Fujian province. In January 1934, Ye was elected to the Central Executive Committee of the Chinese Soviet Republic.

During the Long March of the CCP forces, which commenced in October 1934, Ye played an important political role as well as his usual military role as chief-of-staff of the Military Committee of the CC of the CCP. At the Zunyi Conference in January, the Lianghekou Conference in June, and the critical Maoergai Conference in August 1935, Ye staunchly supported **Mao Zedong**'s strategic leadership against **Zhang Guotao**, and pushed for the northward thrust of the CCP forces into Northern Shaanxi. After the Communist Long March forces, joined by the Fifteenth Red Army group, occupied Northern Shaanxi in late 1935, Ye became a member of the newly formed Northwest Revolutionary Military Committee of the Chinese Worker–Peasant Red Army and chief-of-staff of the reinstated First Front Army. In December 1935, the CCP Central Committee Politburo called for the formation of a "national United Front" against Japan, whose forces had begun their invasion of China in 1931. The Politburo also instructed that the Red Army make plans to cross the Yellow River into Western Shanxi province. Ye was put in charge of this maneuver. At the time, Shanxi was controlled by the Northeast Army of **Zhang Xueliang** and Yang Hucheng, two GMD generals who disagreed with Jiang Jieshi's strategy of ceding territory, especially in Northeast China, to Japan while focusing the force of the GMD military on exterminating the Communists. After a secret meeting with Zhang in April 1936, the CCP Politburo appointed Ye to take the lead in forging cooperative relations with Zhang's Northeast Army. In September, Ye was sent to Xi'an (Zhang's headquarters) to serve as a liaison between the Red Army and Zhang. In this capacity, Ye played an important political part in paving the way for the Xi'an incident in December 1936 and the second CCP–GMD United Front which followed.

At the beginning of China's war against Japan, Ye, as chief-of-staff of the Communist Eighth Route Army, mainly served as chief liaison officer between the Communists and the GMD. He thus had to stay with Jiang Jieshi's government as it retreated in the face of the Japanese onslaught and relocated in various places—Nanjing, Wuhan, Changsha, and, eventually, Chongqing in 1939. In Chongqing from June 1939 onward, Ye served under **Zhou Enlai** in the Communist liaison mission, continuing to promote the United Front strategy and defend the Communist forces' role in the war against Japan. After the position of the liaison office became increasingly untenable in the wake of the "Southern Anhui" in January 1941, Ye was recalled to Yan'an where he resumed active staff duty as chief-of-staff of the Eighth Route Army. For the remainder of the war against Japan, he was engaged in deploying Communist fighting forces in Northern China. He was elected to the Central Committee at the CCP's Seventh Congress in 1945, and as a delegate to the Chinese People's Political Consultative Conference (CPPCC) held in Chongqing in January 1946, Ye played an important role in negotiating the short-lived cease-fire between the CCP and the GMD. During the Third Revolutionary Civil War, which broke out in late 1946, Ye served as deputy chief-of-staff of the People's Liberation Army (PLA) in northern China.

When Beijing fell to Communist forces in early 1949, Ye took charge of the military command of that northern capital and the subsequent peace negotiations with acting Nationalist President **Li Zongren** and his delegates, which broke down in September of that year. Then, as the military situation in southern China rapidly unfolded, Ye returned to his home province of Guangdong to assume the command of the PLA'S Guangdong Military Region. At the founding of the People's Republic of China (PRC) in October he held various military-political positions that made him virtually the most powerful CCP cadre in southern China. He presided over the liberation of Guangdong and Guangxi in October 1949, the takeover of Hainan Island in early 1950, and the subsequent mopping up of local militia resistance and remnants of GMD forces in the southern provinces. In May 1951, the Central Committee of the CCP established the South China Military Region with Ye as its commander. He was also the ranking vice-chairman of the Military Administrative Committee of the Central-South Region, one of the six major regions that made up China's region-based government's administrative structure at the time under the provisions of the Common Program. Ye remained in Guangdong until 1954, when the PRC Constitution came into existence and with it an overhauling of the governmental administrative structure of the country and the abolishing of the regional committees. During these years he had broad oversight for governance of Guangdong, and, in particular, supervised the processes of land reform and urban reconstruction in south China as a whole. In October 1954, Ye was transferred to Beijing and began the next phase of his military-political career, presiding over the training and modernization of the PLA as a new national-defense force. One of Ye's main achievements of this period was the founding of the PLA Military Science Academy in 1958 for which he served as president until 1972. Meanwhile he held high-ranking positions in the CCP, in the PLA structure, and in the National People's Congress (NPC). He was awarded various top-level military decorations and named one of the PLA's ten marshals in 1955.

In an early phase of the Cultural Revolution, Ye played an important role as head of the "work group" that investigated the case of PLA chief-of-staff Luo Ruiqing, and which in April 1966, recommended Luo's dismissal. As the Red Guard movement in 1966 rapidly overstepped what had appeared to be understood, boundaries of the Cultural Revolution as adopted by the Eleventh Plenum of the Eighth CC, as the PLA began to be dragged into the Cultural Revolution, and particularly as Mao Zedong himself, who had instigated the Cultural Revolution, appeared to be poised to intervene to curtail the violence and the devastating impact of the Red Guard movement on crucial state and military institutions, Ye joined a number of senior officials in raising questions about the direction and the continued radicalization of the Cultural Revolution. This sequence of events in 1967, to be labeled by the radicals as a "February Reversal of the Cultural Revolution," triggered a political firestorm in March which rendered many senior cadres, including Ye, vulnerable even after the height of the Red Guard movement had passed. Although Ye survived (largely through the protection of Premier Zhou Enlai) and was even elected to the Politburo in 1969 at the Ninth CCP Congress, he was politically quiet from 1967 until 1971.

Ye's return to a role at center stage of late–Cultural Revolution Chinese politics was played out in the context of the **Lin Biao** affair, first in investigating the activities of Lin's associate, **Chen Boda,** in late 1970 and early 1971, and then, after Lin Biao's defection and death, as head of a reorganized Military Affairs Committee (MAC) looking into and condemning Lin's manipulation of military units for his own aggrandizement. In these roles, he emerged as a Mao loyalist (but an antiradical one) in post–Cultural Revolution politics, aligned with Premier Zhou Enlai and other senior CCP cadres who had managed to survive the violent upheaval of the preceding ten years. Nonetheless, in the years ahead, in the context of the power struggle over the succession of Mao and Zhou, one major test remained on the horizon for Ye. With Zhou's health failing in 1975, Deng Xiaoping was put in charge of running the Chinese government, ostensibly with Mao's blessing. Meanwhile, equally with Mao's approval, the so-called Gang of Four, that is, the leaders of the radical faction, attacked and undermined the leadership and policies of Deng, whom Ye, among others, supported. When Deng was brought down in late 1975, Ye was implicated. After Zhou Enlai's death in January 1976, and with Mao's own health rapidly failing, the Gang of Four launched an attack on Zhou's legacy, but they also criticized **Hua Guofeng,** whom Mao had selected to succeed Zhou as premier.

In the final months of Mao's life, all political factions were preparing for the inevitable showdown that was to come. At this critical juncture, because of his senior standing in the CCP and with his influence over the PLA, Ye emerged as the key factor in a counterforce to the Gang of Four, who had apparently gone as far as to put the Shanghai militia on readiness for the impending struggle. Upon Mao's demise on September 9, 1976, the Gang of Four immediately pressed the issue of their claim to succeeding Mao at Politburo meetings on September 19 and 29, at which they sought to exclude Ye. The action of Mao Yuanxin in calling up an armored division of troops to Beijing on October 2 forced Ye into rapid and decisive action. Ye countermanded the troop maneuver and consulted with Hua Guofeng to settle the issue with the Gang of Four immediately. With China on the verge of being plunged into civil war, Ye, **Li Xiannian,** and Hua held a Politburo meeting on October 5, 1976 which excluded the Gang of Four and its supporters and issued the orders that resulted in the arrest of the Gang the following day. After the purge of the Gang of Four, Ye threw his support to Hua who became chairman of the Party and of the MAC in addition to being the premier. In his short tenure at the helm of Chinese politics, Hua not only displayed a stubborn rigidity in adhering to Mao Zedong Thought and to a continued legitimation of the Cultural Revolution, but was also confronted by a rising tide of sentiment within the CCP and in the country for Deng Xiaoping's return to office and leadership. Although somewhat ambivalent about Deng's return himself, Ye was certainly aware of its inevitability. As Deng became reinstated in his leadership positions in July 1977 at the Third Plenum of the Tenth CC, and in the struggle for power between Deng and Hua in the year and a half that followed, Ye, though publicly loyal to Hua, was rather noncommittal in reality and appeared to have played a role in persuading Hua to agree to readmitting Deng to the leadership. After Hua was in effect removed from his high office at the end of 1980, Ye's role as a power broker in the post–Mao era came to an end. At the June 1981 Sixth Plenum of the Eleventh CC, at which Hua was formally demoted, Ye was absent but sent a letter to announce his agreement with the critique of Hua and the change in leadership. Thereafter Ye performed nominal public duties as senior vice-chairman of the CCP. He resigned from his position and titles in 1984 and died in October 1986.

Ye's leadership role in China, and especially in the PRC after 1949, exemplified the manner in which political outcomes can be and are shaped by the balance of power among factions within the military leadership and command structure. Ideologically, Ye had been stalwart in maintaining a moderate position, but he was never a significant leader in any major ideological trend or initiative; rather, he had served to maintain political and ideological balance within the system by lending support through the considerable weight of his influence in the military, at critical moments when needed, to the ideological center.

REFERENCES: Wolfgang Bartke, *Who's Who in the People's Republic of China* (Armonk, NY, 1981), 474–475; Song Shilun, *Ye Jianying zhuanlue* [A Biography of Ye Jianying] (Beijing, 1987); *Zhonggong renminglu* [Biographies of Chinese Communists] (Taibei, 1978), 815–817.

JOHN KONG-CHEONG LEUNG


**YEN CHIA-KAN.** *See* YAN JIAGAN.


**YUAN SHIKAI** (September 16, 1859–June 6, 1916). Statesman and controversial strongman of Chinese politics, 1895–1916.

The son of a scholar-elite family from Honan province (Xiangzheng xian), Yuan Shikai was a man of action, not a scholar. Although he never received a high degree and bureaucratic rank, he became a top Qing official who surrounded himself with scholars and practical men as advisers. He first rose to prominence as a military attaché to Li **Hongzhang** when he was trying to handle the precarious situation in Korea between 1885 and 1894. In the wake of the first Sino-Japanese War of 1894–1895, while his patron was in disgrace, Yuan pioneered military reforms in creating a small model army in the suburbs of Beijing under the eye of the **Empress Dowager Cixi** and her consort, Ronglu. Yuan was also in touch with the more radical reform movement led by **Kang Youwei** and **Liang Qichao**. During the One Hundred Day crisis of the summer of 1898, Yuan was forced to choose sides. Ever the practical politician, he chose to support the Empress Dowager and Ronglu, thus dooming Kang-Liang and **Emperor Guangxu**. As a reward Yuan was made governor of the important province of Shandong and his career as a high level official was launched.

The next political crisis from which Yuan derived further political benefit was the Boxer Rebellion of 1900–1901. He played a critical role as governor of the province where the peasant rebellion originated. Boxers were butchering foreign missionaries. Under pressure from the German colonialists at Qingdao and elsewhere, Yuan suppressed the rebellion locally and drove the Boxers into neighboring Zhili province where they ultimately, with the support of Ronglu and others, laid seige to the legations in Beijing. The powers reacted with the allied expedition and the Empress Dowager was driven into internal exile to the northwest until 1902. Yuan now emerged as the strong man of the last decade of the dynasty. As governor general of Zhili province and a major figure at court, he wielded more power than any other Chinese official had during the Qing dynasty. Surrounding himself with the most able scholar-officials of the period, like Xu Shichang or Duan Qirui, he led a broad reform movement at both the central government and the provincial level. His most lasting achievements included the creation of the Beiyang army of 60,000 well-trained and equipped soldiers as well as educational reform measures that resulted in the establishment of most of China's major institutions of higher education, as well as women's education, sending of students abroad on a massive scale, and abolition (in 1905) of the examination system. His New Policy or *Xinzheng* reforms are receiving increased attention today as scholars trace the origins of modern police, prison, health care, legal and constitutional reforms.

As the Bismarck of his era, Yuan wielded considerable power domestically and handled most of the delicate negotiations with foreign powers internationally. He was popular with the foreign community in Shanghai and Beijing, in part because he hired a whole retinue of foreign advisers. The jealousies of the Manchu princes brought about his temporary downfall after the death of the Empress Dowager in late 1908. At this point, Yuan shrewdly waited out developments, which included increasing pressure on the dynasty from provincial assemblies as well as avowed revolutionaries like **Sun Yat-sen**. When the dynasty failed to quell a mutiny-rebellion in late 1911, Yuan Shikai dictated the terms for his return to politics and use of the Beiyang army. As the dynasty's last prime minister, he negotiated its bloodless pensioning off as well as his own elevation to the presidency of a new Republic of China with its capital Beijing.

Yuan Shikai's presidency of the Republic should have crowned his career and empowered him to push an institutional modernization agenda forward. Instead it was the most unsatisfying period of his life, ending in tragedy and ridicule. Today to most Chinese, Yuan Shikai is remembered as the petty dictator and proto-warlord who betrayed the Republic of China and the democratic ideals of Sun Yat-sen in order to make himself the emperor-founder of a new dynasty. At the time in the West he was hailed as a reformer and strong man whom China needed to implement economic and social reforms as well as to meet international commitments—financial and otherwise. Reality lies somewhere in between. Yuan tried to centralize and modernize through the exercise of state power. At the same time he had little interest in fostering democracy, going out of his way in 1913–1914 to suppress the press and subvert the fledgling parliament. In the end he was undone by the pressure of the Japanese Twenty-One demands and a growing domestic resistance by elites to his heavy-handed attempts at the exercise of greater centralized controls. By 1916, Yuan had lost power, deserted by his own Beiyang army commanders under the leadership of Duan Qirui and Cai E, and forced out of office.

Yuan died in disgrace in June 1916, with his reputation in tatters. For the rest of the century he has been remembered as the infamous dictator and father of warlords who sold out the 1911 revolution. Only recently has there been renewed interest by Chinese and foreign historians in Yuan's broad-ranging institutional reform record as scholars begin to see in him the origins of later figures, like **Deng Xiaoping**.

REFERENCES: Jerome Ch'en, *Yuan Shih-k'ai: Brutus Assumes the Purple* (Stanford, CA, 1972); Stephen R. MacKinnon, *Power and Politics in Late Imperial China: Yuan Shikai in Tianjin and Beijing* (Berkeley, CA, 1980); Ernest Young, *The Presidency of Yuan Shih-k'ai: Liberalism and Dictatorship in Early Republican China* (Ann Arbor, 1977). Li Zongyi, *Yuan Shikai zhuan* (Beijing, 1980), is the most balanced work in Chinese.

STEPHEN R. MACKINNON

# Z

**ZENG GUOFAN** (posthumous title Wenzheng, November 26, 1811–March 12, 1872). Imperial official; provincial governor general; commissioner for the suppression of the Taiping Rebellion.

Born into a prominent landlord family in the Xiangxiang district of Hunan, Zeng Guofan passed the highest level civil service examinations in 1838 and was awarded the degree of *jinshi*. He was subsequently inducted into the Hanlin Academy, the leading academic institution of imperial China. His career as an imperial and provincial official was shaped by his study of Confucian texts in preparation for the examinations. He exemplified the practicality of the neo-Confucian School of Statecraft, the moral rectitude of the orthodox Song School, and the rigorous literary style of the Tongzheng School. Zeng defended traditional civilization through innovations and introduction of military and economic features of Western civilization.

In 1853, at the behest of the imperial government, Zeng organized local defense forces in his home province Hunan into a provincial militia, known as the Hunan army. Locally financed and led by carefully selected Confucian gentry, the Hunan army was well-disciplined and highly effective, turning back the Western expeditionary force of the Taiping army in Hunan in 1854. During 1855–1856, the Hunan army encountered stiff resistance and suffered serious losses in naval and land battles with the Taipings in the central Yangzi valley. Zeng was surrounded by enemy forces in Jiangxi during much of this time. Shortly after reinforcements reached him in 1856, the Taiping leadership was crippled by a murderous power struggle affording Zeng the opportunity, once again, to take the offensive.

After returning to Hunan to mourn the death of his father, Zeng resumed command of the Hunan army in 1857 and began preparations to retake the Taiping stronghold at Anjing, a strategic Yangzi River port and capital of Anhui province. By the summer of 1859, the Hunan army had expelled the last Taipings from Jiangxi and Zeng moved his command post to Wuchang from where he would launch an attack on Anjing.

In 1860, preparing to strike at Anjing he relocated his headquarters at Qimen in southern Anhui. There he was bottled up by Taiping defenders of Anjing until 1861. Meanwhile, in 1860 the imperial forces attempting to retake the Taiping capital at Nanjing were dealt a crushing defeat by a Taiping army revitalized under new leadership. Desperate, the imperial court sought a new strategic plan and a new commander. On June 8, 1860, Zeng was named governor general of the Liangjiang provinces (Jiangxi, Jiangsu, and Anhui) and imperial commissioner for suppression of the Taipings with wide-ranging administrative, financial, and military authority.

In the summer of 1861, rebel forces were diverted from Qimen by Hunan army units led by **Zuo Zongtang**. Zeng broke through the Taiping investment, and resumed operations against the rebels in southern Anhui. On September 5, 1861, units of the Hunan army commanded by Zeng's brother Zeng Guoquan succeeded in recapturing Anjing. From there, the Hunan army began a drive to clear resistance from southern Anhui in preparation for an assault on the Taiping capital at Nanjing. Supported by the **Empress Dowager Cixi** who had seized power at court during the winter of 1861 and by **Prince Gong**, Zeng was also given control of military operations in Zhejiang.

In the east however, in August 1860, a revitalized Taiping army reached the suburbs of Shanghai where they were repulsed by British- and French-led forces protecting the foreign interests in that port city. The following year, Chinese merchants in Shanghai appealed to Zeng for defense reinforcements. Fearing the further growth of foreign-led military forces in the beleaguered city, Zeng responded to this request ordering one of his staff, **Li Hongzhang** to raise an army in Li's native province Anhui. In April 1862, Li's Anhui army was transported down the Yangzi to Shanghai in steamships rented from foreign firms. Li was named governor of Jiangsu province. By the end of 1862, the Anhui army operating in concert with foreign-led forces succeeded in driving the Taipings from the region surrounding Shanghai. Meanwhile, Zeng had arranged for Zuo Zongtang to direct military operations against the Taipings in Zhejiang. By April 1864, Zuo had cleared that province and retaken the capital at Hangzhou. Concurrently, forces led by Zeng Guoquan advancing from Anjing met determined resistance in the suburbs of Nanjing but finally entered the city in July 1864.

Though scattered resistance persisted until 1866, the fall of Nanjing marked the end of the real threat that the Taipings posed to the Manchu dynasty. Zeng, the architect of the victory, was named a marquis of the first class. In a demonstration of his loyalty to the throne, he demobilized more than 120,000 troops of the Hunan army.

Zeng had assumed his peace-time duties in Nanjing as governor general of the Liangjiang provinces only briefly when the court called upon him in June 1865 to lead the campaign against the Nian rebellion in north China. Zeng's strategy of strengthening village defenses brought little success. In early 1866, he recommended that Li Hongzhang take command of the struggle against the Nian and Zeng, in failing health, returned to Nanjing from where he kept Li's Anhui army supplied with modern arms and ammunition.

The recognition of the efficacy of Western ordnance and steamships and an ill-fated attempt to rent British steamships in 1863 persuaded Zeng to undertake domestic production. After several attempts, in 1865, he established the giant Jiangnan Arsenal and Shipyard in Shanghai, China's first modern machine industry.

In 1870 while serving as governor general of the metropolitan province of Zhili, Zeng was named to investigate the Tianjin massacre—a dispute with France resulting from antiforeign riots in the city of Tianjin. Zeng's conciliatory approach, designed to keep the dynasty from a costly war that he knew it could not win, earned him the disdain of later Chinese nationalists.

Summoned back to the Liangjiang governor general's post in 1871, Zeng together with Li Hongzhang launched the Chinese Educational Mission which sent carefully selected Chinese youth to the United States for extended periods of study. Though the educational aims of the mission were frustrated by conservative opposition and international disputes, like the establishment of the Jiangnan Arsenal, the Chinese Educational Mission represented Zeng's willingness to innovate and adapt features of Western civilization in defense of the dynasty.

Zeng died in March 1872 while serving as Liangjiang governor general. His political leadership is unique in nineteenth-century China. He employed the moral rectitude of a Confucian leader to mobilize his many followers in support of a traditional polity that was eventually transformed by the innovations and adaptations he struggled to introduce.

REFERENCES: Arthur W. Hummel, ed., *Eminent Chinese of the Ch'ing Period (1644–1912)* (Washington, DC, 1944), 771–775; Jonathan Porter, *Tseng Kuo-fan's Private Bureaucracy* (Berkeley, CA, 1972); Zhu Dongan, *Zeng Guofan Zhuan* [Biography of Zeng Guofan] (Chengdu, 1985).

THOMAS L. KENNEDY


**ZHANG CHUNQIAO** (1917–   ). Member of the standing committee of the Politburo of the Chinese Communist Party; vice-premier of the state council of the People's Republic of China; one of the Gang of Four.

The oldest son of a minor government official from Zhuye county, Shandong province, Zhang Chunqiao began a lifelong career in political journalism and propaganda by publishing patriotic essays in the *Shandong Nationalist Daily News* in 1932. After a brief spell of fascination with Fascism he turned to Leninism and joined the Chinese Communist Party (CCP) while working in literary circles in Shanghai in April 1936. After the outbreak of the Sino-Japanese War he moved to Yan'an and the Communist-controlled areas of China, where he remained active as a Party propagandist throughout most of the 1940s.

By 1950, Zhang had returned to Shanghai, and in the mid-1950s he became a member of the Shanghai CCP committee and director of its official newspaper, the *Liberation Daily*. At the beginning of the Great Leap Forward, he rose to national fame as an ideological apologist of egalitarianism. In October 1958, at the direct suggestion of **Mao Zedong**, the *People's Daily* reprinted his article "Eradicate the Ideology of Bourgeois Right" in which he advocated the wholesale abolition of so-called "material incentives" (i.e., various forms of remuneration according to labor), and the establishment of a quasimilitary egalitarian supply system (i.e., a form of remuneration according to "need") as the means whereby China would be able to achieve the rapid transition from Socialism to Communism. In April 1959, he was elected onto the standing committee of the Shanghai CCP committee.

In 1963, Zhang established a close working relationship with Mao's wife **Jiang Qing**, whose attempts to reform the traditional Beijing opera he actively backed as newly appointed director of the Shanghai CCP Propaganda Department. Together with **Yao Wenyuan**, by 1965 he had become part of a small group of confidants upon which Mao relied to launch the Cultural Revolution. In May 1966, he was appointed vice-director of the Central Cultural Revolution group under the CCP Politburo, and began to participate actively in high-level national politics.

In February 1967, Zhang became chairman of the Shanghai Revolutionary Committee, a new body created to supersede the old municipal Party committee. At the National Day celebrations in Beijing in 1968, he ranked number seven among the Party and government leaders present. In April 1969, the Ninth CCP Central Committee elected him into its Politburo. In the early 1970s, while becoming more and more preoccupied with national affairs, he succeeded in retaining considerable control over Shanghai, turning the city into an important power base for himself, Jiang Qing, Yao Wenyuan, and **Wang Hongwen**. In August 1973, at the first plenum of the Tenth CCP Central Committee, he was made a member of the standing committee of the CCP Politburo.

In January 1975, Zhang was appointed director of the People's Liberation Army (PLA) General Political Department and second-ranking vice-premier of the state council. In this latter capacity he delivered a report on the revision of the constitution of the People's Republic of China (PRC) to the

First Session of the Fourth People's Congress. In April 1975 he published "On Exercising All-Round Dictatorship over the Bourgeoisie," in which he presented an authoritative Maoist theoretical justification for the praxis of the Cultural Revolution, as well as reiterated some of his own ideas from the time of the Great Leap Forward about the need to eradicate the "bourgeois right."

On October 6, 1976, four weeks after the death of Mao Zedong, Zhang was arrested in what was essentially a palace coup by a coalition of senior government and military leaders opposed to the Cultural Revolution. Together with Jiang Qing, Yao Wenyuan, and Wang Hongwen (the so-called Gang of Four), he was accused of having attempted to use the Cultural Revolution to undermine China's socialist system in order to pave the way for the restoration of capitalism. When she was told of the fate that had befallen her son, Zhang's eighty-year-old mother committed suicide. On January 23, 1981, at a major trial, Zhang was branded a counterrevolutionary and sentenced to death with a two-year reprieve (a punishment subsequently commuted to life imprisonment). In 1999 he was allegedly still incarcerated in the maximum-security Qincheng Prison outside Beijing.

REFERENCE: Ye Yonglie, *Zhang Chunqiao zhuan* [Biography of Zhang Chunqiao] (Changchun, 1993).

MICHAEL L. SCHOENHALS

**ZHANG GUOTAO** (1897–December 3, 1979). Founding member of the Chinese Communist Party; early labor leader of the Communist movement; major political enemy of Mao Zedong in the 1930s.

Born into a landed Hakka family in Pingxiang county, Jiangxi in 1897, Zhang Guotao received classical training in his hometown and Western education in Nanchang. In 1916 he entered Peking University and was exposed to the New Culture Movement led by **Chen Duxiu**, who became his teacher and lifetime friend. Another mentor who influenced Zhang at the university was **Li Dazhao**, the head librarian.

During the May Fourth Movement of 1919, Zhang served as the director of the speech department of the Beijing Student Association and directed student agitators. Like his teachers, Chen and Li, Zhang in 1920 was impressed with the Bolshevik Revolution and Communism. In that autumn he joined Li's Communist nucleus in Beijing.

Zhang was present at the founding of the Chinese Communist Party (CCP) in Shanghai in 1921, and was elected a Central Committee (CC) member and director of organization. Afterward, he served as director of the China Trade Union Secretariat in charge of the labor movement. In late 1921 and early 1922, he represented the CCP at Comintern meetings in the Soviet Union where he interviewed Lenin. Elected again as a CC member at the Second CCP Congress in 1922, Zhang continued to direct trade union work. Having opposed the Comintern's policy of creating a Communist bloc within the Guomindang (GMD), however, Zhang's status declined and he was excluded from the reorganized Central Executive Committee at the Third CCP Congress in 1923.

Despite his earlier objections to the United Front, Zhang in January 1924 was elected an alternate member of the First GMD Congress' Central Executive Committee. At the Fourth CCP Congress in 1925, he became a member of the Central Bureau and director of the worker and peasant department. During the Northern Expedition in 1926, Zhang directed the Shanghai trade unions and later moved to Wuhan, the center of the Left-wing GMD government. In May 1927, he was elected a standing member of the new Politburo at the Fifth CCP Congress.

In the wake of the Nationalist purge of the CCP in the spring of 1927, Zhang was ordered by the Communist leaders at Wuhan and their Comintern superiors to halt the uprising at Nanchang. But he discovered that it could not be halted, and reluctantly directed the Nanchang Uprising on August 1, 1927, since then known as the founding day of the Red Army.

At the Sixth CCP Congress held in Moscow in 1928, Zhang was elected a Politburo member, and served as the CCP representative to the Comintern until he returned to China in early 1931. Zhang was assigned to direct the Hebei-Henan-Anhui Soviet and serve as political commissar of the Fourth Front Army. In November 1932, under pressure from the GMD suppression campaigns, Zhang and his men retreated to northern Sichuan and Shaanxi. By April 1935, without permission from the CCP Center, Zhang's group abandoned their base and moved to the Sichuan-Xikang border because of attacks from provincial forces. In June, his forces met **Mao Zedong**'s "Long Marchers" at Maogong, Sichuan.

By then Mao had captured the military leadership of the CCP when he became the head of a new three-person Central Military Council at the Zunyi Conference in January 1935. Zhang, however, remained a major leader because he controlled more troops than Mao at their reunion in mid-1935. Refusing to follow Mao's proposal of moving north to Shaanxi, Zhang and his men retreated to Xikang. In October 1935, he established a new "Party Center." In early 1936 however, the GMD troops dislodged these Communists from their base, and in June 1936 Zhang was forced to abolish his "Party Center." In July, he was appointed as secretary of the CCP Northwest Bureau. The remnants of his army reached northern Shaanxi in December 1936.

At the Enlarged Meeting of the Politburo in Yan'an in March 1937, Zhang was denounced for "splittism," "flightism," and "warlordism." In September 1937, he served as the nominal vice-chairman of the Shaanxi-Gansu-Ningxia border government. Anticipating his purge by Mao, Zhang escaped to GMD-controlled areas in early April 1938. On April 18, the Party Center expelled him from the CCP. Soon Zhang was engaged in anti-CCP activities when he worked as director of a "research office on special political issues" in Dai Li's Military Statistics. The agents and graduates from the office were ineffective in fighting the CCP, however.

During the Anti-Japanese War (1937–1945), Zhang served on the Second, Third, and Fourth People's Political Councils but took no active role in them. After the war, he served in 1946 as director of the Jiangxi regional office of the Chinese National Relief and Rehabilitation Administration. In November 1948, he escaped to Taiwan, and in 1949 he moved to Hong Kong. In 1968 he migrated to Toronto, Canada, and passed away there in 1979.

REFERENCES: Howard L. Boorman and Richard Howard, eds., *Biographical Dictionary of Republican China*, vol. 1 (New York, 1968), 77–82; Donald A. Jordan, "Chang Kuo-t'ao," in Edwin P.W. Leung, ed., *Historical Dictionary of Revolutionary China, 1839–1976* (New York, 1992), 35–37; Chang Kuo-t'ao, *The Rise of the Chinese Communist Party, 1921–1938*, 2 vols. (Lawrence, KS, 1970–1971); *Zhongguo gongchandang lishi dacidian: Zonglu, renwu* [A Large Dictionary of CCP History: General Discussion, Personalities] (Beijing, 1991), 343.

JOSEPH K.S. YICK

**ZHANG WENTIAN.** *See* LUO FU.

**ZHANG XUELIANG** (June 4, 1901–October 14, 2001). Leader of the Manchurian army and the Xi'an Incident.

Zhang Xueliang, popularly known as the Young Marshal, was born in Taishan, Liaoning, on June 4, 1901, but Haicheng also in Liaoning has been regarded as his native place. In the words of John Gunther, author of *Inside Asia*, "Young Marshal Chang Hsüeh-liang [Zhang Xueliang] is, I think, the most difficult, the most refractory, the most engaging human being, I have to write about" (p. 223). Some traces of his early life tend to confirm these personal traits as attributed to him by Gunther. He was a born prince, as by the time he reached adolescence, his father, Zhang Zuolin, had become the ruler of the three northeastern provinces (Manchuria). The young Zhang thought of going abroad to study medicine in America, but his father prepared him for a military career probably with the thought that he may succeed him someday.

After graduation from the Northeastern Military Institute, Zhang at the age of twenty was made commander of his father's guards brigade. From that time onward, he with the help of Guo Songling, his teacher at the Military Institute, had remarkable success in training troops and showed much prowess on the battlefield, particularly in the two wars between Zhang Zuolin and **Wu Peifu** (a northern warlord who was then dominating the Beijing government) in 1922 and 1924. Like his father, Zhang had charisma and was able to inspire the devotion of his subordinates, as well as the finesse to judge and control them (probably with the exception of Guo

Songling who staged a revolt against Zhang Zuolin in late 1925, which ended in failure).

With most of the Northeastern Army under his command, Zhang began to be called the Young Marshal, as his father was called the Old Marshal. Raised in the era of the great patriotism movement of May Fourth and dealing with the constant threat of the two great imperialists, Japan and Russia, the Young Marshal was extraordinarily patriotic. With much reluctance, he had to fight against the national Revolutionary Army during the Northern Expedition launched by **Jiang Jieshi** in July 1926. In the Yellow River battle around Zhengzhou in spring 1927, Zhang, with a superior force under his command, withdrew to the north bank of the river instead of fighting. Then he recommended to his father not to stay in North China to fight the revolutionary army as the Japanese wanted him to do, for to do so would only have benefited the Japanese.

When his father was assassinated by the Japanese on June 4, 1928, the Young Marshal seemed to be well prepared to succeed him. But his succession to his father was not without challenge. At one stroke, he eliminated his enemies, Yang Yuting and Chang Yinhuai, thereby making himself the undisputable leader in the northeast. Rejecting both inducement and pressure from Japan, he gave up his semiindependent status for the unification of China by joining the Nanjing government. On the other hand, he devoted himself to reconstructing the northeast: building railways, developing industries, and establishing private and public schools, especially expanding and improving the Northeastern University. He also drastically built up his air force and navy. All this Japan had viewed with alarm that apparently hastened its aggression against the northeast by launching the "September 18" incident in 1931, which developed into the seizure of the whole Manchuria.

Once the Young Marshal joined hands with Jiang Jieshi in 1929, he was increasingly involved in national affairs. In 1930, when **Feng Yuxiang**, joined by **Yan Xishan** and **Wang Jingwei**, fought against Jiang Jieshi in a great civil war, it was the arbitration of the Young Marshal that saved Jiang from defeat. The next year, to answer Jiang's call for the suppression of Shi Youshan's revolt, he dispatched his crack troops to North China with his headquarters set up at Beijing. The Japanese saw this as the golden opportunity to fulfill their long-coveted ambition to seize Manchuria. In pursuance to Jiang's repeated orders that by all means Zhang must restrain his troops not to provoke the Japanese who sought pretext for furthering their aggression, Zhang did not put up fighting, when the Japanese Kwantung Army seized Manchuria, for the loss of which Zhang earned the ignominious title of "nonresistant general." Despite the fact that it was Jiang's order and policy that led to Zhang's nonresistance, as a leader of Manchuria and commander-in-chief of a huge army to defend the national border territories, he cannot be exonerated for the wrong decision and the loss of the northeast, a fact which he later ruefully admitted.

Following the loss of Rehe province to the Japanese in March 1934, under the pressure of public opinion and Jiang's urge, Zhang resigned. Having cured his narcotic habit, together with his Australian adviser William Donald he went on a European tour. In Europe, he was much impressed by the revival of Germany and Italy under Fascism. Upon learning of the Fujian revolt in December 1933, he sailed for Shanghai, where he arrived in early January 1934.

Refreshed by his European tour, the Young Marshal regained his health and was filled with new ideas, particularly Fascism. Once again he became Jiang's most favored and valuable partner, as his Northeastern army, still 300,000 men strong, could be used to suppress the Communists, the arch-enemy of Jiang, while his Fascist ideology would bolster Jiang's aspiration to dictatorship. Most concerned for recovering his lost homeland, the Young Marshal reluctantly assumed responsibility for suppressing the Red Army and found Jiang's persistent policy of "internal pacification before resistance against external aggression" contradictory to the best interest of the nation, whose enemy was none other than the Japanese. More and more, he was leaning toward the student and the national salvation movements. Further his think tank comprised half a dozen highly educated men, notably Du Zhongyuan and Gao Chongmin, who were all opposed to continuing the civil war, but rather inclined to form a United Front with the Chinese Communists and others to fight Japan. When the Young Marshal with his major force transferred to the northwest with Xi'an as his headquarters and after suffering some heavy losses in fighting the Red Army, he decided to ally with the Communists rather than to continue Jiang's "suppression and encirclement" campaign against the Red Army. In this new approach to the national problem, he was joined by General Yang Hucheng and his Northwestern Army in early 1936.

Failing to persuade Jiang to change his policy by suspending the civil war and uniting the nation to fight Japan, Zhang–Yang staged the "remonstration with military force" (*Bing-jian*) to put Jiang under house arrest in Xi'an on December 12, 1936. Two weeks later, having given verbal promise to the Zhang–Yang demands, Jiang was set free and returned to Nanjing accompanied by the Young Marshal, who turned out to be a captive of Jiang's for over 50 years, the longest confinement in history. Ignoring law and human morality, Jiang Jieshi and his son Jingguo obdurately kept "the tiger instead of allowing it to return to the mountain." Zhang and his faithful wife Zhao Yidi had long been converted to Christianity and were diligent in God's work. It was the next president, **Li Denghui**, another professed Christian, who set the Young Marshal free on the ninetieth anniversary of his birth. Insouciant to mundane affairs and politics, Zhang lived in the paradise of Hawaii from 1995 until his death on October 14, 2001.

REFERENCES: Zhang Kuitang, *Zhang Xueliang zhuan* [Biography of Zhang Xueliang] (Beijing, 1991); Tien-wei Wu, *The Sian Incident: A Pivotal Point in Modern*

*Chinese History* (Ann Arbor, 1976); Zhang Youkun and Qian Jin, eds., *Zhang Xueliang nian pu* [Chroncicle of Zhang Xueliang] (Beijing, 1996), 2 vols.

TIEN-WEI WU

**ZHANG ZHIDONG** (September 2, 1837–October 4, 1909). Scholar; leading official in the last two decades of the Qing; conservative reformer.

A native of Nanpi, Zhili, Zhang Zhidong was born into a family that had produced officials for three successive generations. With an excellent classical education, he placed first in the *juren* examinations at age fifteen (1852). He placed third in the palace examination in 1863 following a reappraisal of his papers by the **Empress Dowager Cixi**. After having served as a compiler of the Hanlin Academy for three years, he held several positions connected with the civil service examinations in the provinces. As director of education for Sichuan in 1873–1876, he founded the *Zunjing shuyuan* (Revere the Classics Academy) and promoted traditional education. He also authored a handbook on study and composition, and an annotated bibliography on important works. The latter examined more than 2,000 works, but only eight had anything to do with the geography of the West and none dealt with its civilization. In both volumes he insisted on the scholar's adherence to Confucian morality. He returned to Beijing in 1876, first as a tutor in the imperial academy and then a registrar in the state archives.

Two events in 1879 earned him fame and recognition by the Empress Dowager Cixi. The first concerned Wu Kedu, a secretary in the Board of Civil Appointments, who took his own life in protest against Cixi's breach of dynastic law when choosing the new emperor in 1875. As the empire took note of Wu's action, Zhang wrote an obsequious memorial in defense of the Empress Dowager. The second was the vast concessions given to Russia by Chonghou when trying to settle the dispute over the Yili region. Zhang, now identified as a member of the Qingliu group who took it upon themselves to defend traditional values and made bold commentaries on current issues, wrote a searing memorial attacking Chonghou, demanding his execution and the repudiation of the treaty. Faced with strident Chinese resistance, the Russians agreed to reopen negotiations. As the Chinese were able to recover much of the lost grounds in the subsequent Treaty of St. Petersburg, Zhang was rewarded with rapid promotions, culminating in the governorship of Shanxi in 1882.

Having just emerged from a great famine that affected much of north China, Shanxi was in a terrible state. Conditions were made worse by widespread official corruption. Zhang punished the key offenders and then introduced a variety of reforms, forgiving delinquent taxes, supporting Confucian learning, promoting the colonization of Inner Mongolia, and checking the growth and smoking of opium. But the reforms withered with his departure for the viceroyalty of Liang Guang in August 1884.

Since the early 1880s the French had renewed their advance in Vietnam. Their seizure of Hanoi in April 1882 had jogged the Chinese out of inaction. As negotiations for peace collapsed, Zhang advocated a forward policy. He tried turning Vietnam into China's first line of defense, and sent military aid to Liu Yongfu's Black Flags. In the end, China simply did not have the power to resist France; Zhang's policy, however correct, proved unrealistic.

Following China's defeat, Zhang, now the governor general of two important coastal provinces in the south—Guangdong and Guangxi—became convinced of the need for defense and economic modernization. He established an academy for training naval and army officers, an arsenal for making shells and small arms, both in 1887, and two years later, made plans for the creation of an arsenal and a large-scale iron foundry. On the economic front, he reformed the tax collection system, established China's first modern mint, and set up two textile mills. Of particular note, too, was his founding of the Guangya Academy and its associated publishing house, promoting traditional learning and making available major works mainly by Qing scholars. When he left for the viceroyalty of Hu Guang in December 1889, he left a legacy of energetic and honest government, buttressed by a surprisingly healthy treasury.

From December 1889 to August 1907, with the exception of two short periods, Zhang was the governor general of Hunan and Hubei. His appointment was in large part the result of his support for the building of a railway trunk line from Beijing to Hankou. The project had to be temporarily shelved soon after because of funding problems. Meanwhile, he moved the equipment he ordered when viceroy at Guangzhou and set up an iron foundry at Hanyang, across the river from his yamen (government office). To provide ore for the foundry, he opened an iron mine at Daye in 1894. The two were subsequently linked with the Pingshan coal mine in Jiangxi to form the Hanyeping Company in 1908. His other industrial accomplishments included a mint, cotton mills, silk factories, and tanneries.

In the early 1890s, a series of attacks on missionaries and their properties occurred in the Yangzi provinces. Zhang cooperated with **Liu Kunyi**, the Liang Jiang governor general, in quelling the riots and avoided potential hostilities with the powers. By this time, he had become far more appreciative of the West, ordering translations of Western works on geography, education, government, commerce, legal code, and even customs and religion. Workers were also sent to Belgium to study iron and steel production.

After the outbreak of the Sino-Japanese War (1894–1895), Zhang was appointed acting governor general of Liang Jiang as Liu Kunyi was ordered to help defend the North. During his brief tenure at Nanjing, Zhang built schools and made proposals for naval development, a national postal system, and a railway network. These broadly based reform proposals greatly enhanced his national stature as he returned to Wuchang.

China's defeat in 1895 rekindled the fervor for reform. Zhang favored education and administrative reforms—he introduced a new curriculum in schools, sent students to Japan, and cut superfluous government jobs. He parted ways with **Kang Youwei** partly because of changing political winds in Beijing but mainly because of fundamental philosophical differences. Zhang found the idea of empowering the nonofficial elite in politics (*minquan*) too threatening to central authority. In April 1898 he published his treatise, *Quanxue pian* (Exhortation to Learn), advocating selective retention of China's heritage and the use of Western ideas and tools to build national strength. In this elaboration of the *ti-yong* formula, he went beyond a narrow refutation of Kang and the limitations of the goals of the "self-strengthening" era.

In the reaction that followed the Hundred Day Reform, Zhang, perhaps because of his good relations with the Empress Dowager, was silent over the latter's attempt to dethrone **Emperor Guangxu**. But in the Boxer Uprising, he joined Liu Kunyi in ignoring Cixi's declaration of war, electing to interpret her edict as an order to keep peace within his jurisdiction and confine hostilities to the north. This "neutrality" gained the support of the powers as he suppressed the Boxers and other rebels in his jurisdiction.

After 1900 Zhang emerged as the foremost spokesman for a comprehensive reform movement. In July 1901 he and Liu Kunyi submitted concrete proposals for reform in the school system, civil service examinations, governmental institutions, administrative practices, and for the introduction of Western methods (*xifa*). He spent nearly a year in Beijing in 1903 to lobby for a program of national reform. In his own viceroyalty, he had pushed reform to such a stage that by 1905 he, however reluctantly, was ready to entertain the idea of a constitutional government. The new national goals such as the rights recovery campaign to regain control over railways and mining projects simply could not be achieved without support from the new and increasingly assertive local elites.

In September 1907 Zhang was appointed to the grand council. Contrary to popular belief, he was not so much "kicked upstairs" as being placed in a critical position at a time when reforms acquired an increasingly national dimension. In 1908 he was also given charge of building the Guangzhou-Hankou railway, the rights to which he had wrestled from American hands three years earlier. But the project was mired in interprovincial squabbles as well as bickering among the imperialist powers over a loan to the Chinese as Zhang died in office.

The other big, vexing issue in Zhang's last years concerned the establishment of a constitutional government. Zhang had joined **Yuan Shikai** in 1905 to urge a mission to study the constitutional systems in foreign countries. But Zhang was opposed to yielding too much power to the gentry. To him, constitutional government was merely a means to a powerful state. But as he tried to preserve the authority of the court, he also became increasingly despondent over the leadership of the regent, Prince Chun. Thus, despite the abolition of distinctions between the Chinese and the Manchus in 1907, an imperial decision in which Zhang had played a part, large numbers of Manchus were appointed to high positions in the name of reform.

Zhang was an energetic and honest administrator. His long career was marked by major shifts in ideas on reforms and foreign policy as dictated by his patriotism and loyalty to the throne. But his political behavior was also guided by an unusual allegiance to the Empress Dowager, which led to charges of opportunism and betrayals, especially by the more radical reformers. His influence finally waned with the almost simultaneous passing of the Empress Dowager and the Guangxu emperor in 1908. By this time, however, though still a voice for reform within the government, he had also fallen behind the times.

REFERENCES: William Ayers, *Chang Chih-tung and Educational Reform in China* (Cambridge, MA, 1971); Daniel H. Bays, *China Enters the Twentieth Century: Chang Chih-tung and the Issues of a New Age, 1895–1909* (Ann Arbor, 1978); Li Guoqi, *Zhang Zhidong di waijiao zhengce* [Zhang Zhidong's Foreign Policy] (Taibei, 1970).

DAVID PONG

**ZHAO ZIYANG** (October 17, 1919–   ). Premier; Chinese Communist Party general secretary.

Born Zhao Xiusheng to a landlord and grain merchant family in Hua County, Henan, Zhao Ziyang is not known to have been formally educated beyond secondary school though he was said to be well-versed in Marxism Leninism. Zhao's career was a string of seeming meritocratic promotions involving Party work in agriculture. Capable leadership of economic reform led to his appointment as prime minister (September 1980–April 1988) and as general secretary (January 1987–May 1989). He was removed from the inner circle during the Tiananmen episode.

Zhao joined the Party at age nineteen. In the early years of the People's Republic of China (PRC), when Zhao was in his thirties and forties, he focused on rural affairs in Guangdong. He served under powerful regional leader Tao Zhu, and became known to other elite figures, as secretary general of the higher South Party China Sub-Bureau from 1951–1954, and with Tao in the still higher Party Central-South Bureau. In early 1965 he replaced Tao as first secretary of the Guangdong Province Party Committee.

When the Cultural Revolution broke out, at age forty-seven, Zhao's prominence all but guaranteed he would become a prominent target. Red Guard groups held him under house arrest and questioned him for months at mass criticism rallies, but reportedly met their match in open debate. Zhao refused to bend, and earned much respect for perseverence and for besting his accusers at ideological arguments.

At the end of the Cultural Revolution decade, at fifty-six, Zhao was made first Party secretary in populous Sichuan, hard hit by the previous tumultuous decade and home of **Deng Xiaoping**. He attracted attention for stimulating revival of farm production by promoting rural free markets, private plots, decentralized land ownership and accounting, and a so-called household responsibility system. Deng recruited him to the new post–Mao leadership team at the center.

At age sixty (September 1979) Zhao was added to the Politburo, and in February 1980 to its standing committee, making up part of a narrow pro-reform majority on both leadership bodies. The following April he became vice-premier of the state council, and in September replaced **Hua Guofeng** as premier. As Deng Xiaoping approached eighty, Zhao and another Deng protégé, **Hu Yaobang**, emerged as rivals ro succeed Deng at the top. Zhao's approach to reform emphasized productivity incentives within a political framework of continued central planning and administrative control. Hu's approach emphasized decentralization of budgets and decision-making to localities and enterprise managers. Conservative leaders fearing reform might cause central authority to weaken were suspicious of both but marginally preferred Zhao.

By 1987 bitter infighting led Deng to shift support tentatively to Zhao Ziyang. Zhao was named Party general secretary after conservatives forced out Hu. Zhao failed to win enough support from conservative People's Liberation Army (PLA) commanders to be appointed chair of the Military Affairs Commission (MAC). And conservative **Li Peng** assumed Zhao's old job as premier. Over the next two years Deng remained aloof from debates between Li and Zhao over the next phase of reform, and withheld explicit expression of confidence in Zhao himself. Zhao's proposals to separate Party and government, and move on enterprise reform, apparently went farther than Deng was prepared to go. Intellectuals wrote praise of Zhao's visions, implying of course that Deng was getting behind the times.

In 1989 he turned seventy. At Hu's death in April he delivered the eulogy. As "democracy" protests swelled in Beijing and other cities, angering control-minded conservatives, he urged a soft hand in dealing with them. In particular, Zhao ardently supported protesters' demands for an end to rampant official corruption. After Deng decided to get tough with protesters, Zhao was isolated, and after the June 4 crackdown he was dismissed as general secretary; his closest associates were imprisoned. He lived thereafter under house arrest as the leading symbol of anticorruption and more liberal politics, both views widely popular in China.

REFERENCES: Richard Baum, *Burying Mao* (Princeton, NJ, 1994); Donald W. Klein and Anne B. Clark, *Biographic Dictionary of Chinese Communism, 1921–1965*, vol. 1 (Cambridge, MA, 1971), 93–94; David Shambaugh, *The Making of a Premier: Zhao Ziyang's Provincial Career* (Boulder, CO, 1984); Zhao Wei, *Zhao Ziyang zhuan* [Biography of Zhao Ziyang] (Hong Kong, 1984).

GORDON BENNETT

**ZHOU ENLAI** (Chou En-lai, March 5, 1898–January 8, 1976). First People's Republic of China (PRC) premier and foreign minister; Chinese Communist Party (CCP) vice-chairman; member of CCP Politburo since 1927.

Zhou Enlai was the firstborn of a prominent gentry family in Huaian, Jiangsu on March 5, 1898. Despite a turbulent childhood he was exposed to a cultured and supportive Confucian environment in Jiangsu until he was twelve. He then moved to Shanghai and to Manchuria where he was reared by uncles during the teen years and where exposure to harsher weather and social experiences (as a light-skinned southerner) broadened his outlook. He attended and achieved distinction at Nankai Middle School where he was befriended by influential school president Zhang Boling and where he was very active in student publications, organizations, and in dramatic productions in some of which he successfully played female roles. He spent two years in Japan and while he does not seem to have attended universities there as some biographers claim, he was, however, introduced to Marxism by Kawakami Hajime. Zhou returned to China at the time of the May Fourth incident in 1919 and enrolled in the initial class of the new Nankai University.

Political action now consumed him, leaving little time to attend classes. Zhou wrote for and edited student publications and helped to establish the *Juewushe* (Awakening Society) which subsequently became one of the several nuclei for the Chinese Communist Party (CCP) after its establishment in 1921. Zhou continued to display a self-effacing willingness to let others take the leading positions in such organizations and activities, a trait that would remain a personal characteristic throughout his long career. In Tianjin he was jailed for six months in 1920, but later that year departed for France in a work-study program, where he again engaged heavily in political work among Chinese students. He formally joined the CCP in 1922, helping to establish that June the Chinese Youth Communist Party in Europe, as an overseas branch of the CCP. He was also very active in the Guomindang (GMD) in Europe during the initial period of collaboration between the two parties and was a special correspondent from Europe for the Catholic publication *Yishibao* in Tianjin. While abroad, he resided mostly in Paris and Berlin, but traveled to England and Belgium, the overall experience contributing to his intellectual growth and cosmopolitanism although the full potential of such growth was limited by his deepening commitment to Marxism.

In 1924, Zhou returned to China, immediately taking up important posts in Guangzhou. He served as occasional aide to Soviet military adviser Galen (General Vassily Blucher), but most important, Zhou became head of the GMD's Huangpu (Whampoa) Military Academy Political Department. He distinguished himself in important political roles in the two military campaigns that secured Guangzhou from the latent threat of warlord **Chen Jiongming**. In 1925, Zhou married **Deng Yingchao**; the couple had met as fellow activists in the Awakening Society in Tianjin. Following the *Zhong-shan* incident of March 1926 Zhou was relieved of his GMD posts. In the internal CCP debate regarding an appropriate response to this initial, relatively mild GMD crackdown, Zhou upheld the Comintern line of continued cooperation with the GMD. When the revolutionary army occupied Wuhan in late 1926 he was made head of the CCP's new military department. He played a prominent role in organizing the massive strike of March 21, 1927 in Shanghai that facilitated the city's seizure by **Jiang Jieshi**'s army. He was exceedingly fortunate to escape when on April 12 Jiang suddenly smashed the CCP in Shanghai.

Zhou now went to Wuhan where the Communists continued to implement the Comintern line by working with the Left GMD. He attended the CCP's Fifth Congress in late April–early May 1927 at which time he became a member of the Central Committee (CC) and its Politburo. Shortly after this, the Left GMD also turned on the Communists. Zhou then became one of the organizers of the Nanchang Uprising on August 1, 1927. In the aftermath of this disastrous operation, he came down with malaria and went to Hong Kong for a time to recuperate. In mid-1928, he went to Moscow to attend the Sixth CCP Congress, following which he came to be second in influence only to the powerful **Li Lisan**. Zhou was also elected a candidate member of the executive committee of the Comintern at its July–September 1928 Sixth Comintern Congress. He returned to China by late 1928, but in early 1930 went back to Moscow as the effective head of the CCP delegation to the Comintern. When the Chinese Red Army failed that summer in its attempt to take and hold Changsha, Zhou returned to China for the convening of the Third Plenum in September that would make Li Lisan the scapegoat. Zhou waffled in his criticism of Li, yet was reelected to his positions at the next plenum in January 1931 after Li Lisan's removal from power.

In 1931, Zhou joined **Mao Zedong** and **Zhu De** in Ruijin, Jiangxi, where he was elected to important political and military positions in the Chinese Soviet Republic. He often opposed Mao during this period, particularly on military matters, and for a time succeeded in overriding Mao. But the tactics endorsed by Zhou eventually resulted in the loss of the Soviet Republic. In January 1935, at Zunyi in Guizhou, Mao assumed effective command of the exodus from Jiangxi that would now come to be known as the Long March. Once again, however, the agile Zhou demonstrated that he could adjust to new leadership, tactically accepting a less-prominent position. Thus ensued the collaboration with Mao that would last some 40 years to the end of Zhou's life.

Zhou won international attention when he successfully negotiated the release of Jiang Jieshi during the Xi'an incident of December 1936, and afterward the agreement for a Second CCP–GMD United Front. He continued to act as liaison to the Nationalist government during the War of Resistance against Japan. He was the principal representative of the CCP in the unsuccessful efforts of American General George C. Marshall to mediate between the CCP and the GMD in the early postwar period. He provided surrender terms to Nationalist Acting President **Li Zongren** in early 1949, which when rejected, led to the decisive Communist military victory on the Chinese mainland.

By mid-1949, Zhou turned his attention to participating in the formation of a new government for China, initially as vice-chairman under Mao of the reconstituted Chinese People's Political Consultative Conference, which body then formally established the People's Republic of China (PRC). Zhou became the premier (until his death) of the new government and its first minister of foreign affairs (until 1958). Thus Zhou was responsible for administering the government and was its chief diplomat in dealing with foreign governments, tasks he devoted himself to with incredible energy and finesse for the next quarter century despite tremendous problems and frustrations.

Zhou was in the international limelight again as a pallbearer at Joseph Stalin's funeral in March 1953, and his visit to Moscow was instrumental in bringing about a three-year honeymoon period in Sino-Soviet relations. He played an important role in achieving the much-delayed 1953 armistice in Korea. In May 1954 he again showed his impressive diplomatic skills at the Geneva Conference on Indochina. The following April 1955 saw his greatest triumph (prior to 1972) at the meeting of 29 nonaligned nations in Bandung, Indonesia.

Zhou's role in both the disastrous Great Leap Forward of the late 1950s and in the chaotic Great Proletarian Cultural Revolution beginning in 1966 was controversial inasmuch as he appeared to support Mao's radical policies, exhibiting considerable zeal in doing so. In the 1960s, in particular, Zhou decisively sided with Mao in the struggle against so-called revisionists and capitalist roaders, including the relatively pragmatic **Liu Shaoqi**. Even so, he used his negotiating skills to keep the government functioning during the chaos of the Cultural Revolution and to protect many of his own, primarily, government cadres. It bears noting, however, that his ability or willingness to protect others did not include his own adopted daughter, Sun Weishi, who was tortured to death by Red Guards. At the Nineth Party Congress in April 1969, Zhou was named Party secretary general (Mao was chairman). He was ranked third in the Party hierarchy, after his chief rival, the now second-ranked **Lin Biao** who was named Mao's successor in 1969 but who would be eliminated only two and a half years later.

During China's protracted domestic political crisis, Zhou personally played a major role in guiding the country out of its isolation and was notably successful in achieving rapprochement with the United States in

1972, in gaining admission to the United Nations in 1971, and in establishing or restoring diplomatic relations with dozens of nations during the early 1970s.

Zhou's diplomatic success sharpened the rivalry with Lin Biao, with whom Zhou disagreed on both domestic and foreign policy issues. Zhou then had a major role in the sudden demise of Lin Biao in September 1971. The militarily sagacious Lin was no match for Zhou, politically. Zhou's official explanation of the Lin Biao incident, which he delivered at the Tenth Party Congress in 1973, was unsatisfactory, raising as many questions as it purported to answer. Nevertheless, Zhou was politically strengthened at this congress, having been elevated to the second position in the Party hierarchy.

Subsequently, as he sought to rehabilitate cadres who had been targeted during the early Cultural Revolution and to restore regular government, Zhou also had to struggle with the radical Gang of Four, including Mao's wife, **Jiang Qing**. The radicals, frustrated by Zhou, attacked him indirectly in a widespread and intensive campaign to criticize Confucius that was eventually merged with a campaign to criticize Lin Biao. Already exhausted by the extraordinary burdens of the Cultural Revolution, Zhou soon weakened physically.

After being bedridden for many months, during which time he continued to work and was consulted, Zhou died of cancer on January 8, 1976 at the age of seventy-eight. **Deng Xiaoping**, whom Zhou had made his expected successor, gave the funeral oration on January 15 in the Great Hall of the People. Mao rather conspicuously absented himself from this ceremony. Zhou's ashes were scattered throughout China in accord with his request.

REFERENCES: Donald W. Klein and Anne B. Clark, *Biographic Dictionary of Chinese Communism, 1921–1965*, vol. 1 (Cambridge, MA, 1971), 204–219; Chae-Jin Lee, *Zhou Enlai: The Early Years* (Stanford, CA, 1994); David Wilson, *Zhou Enlai: A Biography* (New York, 1984).

STEPHEN UHALLEY, JR.

**ZHOU FOHAI** (May 29, 1897–February 28, 1948). Founding member of the Chinese Communist Party; Guomindang theorist; collaborator during the Sino-Japanese War, 1937–1945.

Born to an official family in Hunan province, Zhou displayed his talents and ambition early in his life. He went to Japan to study in 1917, enrolling first in high school and then in Kyoto Imperial University. While in Japan, Zhou became interested in Marxism and politics. He wrote extensively on Socialist ideas and became known among radical Chinese intellectuals. In 1921 he returned to Shanghai to attend the founding meeting (i.e., the First National Congress) of the Chinese Communist Party (CCP) and was elected the Party's deputy leader.

As his study came to a close in 1924, Zhou went to Guangzhou at the invitation of Dai Jitao to work for the recently reorganized Guomindang

(GMD). It was the heyday of the United Front between the GMD and the CCP, but Zhou's new career in the GMD and his new ideological orientation soon alienated him from his fellow Communists. Later that year he withdrew from the CCP and, under the influence of Dai, became a fierce critic of the Communists. In late 1925, Zhou left Guangzhou in protest against the increasing Communist influence there. He then participated in the formation of the Western Hills Faction, an anti-CCP splinter group in the GMD, in Shanghai.

During the Northern Expedition, Zhou briefly served at the Wuhan branch of the GMD's Central Military Academy, but returned to Shanghai when the GMD was divided between the Nanjing and the Wuhan camps in early 1927. He was quickly recruited by **Jiang Jieshi** into the Right-wing Nanjing regime, and from then on became a loyal supporter of Jiang. As the United Front collapsed and Jiang emerged victorious in the ensuing power struggle, Zhou's political fortune also rose. His influential treatise, *The Theoretical System of the Three People's Principles*, published in 1928, firmly established him as a leading theorist and propagandist in Jiang's entourage.

In the early years of the Nanjing government, Zhou served as a trusted and able assistant to Jiang as Jiang tackled a series of political and military challenges to his new leadership. For his service Zhou was rewarded with a membership in the GMD's Central Executive Committee in 1931. In the years that followed, he was also given a number of important Party and governmental posts in Nanjing and in the province of Jiangsu. He developed close ties with the Chen brothers, Guofu and Lifu, who controlled the Party machine on behalf of Jiang, and was generally regarded as a member of the CC clique.

When the Sino-Japanese War broke out in 1937, Zhou was deputy head of the GMD's Department of Propaganda. While his official responsibility was to promote China's war effort, in private he was extremely pessimistic about the possible outcome of the war. In early 1938, with Jiang's approval, Zhou sent Gao Zongwu, an official in the Foreign Ministry, to Hong Kong in search of opportunities for negotiating peace with Japan. Progress was made during Gao's mission, but Jiang's hesitation as well as policy shifts in the Japanese government led Zhou to believe that **Wang Jingwei**, Jiang's deputy and arch rival in the GMD, was the ideal person to lead the peace effort. Wang welcomed Zhou's proposal. Later that year Zhou arranged and accompanied Wang's secret departure from Chongqing. Wang then announced his peace plan in Hanoi in December, and in April 1939 he and Zhou moved to Shanghai for further negotiations with the Japanese.

During the following months, Zhou was Wang's principal adviser and key representative in the peace negotiations. He also strongly supported the organization of a collaborationist regime by Wang in the occupied areas. When that regime was established in Nanjing in March 1940, Zhou served concurrently as its deputy premier (vice-head of the Administrative Yuan), finance minister, police minister, and president of its Central Reserve Bank. From 1940 to 1945, Zhou was probably the most powerful person, other than Wang himself, in the Nanjing regime. Aside from gathering a significant personal following, he organized an armed force, the "Tax Police Corps," and placed it under his own command. After the outbreak of the Pacific War, however, Zhou lost faith in the collaboration effort and began to seek understanding from his old boss, Jiang Jieshi. He secretly reestablished contacts with Chongqing through Jiang's chief of intelligence, Dai Li. In 1944, following Wang's death, Zhou became the regime's mayor of Shanghai but continued to work for the Chongqing government. Zhou was arrested and sentenced to death on charges of high treason after Japan's surrender. His sentence was commuted to life imprisonment by Jiang in 1947, but he died of illness in a Nanjing prison several months later.

REFERENCES: "Chou Fo-hai," in Howard L. Boorman and Richard C. Howard, eds., *Biographical Dictionary of Republican China*, vol. 1 (New York, 1967); Cai Dejin, ed., *Zhou Fohai riji* [Diary of Zhou Fohai] (Beijing, 1986); Susan Marsh, "Chou Fo-hai: The Making of a Collaborator," in Akira Iriye, ed., *The Chinese and the Japanese* (Princeton, NJ, 1980).

                                                                WANG KE-WEN

## ZHOU SHUREN. *See* LU XUN.

**ZHU DE** (November 30, 1886–July 6, 1976). Founder of the Red Army; marshal; Politburo member; chairman, standing committee of the National People's Congress.

Zhu De was born in Yilong County, Sichuan, to a tenant family which had relocated from Guangdong, hence he was raised with a knowledge of both the Sichuanese and Cantonese dialects. Zhu attended middle school in Shunqing (later Nanchong), higher normal school in Chengdu where he studied physical education. In 1909, he enrolled in the new Yunnan Military Academy, where he secretly joined **Sun Yat-sen**'s revolutionary *Tongmenghui* and the *Kelaohui* secret society.

While stationed in Kunming, Yunnan, Zhu participated in the October 1911 revolution, and in the following year joined the Guomindang (GMD). He also participated in the 1916 civil war against **Yuan Shikai**'s monarchical ambition. He spent the next several years in southwest Sichuan commanding a brigade of the Yunnan Army on behalf of Sichuan governor Cai O, and living the dissolute life of a petty warlord. In 1920, he returned to Yunnan where he was appointed provincial commissioner of public security the following year. The vicissitudes of warlord politics soon forced him to withdraw to the Sichuan-Tibet border area. But in early 1922 he went to Shanghai where he was cured of the opium habit. Having already read revolutionary literature in recent years and greatly influenced by a friend,

Sun Pingwen, Zhu at this time met with Sun Yat-sen and **Chen Duxiu**, although Chen responded coolly to his request for admission into the Chinese Communist Party (CCP).

In his mid-thirties, Zhu went to Europe in late 1922. Soon after arriving in Berlin he met **Zhou Enlai** and joined the CCP. After studying both German and Marxism for several months, he attended lectures in 1923–1924 at the University of Gottingen, although he considered this less useful than his visits to factories and other sites in various cities of Germany. In 1924 he edited the GMD's *Zhengzhi zhoupao* (Political Weekly) in Berlin. After being arrested briefly on two occasions in 1925, he was quickly deported to the USSR. Here he studied at the University of the Toilers of the East in Moscow.

Zhu returned to China just in time for the Northern Expedition. He played a useful role in that campaign by persuading the powerful Sichuan warlord General Yang Sen to join the revolutionary cause. However, Yang Sen soon afterward betrayed the Communists, and Zhu narrowly avoided arrest. Zhu then went to Nanchang, Jiangxi, where a former student gave him important positions including those of chief public security officer and deputy army commander. Thus was Zhu De well-placed strategically when the CCP, having been expelled by the Guomindang (GMD) in Shanghai in April and then in Wuhan in July 1927, staged the Nanchang Uprising of August 1, 1927. In the aftermath of this historic but disastrous event, Zhu's forces were reduced to a few hundred men, poorly armed. By January 1928 his modest forces captured Yizhang in southern Hunan and publicly proclaimed themselves to be a Communist, rather than a GMD, military unit. In the spring of 1928 **Mao Zedong** abandoned his precarious base at Jinggangshan and joined forces with Zhu. The combined force of about 10,000 men now reoccupied Jinggangshan where they formally established the Fourth Red Army. In this difficult early period of establishing a base in the mountains (eventually centered at Ruijin, Jiangxi, formally the seat of the Chinese Soviet Republic beginning in November 1931), Mao and Zhu forged a cooperative relationship, with Zhu subordinate to Mao. Both men opposed the **Li Lisan** line of fruitlessly attempting to take large cities during 1930, although they grudgingly complied for a time. Zhu also sided with Mao during the Futian incident (a revolt directed against Mao) late that year, a critical juncture because it coincided with an imminent assault from the first of Jiang Jieshi's five annihilation campaigns against the Communist stronghold. Zhu was preoccupied by these successive campaigns, successfully turning all of them back except the last one when the Communists were forced to abandon the Jiangxi Soviet in late 1934. Zhu was made a member of the Politburo sometime during the period of the Jiangxi Soviet. In addition, he sat on the Soviet's political cabinet, and chaired its Central Revolutionary Military Council. Zhu was commander-in-chief of the famed and perilous Long March which relocated the Communists in Shaanxi a year later, although at the outset of the flight from Jiangxi Zhou Enlai was the chairman of the important Party Military Affairs Committee. Zhu became a vice-chairman of this committee. After Mao resumed the Long March to Shaanxi, Zhu remained for a time with **Zhang Guotao**, which gave rise to conflicting stories that Zhu and Mao either disagreed with each other at the time or the militarily stronger forces of Zhang detained Zhu. In any case, Zhu rejoined Mao in Shaanxi in the fall of 1936 and resumed overall command of the Red Army.

Following the renewed cooperation between the CCP and GMD Zhu was named deputy commander of the Second War Zone, and commander of the Eighth Route Army, as the Red Army was now redesignated. Following Japan's invasion of North China in July 1987, he was at the front much of the time until the end of 1939 when he was ordered back to Yan'an where he stayed throughout the remainder of the war against Japan. He concentrated his attention now on measures to deal both with the GMD's new siege of Yan'an and the pressure exerted by the Japanese. After the American Dixie Mission was established in Yan'an in 1944, a number of American officials and journalists interviewed Zhu. They generally admired his modest manner and apparent lack of political dogmatism.

Following the victory over Japan, and as the Chinese civil war resumed despite the effort of the Marshall Mission to avert it, the Communist military units were redesignated the People's Liberation Army (PLA) and Zhu continued as commander-in-chief. After Yan'an fell to the Nationalists in March 1947, Zhu eventually relocated the headquarters in Xipaipo village which was near Shijiazhuang in southwest Hebei in time for Mao's arrival in May. By now the war was turning decisively in favor of the Communists and this was happening much more quickly than either Mao or Zhu had anticipated. Victory came within the next several months. On October 1, 1949 Mao pronounced the establishment of the People's Republic of China (PRC) and Zhu was accorded a place of honor at the ceremony on Tiananmen Square.

During the 1950s and early 1960s, Zhu was frequently active in the several high positions that he held. He was elected regularly from Sichuan province to the National People's Congress (NPC) after it was established in 1954. That year he relinquished command of the PLA. Five years later, by 1959, he no longer had any formal military position but retained the title of marshal. He was appointed chairman of the standing committee of the NPC in 1959 and was elected to the position in January 1965, and reelected in January 1975. During this tumultuous decade, Zhu was in his eighties and mostly stayed clear of politics, being on hand for ceremonial occasions only.

Zhu De died on July 6, 1976 at ninety years of age. He had been well enough to meet with visiting Australian Prime Minister Malcolm Fraser only a couple of weeks before his death (and after the infirm Mao was no longer seeing foreigners). Interestingly, Zhu outlived Zhou Enlai by six months while Mao lived only two months longer than Zhu.

REFERENCES: Donald W. Klein and Anne B. Clark, *Biographic Dictionary of Chinese Communism, 1921–1965*, vol. 1 (Cambridge, MA, 1971), 245–254; Agnes Smedley, *The Great Road: The Life and Times of Chu Teh* (New York, 1956).

STEPHEN UHALLEY, JR.

**ZHU RONGJI** (1928–   ). Party chief for Shanghai; Politburo member, vice-premier, and premier since 1998.

Zhu Rongji represents the new generation of leaders in the post-Deng China. This new corps of top leaders may be described as the technocratic elite. Zhu Rongji was a graduate of the prestigious Tsinghua (Qinghua) University, China's MIT, with an electrical engineering degree. While serving as a Politburo member in the Party and a vice-premier in the central government, he had been concurrently the dean of Tsinghua's School of Economic Management until 2001. Since 1992 he has been regarded as the "czar" of China's economic policy and management.

Zhu was born in 1928 of a poor family in Changsha, Hunan province. It was through his diligence and hard work that he was able to graduate from Tsinghua University. In 1949, while still an undergraduate, Zhu Rongji joined the Communist Party as a leader in the university student association. Upon graduation he joined the provincial government in the northeast as a planning officer. In 1957–1958 he was caught in the antirightist campaign waged by **Mao Zedong;** Zhu was then labeled a "rightist" and was expelled from the Party. For about seven years, from 1958 to 1965, he languished as a "downward transfer" cadre member doing manual labor in the countryside. He returned briefly to a government position as a planner and engineer, but was again banished to the countryside during the Cultural Revolution.

He returned to the government planning office in 1975 and in 1979 was rehabilitated as a Party member. By 1982 Zhu, as a top-level engineer, had assumed the directorship for economic planning. As mentioned earlier, two years later he was appointed concurrently as a professor in the newly established School of Economic Management at Tsinghua advising doctoral candidates.

In 1987 Zhu was transferred to Shanghai to serve as deputy Party secretary under **Jiang Zemin,** then the mayor of Shanghai. Zhu succeeded Jiang as mayor in 1988 when the former was made the Party secretary for Shanghai. Together Jiang and Zhu kept the Shanghai student demonstration at a manageable level prior to the Tiananmen crackdown in Beijing, which occurred on June 4, 1989. Zhu Rongji and Jiang Zemin were able to avoid calling in the troops to suppress the student demonstrators. Instead, they relied on the industrial workers to provide discipline and keep order in the streets.

When Jiang Zemin was chosen to succeed **Zhao Ziyang** as the Chinese Communist Party (CCP) chairman after the 1989 crackdown, Zhu held concurrently the positions of Party secretary and mayorship of Shanghai. At the 1991 Party congress, Zhu was elevated to Politburo membership. A year later he was chosen as one of the vice-premiers for the state council by the National People's Congress (NPC). Because of his managerial skill, Zhu was appointed concurrently the governor for the central bank to curb the overheated economy. Since 1991–1992 political power has been shifted to former leaders from Shanghai dominated by Jiang Zemin and Zhu Rongji. By the time the Ninth NPC met in March 1998 Zhu had emerged to become the new premier replacing **Li Peng**.

As the new premier Zhu proposed several major reforms in an effort to improve China's economy in order to avoid a financial meltdown which was faced by a number of Asian nations. In addition, Zhu originally wanted to downsize China's bloated bureaucracy by merging or eliminating the number of ministries and their personnel—he had approval from the 1998 NPC to reduce the ministries and commissions from 40 to 29, and a 50% cut in personnel.

However, his ambitious reform plan has since been put on hold, but he has not abandoned entirely the process of reform which has met with opposition from within and the fear of possible impact on China's economy because of the Asian financial meltdown.

Zhu Rongji has little tolerance for subordinates who are evasive and sloppy in their work style. He can be very blunt and direct to the point of asking questions about government operations and demanding answers from officials. While this working style has been considered a strength by many, it nevertheless has perhaps antagonized the ossified bureaucracy whose support Zhu needs in implementing the reforms. In addition, Zhu Rongji still has to contend with the neoconservative and Left-leaning elements in the Party and the government. It will take time for Zhu to dislodge the "local protectionism" exhibited by provincial officials toward some of his reform policies.

Zhu has been criticized for advocating the South Korean model of building up the more efficient big state-owned enterprises for export-growth purposes—the so-called "big group strategy." Zhu has advised Party chief Jiang Zemin, chairman of the powerful Military Affairs Commission which exercises Party control over the military, to force the military to relinquish its vast business undertakings and devote its efforts mainly to combat preparedness. While the decision has the support of China's top military leaders, it has generated protests and discontent from those in the middle level of the officer corps.

Zhu Rongji most likely would not be a contender to succeed Jiang Zemin, who will have to vacate the Party chief position by 2003. Because of his age—Zhu will be seventy-five by then—in accordance with recently adopted Party rules, he is not eligible for top Party government positions.

Zhu Rongji speaks fluent English and has made a favorable impression on Western diplomats and businessmen alike.

REFERENCES: Matt Forney and Pamela Yatsko, "Who's the Boss?" *Far Eastern Economic Review* (March 5, 1998), 10–14; Li Guocheng, *CCP's Top Leadership Group* (Hong Kong, 1990, in Chinese), 66–69; Cheng Li, "University Networks and the Rise of Qinghua Graduates in China's Leadership," *The Australian Journal of Chinese Affairs*, no. 32 (July 1994), 21–22; James C.F. Wang, *Contemporary Chinese Politics*, 6th ed. (Upper Saddle River, NJ, 1999); Gao Xin and Hop In, *The Most Powerful People of CCP* (Hong Kong, 1998, in Chinese), 96–125.

JAMES C.F. WANG

**ZUO ZONGTANG** (posthumous title Wenxiang, November 10, 1812–September 5, 1885). Provincial official and military leader of the Qing dynasty.

Born to a family of limited economic means in the Xiangyin district of Hunan, Zuo Zongtang passed the provincial civil service examinations for the degree of *juren*, but failed repeatedly the metropolitan examinations. His early years were devoted to teaching, farming and, by the 1850s, to local defense against the Taiping rebels. After 1852 he served on the military staffs of several governors of Hunan earning a reputation as an able defensive strategist. In 1860 he decisively defeated Taiping forces in Jiangxi and southern Anhui enabling **Zeng Guofan**'s forces to break through the Taiping lines at Qimen. On the recommendation of Zeng, Zuo was named governor of Zhejiang province in 1862. In 1863, he was appointed governor general of Fujian and Zhejiang. During the next few years he cooperated with a French-led force under the command of Prosper Giquel to clear the province of Taipings, retaking the capital Hangzhou in April 1865, a feat that earned him an earldom of the first rank. After the fall of the Taiping capital at Nanjing in July 1864, Zuo directed mopping up operations against fleeing Taiping remnants in South China until 1866.

Zuo admired the swift, well-armed steamships employed by the French and tried to replicate their production. An experimental vessel built by Chinese engineers from his staff at Hangzhou in 1864 was a disappointment but the experience led Zuo in 1867 to establish the Fuzhou Dockyard on the Min River near Fuzhou. There foreign advisers led by Giquel and Paul d'Aiguebelle supervised a Chinese workforce employing Western methods and technology to build modern steam-powered vessels comparable to those produced in European shipyards.

In September 1866, before the Fuzhou Dockyard had entered production, Zuo was named governor general of Shaanxi and Gansu provinces in northwestern China where a Muslim insurrection had been underway since 1864. He determined first to move against a western branch of the Nian rebels who had moved from Shanxi into Shaanxi in 1866 linking up with the Muslims. Zuo's forces pursued the Nian eastward across north China into the metropolitan province of Zhili where they threatened the imperial capital, Beijing. For thus imperiling the imperial court, Zuo was stripped of his earldom. It was not until the summer of 1868 that Zuo's army, acting in concert with **Li Hongzhang**'s Anhui army, finally defeated the Nian in northern Shandong.

Zuo, once again enjoying the favor of the court, was restored to his former rank. He moved westward where Muslim rebels controlled most of Shaanxi, Gansu, Ningxia, and Xinjiang. Clearing the Muslim rebels from Shaanxi and most of Gansu by 1872, he established China's first modern woolen mill at Lanzhou in Gansu. Logistical needs led him to establish aresenals at Xi'an in Shaanxi and at Lanzhou. Muslims in Xinjiang seizing the opportunity provided by widespread unrest in China's northwest rebelled in 1864 under the Muslim Chieftain Yakub Beg. In 1872 Yakub Beg's regime received international recognition from Great Britain which regarded Xinjiang as a buffer between Tsarist Russia and British interests in South Asia. In 1871, Russia had occupied the fertile Yili River valley in Northwest Xinjiang and the next year the tsar extended recognition to the regime of Yakub Beg.

Zuo's campaign to regain control of Xinjiang from Yakub Beg and his European allies was delayed by a policy dispute over allocation of resources by the imperial government. Li Hongzhang and his supporters argued for first priority for maritime defense along China's east coast while Zuo and his followers advocated for the importance of frontier defense in the northwest. Resources for the campaign to retake Xinjiang were finally allocated in 1875. Zuo moved from his headquarters in Gansu into Xinjiang in 1876 securing the northern half of the territory by the end of the year and crushing Yakub Beg's regime in the south in 1877. Diplomatic efforts to force Russia to relinquish control of the Yili River valley resulted in the Treaty of Livadia which actually ceded 70% of the Yili region to Russia. Infuriated by the ineptitude of the envoy who negotiated the treaty, the court rejected it and dispatched Marquis Zeng Jice (oldest son of **Zeng Guofan**) to St. Petersburg to renegotiate. Zuo called for a firm response to the Russian attempt to take over valuable Chinese territory and moved his forces into position to confront the Russian forces in Yili if Marquis Zeng's negotiation failed. In the summer of 1880, the court, fearing a showdown with Russia, recalled Zuo to Beijing. Zeng Jice's renegotiation proved successful in regaining most of the Yili valley for China in the Treaty of St. Petersburg in early 1881. Zuo's resolute stand during the crisis encouraged those who favored a firm policy in dealing with foreign powers. It also led to the incorporation of Xinjiang as a province in 1884.

Posted to Nanjing as Liangjiang governor general in 1882, Zuo had barely initiated a program of administrative reform and economic development when he was placed in charge of military affairs in the fighting that erupted between Chinese and French forces in Vietnam in 1883. The following year when the French sunk 11 Chinese vessels in the Min River and leveled the Fuzhou Dockyard, China formally declared war and placed Zuo in command of military operations. As Zuo readied a force to relieve Taiwan which had come under French attack, China accepted French terms for peace in June 1885. Zuo died three months later on September 5.

Although Zuo's military operations in the northwest were known for their ruthlessness and violence, as a political leader he introduced administrative reforms, agricultural development, industrial modernization, and education providing the basis for Xinjiang's incorporation as a province. In the 1870s he waged a bitter policy struggle against Li Hongzhang and others to place the highest priority on defense of China's inner Asian frontier rather than on maritime defense. Though Zuo's position prevailed, by the close of the century it was clear that China's most serious security concern was maritime defense.

REFERENCES: Arthur W. Hummel, ed., *Eminent Chinese of the Ch'ing Period* (Washington, DC, 1944); Dai Yi and Lin Yanjiao, eds., *Qinqdai renwu zhuangao* [Draft Biographies of Figures from the Qing Period], second collection, II (Shenyang, 1984).

THOMAS L. KENNEDY

# Chronology

| | | |
|---|---|---|
| 1839 | Nov. 3–13 | Chinese war junks clash with British warship at Chuanbi near Guangzhou. Opium War breaks out in Guangzhou areas. |
| 1840 | June | British forces under Rear Admiral George Elliot blockade Guangzhou and then sail north. |
| | Oct. 3 | Lin Zexu is relieved of his Imperial Commissionership by Emperor Daoguang. |
| 1842 | Aug. 24 | The Opium War ends with the signing of the Treaty of Nanjing. |
| 1843 | | Hong Xiuquan begins to preach Christianity in his native village in Hua County, Guangdong. His followers include cousin Hong Ren'gan and Feng Yunshan. |
| 1847 | July 21 | Hong Xiuquan and Feng Yunshan set up the Bai Shang-Di hui (God Worshippers Society). |
| | Aug. | Hong Xiuquan arrives at Zijinshan, Guangxi, where Feng Yunshan has been preaching since 1845. The number of "God Worshippers" has grown to 2,000. Hong is joined by Yang Xiuqing, Xiao Chaoqui, Wei Changhui, and Shi Dakai. |
| 1851 | Jan. 11 | Hong Xiuquan declares revolution against the Qing dynasty and establishes the Taiping Tianguo (Heavenly Kingdom of Great Peace) at Jintian Village, Guiping County, Guangxi. |

| | | |
|---|---|---|
| 1853 | March 20 | Taiping armies capture Nanjing and designate it as the capital. |
| | May 8 | Northern Expedition of the Taipings is launched to topple the Qing dynasty. |
| 1854 | Feb. 25 | The Hunan Army (Xiangjun), established under the command of Zeng Guofan, sets out for Hubei to meet the Taipings. |
| 1856 | Sept. 2 | Civil strife reaches a climax in Taiping's capital, Tianjing (Nanjing). Dong Wang, Yang Xiuqing, and their subordinates are slaughtered by Wei Changhui (Bei Wang). |
| 1859 | April 22 | Hong Ren'gan arrives at Tianjing and is appointed as the prime minister. Hong and Li Xiucheng, a talented general, are responsible for upholding the Taiping movement in the last phase until 1864. |
| 1861 | March 11 | The Zongli Yamen (Office for General Management) is established at the suggestion of Prince Gong. This action marks the first step of the Self-Strengthening Movement. |
| | Nov. | Empress Dowager Cixi and Prince Gong initiate a coup. They become coregents of Emperor Tongzhi (r. 1862–1874). |
| 1863 | March | Charles G. (Chinese) Gordon, an English officer, is named commander of the "Ever-Victorious Army." He battles with the Taipings in the lower Yangzi areas until May 1864. |
| 1864 | June 1 | Tian Wang, Hong Xiuquan, commits suicide at age fifty-two. His oldest son, Hong Tian Guifu, succeeds to the throne. |
| | July 19 | After a two-year siege by Zeng Guoquan, Tianjing falls to the Qing Army. The Taiping Revolution comes to an end. |
| 1870 | Aug. 29 | Li Hongzhang is promoted to be the governor general of Zhili. He becomes the pivot of the Self-Strengthening Movement and foreign policy. |
| | Nov. 12 | Li Hongzhang is appointed the high commissioner of the Northern Ocean. |
| 1872 | Aug. | For the first time, on the recommendation of Zeng Guofan and Li Hongzhang, 30 teenage students are sent to the United States to study. |
| 1877 | Feb. | The first Chinese embassy is set up in London with Guo Songtao as ambassador to England. |

| 1878 | Jan. | The Qing army, under the command of Zuo Zongtang and Liu Jintang, recovers Xinjiang except the Yili valley. |
|------|------|------|
| 1881 | Feb. 24 | The Treaty of St. Petersburg is signed, with Russia agreeing to return Yili. |
| 1882 | July 23 | Domestic insurrection erupts in Korea, and Yuan Shikai is ordered to station there. Li Hongzhang begins to follow a positive policy to counter Japanese influence in Korea. |
| 1884 | Dec. 4 | In Korea, the Japanese minister and pro-Japanese group stage a coup. Yuan Shikai puts down this rebellion and rescues the king of Korea. |
| 1887 | Nov. | Guangxue hui (the Society for the Diffusion of Christianity and General Knowledge among the Chinese, SDK) is established by missionaries and foreigners in Shanghai. |
| 1894 | Aug. 1 | China and Japan declare war on each other. |
| | Nov. 24 | Sun Yat-sen organizes the first revolutionary group, the Revive China Society (Xing Zhonghui), in Honolulu. |
| 1895 | April 17 | The Treaty of Shimonoseki is concluded between China and Japan. It includes the cession of Taiwan, the Pescadores, and the Liaodong peninsula to Japan. Korea is also recognized as an independent state. Japanese are granted the privilege of manufacturing in China. |
| | May 25 | The Republic of Taiwan is established with Tang Jinsong as president. Taiwanese organize militia to resist the Japanese takeover. |
| | Aug. | Qiangxue hui (the Society for the Study of National Strengthening) is set up by Kang Youwei in Beijing to promote reform movement. |
| | Oct. 26 | The Guangzhou uprising, the first of its kind that is led by Sun Yat-sen, fails. |
| | Dec. | Yuan Shikai is ordered to train a new army at Xiaozhan, Tianjin. Leaders of this army become the forebears of Beiyang clique. |
| 1896 | Oct. 11–23 | Sun Yat-sen is kidnapped by officials of the Qing embassy in London. After release, he gains a reputation as the leader of the Chinese Revolutionary Party. |
| 1897 | May–Aug. | During his exile in Europe, Sun Yat-sen develops the theory of the Three People's Principles (*San Min Zhu Yi*)— the Principle of the People's National Consciousness (*Minzhu*), the Principle of the People's Rights (*Minquan*), and the Principle of the People's Livelihood (*Minsheng*). |

| | Oct. 30 | Shiwu xuetang (the School of Current Affairs) is founded in Changsha by reform-minded gentry and provincial government officials. Liang Qichao is invited to be the chief instructor. |
|---|---|---|
| 1898 | June 11 | The Hundred Day Reform begins. At the urging of Kang Youwei and Liang Qichao, Emperor Guangxu issues edicts to reform the government, education, industry, and international cultural exchange. |
| | Sept. 21 | The Hundred Day Reform ends with a coup that is instigated by Empress Dowager Cixi and the conservatives. Kang Youwei and Liang Qichao flee to Japan. Six Martyrs—Yang Shenxiu, Kang Guangren, Yang Rui, Lin Xu, Liu Guangdi, and Tan Shitong—are executed. |
| 1899 | July 15 | Kang Youwei establishes the Emperor Protection Society (*Bao-huang hui*) in Canada. |
| 1900 | Oct. 8–22 | The Huizhou (*Waichow*) Uprising, led by Xing Zhonghui member Zheng Shiliang, fails because of a shortage of supplies. |
| 1901 | April 21 | The Superintendency of Political Affairs (*Dupan zhengwu chu*) is formed to initiate political reform by the Qing government. |
| | Nov. 7 | Li Hongzhang dies. Yuan Shikai succeeds Li's post of governor general of Zhili. |
| 1902 | April 27 | Zhongguo jiaoyu hui (the China Education Association) is set up by Cai Yuanpei and Zhang Binlin. |
| 1903 | June | The *Jiangsu Tribune* (Su Bao) case occurs. Its editor, Zhang Binlin, and the author of *The Revolutionary Army* (Geming jun), Zou Rong, are under arrest. Zou Rong later dies in prison. |
| | Nov. | Huang Xing and Song Jiaoren organize the China Revival Society (Hua-Xing hui) at Changsha. |
| 1905 | Aug. | The Qing government announces the abolition of the civil service examination. |
| | Aug. 20 | In order to unify different revolutionary groups including the Xing Zhonghui, Guangfu hui, and Huaxing hui, the Chinese United League (Zhongguo Tongmeng hui) is formed in Japan. Sun Yat-sen is elected chairman, and Huang Xing becomes chief of the executive department. |
| | Nov. 26 | *Min Bao* is founded in Japan and serves as the official newspaper of the Tongmeng hui. |

| | Dec. | The Qing government sends a mission to investigate constitutionalism around the world. |
|---|---|---|
| 1906 | Sept. | The Qing government announces preparations for the establishment of a constitutional monarchy. |
| 1907 | May 22–Dec. | Uprisings of Chaozhou (Huanggang), Huizhou, Anqing, Qinchou, Lianzhou, Fangcheng, and Zhennanguan, almost all located in southern China and border areas, fail. |
| 1908 | March | Uprisings of Qinzhou, Lianzhou, and Hekou fail again. |
| | Aug. 27 | The Qing government issues the Outline of Constitution. |
| | Dec. 2 | Emperor Puyi succeeds to the throne. |
| 1910 | Feb. 12 | The Guangzhou Uprising, instigated by Tongmeng hui members in the New Army (xinjun), takes place. |
| 1911 | April 27 | The Guangzhou Uprising, led by Huang Xing, fails and results in the death of 72 Huanghua gang martyrs. |
| | Oct. | Yuan Shikai is ordered by the Qing government to suppress the rebellion. He adopts the strategy of killing two birds with one stone, that is, putting pressure on both revolutionaries and Manchu aristocrats. |
| | Oct. 10 | Revolutionaries in the New Army succeed in taking Wuchang. Hanyang and Hankou fall during the following days. Li Yuanhong is drafted to be the military governor of Hubei. Within one and a half months, 15 provinces declare independence. |
| 1912 | Jan. 1 | The Republic of China is established in Nanjing, and Sun Yat-sen is inaugurated as provisional president. |
| | Feb. 12 | Qing Emperor Puyi announces abdication of the throne. |
| | Feb. 13 | Sun Yat-sen tenders his resignation to the provisional senate. |
| | Feb. 15 | Yuan Shikai is elected provisional president by the provisional senate. |
| | March 10 | Yuan Shikai is inaugurated as provisional president in Beijing. |
| | March 11 | The provisional constitution is promulgated. |
| | Aug. 25 | Tongmeng hui, allied with four other small parties, is reorganized into the Guomindang (the Nationalist party) with Sun Yat-sen as its chairman and Song Jiaoren as its deputy chairman. |

| | | |
|---|---|---|
| 1913 | March 20 | Afraid of the domination of parliament by the Nationalist party, Yuan Shikai orders the assassination of Song Jiaoren in Shanghai. |
| | July 12 | Li Liejun, military governor of Jiangxi, declares independence. The Second Revolution, instigated by the Nationalist party against Yuan Shikai, breaks out. |
| | Sept. | The Second Revolution fails, and Sun Yat-sen goes into exile to Japan. |
| 1914 | Jan. 10 | Yuan Shikai dissolves the parliament. |
| | July 8 | Sun Yat-sen reorganizes the Nationalist party into the Chinese Revolutionary Party (Zhonghua keming dang) in Japan and continues fighting against Yuan Shikai. |
| 1915 | | Hu Shi and Zhao Yuanren promote the *Bai-hua* (plain language) movement while they are students in the United States. |
| | Aug. | Dr. Frank J. Goodnow publishes an article to endorse Yuan's monarchical movement. |
| | Sept. 15 | Chen Duxiu founds the *Youth Magazine* (Qingnian zashi) in Shanghai. It is renamed the *New Youth* (Xin Qingnian) the next year. |
| | Nov. 20 | The National People's Representative Assembly, manipulated by Yuan, disregards the constitution and unanimously approves monarchy. |
| | Dec. 12 | Yuan Shikai accepts the throne. |
| 1916 | March 22 | Under pressure from revolutionaries and his own generals, Yuan Shikai gives up the monarchy. |
| | June 6 | The warlord period begins with the death of Yuan Shikai. |
| | Dec. | Cai Yuanpei is appointed chancellor of National Peking University, which becomes the center of intellectual ferment. |
| 1917 | July 1–12 | Zhang Xun, military governor of Anhui, who is summoned by President Li Yuanhong to counterbalance the power of Prime Minister Duan Qirui, restores the abdicated Qing emperor, Puyi, to the throne. Under attacks from the warlords, the Restoration Movement ends within 12 days. |
| | Aug. | Sun Yat-sen establishes a military government in Guangzhou and starts the Constitution Protection Movement (Hufa yundong, protecting the 1912 provisional constitution). |

1918   May 4      Sun Yat-sen is forced out of the military government and lives in Shanghai where he devotes himself to writing the *Outline of National Reconstruction* (Jianguo fanglüe).

       May 15     Lu Xun publishes the "Diary of a Madman" in the *New Youth*.

       Autumn     The New Tide Society (Xinchao she) is founded. Among its members are Li Dazhao, Qu Qiubai, Zhang Guotao, and Mao Zedong.

1919   May 4      Students in Beijing rally to protest the decision of the Versailles Peace Conference on the issue of Shandong. Mass demonstrations break out throughout China.

       Sept. 16   Zhou Enlai organizes the Awakening Society (Juewu she) in Tianjin.

       Oct. 10    Sun Yat-sen reorganizes the Chinese Revolutionary party into the Chinese Nationalist Party (Zhongguo guomin dang, GMD).

1921   April      A republican government, headed by Sun Yat-sen, is established in Guangzhou versus the government in Beijing, which is dominated by the Zhili and the Fengtian cliques.

       July 23–31 The First Congress of the Chinese Communist party is held in Shanghai and Jiaxing. The party is led by Chen Duxiu, as general secretary, and Li Dazhao. Zhang Guotao, Li's student, is head of the Department of Organization.

       Dec.       Lu Xun publishes the "True Story of Ah Q."

1922   June 16    Chen Jiongming leads a mutiny, and Sun Yat-sen is forced out of Guangzhou.

       Aug.       The CCP Central Committee concludes the policy of permitting individual Communists to join the GMD. Li Dazhao becomes the first CCP member to join the GMD. This is the first United Front between CCP and GMD.

       Sept.      GMD leaders approve the policy of "alliance with the Soviet Union, admission of the Communists" (*lianE rong-Gong*).

1923   Jan. 26    Sun Yat-sen and Adolf Joffe, the Soviet representative, issue a joint manifesto. In this manifesto, both of them agree that the Communist organization and the Soviet system are not suitable for China. But China can rely on Soviet assistance to achieve the goal of national unification and independence.

       Aug. 10    Jiang Jieshi leads a GMD delegation to the Soviet Union.

1924   Jan. 20–30    The First National Congress of GMD is held in Guangzhou. Communists are appointed to several key positions of the reorganized GMD.

       May 3         The Huangpu Military Academy is founded. Jiang Jieshi is appointed principal and Liao Zhongkai, party representative. CCP members, like Zhou Enlai and Ye Jianying, serve as acting director of the Political Education Department and instructor, respectively.

1925   March 12      Sun Yat-sen dies in Beijing. The GMD leadership falls to Wang Jingwei and Hu Hanmin.

       July 1        The Nationalist government is established in Guangzhou with Wang Jingwei as chairman.

       Nov.          Fifteen rightist GMD executive and supervisory committee members form a Western Hills (Xishan) faction in Beijing against the *lianE rongGong* policy.

1926   March 20      The warship *Zhongshan* incident occurs, and that is Jiang Jieshi's first break with the Communists.

       July          Jiang Jieshi is appointed commander-in-chief of the Northern Expedition Army. The Nationalist government begins the mission to unify China.

       Sept.         The Northern Expedition Army occupies Wuhan and crushes the major forces of Wu Peifu.

1927   Jan.          The Nationalist government moves to Wuhan.

       March         The Northern Expedition Army takes Shanghai and Nanjing.

       April 12      Jiang Jieshi orders the purge of Communists. With the help of Hu Hanmin, he establishes another Nationalist government in Nanjing. The Wuhan government is controlled by leftist GMD members (headed by Wang Jingwei), Soviet advisers (like Michael Borodin), and the CCP.

       July 15       The Wuhan Nationalist government announces its split with the CCP. It reunites with the Nanjing government afterward. The First United Front between the GMD and the CCP ends.

       Aug. 1        The Communist Nanchang Uprising fails.

       Aug. 7        In a provisional Politburo meeting, Qu Qiubai replaces Chen Duxiu as general secretary of the CCP. The CCP adopts a new policy of riot and uprising.

| | Sept.–Oct. | Mao Zedong leads the Autumn Harvest Uprising in Hunan and Hubei. He then retreats to the Jinggang Mountain in the border areas of Hunan and Jiangxi. |
| | Oct. | Peng Pai establishes the first Soviet government in Haifeng and Lufeng, Guangdong. |
| | Dec. 11 | The Guangzhou Uprising by the CCP fails. |
| 1928 | Feb. | With the support of Feng Yuxiang and Yan Xishan, Jiang Jieshi resumes the Northern Expedition. |
| | April | Zhu De and Chen Yi join Mao Zedong's forces at Jinggang Mountain and form the Fourth Red Army. |
| | June–July | The Sixth Party Congress of the CCP is held in Moscow. Because of the failure of many uprisings, Qu Qiubai is replaced by Xiang Zhongfa and Li Lisan. |
| | Oct. | An Outline of Political Tutelage and the five-yuan structure are proclaimed. Jiang Jieshi is elected president of the Nationalist government in Nanjing. |
| | Dec. 29 | Zhang Xueliang announces his support of the Nationalist government. Major parts of China are now united. |
| 1929 | June | In the Second Plenum of the Sixth CCP Central Committee, the Li Lisan line is formed. Li recognizes the coming of a new tide of revolution and urges CCP members to instigate strikes and military attacks in the cities. |
| | Dec. 28 | Mao Zedong makes his report on the "Rectification of Incorrect Ideas in the Party" at the Gutian Conference in Fujian. |
| 1930 | April–Nov. | Yan Xishan, Feng Yuxiang, and Li Zongren rebel against the Nationalist government. Civil war erupts in north and central China. |
| | Dec. | Mao Zedong strikes down a large number of opponents during the Futian incident, but formal party leadership is bestowed elsewhere. |
| 1930–1931 | Dec.–Jan. | Jiang Jieshi launches the First Campaign of Encirclement and Suppression against the Communists in Jiangxi. |
| 1931 | Jan. | After criticism of the failure of the Li Lisan line in the Fourth Plenum of the Sixth CCP Central Committee, Chen Shaoyu (Wang Ming), Qin Bangxian (Bo Gu), and the so-called Twenty-Eight Bolsheviks take over the Politburo. |
| | April–May | The Second Campaign of Encirclement and Suppression is launched. |

|  | July–Sept. | The Third Campaign of Encirclement and Suppression is launched. |
|---|---|---|
|  | Sept. 18 | The Japanese Kwantung Army attacks Chinese military camps and occupies Mukden. Manchuria is occupied by Japan. |
|  | Nov. 7–20 | The First All-China Congress of the Soviets is held in Ruijin, Jiangxi. A Soviet Republic is established with Mao Zedong as chairman of the Central Executive Committee of the All-China Soviet Government, as well as chairman of the Council of People's Commissars. |
| 1932 | March 9 | Manchukuo, headed by the last Qing Emperor Puyi, is established by the Japanese. |
| 1933 | Jan. | The CCP Central Committee moves from Shanghai to Jiangxi. |
|  | Jan.–April | The Fourth Campaign of Encirclement and Suppression is launched. |
| 1933–1934 | Oct.–Oct. | The Fifth Campaign of Encirclement and Suppression is launched. |
| 1934 | Jan. | In the Second All-China Congress of the Soviets, Mao Zedong loses his power to the Twenty-Eight Bolsheviks. Zhang Wentian takes Mao's chairmanship of the Council of People's Commissars. |
|  | July–Sept. | Mao Zedong is under house arrest by the Twenty-Eight Bolsheviks. |
| 1934–1935 | Oct.–Oct. | The Long March begins. Because of Comintern representative Li De's incorrect military strategy, the CCP starts a 25,000 *li* (6,000 miles) retreat, along southwest and west China, and finally reaches northern Shaanxi. |
| 1935 | Jan. | In the Zunyi (Guizhou) Conference, with the support of Zhu De and other military commanders, Mao Zedong criticizes the current leadership and regains power from the Twenty-Eight Bolsheviks. |
|  | July | In the Maoergai Conference, at the border of Sichuan, Qinghai, and Gansu, the First Front Red Army, under Mao Zedong and other Central Committee members from the Jiangxi Soviet, splits with the Fourth Front Red Army, which is led by Zhang Guotao. Mao heads north, and Zhang heads west. |
|  | Aug. 1 | CCP issues a manifesto of the Anti-Japanese United Front and begins to show a willingness to cooperate with the Nationalist government against Japanese aggression. |

| | | |
|---|---|---|
| 1936 | Dec. 12 | The Xi'an Incident occurs. Zhang Xueliang and Yang Hucheng end the campaign against the Red Army and kidnap Jiang Jieshi in Xi'an. |
| | Dec. 25 | Upon the intervention of the Soviet Union and the CCP, Jiang Jieshi is released and Zhang Xueliang is put under house arrest by Jiang. The war against the Communists in northern Shaanxi is terminated. |
| 1937 | July 7 | The Japanese Army attacks the Chinese garrison and occupies Wanping, Hobei. It is called the Marco Polo Bridge (Lugouqiao) Incident. The Sino-Japanese War begins. |
| | July 15 | The CCP issues a "Together We Confront the National Crisis" (Gongfu guonan) manifesto and pleads for cooperation with the GMD. |
| | Aug. | The Communist Red Army in Shaanxi is reorganized into the Eighth Route Army, led by Zhu De and Peng Dehuai. |
| | Dec. | Nanjing is taken by the Japanese Army. The Rape of Nanjing takes place when Japanese soldiers massacre more than 200,000 Chinese civilians. The Nationalist government retreats to Chongqing. |
| | Dec. | The Communist Red Army south of the Yangzi River is reorganized into the New Fourth Army, and is led by Ye Ting and Xiang Ying. |
| 1938 | Oct. 25 | The Nationalist government orders the evacuation of Wuhan. The fall of Wuhan ends the first phase of the war. |
| | Dec. 18 | Wang Jingwei issues a statement in Hanoi and starts the peace movement with Japan. |
| 1940 | March | Wang Jingwei establishes a puppet government in Nanjing. |
| 1941 | Jan. | The frictions between CCP and GMD forces in Japanese-occupied areas reach a climax. The New Fourth Army is disbanded by the GMD. The New Fourth Army Incident ends the Second United Front between the two parties. |
| | Dec. 7 | The Japanese Navy attacks Pearl Harbor. The Pacific War begins. |
| 1942 | Feb. | A Rectification Movement, which is designed to correct the subjectivism, sectarianism, and formalism in ideology, party organization, and literature, begins in Communist-controlled areas. |
| | May 2–23 | A Forum on Art and Culture is convened at Yan'an and Mao Zedong postulates several guidelines that literary people are to follow. |

| 1943 | Dec. 1 | After the meeting of Jiang Jieshi, Winston Churchill, and Franklin D. Roosevelt in Cairo, a declaration is issued to demand the unconditional surrender of Japan and the return of Manchuria and Taiwan to China. |
| 1945 | April 23 | The Seventh National Party Congress of the CCP is held in Yan'an. Mao Zedong's leadership is firmly consolidated at this meeting. |
| | Aug. 10–11 | Zhu De orders the PLA to accept Japanese surrender and to seize military strongholds. Civil war breaks out in China. |
| | Aug. 14 | Japan officially surrenders. |
| | Aug. 28–Oct. 10 | Mao Zedong leads a delegation to Chongqing to negotiate with Jiang Jieshi about postwar political and military arrangements. |
| | Dec. | General George C. Marshall arrives in China to mediate between the GMD and the CCP. |
| 1946 | Jan. 10–31 | The Political Consultative Conference is convened in Chongqing. All participants agree on forming a multiparty state council, a cabinet system, and a provincial government. |
| | July–Oct. | Nationalist forces advance and win major battles against the Communist PLA. |
| | Nov. 25 | Defying the CCP's nonrecognition, the National Assembly is held in Nanjing. A new constitution is adopted on December 25 of the same year. Later, the National Assembly elects Jiang Jieshi as president and Li Zongren as vice-president. |
| 1947 | Jan. 6 | U.S. mediation fails, and General George C. Marshall is recalled by President Harry Truman. |
| | Feb. 28 | The Taiwanese rebel against the GMD ruling in Taiwan. |
| | March | Nationalist forces capture Yan'an. |
| | July | From this point on, the PLA advances to Honan, Hobei, and gets an upper hand in the civil war. |
| | Oct. | The Outline of Agrarian Law is promulgated by the CCP, and land reform is formalized in "liberated areas." |
| | Oct.–Dec. | Lin Biao's forces gain a major victory in Manchuria. |
| 1948 | Sept. | The PLA, under Chen Yi, occupies Shandong. |
| 1948–1949 | Oct.–Jan. | The Battle of Huai-Hai (Anhui) is a major defeat of the Nationalist forces. |

| 1948 | Nov. | The Manchurian campaign ends with the victory of the Communists. |
|------|------|------|
| 1949–1953 | | Land reform in Taiwan is sponsored by Governor Chen Cheng. This reform is divided into three stages—37.5% rent reduction, sales of public land, and land to the tillers. |
| 1949 | Jan. | The garrison of Beijing and Tianjin surrenders to the PLA. |
| | Jan. 21 | Jiang Jieshi resigns from the presidency. |
| | April 21 | The PLA crosses the Yangzi River. |
| | April 23 | Nanjing is taken by the PLA. The Nationalist government, headed by acting president Li Zongren, moves to Guangzhou. |
| | Sept. 21 | The People's Political Consultative Conference is held by the CCP and pro-Communist parties in Beijing. An Organic law of the Central People's Government and a Common Program are adopted. |
| | Oct. 1 | Mao Zedong proclaims the formal inauguration of the People's Republic of China. |
| | Dec. 16 | Mao Zedong visits the Soviet Union and announces his "lean to one side" policy. |
| 1950 | March 1 | Jiang Jieshi resumes the presidency of the Republic of China in Taiwan. Taibei becomes the temporary capital. |
| | Oct. 14 | The PLA under Peng Dehuai crosses the Yalu River and participates in the Korean War. The U.S.-China relationship is severed. |
| 1950–1953 | Nov.– | The Resist-America Aid-Korea Campaign is launched. |
| 1952 | Jan. | The Five-Anti (*Wu-fan*) Movement against bribery, tax evasion, theft of state property in carrying out government contracts, theft of state economic secrets, against cheating on workmanship and materials targets the business community. |
| | Jan. 1 | The Three-Anti (*San-fan*) Movement against corruption, waste, and bureaucratism in the Communist party commences. |
| 1953 | | The First Five-year Plan officially starts. Actually, it is not put into practice until two and a half years later. |
| 1954 | Feb. | Gao Gang and Rao Shushi, two senior party leaders, are charged with antiparty activities and are expelled from office. |

|  |  |  |
|---|---|---|
| | April 26 | Zhou Enlai leads a delegation to the Geneva Conference to discuss the issues of Korea and Indochina. |
| | Sept. 15–28 | The First National People's Congress is convened in Beijing and adopts a state constitution. |
| 1955 | Jan. | The Hu Feng Affair erupts and brings another purge in the cultural and educational circle. |
| | April 18–24 | A Chinese delegation headed by Zhou Enlai participates in the Bandung Conference in Indonesia. The peaceful co-existence policy is posted. |
| | July | Mao Zedong pushes forward the once-slackened cooperative movement by rallying support from provincial party leaders. |
| 1955–1956 | Oct.– | Socialization of private-owned enterprise begins. Capitalists are virtually transformed into managers of their own shops and factories. |
| 1956 | May 2 | Mao Zedong declares the "Let One Hundred Flowers Blossom, Let One Hundred Schools Contend" policy and asks intellectuals as well as "democratic" party members to criticize state policy. |
| | June 15–30 | The Model Ruling for a Socialist Agricultural Producers' Cooperative is promulgated at the third session of the First National People's Congress. By the end of this year, more than 90% of rural households join the cooperatives. |
| | Sept. 7–27 | The Eighth Party Congress is convened. A retrenchment policy of agricultural collectivization and collective leadership is formulated. |
| 1957 | June | The Hundred Flowers Campaign ends with the Anti-Rightist Movement against intellectual dissidents. |
| 1958 | May 5–23 | In the Second Plenum of the Eighth Party Congress, a General Line of Socialist Construction, that is, construction based on the principle of more, faster, better, and more economically is established. |
| | Aug. 4–13 | After Mao Zedong inspects and praises several model communes, the People's Communes mushroom all over China. |
| | Oct. | A movement to build backyard furnaces is promoted by the government. |
| | Nov. | In order to free women from traditional household work, mass dining halls and nurseries are built in the People's Communes. |

| 1958–1960 | | The period of the Great Leap Forward begins. A new strategy of development—Walking on Two Legs—is put into practice. |
|---|---|---|

1959–1961      Owing to the dislocation of economic resources, which is caused by the policy of the Three Red Banners (the Great Leap Forward, the General Line, and the People's Communes) and bad weather, China experiences a severe economic depression.

1959    March 17–31    Tibetans rebel against the Chinese Communists' ruling. The Dalai Lama goes into exile to India.

         April 27    At the Second National People's Congress, Liu Shaoqi is elected state chairman.

         Aug.    Defense minister Peng Dehuai criticizes Mao's policy of the Great Leap Forward and the People's Communes in the Lushan Conference of the Politburo.

         Sept. 17    Peng Dehuai is dismissed from the Ministry of Defense and is replaced by Lin Biao.

1960    Aug.    General Secretary Nikita Khrushchev recalls all Soviet technical advisers in China. The Sino-Soviet relationship is severed over the issues of Communist ideology, leadership in the Communist bloc, as well as China's internal politics.

1961      Wu Han first publishes the story "Hai Rui Scolds the Emperor" in the *People's Daily* in June 1959. It is rewritten into a historical play, "Hui Rui Dismissed from Office," and is put on stage in the early part of the year.

1962    Jan.    Two policies—Three Privates and One Guarantee (*Sansi yibao*) and Three Reconciliations and One Reduction (*Sanhe yishao*)—are endorsed and implemented by Liu Shaoqi and Deng Xiaoping.

         Sept. 24–27    The Tenth Plenum of the Eighth Central Committee is held in Beijing. In this meeting, Mao Zedong reminds his fellow comrades: "Never forget class struggle." His concern is about the present development of ideology toward the restoration of "capitalism, feudalism, and revisionism."

1962–1965    Sept.    Another Socialist Education Movement is launched in the countryside. This campaign aims at corrupt local cadres and capitalist tendency. But it is resisted by local as well as central officials, such as Peng Zhen, mayor of Beijing.

1963    Feb.    The Learn from Lei Feng Campaign begins. Later, Mao Zedong even asks the entire country to learn from the PLA. Lin Biao emerges as a strong supporter of Mao Zedong.

1964  June        In the Beijing Opera Festival on Contemporary Themes, Jiang Qing promotes her revolutionary drama.

                  A cultural Rectification Campaign is launched but is blocked by Peng Zhen, head of the Five-Person Cultural Revolution Group.

      Dec.        At the Third National People's Congress, Zhou Enlai proposes the Four Modernizations scheme.

1965  Nov. 10     Under the direction of Mao Zedong, Yao Wenyuan publishes an article entitled "Comment on the Newly Composed Historical Play 'Hai Rui Dismissed from Office' " in *Wenhui Bao* in Shanghai. This article starts the Great Proletarian Cultural Revolution.

      Dec.        Because of the disagreement with Lin Biao's war thesis, Lo Ruiqing is dismissed as PLA chief-of-staff and becomes the first victim of the Cultural Revolution.

1966  Feb.        Peng Zhen brings forward the February Outline Report and tries to counter the allegation from the Maoists. But this report is opposed by another document from the Forum on the Work in Literature and Art for the Armed Forces in April.

      April 18    The *Liberation Army Daily* publishes: "Hold High the Great Red Banner of Mao Zedong's Thought and Actively Participate in the Great Socialist Cultural Revolution." This shows the PLA's support of Mao.

      May 16      In the enlarged Politburo meeting, the February Outline Report is overruled. Peng Zhen is dismissed, and a new Central Cultural Revolutionary Committee is formed, with Chen Boda as its chairman and Jiang Qing as vice-chairwoman.

      Aug. 1      Lin Biao is promoted to the first vice-chairmanship of the party.

      Aug. 1–12   In the Eleventh Plenum of the Eighth Central Committee, Mao Zedong attacks those who are "taking the capitalist road," namely, Liu Shaoqi and Deng Xiaoping, and he also announces the creation of the Red Guards (Hong weibing).

      Aug. 5      Mao Zedong writes his own first wall poster: "Bomb the Headquarters."

      Aug. 18     A Decision Concerning the Great Proletarian Cultural Revolution (Sixteen Points) is issued.

| | | |
|---|---|---|
| | Aug. 18–31 | A campaign aimed at destroying Four Olds (old thoughts, old culture, old customs, old habits) is launched. |
| | Nov. | Liu Shaoqi and Deng Xiaoping become the known targets of wall poster attacks. |
| 1967 | Jan. | Under the Maoists' support, the Shanghai worker coalition, headed by Wang Hongwen, seizes control of the city and establishes the Shanghai Commune in February. Later, it is changed into the Shanghai Revolutionary Committee. |
| | Jan. | The PLA intervenes in the Cultural Revolution to restore order. Revolutionary Committees, including regional PLA commanders, party cadres, and radicals, are formed. |
| | Feb. | Top-ranking leaders of the party criticize the policy of the Cultural Revolution, which is known as the "February Countercurrent." |
| | March | A case of 61 renegades in which Liu Shaoqi is involved is revealed. |
| | July–Aug. | Liu Shaoqi and Deng Xiaoping are subject to intensified mass-struggle meetings and, finally, are placed under house arrest. |
| | Aug. | A campaign aimed at the May 16 Antirevolutionary Corps is launched against the ultraleftist tendency of some Maoists. |
| 1968 | Aug. 12– Sept. 25 | Mao Zedong's Thought Worker Propaganda Teams begin to move into university campuses and restore order. |
| | Sept. | By now, Revolutionary Committees have seized the power of all provinces, autonomous regions, and large municipalities. |
| | Oct. | The Twelfth Plenum of the Eighth Central Committee confirms that Liu Shaoqi has been ousted from all party and government posts. He dies in humiliation one year later. |
| | Oct. 13 | May 7 cadre schools are established to reeducate party cadres as well as intellectuals through hard labor. |
| | Dec. | Mao Zedong decides to reduce the disturbances of the Red Guards; they are sent down to the countryside to learn from the peasants. |
| 1969 | April | In the Ninth Party Congress, military commanders and leaders of the Cultural Revolutionary Group gain power in the Central Committee. Lin Biao is designated as Mao's successor. |

| | | |
|---|---|---|
| 1970 | Aug. | In the Second Plenum of the Ninth Central Committee at Lushan, Mao Zedong and Lin Biao openly split on the issues of state chairmanship and the thesis of genius. |
| | Dec. | Mao Zedong, allying with Zhou Enlai, launches a campaign to criticize Chen Boda as well as other Lin Biao supporters. |
| 1971 | March | Lin Liguo, Lin Biao's son, and other conspirators gather in Shanghai and plan the "571 Engineering Outline" for armed uprising. |
| | July 9 | Henry Kissinger visits Beijing. U.S. President Richard Nixon announces that he will visit China. |
| | Aug.–Sept. | Mao Zedong inspects the central and southern provinces to dissuade regional PLA commanders from supporting Lin Biao. |
| | Sept. 13 | When Lin's plot is discovered, he and his conspirators fly to the Soviet Union, but the airplane crashes in the Mongolian People's Republic. |
| | Oct. 15 | The People's Republic of China is admitted into the United Nations and replaces the seat of the Republic of China. |
| | Dec. | The Anti–Lin Biao Campaign is launched. More than 100 central and provincial party as well as military leaders are purged. |
| 1972 | | Yan Jiagan, vice-president of the Republic of China in Taiwan, and Jiang Jingguo, the premier and oldest son of Jiang Jieshi, begin a process of power transfer within the GMD. |
| | Feb. 21 | President Richard Nixon visits China. The Shanghai Communiqué opens a new page of Sino-American relations. |
| | Sept. 25 | Japanese Prime Minister Tanaka Kakuei visits China. China and Japan agree to establish diplomatic relations. |
| 1973 | March | Owing to Zhou Enlai's failing health, Deng Xiaoping is rehabilitated to the vice-premiership to help Zhou. |
| | Aug. 24–28 | In the Tenth Party Congress, Jiang Qing, Zhang Chunqiao, Yao Wenyuan, and Wang Hongwen, later called the Gang of Four, are elected into the Politburo. |
| 1973– 1974 | Aug.– Jan. | The Anti-Lin, Anti-Confucius Campaign is launched. The Cultural Revolutionary Group uses this movement to harass Zhou Enlai who represents the group of moderate party cadres. |

| 1975 | Jan. 13–17 | In the Fourth National People's Congress, struggle between the moderate party elders and the Cultural Revolutionary Group continues. A plan of Four Modernizations is revealed. |
| | April 5 | Jiang Jieshi dies in Taiwan, and Yan Jiagan succeeds to the presidency. |
| | Aug. | The campaign criticizing the novel *Water Margin* is launched. The Cultural Revolutionary Group attacks Zhou Enlai and Deng Xiaoping. |
| 1976 | Jan. 8 | Zhou Enlai dies. |
| | April 5 | The Tiananmen Square incident breaks out in Beijing. The Cultural Revolutionary Group violently suppresses demonstrators who support Deng Xiaoping and oppose the Gang of Four. |
| | April 7 | Hua Guofeng, the former party chairman of Hunan province and minister of public security, is appointed premier to succeed Zhou Enlai. At the same time, Deng Xiaoping is dismissed from all party and government posts. |
| | July 6 | Zhu De dies. |
| | July 28 | The Tangshan (Hobei) earthquake causes more than 700,000 casualties. |
| | Sept. 9 | Mao Zedong dies, and the succession crisis reaches its climax. |
| | Oct. 6 | Jiang Qing, Chang Chunqiao, Yao Wenyuan, and Wang Hongwen are under arrest in a coup that is initiated by Hua Guofeng, Deng Xiaoping, and Ye Jianying. Hua Guofeng becomes chairman of the CCP and chairman of the party's military commission. The Great Proletarian Cultural Revolution officially ends. |
| 1977 | Feb. 7 | The pro-Maoist "two whatevers" are launched by the *People's Daily*. |
| | March | The "two-whatevers" are reaffirmed by the Central Work Conference. Chen Yun and Wang Zhen order the rehabilitation of Deng Xiaoping. |
| | July | Deng Xiaoping is restored to the Politburo standing committee by the Tenth Party Congress. Hua Guofeng's position as Mao's successor is validated. |
| | Aug. | Deng Xiaoping promotes major reforms and praises intellectuals during the Science and Education Work Forum. |

| 1978 | May 12 | Leftist ideological orthodoxy is attacked in a *People's Daily* editorial. |
| | July 1 | A speech given by Mao in 1962 was reprinted in order to show the mistakes that he had made in a further attempt to prove his ignorance to his still-loyal subjects. |
| | April–June | Deng Xiaoping criticizes Leftist Party leaders at the All-Military Conference on Political Work. |
| | Oct. | Beginning of the Democracy Wall movement in Beijing. |
| | Nov. | Debate begins over "criterion of truth." Deng Xiaoping speaks about focusing Party work on Socialist modernization. |
| | Dec. | Major agricultural and economic reforms are instituted. |
| 1979 | Jan. | The Democracy Wall movement reaches a peak in Beijing. Deng Xiaoping visits the United States. |
| | Feb. 17 | China invades Vietnam. |
| | March 5–16 | Chinese troops withdraw from Vietnam. Deng Xiaoping gives a speech stressing the importance of "Upholding the Four Cardinal Principles." Wei Jingsheng is arrested. |
| | April | Party conservatives criticize the reforms inaugurated by the December Third Plenum. |
| | | A proposal is made for a three-year period of readjustment. |
| | Sept. | Zhao Ziyang is promoted to the Politburo and senior cadres are added to the CCP Central Committee. Revisions are made in agricultural policies. |
| 1980 | Feb. 23–29 | Zhao Ziyang and Hu Yaobang are named to the Politburo. The Party secretariat once again becomes the de facto decision-making body of the Party. The radicals Ji Dengkui, Wu De, Chen Xilian, and Wang Dongxing are removed from their Party posts. |
| | April | Party Propaganda Department is verbally attacked by Hu Qiaomu. |
| | May | Deng attacks feudalism in the Party. |
| | June | Politburo meeting is held to discuss eliminating "feudalism" from the Party. |
| | Sept. | Zhao Ziyang replaces Hua Guofeng as premier. Bicameral NPC and tricameral CCP are discussed. Institutional political reform is endorsed by Deng Xiaoping. |

New open door policies are brought to Guangdong and Fujian provinces.

Nov.     Deng Xiaoping is put in charge of the CCP Central Military Commission. The trial for the Gang of Four begins. The "struggle against bourgeois liberalization" is established by Hu Qiaomo. Deng Xiaoping, Chen Yun, and Zhao Ziyang endorse economic entrenchment.

1981  March    "Struggle against bourgeois liberalization" is brought up by Deng Xiaoping for the first time. The state council calls for a diversified agricultural economy.

July     The Special Economic Zones are attacked by Party conservatives.

July 27  Mao Zedong's excesses during the Cultural Revolution are criticized in "Resolution on Certain Questions in the History of Our Party." Hu Yaobang is made Party chairman.

Aug.     Attacks on "bourgeois liberalization" are discussed at the Forum on Problems on the Ideological Battlefront.

Dec.     Chen Yun Criticizes Hu Yabong's supposed mistakes in economic policy.

1982  Jan.     Hu Yaobong calls for foreign investing in China's economic modernization. Chen Yun states that economic planning must remain the superior system in the countryside.

Feb.     Hu Yaobang addresses corruption in the Party. There is an open forum on Guangdong and Fujian provinces.

April    Harsh punishments are called for on those who commit "economic crimes."

July     Topic of Politburo meeting is how to end life tenure for leaders.

Aug.     Hua Guofeng launches an attack on the slogan "practice is the sole criterion of truth."

Sept.    The Twelfth Party Congress meets. The position of Party chairman is abolished and replaced by general secretary. The Central Military Commission's chairmanship becomes stronger.

Dec.     The importance of raising conflicting viewpoints at inner-Party meetings is brought up during Politburo meeting.

1983  Jan.     Hu Yaobang and the leftist leader Deng Liqun disagree over the purpose of ideology in China's modernization.

|  | March | Zhou Yang brings up the role of alienation and humanism in a Socialist society. |
|---|---|---|
|  | Oct. | Chen Yun calls for a purging of the "three categories of people." |
|  | Nov. | The "antispiritual pollution campaign" is narrowed down to art and literature. |
| 1984 | Jan. | Deng Xiaoping continues to show his support for economic reform while touring southern Special Economic Zones. |
|  | Feb. | Discussion of open-door policy takes place. |
|  | March–April | Fourteen new coastal cities are opened to foreign investment. |
|  | April | *People's Daily* newspaper denounces the Cultural Revolution. |
|  | June | Document Number One in the Central Committee is established which states that improvements need to be made in the rural responsibility system. |
|  | Sept. 26 | China and Great Britain sign an agreement stating that Hong Kong will be returned to China on July 1, 1997. |
|  | Oct. | "Resolution on the Structural Reform of the Economy" is the liberal beginning of the urban reforms. |
|  | Dec. | The Fourth Conference of the All-China Writers' Association held in Beijing grants writers more creative freedom. |
| 1985 | Jan. | An expansion of the free rural economy is called by the CCP and the state council. |
|  | March | The National Forum on Science and Technology in Beijing orders radical changes. Attempts at price reforms begin. |
|  | May | The size of the Chinese army is reduced by over one million troops. |
|  | June | The administrative segment of the people's communes are fully restructured. |
|  | Sept. | Chen Yun attacks Party members for lacking Communist principles. |
| 1986 | Jan. | Central Cadres Conference focuses on the unstable national economy and reproaches Party administrators for their "lax" work behavior. |
|  | June | Deng Xiaoping gives a speech on the necessary reform of China's political structure. |

|        |            |                                                                                                                                                                                                                                                                                                      |
|--------|------------|--------------------------------------------------------------------------------------------------------------------------------------------------------------------------------------------------------------------------------------------------------------------------------------------------------|
|        | Sept.      | Sixth plenum of the Twelfth Party Congress sanctions the "Resolution on the Guiding Principles for Construction of Socialist Spiritual Civilization."                                                                                                                                                   |
|        | Dec.       | Mass student demonstrations break out in Hefei and Anhui province, as well as Beijing and other cities. Hu Yaobang is reproached by Deng Xiaoping for his handling of the Party's liberal intellectuals.                                                                                                |
| 1987   | Jan. 17    | Hu Yaobang is dismissed from his position as general secretary of the CCP. Fang Lizhi, Liu Binyan, and Wang Ruowang are discharged from the CCP for supporting "bourgeois liberalization."                                                                                                             |
|        | April      | The CCP gains control over semi-independent newspapers, while leftists continue their criticism of "bourgeois liberalization."                                                                                                                                                                        |
|        | July       | Zhao Ziyang initiates plans for political reform.                                                                                                                                                                                                                                                     |
|        | Oct. 25–Nov. 1 | Zhao Ziyang is named general secretary to the CCP by the Thirteenth Party Congress. The "General Program for Political Reform" is also instituted, which creates a restructuring of the government, including a separate Party and government and an independent judiciary. Decisions on economic matters are reallocated to the state from the CCP. |
|        | Oct.–Nov.  | Zhao Ziyang announces that China is in the "primary stage" of Socialism. The Politburo becomes the decision-making center of the CCP. Party administrations that were founded in the 1950s are eradicated.                                                                                              |
| 1988   | March      | A professional civil service is proposed by Zhao Ziyang.                                                                                                                                                                                                                                              |
|        | March–April | Li Peng is made the state premier, Yang Shangkun the president, and Wang Zhen the vice-president. Inflation is becoming a threat to the state.                                                                                                                                                         |
|        | July       | *Seeking Truth* is established, taking the place of *Red Flag*.                                                                                                                                                                                                                                       |
|        | Aug.       | Price reform begins as an effort to control inflation, however a stream of panic-buying squelches the reform efforts.                                                                                                                                                                                 |
|        | Sept.      | An emphasis is placed on controlling China's economy.                                                                                                                                                                                                                                                 |
| 1988–1989 | Dec.–Feb. | Petitions are circulated with the goal of attaining amnesty for China's political prisoners.                                                                                                                                                                                                          |
| 1989   | April 15   | Hu Yaobang dies.                                                                                                                                                                                                                                                                                      |
|        | April 22   | Crowds of students gather in the Tiananmen Square to mourn the death of Hu Yaobang.                                                                                                                                                                                                                    |

| | | |
|---|---|---|
| | April 26 | Student demonstrations are condemned in a *People's Daily* editorial, based on the words of Deng Xiaoping, who called them "antiparty, anti-Socialist turmoil." |
| | May 17 | Zhao Ziyang speaks in favor of the student movement. Hundreds of journalists demand freedom-of-the-press rights. Student hunger strikes begin in Tiananmen Square. Soviet leader Mikhail Gorbachev arrives in Beijing. |
| | May 19 | Zhao Ziyang unsuccessfully urges the students to end their hunger strikes. |
| | May 20 | Martial law is declared as a result of the student demonstrations. |
| | June 3–4 | The Tiananmen Square incident occurs. |
| | June 23 | Zhao Ziyang is removed from all of his posts. Jiang Zemin becomes the Party's general secretary. |
| | Nov. 1 | Deng Xiaoping resigns as chairman of the CCP Military Affairs Commission (MAC). |
| | Dec. | Romania's Communist government is overthrown. |
| 1990 | Jan. | Chinese government is alarmed by the collapse of the Communist government in Romania and police are put on watch. A two-year economic recovery program is implemented. |
| | March | Li Peng states that "hostile elements" must be kept under tighter control. |
| | April | Jiang Zemin becomes the chairman of the state MAC. Basic Law is passed for Hong Kong. |
| | June | Wang Zhen refers to moderates in the government as "hostile anti-Party forces." |
| | Oct. | A new campaign is launched against crime and influences such as pornography. |
| | Dec. | The Eighth Five-Year Plan is in construction and calls for stability and self-reliance. |
| 1991 | Jan.–Feb. | 1989 prodemocracy-movement participants are put on trial. |
| | March | Attempts to decentralize the economy are made by Li Peng. |
| | April | Zhu Rongji and Zou Jiahua are named vice-premiers. |

|       | May       | Journalists are required to spread Marxism Leninism by a new press code. All Party and government officials are warned by secret emergency directive to protect China from hostile forces that threaten to overthrow the government. |
|-------|-----------|---|
|       | Aug.      | An attempted coup against Mikhail Gorbachev is unsuccessful. |
|       | Sept.     | "Realistic Responses and Strategic Options for China Following the Soviet Union Upheaval" is written by Chen Yun. |
|       | Oct.      | The George Bush administration is accused of trying to bring about Communist collapse. |
| 1992  | Jan.      | Deng Xiaoping calls for additional economic reforms. |
|       | Feb.      | The *People's Daily* launches an attack on hard-line views and states a need for additional economic reforms. |
|       | March     | Conflicts occur between those who support economic reforms and conservatives who are attempting to reverse economic reforms. The budget deficit reaches 3.8 billion for 1992. There is a 13% military spending increase. |
|       | April     | The Three Gorges Dam project is approved by the NPC. |
|       | June      | Liberal scholars meet to discuss the corruption of hardliners in the CCP. Over one million workers are laid off from failed state enterprises. |
|       | Aug.      | Industrial workers begin strikes. |
|       | Oct.      | The plan of a "socialist market economic system" is introduced into China to try to ensure success in their future development. Yang Shangkun is dismissed by the CCP MAC. Deng Xiaoping urges people to follow the "three don'ts." |
| 1993  | March 13  | Wang Zhen dies. |
|       | March 27  | Jiang Zemin is appointed president of the PRC. |
|       | April     | China becomes the world's fastest growing economy, according to the World Bank. |
|       | June      | Taxes and other outrageous fees lead to peasant riots in Sichuan province. |
|       | Aug.      | Chinese companies are charged with selling missile technology to Pakistan and as a result the United States dictates trade sanctions on both countries. |

| | | |
|---|---|---|
| | Oct. | Hong Kong Governor Chris Patten announces that he does not have China's support to institute democratic political reforms in Hong Kong. |
| | Dec. 9 | The anniversary of Mao's Zedong's one hundredth birthday. |
| 1994 | March | Serious crimes, such as murder, robbery, and rape, as well as economic crimes, increase drastically. PRC-Taiwan relations are in straits after Taiwanese tourists in Zhejiang province are robbed and killed. |
| | May | Chinese intellectuals request a reevaluation of the 1989 democracy movement. China is awarded the Most Favored Nation Status by the Clinton administration. |
| | June | China's Foreign Ministry advises the North Korean government to refrain from "fruitless military conflict." |
| | Oct. | A confrontation occurs between a U.S. Navy aircraft and a Chinese submarine in the Yellow Sea. |
| 1995 | Feb. | Chinese intellectuals circulate a petition calling for political reform. |
| | April 10 | Chen Yun dies. |
| 1996 | March | The first direct presidential election in Chinese history occurs in Taiwan. |
| 1997 | Feb. 19 | Deng Xiaoping dies at the age of 93. |
| | July 1 | China regains control of Hong Kong. |
| | Sept. 12 | Jiang Zemin gives a report on foreign policy at the Fifteenth National Congress of the Chinese Communist Party. |
| | Oct. | Jiang Zemin visits the United States. |
| 1998 | Feb. 4 | Chinese and Japanese defense ministers meet for the first time in over ten years to discuss military associations. |
| | Feb. 27 | A plan is hatched to dismantle the corrupt Chinese bureaucracy by downsizing four million government jobs over the next three years. |
| | March 19 | Premier Zhu Rongji holds his first press conference on China's domestic situation. |
| | April 2 | China and the European Union strengthen their relations by sharing common viewpoints regarding the Asian economic crisis. |
| | May 18 | Floods kill 20 people and do approximately $31 million worth of damage in southern China. |

| | | |
|---|---|---|
| | June 27 | Jiang Zemin meets with President Bill Clinton in Beijing for formal talks. |
| | July 19 | Floods have killed 760 people in China since the beginning of the year. |
| | Oct. 1 | The PRC's forty-ninth anniversary is celebrated in Tiananmen Square. |
| | Oct. 15 | China and Taiwan hold a monumental meeting where they agree to send a negotiator to the island. |
| | Oct. 28 | Zhao Ziyang reappears in the Chinese media. |
| | Nov. 25 | Sino-Japanese Summit. Jiang Zemin is the first Chinese president since 1949 to visit Japan. |
| | Dec. 5 | Nationalists win the mayoral election for the first time, paving the way for the upcoming presidential election in 2000. |
| 1999 | Jan. 11 | China and the United States discuss human rights for the first time in five years. |
| | April 7 | President Bill Clinton speaks on U.S. policy toward China. |
| | Dec. 20 | China regains control of Macao from Portugal. |
| | | China boasts the second largest economy in the world, coming second to the United States. |
| 2000 | March | The Nationalists lose the presidential election in Taiwan to the pro-independence Democratic Progressive Party. |
| | Nov. 23 | The United States and China reach an agreement stating that while China would not sell nuclear missile technology, the United States would allow China to launch United States satellites. |
| | 30 | U.S. Secretary of Defense Walter Slocomb speaks with top military officials in Beijing, showing the furthering improvement in U.S.-China relations. |
| 2001 | Jan. | Anson Chen (Anson Chan Fang On-sang) announces her resignation as the Chief Secretary of the Hong Kong Special Administrative Region government. |
| | March 22 | During a meeting at the White House Chinese Vice-Premier Qian Qichen warns newly elected U.S. President George W. Bush not to sell weapons to Taiwan. |

| | |
|---|---|
| April 1 | A U.S. Navy surveillance plane is forced to make an emergency landing after colliding with a Chinese fighter jet. The Chinese pilot is killed in the crash. The U.S. crew and the plane are held in China. The Chinese demand a formal apology before the crew members are returned. |
| April 11 | U.S. crew is released and heads home. The U.S. jet is still not returned. The United States issues an apology for the death of the fighter jet pilot and for making an unauthorized landing. |
| July 1 | Jiang Zemin presents his "July 1" speech at the eightieth anniversary of the CCP. His speech includes the "Three Representatives Theory," to become an amendment of the CCP Party constitution. He also announces that Chinese capitalists can join the CCP as members. |
| July 13 | Beijing wins the bid to hold the 2008 Olympic Games. |
| Sept. 30 | Li Denghui (Lee Teng-hui) is expelled from the GMD in Taiwan. |
| Oct. 14 | Zhang Xueliang dies in Hawaii. |
| Nov. 10 | The World Trade Organization (WTO) accepts China as a member. |

# Modern Chinese Political Leaders

## LEADERS OF THE IMPERIAL GOVERNMENT/PERIOD

Chen Baochen

Cixi, Empress Dowager

Daoguang, Emperor

Ding Richang

Feng Yunshan

Gong, Prince (Gong Wang or Yisin)

Guangxu Emperor

Hong Xiuquan

Hu Linyi

Kang Youwei

Li Hongzhang

Li Xiucheng

Liang Qichao

Lin Zexu

Liu Kunyi

Puyi (Aisin Gioro Puyi, Henry Puyi)

Shen Baozhen

Sheng Xuanhuai

Shi Dakai

Tan Sitong

Tongzhi, Emperor

Weng Tonghe
Xiao Chaogui
Yang Xiuqing (Silung)
Yuan Shikai
Zeng Guofan (Wenzheng)
Zhang Zhidong
Zuo Zongtang (Wenxiang)

## LEADERS OF THE REPUBLICAN GOVERNMENT/PERIOD

Chen Cheng (Ch'en Ch'eng)
Chen Gongbo
Chen Jiongming
Feng Yuxiang
Fu Zuoyi
Hu Hanmin
Huang Xing
Jiang Jieshi (Chiang Kai-shek)
Jiang Jingguo (Chiang Ching-kuo)
Kong Xiangxi, Chauncey (H.H. Kung)
Li Denghui (Lee Teng-hui)
Li Yuanhong
Li Zongren
Lian Zhan (Lien Chan)
Liang Qichao
Song Meiling (Soong May-ling)
Song Qingling, Rosamond
Song Ziwen, Paul (T.V. Soong)
Sun Ke (Sun Fo)
Sun Yat-sen (Sun Yixian)
Wang Jingwei
Wu Peifu
Yan Jiagan (Yen Chia-kan)
Yan Xishan
Yuan Shikai
Zhang Xueliang
Zhou Fohai

## LEADERS OF THE COMMUNIST GOVERNMENT/PERIOD

Bo Gu (Qin Bangxian)
Chen Boda
Chen Duxiu
Chen Gongbo
Chen Yun
Deng Xiaoping
Deng Yingchao
Dong Biwu
Gao Gang
Hu Yaobang
Hua Guofeng
Jiang Qing
Jiang Zemin
Li Dazhao
Li Lisan
Li Peng
Li Xiannian
Lin Biao
Liu Shaoqi
Lu Xun (Zhou Shuren)
Luo Fu (Zhang Wentian)
Mao Zedong (Mao Tse-tung)
Qian Qichen
Qu Qiubai
Rao Shushi
Song Qingling, Rosamond
Ulanfu
Wan Li
Wang Hongwen
Wang Ming (Chen Shaoyu)
Yang Shangkun
Yao Wenyuan
Ye Jianying
Zhang Chunqiao
Zhang Guotao
Zhao Ziyang

Zhou Enlai (Chou En-lai)
Zhou Fohai
Zhu De
Zhu Rongji

## LEADERS OF LOCAL GOVERNMENTS

Chen, Anson (Anson Chan Fang On-sang)
Chen Cheng (Ch'en Ch'eng)
Dong Jianhua (Tung Chee Hwa)
Jiang Jingguo (Chiang Ching-kuo)
Li Denghui (Lee Teng-hui)
Lian Zhan (Lien Chan)
Yan Jiagan (Yen Chia-kan)

# Glossary

| | |
|---|---|
| Bo Gu (Qin Bangxian) | 博古(秦邦憲) |
| Chen, Anson (Anson Chan) | 陳方安生 |
| Chen Baochen | 陳寶琛 |
| Chen Boda | 陳伯達 |
| Chen Cheng | 陳誠 |
| Chen Duxiu | 陳獨秀 |
| Chen Gongbo | 陳公博 |
| Chen Jiongming | 陳炯明 |
| Chen Yun | 陳雲 |
| Cixi, Empress Dowager | 慈禧 |
| Daoguang, Emperor | 道光 |
| Deng Xiaoping | 鄧小平 |
| Deng Yingchao | 鄧穎超 |

| | |
|---|---|
| Ding Richang | 丁日昌 |
| Dong Biwu | 董必武 |
| Dong Jianhua (Tung Chee Hwa) | 董建華 |
| Feng Yunshan | 馮雲山 |
| Feng Yuxiang | 馮玉祥 |
| Fu Zuoyi | 傅作儀 |
| Gao Gang | 高崗 |
| Gong, Prince | 恭親王 |
| Guangxu, Emperor | 光緒 |
| Hong Xiuquan | 洪秀全 |
| Hu Hanmin | 胡漢民 |
| Hu Linyi | 胡林翼 |
| Hu Yaobang | 胡耀邦 |
| Hua Guofeng | 華國鋒 |
| Huang Xing | 黃興 |
| Jiang Jieshi (Chiang Kai-shek) | 蔣介石 |
| Jiang Jingguo (Chiang Ching-kuo) | 蔣經國 |
| Jiang Qing | 江青 |
| Jiang Zemin | 江澤民 |
| Kang Youwei | 康有爲 |
| Kong Xiangxi, Chauncey | 孔祥熙 |
| Li Dazhao | 李大釗 |
| Li Denghui (Lee Teng-hui) | 李登輝 |
| Li Hongzhang | 李鴻章 |
| Li Lisan | 李立三 |

| | |
|---|---|
| Li Peng | 李鵬 |
| Li Xiannian | 李先念 |
| Li Xiucheng | 李秀成 |
| Li Yuanhong | 黎元洪 |
| Li Zongren | 李宗仁 |
| Lian Zhan (Lien Chan) | 連戰 |
| Liang Qichao | 梁啓超 |
| Lin Biao | 林彪 |
| Lin Zexu | 林則徐 |
| Liu Kunyi | 劉坤一 |
| Liu Shaoqi | 劉少奇 |
| Lu Xun (Zhou Shuren) | 魯迅 |
| Luo Fu (Zhang Wentian) | 洛甫(張聞天) |
| Mao Zedong (Mao Tse-tung) | 毛澤東 |
| Puyi | 溥儀 |
| Qian Qichen | 錢其琛 |
| Qu Qiubai | 瞿秋白 |
| Rao Shushi | 饒漱石 |
| Shen Baozhen | 沈葆楨 |
| Sheng Xuanhuai | 盛宣懷 |
| Shi Dakai | 石達開 |
| Song Meiling (Soong May-ling) | 宋美齡 |
| Song Qingling, Rosamond | 宋慶齡 |
| Song Ziwen, Paul (T.V. Soong) | 宋子文 |
| Sun Ke (Sun Fo) | 孫科 |

| | |
|---|---|
| Sun Yat-sen (Sun Yixian) | 孫逸仙 |
| Tan Sitong | 譚嗣同 |
| Tongzhi, Emperor | 同治 |
| Ulanfu | 烏蘭夫 |
| Wan Li | 萬里 |
| Wang Hongwen | 王洪文 |
| Wang Jingwei | 汪精衛 |
| Wang Ming (Chen Shaoyu) | 王明(陳紹禹) |
| Weng Tonghe | 翁同龢 |
| Wu Peifu | 吳佩孚 |
| Xiao Chaogui | 蕭朝貴 |
| Yan Jiagan (Yen Chia-kan) | 嚴家淦 |
| Yan Xishan | 閻錫山 |
| Yang Shangkun | 楊尚昆 |
| Yang Xiuqing | 楊秀清 |
| Yao Wenyuan | 姚文元 |
| Ye Jianying | 葉劍英 |
| Yuan Shikai | 袁世凱 |
| Zeng Guofan | 曾國藩 |
| Zhang Chunqiao | 張春橋 |
| Zhang Guotao | 張國燾 |
| Zhang Xueliang | 張學良 |
| Zhang Zhidong | 張之洞 |
| Zhao Ziyang | 趙紫陽 |
| Zhou Enlai (Chou En-lai) | 周恩來 |

| | |
|---|---|
| Zhou Fohai | 周佛海 |
| Zhu De | 朱德 |
| Zhu Rongji | 朱鎔基 |
| Zuo Zongtang | 左宗棠 |

# Bibliography

*Editor's Note*: Please also refer to the "References" section of each entry for further and more specific bibliographical suggestions.

Bachman, David. *Bureaucracy, Economy and Leadership in China: The Institutional Origins of the Great Leap Forward*. New York: Cambridge University Press, 1991.

Bailey, Paul John. *China in the Twentieth Century*. Oxford: Basil Blackwell, 1988.

Barnett, A. Doak. *China on the Eve of the Communist Takeover*. Boulder, CO: Westview Press, 1985. (Orig. pub. in 1963.)

Bartke, Wolfgang. *A Biographical Dictionary and Analysis of China's Party Leadership, 1922–1988*. New York: K.G. Saur, 1990.

Bartke, Wolfgang. *Who's Who in the People's Republic of China*. 2nd ed. Munich: K.G. Saur, 1987.

Bianco, Lucien. *Origins of the Chinese Revolution, 1915–1949*. Trans. Muriel Bell. Stanford, CA: Stanford University Press, 1971.

Boorman, Howard L., and Richard C. Howard, eds. *Biographical Dictionary of Republican China*. 5 vols. New York: Columbia University Press, 1967–1979.

Bown, Colin, and Tony Edwards. *Revolution in China, 1911–1949*. Portsmouth, NH: Heinemann Educational Books, 1974.

*The Cambridge History of China*. See under vol. editors: Vol. 10: Fairbank, John King ed.; Vol. 11: Fairbank, John King, and Kwang-Ching Liu, eds.; Vol. 12: Fairbank, John King, and Denis Twitchett, eds. Vol. 13: Fairbank, John King, and Albert Feuerwerker, eds.; Vol. 14: MacFarquhar, Roderick, and John King Fairbank, eds. Cambridge: Cambridge University Press.

Cavanaugh, Jerome. *Who's Who in China, 1918–1950: With an Index*. Hong Kong: Chinese Materials Center, 1982.

Chan, F. Gilbert, and Thomas H. Etzold, eds. *China in the 1920s: Nationalism and Revolution*. New York: New York Viewpoints, 1976.

Chang, Kia-ngau. *The Inflationary Spiral: The Experience in China, 1939–1950*. Cambridge, MA: MIT Press, 1958.

Chang, Parris. *Power and Policy in China*. Dubuque, IA: Kendall/Hunt, 1990.

*Chinese Communist Who's Who*. 2 vols. Taibei: Institute of International Relations, 1970–1971.

Cohen, Paul A. *Discovering History in China: American Historical Writings on the Recent Chinese Past*. New York: Columbia University Press, 1984.

Cole, James H. *Twentieth Century China: An Annotated Bibliography of Reference Works in Chinese, Japanese and Western Languages*. 2 vols. Armonk, NY: M.E. Sharpe, 2001.

Dirlik, Arif. *The Origins of Chinese Communism*. New York: Oxford University Press, 1986.

Dirlik, Arif. *Revolution and History: The Origins of Marxist Historiography in China, 1919–1937*. Berkeley: University of California Press, 1987.

Dittmer, Lowell. *China's Continuous Revolution: The Post Liberation Epoch, 1949–1981*. Berkeley: University of California Press, 1987.

Domes, Jurgen. *Die Kuomintang-Herrschaft in China* [Guomindang Rule in China]. Hanover: Niedersachsische Landeszentrale fur Politische Bildung, 1970.

Embree, Ainslie T., ed. *Encyclopedia of Asian History*. 4 vols. New York: Scribner, 1988.

Esherick, Joseph, and Mary Backus Rankin. *Chinese Local Elites and Patterns of Dominance*. Berkeley: University of California Press, 1990.

Fairbank, John King. *The Great Chinese Revolution, 1800–1985*. New York: Harper and Row, 1986.

Fairbank, John King, ed. *The Cambridge History of China. Vol. 10: Late Qing, 1800–1911, Part 1*. Cambridge: Cambridge University Press, 1978.

Fairbank, John King, Mastaka Banno, and Sumiko Yamamoto. *Japanese Studies of Modern China: A Bibliographical Guide to Historical and Social Science Research on the Nineteenth and Twentieth Centuries*. Cambridge, MA: Harvard University Press, 1971.

Fairbank, John King, and Albert Feuerwerker, eds. *The Cambridge History of China. Vol. 13: Republican China, 1912–1949, Part 2*. Cambridge: Cambridge University Press, 1986.

Fairbank, John King, and Kwang-Ching Liu, eds. *The Cambridge History of China. Vol. 11: Late Qing, 1800–1911, Part 2*. Cambridge: Cambridge University Press, 1980.

Fairbank, John King, and Edwin O. Reischauer. *China: Tradition and Transformation*. Boston: Houghton Mifflin, 1978.

Fairbank, John King, and Denis Twitchett, eds. *The Cambridge History of China. Vol. 12: Republican China, 1912–1949, Part 1*. Cambridge: Cambridge University Press, 1983.

Fewsmith, Joseph. *Elite Politics in Contemporary China*. Armonk, NY: M.E. Sharpe, 2000.

Franke, Wolfgang. *A Century of Chinese Revolution, 1851–1949*. Trans. Stanley Rudman. New York: Columbia University Press, 1986.

Gamer, Robert E. *Understanding Contemporary China*. Boulder, CO: Lynne Reinner, 1999.

Gasster, Michael. *China's Struggle to Modernize*. New York: McGraw Hill, 1972.

Gray, Jack. *Rebellions and Revolutions: China from the 1800s to the 1980s*. New York: Oxford University Press, 1990.

Gray, Jack, ed. *Modern China's Search for Political Form*. London: Oxford University Press, 1969.

Greider, Jerome B. *Intellectuals and the State in Modern China: A Narrative History*. New York: Free Press, 1981.

Guoshiguan Zuanjizhu, ed. *Guoshiguan xuanchang gemingrenwuzhuanji shiliaohuibian* [A Classified Compilation of Nationalist Biographical Source Materials Currently in Academia Historica]. Taibei: Guoshiguan, 1988.

He, Ganzhi, ed. *Zhongguo xiandai gemingshi* [History of Contemporary Chinese Revolution]. Shanghai: Renmin chubanshe, 1985.

He, Henry Yuhuai. *Dictionary of the Political Thought of the People's Republic of China*. Armonk, NY: M.E. Sharpe, 2000.

He, Qing, ed. *Zhonghua renmin gongheguo shi* [History of the People's Republic of China]. Beijing: Gaodeng jioyu chubanshe, 1999.

Hsü, Immanuel C.Y. *The Rise of Modern China*. 6th ed. New York: Oxford University Press, 2000.

Hsueh, Chun-tu. *The Communist Movement: An Annotated Bibliography of Selected Materials in the Chinese Collection of the Hoover Institution of War, Revolution and Peace*. 2 vols. Palto Alto, CA: Hoover Institution on War, Revolution and Peace, Stanford University, 1960–1962.

Hu, Hua. *Zhonggong dangshi renwuzhuang* [Biographies from Chinese Communist Party History]. 37 vols. Xi'an: Shaonxi renmin chubanshe, 1980.

Hummel, Arthur W., ed. *Eminent Chinese of the Ch'ing Period (1644–1912)*. 2 vols. Washington, DC: U.S. Government Printing Office, 1943–1944.

Ichiko, Chuzo. *Kindai Chugoku no seiji to shakai* [The Politics and Society of Modern China]. Tokyo: Tokyo Daigaku, 1971.

Issacs, Harold R. *The Tragedy of the Chinese Revolution*. Stanford, CA: Stanford University Press, 1961.

Jing, Dexing, and Chen Wanan, eds. *Zhongguo gemingshi cidian* [Dictionary of Chinese Revolutionary History]. n.p.: Henan Daxue Chubanshe, 1986.

Johnson, Chalmers A. *Peasant Nationalism and Communist Power: The Emergence of Revolutionary China*. Stanford, CA: Stanford University Press, 1962.

Kamper, Thomas. *Mao Zedong, Zhou En-lai and the Evolution of the Chinese Communist Leadership*. Copenhagen: Nordic Institute of Asian Studies, 1999.

Kaplan, Fredric M., and Julian M. Sobin. *Encyclopedia of China Today*. 3rd ed. New York: Harper and Row, 1980.

Klein, Donald, and Anne B. Clark, eds. *Biographic Dictionary of Chinese Communism, 1921–1965*. 2 vols. Cambridge, MA: Harvard University Press, 1971.

Kuo, Tai-chun, and Ramon H. Myers. *Understanding Communist China: Communist China Studies in the United States and Republic of China, 1949–1978*. Stanford, CA: Stanford University Press, 1986.

Leung, Edwin Pak-wah. *Historical Dictionary of the Chinese Civil War*. Lanham, MD: Scarecrow Press, 2002.

Leung, Edwin Pak-wah, ed. *Historical Dictionary of Revolutionary China, 1839–1976*. Westport, CT: Greenwood Press, 1992.

Leung, Edwin Pak-wah, and Philip Leung, eds. *Modern China in Transition*. Claremont, CA: Regina Books, 1995.

Leung, Edwin Pak-wah et al., eds. *Papers of the International Conference on the 50th Anniversary of the War of Resistance*. Taibei: Academia Historica, 1997.

Lewis, John Wilson. *Leadership in Communist China*. Ithaca, NY: Cornell University Press, 1963.

Lewis, John Wilson, ed. *Party Leadership and Revolutionary Power in Asia*. Cambridge: Cambridge University Press, 1970.

Li, Chien-nung. *The Political History of China, 1840–1928*. Ed. Ssu-yu teng and Jeremy Ingalls. Stanford, CA: Stanford University Press, 1956.

Li, Xin et al., eds. *Minguo renwuzhuan* [Biographies of Republican China]. 2 vols. Beijing: Zhonghua, 1978–1980.

Li, Yuming. *Zhonghua renmin gongheguoshi cidian* [Historical Dictionary of the People's Republic of China]. Beijing: Zhongguo guoji guanbe chubianshe, 1989.

Liu, Bao. *Xiandai Zhongguo renwuzhi* [Biographies of Contemporary Chinese Leaders]. Macao: Dadi chubanshe, 1973.

*Liushinianlai de Zhongguo jingdaishi yanju* [Historical Studies on Modern China in the Past 60 Years]. 2 vols. Taibei: Zhongyang yanjuyuan jindaishi yanjushue, 1989.

Lorenz, Richard, ed. *Umwalzung einer Gesellschaft. Zur Sozialgeschichte der Chinesischen revolution (1911–1949)* [Transformation of a Society: Concerning the Social History of the Chinese Revolution, 1911–1949]. Frankfurt: Suhrkamp, 1977.

Ma, Hongwu et al., eds. *Zhongguo gemingshi cidian* [Dictionary of the Chinese Revolutionary History]. Beijing: Dongan chubanshe, 1988.

MacFarquhar, Roderick, and John King Fairbank, eds. *The Cambridge History of China. Vol. 14: The People's Republic, the Emergence of Revolutionary China, 1949–1965, Part I*. Cambridge: Cambridge University Press, 1987.

Mackerras, Colin. *Modern China: A Chronology from 1942 to the Present*. San Francisco: W.H. Freeman, 1982.

Meisner, Maurice. *Li Ta-chao and the Origins of Chinese Marxism*. Cambridge, MA: Harvard University Press, 1980.

Meisner, Maurice. *Mao's China: A History of the People's Republic*. New York: Free Press, 1977.

Melby, John F. *The Mandate of Heaven: A Record of Civil War in China, 1945–1949*. Toronto: University of Toronto Press, 1968.

Moise, Edwin E. *Modern China: A History*. London: Longman, 1986.

Murphey, Rhoads. *East Asia: A New History*. New York: Addison Wesley Longman, 1997.

Nathan, Andrew J. *Modern China, 1940–1972: An Introduction to Sources and*

*Research Aids.* Ann Arbor: Center for Chinese Studies, University of Michigan, 1973.

Nee, Victor, and James Peck, eds. *China's Uninterrupted Revolution: From 1840 to the Present.* New York: Pantheon Books, 1975.

Perry, Elizabeth. *Challenging the Mandate of Heaven: Social Protest and State Power in China.* Armonk, NY: M.E. Sharpe, 2001.

Perry, Elizabeth. *Rebels and Revolutionaries in North China, 1845–1945.* Stanford, CA: Stanford University Press, 1980.

*A Pictorial History of the Republic of China: Its Founding and Development.* 2 vols. Taibei: Modern China Press, 1981.

Pong, David, and Edmund S.K. Fung. *Ideal and Reality: Social and Political Change in Modern China, 1860–1949.* Lanham, MD: University Press of America, 1985.

Rankin, Mary Backus. *Early Chinese Revolutionaries.* Cambridge, MA: Harvard University Press, 1971.

Robottom, John. *China in Revolution: From Sun Yat-sen to Mao Tse-tung.* New York: McGraw-Hill, 1971.

Rozman, Gilbert. *Modern China and Its Revolutionary Process: Recurrent Challenges to the Traditional Order, 1850–1920.* Berkeley: University of California Press, 1986.

Rozman, Gilbert, ed. *The Modernization of China.* New York: Free Press, 1982.

Scalapino, Robert, and George Yu. *Modern China and Its Revolutionary Process: Recurrent Challenges to the Traditional Order, 1850–1920.* Berkeley: University of California Press, 1985.

Schiffrin, Harold. *Sun Yat-sen and the Origins of the Chinese Revolution.* Berkeley: University of California Press, 1968.

Shaw, Yu-ming, ed. *Reform and Revolution in Twentieth Century China.* Papers from the Third Sino-European Conference. Taibei, September 1–6, 1986. Taibei: Institute of International Relations, National Chengchi University, 1987.

Sheridan, James E. *China in Disintegration: The Republican Era in Chinese History, 1912–1945.* New York: Free Press, 1975.

Sih, Paul K.T., ed. *The Strenuous Decade: China's Nation-Building Efforts, 1927–1937.* Jamaica, NY: St. John's University Press, 1970.

Skinner, G. William, ed. *Modern Chinese Society: An Analytical Bibliography. Vol. 1: Publications in Western Languages, 1644–1972.* Stanford, CA: Stanford University Press, 1973.

Skinner, G. William, and Winston Hsieh, eds. *Modern Chinese Society: An Analytical Bibliography. Vol. 2: Publications in Chinese, 1644–1969.* Stanford, CA: Stanford University Press, 1973.

Skinner, G. William, and Shigeaki Tomita, eds. *Modern Chinese Society: An Analytical Bibliography. Vol. 3: Publications in Japanese, 1644–1971.* Stanford, CA: Stanford University Press, 1973.

Spence, Jonathan. *The Gate of Heavenly Peace: The Chinese and Their Revolution, 1895–1980.* New York: Viking Press, 1981.

Spence, Jonathan. *The Search for Modern China.* New York: Norton, 1990.

Strong, Anna L. *China's Millions: The Revolutionary Struggles from 1927 to 1935.* Freeport, NY: Books for Libraries Press, 1973.

Sullivan, Lawrence R. *Historical Dictionary of the People's Republic of China, 1949–1997*. Lanham, MD: The Scarecrow Press, 1997.

Teng, Ssu-yu. *Historiography of the Taiping Rebellion*. Cambridge, MA: Harvard University Press, 1962.

Terrill, Ross. *The Whiteboned Demon: A Biography of Madam Mao Zedong*. New York: William Morrow, 1984.

Uhalley, Stephen. *A History of the Chinese Communist Party*. Stanford, CA: Hoover Institution Press, 1988.

Vohra, Ranbir. *China's Path to Modernization: A Historical Review from 1800 to the Present*. 3rd ed. Upper Saddle River, NJ: Prentice-Hall, 2000.

Walp, Herbert. *Asian Leaders: A Bibliography*. Huntington, NY: Nova Science Publishers, 2001.

Wang, James C.F. *Contemporary Chinese Politics*. 6th ed. Upper Saddle River, NJ: Prentice-Hall, 1999.

Wang, Ke-wan. *Modern China: An Encyclopedia of History, Culture and Nationalism*. New York: Garland, 1998.

Wang, Y.C. *Chinese Intellectuals and the West, 1872–1949*. Chapel Hill: University of North Carolina Press, 1966.

Wei, Xiumei. *Qingji zhiguanbiao* [Tables of Late Qing Government Offices, with Biographies]. 2 vols. Taibei: Zhongyang yanjuyuan jindaishiyanju shue, 1977.

Weston, Anthony. *The Chinese Revolution*. Ed. Malcolm Yapp et al. St. Paul, MN: Greenhaven Press, 1980.

*Who's Who in Communist China*. 2nd ed. 2 vols. Hong Kong: Union Research Institute, 1966.

Wright, Mary C. *The Last Stand of Chinese Conservatism: The T'ung-chih Restoration, 1862–1874*. New York: Antheneum, 1966.

Wu, Tien-wei. *Lin Biao and the Gang of Four: Contra-Confucianism in Historical and Intellectual Perspective*. Carbondale: Southern Illinois University Press, 1983.

Wu, Xiangxiang. *Minguo bairenzhuan* [One Hundred Biographies from the Republican Period]. Taibei: Zhuanji wenxueshe, 1971.

Wu, Xiangxiang. *Minguo renwu liezhuan* [Biographies from the Republican Period: A Sequel to *Mingguo bairenzhuan*]. Taibei: Zhuanji wenxueshe, 1986.

Zeng, Fanguang. *Zhongguo gemingshi biaojie* [Explanatory Tables of China's Revolutionary History, 1840–1956]. Changsha: Hunan renmin chubanshe, 1988.

Zhang, Yufa, and Zhang Ruide, eds. *Zhongguo xiandai zhizuan chongshu* [Collections of Contemporary Chinese Autobiographies]. Taibei: Zhongyang yanjuyuan shanzhuyi yanjushuo, 1989.

*Zhonggong renminlu* [Collected Biographies of Chinese Communist Leaders]. Taibei: Zhonghua mingguo guojiguanxi yanjushue, 1967.

Zhou, Linong. *Shiji zhijiao de Zhongguo* [China at the Turn of the Century]. Hong Kong: Wentong chubanshe, 1997.

# Index

# About the Contributors

GORDON BENNETT, Department of Government, University of Texas

GERALD W. BERKLEY-COATS, East Asian Studies, University of Guam

HENRY Y.S. CHAN, Department of History, Moorhead State University

CHIU-YEE CHEUNG, Department of Asian Languages and Studies, University of Queensland, Australia

CINDY YIK-YI CHU, Department of History, Hong Kong Baptist University

PENG DENG, Department of History, High Point University

HUNG-YOK IP, Department of History, Oregon State University

THOMAS L. KENNEDY, Department of History, Washington State University

YEE-CHEUNG LAU, Department of History, The Chinese University of Hong Kong

TA-LING LEE, Department of History, Southern Connecticut State University

JOHN KONG-CHEONG LEUNG, Department of History, Northern Arizona University

STEPHEN R. MacKINNON, Department of History, Arizona State University

RAMON H. MYERS, Hoover Institution, Stanford University

TERENCE PANG TIM TIM, Department of English, Lingnan University, Hong Kong

DAVID PONG, Department of History, University of Delaware

MURRAY A. RUBINSTEIN, Department of History, Baruch College, City University of New York

MICHAEL L. SCHOENHALS, Centre for East and Southeast Asian Studies, Lund University, Sweden

YI SUN, Department of History, University of San Diego

ANTHONY Y. TENG, Department of History, Rhode Island College

STEPHEN UHALLEY, JR., Department of History, University of Hawaii

JAMES C.F. WANG, Department of Political Science, University of Hawaii at Hilo

WANG KE-WEN, Department of History, St. Michael's College

LYNN T. WHITE III, Department of Politics, Princeton University

TIEN-WEI WU, Department of History, Southern Illinois University

JOSEPH K.S. YICK, Department of History, Southwest Texas State University

# About the Editor

EDWIN PAK-WAH LEUNG is Professor of Asian Studies, Director of the Asian Studies Graduate Program, Associate Chairman of the Department of Asian Studies, and Senior Fellow of the Asia Center at Seton Hall University. Dr. Leung has taught at the University of Hong Kong, Hong Kong Polytechnic University, Peking (Beijing) University, Zhejiang University, Wuhan University, and the University of California at Santa Barbara. He was also a research fellow at the University of California at Berkeley, the University of California at Los Angeles, the University of Michigan, Columbia University, and the Chinese University of Hong Kong. Dr. Leung's published works include *Historical Dictionary of the Chinese Civil War* (2002), *Papers of the International Conference on the 50th Anniversary of the War of Resistance* (1997), *Modern China in Transition* (1995), *Historical Dictionary of Revolutionary China, 1839–1976* (*Choice* Outstanding Academic Book) (Greenwood, 1992), *Modern Changes in Chinese Diplomacy* (1990), and *Ethnic Compartmentalization and Regional Autonomy in the People's Republic of China* (1982).